# Contents

# PART II: FINDING A JOB ABROAD

# PART III: COUNTRY GUIDE ...........................................................104

# Health
## PROFESSIONALS
# Abroad

## Tim Ryder

Revised and updated by
## Ian Collier

Published by Vacation Work, 9 Park End Street, Oxford
www.vacationwork.co.uk

**Health Professionals Abroad**

First edition 1997 Tim Ryder
Second edition 2000 Ian Collier

Copyright © Vacation Work, 2000

ISBN 1 85458 227 5 (softback)

Cover Design by
Miller Craig & Cocking Design Partnership


Publicity co-ordinator: Roger Musker


Typeset by WorldView Publishing Services (01865-201562)


Printed by William Clowes Ltd., Beccles, Suffolk, England

# Preface

The term 'health professional' is a deliberate umbrella term, as it includes scores of specialised jobs. These range from the more obvious professions – such as medicine, nursing and dentistry – to the more specialised fields that are as essential to modern health care as well built hospitals and clinics – for example, radiography, pharmacy and physiotherapy. The term also includes the variety of vital support and administrative roles, and the seperate specialisations of 'alternative' medicine. This variety is reflected in this book, and in the opportunities of different kinds that it describes.

Currently the demand for trained staff to supply health care is not matched by the numbers of qualified personnel available in many countries around the world. For many health professionals disillusioned with rampant bureaucracy, dull weather, a lack of adequate facilities or no prospects for professional growth and promotion this is a good thing as it provides an opportunity to work somewhere else. This book is intended to help in that regard, and while the British government has recently moved to stop health authorities hiring foreign staff en masse to fill staffing needs, there is nothing to stop individual professionals from applying directly or through agencies.

For those who worry about the draining of trained staff away from developing nations, the second section of the book has details of two types of agency. Those employment agencies that place staff in developed nations and those non-government organisations (NGOs) that work to relieve the health-related problems of developing countries, often provide a key component of a nation's health service in the process. Usually the motives of these NGOs are primarily humanitarian, although there are also many religious organisations who provide health care as part of their evangelical activities. There are also many agencies who send health staff into regions affected by war, famine and other disasters – the internationally renowned organisation Médecins sans Frontières is a good example.

This complex situation means that there are demands for all types of health professional in countries around the world. The aim of this book is to provide those staff interested in working overseas with information on the organisations involved in matching health staff with opportunities abroad, and to provide information on the employment situation in the health sectors of various countries.

Whatever your specialisation in the health field, *Health Professionals Abroad* is a book intended to provide its readers with the information they will need when looking for work abroad.

Ian Collier
Oxford, February 2000

# Acknowledgments

I would like to thank all of the people and organisations who helped me during the course of my research for this book. I would especially like to mention Scott Adams, Dawn Boyall, Anke Büttner, Maike Büttner, Lara Croft, Annariita Kottonen, Ann Lundberg, Arthur Osteen PhD, Lee Randall, Tim Ryder, author of the first edition, Enid Segall, Martina Stanley, Soile Tammisto, Michael Waters, and Julian Winston.

# PART I

## Types of Health Professional

# INTRODUCTION

The purpose of this part of *Health Professionals Abroad* is to provide descriptions of the main health professions covered in the later sections. Information on training, qualifications and sources of further information is also included. Professional organisations are important in this respect, and can often provide very useful information on what working in their field involves.

What people working in a particular profession do can often vary significantly between countries, and people doing essentially the same job can have quite different job titles in different parts of the world. The Country Guides in Part III include information on these variations. They also include details of professional organisations and other sources of information for some of the more specialised jobs described below.

# Mainstream Medicine

## DOCTORS

Working as a doctor is perhaps the quintessential health profession, although the term actually covers people working in a wide range of specialised medical disciplines. For all of them, however, a rigorous, lengthy period of training is a prerequisite.

## TRAINING

There are 27 medical schools in the UK, and competition for places is exceptionally keen. The basic medical course lasts for 5 years, and is divided into pre-clinical and clinical parts. The first 2 years are concerned with basic medical sciences; the last 3 years are spent mainly in teaching hospitals. After successfully completing qualifying examinations at the end of the course, doctors enter a further pre-registration year, working under supervision as house officers in general hospitals. After completing this year satisfactorily they can register with the General Medical Council; they are then entitled to practise. Following further postgraduate training, they can work in either a hospital, general practice or community medicine.

There are 125 medical schools in the USA, and medical education differs from many countries in that students complete their pre-medical education before entering medical school. This means that nearly all students have Bachelor's degrees before entry. Medical school education lasts for 3 years, with the curriculum divided, as in the UK, into study of basic sciences followed by clinical sciences. Entry requirements are set out in *Medical School Admission Requirements: US and Canada*. Canadian medical schools, of which there are 16, are accredited by the same independent agency and to the same standards as those in the USA, with similar curriculae. Following completion of medical school, graduates undertake periods of graduate medical education, known as residencies – the length of residency varying from 3 to 7 years, according to the speciality studied. There is no education programme for general practice, in the USA general practitioners are known as primary care physicians. Physicians who plan to undertake primary care practice need to complete three years of graduate education and obtain speciality board certification. Admission to practice is regulated by 54 licensing jurisdictions or State Medical Boards. These 54 Medical Boards have adopted as a licensing examination the USMLE, this is prepared by a private organisation, the National Board of Medical Examiners, and is a three-step examination for medical licensure. This is used to examine graduates of medical schools, and to certify graduates of foreign medical schools, for licensing and entry to practice. Enrolled students or graduates of institutions listed in the *World Directory of Medical Schools* are eligible to take the first two parts of the examination. The individual state's medical licensing authorities administer part three of the examination, and so passing it in one state merely means that you are licensed in that state and will have to undergo an additional licensing procedure if you move to another state or licensing jurisdiction.

# HOSPITAL DOCTORS

In the UK approximately 25% of doctors work in hospitals. Furthermore the great majority of newly qualified doctors begin their careers working in a hospital within the National Health System. The first four grades for hospital medical staff – house officer, senior house officer, registrar and senior registrar – are training posts; doctors work up through these levels, under the supervision of a consultant responsible for their postgraduate training. Working as a house officer is extremely demanding, and can currently require up to 80 hours per week. While working in these training posts, doctors combine work with postgraduate study and further examinations. Postgraduate training generally consists of about 3 years of general training in areas relevant to the doctor's eventual specialty, followed by 4 years of specialist training, usually in a senior registrar post. After this doctors are eligible for consultant positions.

## Consultants

Consultants are the most senior grade of hospital doctor. They are doctors who have specialised in one particular branch of medicine and who have ultimate and continuing clinical responsibility for their patients.

There are a huge number of specialties, but the main groupings are surgery, medicine, pathology and psychiatry. Specialisations that do not fit under these categories include anaesthetics, radiology, radiotherapy, gynaecology and obstetrics.

Broadly speaking surgery is concerned with patients who need operations, medicine with patients who do not. There are numerous sub-specialties within each: in surgery these include accident and emergency (A & E), general surgery, neurosurgery, ophthalmology, plastic surgery and urology, as well as others; in medicine they include audiology, cardiology, dermatology, diseases of the chest, general medicine, neurology, nuclear medicine and paediatrics, among many more. Some medical specialties are concerned with acute illnesses and relatively well defined curative treatment; others with longer-term illness and the more protracted treatment that they require.

Pathology is the study of disease; most of the work is laboratory-based and contact with patients is usually in an advisory capacity, working with the doctors treating them. Again there are several sub-specialties. Most pathologists work in laboratories attached to hospitals. Laboratory technicians are employed to carry out tests, and pathologists interpret the results.

Anaesthetics is concerned with the variety of methods of anaesthesia used for operations, and for pain control in such areas as intensive care. Anaesthetists can work across a range of areas or specialise in one branch, in which case they may be more actively involved in dealing with patients.

Radiology is concerned with the taking of X-rays for both diagnostic and investigative purposes and involves considerable variety. Interpretation of X-ray photographs is an important part of the work. Radiotherapy mainly involves providing cancer patients with radiation treatment. Interaction with patients forms a key part of the radiotherapist's job, as the radiotherapist is involved with them throughout the course of their illness and its treatment.

Obstetrics is concerned with childbirth and the treatment of women before and after childbirth. Technological advances have greatly affected the obstetrician's work – for example, it is now possible to monitor a pregnancy in impressive visual detail. Gynaecology is a related specialisation, concerned with the diseases and hygiene of women.

In the USA primary care physicians treat their own patients in a hospital rather than turning them over to a hospital staff physician. Because primary care physicians work in hospitals they must meet the requirements established by a hospital's medical staff, these are frequently more demanding than the requirements for licensure. Specialists join in with patient treatment as necessary or in consultation with the patient's primary care physician. As US physicians are licensed to practice medicine, not a specific branch of medicine, a hospital staff appointment delineates the scope of practice, and thus the speciality learned is part of the appointment rather than a pre-determined career path.

## DOCTORS IN THE COMMUNITY

The alternative for doctors to working in a hospital is to work in the community. More than half of all medical graduates in the UK enter general practice. Approximately 90% of GPs now work in group practices, each of which is staffed by a primary health care team, which includes nurses, health visitors and often social workers. All doctors wishing to become GPs need to undergo 3 years of postgraduate training, which includes a year's experience as a trainee in general practice.

Doctors can also work in the Community Health Service, which is based in local clinics. Here much of the work is concerned with preventive care. Registered doctors can work in this field without undertaking further postgraduate training. They work in a similar way to GPs, except that they are restricted to their specialist areas and can not prescribe medicines.

District health authorities employ public health physicians who help to evaluate the health needs of local populations and planning appropriate services. Before beginning specialist training in this area, doctors complete 3 years of clinical work in a variety of settings. Public health physicians do not have direct contact with patients.

In the USA general practitioners are becoming rare, as they are increasingly being replaced by family practitioners who have received more intensive training.

# A NEW LIFE ABROAD!

### How often have you pictured yourself living abroad? Enjoying a brand new lifestyle somewhere new and different?

It's an ambition you share with lots of people, of all ages and backgrounds.

But most fall at the first hurdle, unsure where to start and daunted by the prospect of cutting through all the red tape and bureaucracy that is involved. What a pity they didn't know about First Point International.

Whether you'd like to work, run your own business or even spend your retirement abroad, First Point will secure that crucial visa and provide all the advice and practical assistance you're likely to need.

**YOUR NEXT STEP**

To find out how you could soon be on your way to a new life abroad, call or send for our Information Pack today.

# +44 (0)20 7724 9669
(24 Hours.) Please quote ref. HPA

**www.firstpointinter.com**
**info@firstpointinter.com**

## FURTHER INFORMATION

The medical association in your country will be able to provide careers information and addresses of medical schools. In the UK an essential source of further information is the British Medical Association's publication *Medical Careers – A General Guide* (see page 254), and the place to look for vacancies for doctors is the *British Medical Journal*.

*American Medical Association:* 515 North State Street, Chicago, Illinois 60610, USA (tel +1-312-464-4677; fax 312-464-4567; Website www.ama-assn-org).

*British Medical Association:* BMA House, Tavistock Square, London WC1H 9JP, UK (tel 020-7387 4499; fax 020-7383 6454; Website http//web.bma.org.uk).

*Australian Medical Association:* PO Box E115, Queen Victoria Terrace, Parkes ACT 2600, Australia (tel +61-6-270 5400; fax 06-270 5499; Website www.ama.com.au).

*Canadian Medical Association:* 1867 Alta Vista, Ottawa, Ontario K1G 3Y6, Canada (tel +1-613-731-9331; e-mail cmamsc@cma.ca Website www.cma.ca).

*New Zealand Medical Association:* PO Box 156, Wellington 1, New Zealand (tel +64-4-472 4741; fax 04-471 0838; e-mail nzma@nzma.org.nz Website www.nzma.org).

*South African Medical Association:* PO Box 74789 Lynnwood Ridge, Pretoria 0040, South Africa (tel +27-12-481 2000; fax 012-481 2100).

*World Medical Association:* BP 63, F-01212 Ferney-Voltaire Cedex, France (tel +33-50 40 75 75; fax 50 40 59 37; info@wma.net Website www.wma.net); contact the WMA for a list of medical associations around the world.

## MEDICAL CLERICAL WORK

In addition to the health professionals trained in the key medical and related areas described elsewhere in this section, there are a huge number of staff working in health services providing essential administrative, organisational and secretarial support. While these staff are not health professionals in the same sense as, say, dentists and dietitians, they require in-depth knowledge of how health systems are structured and managed, and often of medical terminology and of particular specialisations. Such positions include medical secretaries, clinic clerks, ward clerks, out-patient receptionists, medical records staff, personal assistants and general administrators. Medical secretaries, for example, may work for an individual consultant or a particular hospital department. Clerical staff work in health care facilities ranging from doctors' surgeries to general hospitals, with rates of pay varying accordingly between £8000 and £18000.

Clerical work in this field requires gaining experience in an appropriate health care environment; commercially gained experience is generally inadequate. In the UK, medical secretaries can obtain the qualification of the Association of Medical Secretaries, Practice Managers, Administrators and Receptionists (AMSPAR). The Association can also provide information on working in the field.

*Association of Medical Secretaries, Practice Managers, Administrators and Receptionists:* Tavistock House North, Tavistock Square, London WC1H 9LNH, UK (tel 020-7387 6005; fax 020-7387 2648; e-mail amspar@atlas.co.uk).

# Nursing & Midwifery

## NURSING

Nurses are responsible for assessing an individual patient's nursing needs, planning an appropriate programme of care, delivering that care and evaluating the results, adjusting the plan of care as the patient's needs change.

Nurses need an array of attributes – they have to be able to comfort the distressed, reassure the anxious and explain to the confused. They are not only concerned with the person they are caring for; they also support family and friends, who can be just as worried as the patient. Increasingly nurses need to have a deeper knowledge of the science and art of nursing than before, and be competent to practice in their field.

The term 'nursing' is often used to refer to general nursing, or the nursing of physically ill adults. Adult nursing is concerned with providing appropriate care for people with chronic and acute physical illness, both in the community and in hospital. In the community the nurse could be attached to a district nurse, health visitor, a general practice or a community health centre; in hospital the nurse works in general medical and surgical wards as well as in more specialised areas. Nurses work at the centre of a multi-disciplinary team that includes doctors, physiotherapists, occupational therapists, pharmacists, dietitians and many others. The nurse usually has the closest and most extended contact with the patient.

There are other important branches of nursing apart from adult nursing, however. Mental health nurses, for example, look after people with psychiatric problems, and may be based either in hospital units or out in the community (in the UK, mental health problems are increasingly addressed in a person's own home). They work as part of a team including psychiatrists, social workers and other health and social care professionals. A key part of the mental health nurse's role is the formation of therapeutic relationships with individuals and their families. Their work includes supporting people with serious or long-term mental illness, in addition to people who reach a crisis in their life and find they are not able to cope.

Learning Disabilities nurses are trained in techniques to help children and adults with learning disabilities reach their full potential; they work in a multidisciplinary team, usually in the community. This is increasingly the case in the UK, where community-based care has shifted the emphasis of care away from hospitals.

Children's nurses gain experience in the care of children from the very young to the adolescent. Much of the nurse's role is taken up in teaching and supporting the parents, who carry out a great deal of the care. A growing number of paediatric nurses are now based permanently in the community with the primary health team.

A number of career options are available to qualified nurses. Many nurses develop their careers by specialising in one of the many areas covered by post-registration courses. Clinical specialists can work in hospital and/or in the community. For example, a nurse from the children's branch could specialise in cancer treatment or neonatal care. Many nurses choose to move from hospital into the community, offering nursing care, support and advice to people at home. Nurses in this field clearly need to have a good understanding of how their community works. There are 8 branches of community specialist practice. These include home/district nursing, health visiting and so on. The post registration education and practice for each is at no less than degree level, and would be at least one academic year, made up of 50% theory and 50% practice. Nurses in the community may work as nurses, undertake further training to become health visitors, or be attached to a GP's surgery.

In the UK higher education institutions (ie universities) offer a three-year diploma programme, in which students follow a common foundation and then specialise in one of the four branches mentioned above. There are also a number of degree courses. Registration is with the UK Central Council for Nursing, Midwifery and Health Visiting (UKCC). Further information is available from the appropriate national board (see addresses below).

Nurses trained within Europe have freedom of movement, but those who gained nursing qualifications outside Europe need to write to the UKCC, for information on Registration and possible further experience and assessment of this prior to practising in the UK and Northern Ireland. Information on nursing in specific countries is available in the UK from the Royal College of Nursing International Office, including details of employment prospects, work permits and nurse registration requirements. The RCN library is the largest nursing library in Europe, and full RCN members can request literature searches on specific aspects of nursing abroad. Some RCN members list their details on the International Offices's Open Register of members living and working abroad, and the Office may be able to put you in touch with someone with first-hand experience of the country that you want to work in.

In the USA there are two ways to become a registered nurse (RN): by graduating from a four-year university programme with a baccalaureate degree (BSN) in nursing; or from a two-year college programme with an associate degree in nursing (ADN).

In the UK good journals to consult for advertisements for employment opportunities abroad are the *Nursing Standard* and *Nursing Times*.

## Health Visitor

Health visiting is a specialised area of nursing, focused on promoting health in the community.

The health and welfare of children is a traditional and continuing aspect of health visitors' work – for example, helping parents prepare for a birth and addressing health problems affecting children. Examples of other types of work carried out by health visitors include providing guidance in parenting skills; paying 'listening visits' to mothers who have post-natal depression; helping the family of someone who is terminally ill to cope; counselling on sexual health (for example, in the case of teenage pregnancies, or discussing the risks of AIDS); and helping to improve nutrition among families who have been identified as being at risk.

Health visitors need to know the community in which they work well; for example, who has special needs and who might benefit from a visit. They need to be receptive to the health needs of individuals and the community. Stimulating an awareness of health in the community is another important aspect of the job.

Health visitors are also involved in setting up 'health enhancement' activities in the community – for example, groups for people wanting to stop smoking. They are involved in improving the planning and provision of services. They often work in close partnership with other health professionals, such as district nurses, midwives, school nurses and GPs, as well as social workers. They may be based in a local health centre or in a GP's practice.

In the UK you need to have UKCC Registration parts 1 or 10 or equivalent, a qualification including English, Welsh, or History as a subject and the equivalent of 5 GCSEs plus experience on the UKCC Register of sufficient length to have consolidated pre-registration training and experience – this requirement reflects the maturity and experience needed for the job. Since 1998 all health visitors' courses have been at degree level (51 weeks full-time). Those successfully completing the course can register with the UK Central Council for Nursing, Midwifery and Health Visiting.

## Further Information

*American Nurses Association Inc:* 600 Maryland Avenue, SW, Suite 100W, Washington DC 20024-2571 (tel +1-202-651-7134; fax 202-651-7001; Website www.nursingworld.com).

*Royal College of Nursing:* 20 Cavendish Square, London W1M 0AB, UK (tel 020-7409 3333; fax 020-7355 1379; Website www.rcn.org).

*Australian Nursing Federation:* Level 2, 21 Victoria Street, Melbourne VIC 3000, Australia (tel +61-9369 5211; fax 03-9652 0567; Website www.anf.org).

*Canadian Nurses' Association:* 50 The Driveway, Ottawa, Ontario K1P 1E2, Canada (tel +1-613-237-2133; fax 613-237-3520; e-mail prr@cna-nurses.ca Website www.cna-nurses.ca).

*New Zealand Nurses Organisation:* PO Box 2128, Wellington, New Zealand (tel +64-4-385 0847; fax 04-382 9993).

*International Council of Nurses:* 3 place Jean-Marteau, 1201 Geneva, Switzerland (tel +41-22-908 0100; fax 022-908 0101; e-mail webmaster@icn.ch Website www.icn.ch).

## UK National Boards

*United Kingdom Central Council for Nursing, Midwifery and Health Visiting:* 23 Portland Place, London, W1N 3JT, UK (tel 020-7333 9333; fax 020-7636 6935; Website www.ukcc.org.uk in English, French, German and Spanish).

*English National Board for Nursing, Midwifery and Health Visiting (Careers Service):* Victory House, 170 Tottenham Court Road, London W1P 0HA, UK (tel 020-7388 3131; fax 020-7383 4031; Website www.enb.org.uk ).

*National Board for Nursing, Midwifery and Health Visiting for Northern Ireland:* Centre House, 79 Chichester Street, Belfast BT1 4JE, UK (tel 01232-238152; e-mail enquiries@nbni.n-i.nhs.uk Website www.n-i.nhs.uk/NBNI/index.htm).

*National Board for Nursing, Midwifery and Health Visiting for Scotland (Careers Information Team):* 22 Queen Street, Edinburgh EH2 1NT, UK (tel 0131-225 2096; fax 0131-226 2492; Website www.nbs.org.uk).

*Welsh National Board for Nursing, Midwifery and Health Visiting:* 2nd Floor, Golate House, 101 St Mary Street, Cardiff CF1 1DX, UK (tel 02920-261400; fax 02920-261499; e-mail info@wnb.org.uk Website www.wnb.org.uk).

# MIDWIFERY

Although a significant part of a midwife's work is delivering babies in a variety of settings, there are many other important aspects to the profession. Throughout pregnancy and in the days following a birth, midwives support, advise and care for women, their partners and babies helping them to manage the pregnancy, maintain good health and prepare for being parents.

The midwife is also involved in the care of the pregnant woman in the months before the birth. Regular visits to the antenatal clinic allow the midwife to build up a rapport with the mother-to-be and her partner. The midwife is often the primary contact for the expectant mother, and has an important role in liaising with other health professionals such as the GP, obstetrician and health visitor. Where there are problems with a pregnancy, the midwife must know when to bring in the appropriate medical help.

The midwife is also responsible for helping to care for the infant for up to 4 weeks after the birth, advising on babycare, feeding and general health issues. When mothers and babies are discharged from the maternity unit they will be referred to a midwife near their home for continuing care.

In labour wards, midwives and doctors work closely together. Midwives provide support and care during labour, and must also be adept with the increasing amount of technology now available to them. Midwives also work in high-technology neonatal units, providing intensive care for babies who are small or sick; in this area a midwife's ability to counsel and support distressed parents is particularly important.

Outside hospitals and clinics, midwives provide antenatal, intranatal and postnatal care to women and families within hospitals, clinics and in the community including delivering babies at home.

In the UK student midwives follow a three-year programme of education leading to qualification as a midwife and the award of a diploma or degree at higher education level. Minimum entry requirements are five GCSE passes.

It is not essential to train as a nurse before becoming a midwife, but some midwives are also qualified nurses. Registered nurses can take an 18-month programme to become a midwife. Training involves experience in both hospital and community settings, where antenatal, labour and postnatal care is provided. In addition to learning practical skills, theoretical study in anatomy, physiology, sociology and psychology is important. Further training can lead to specialisation in such areas as intensive care of the newborn, family planning and clinical teaching.

In the USA certified nurse-midwives are educated in both nursing and midwifery. Before entering one of the many nurse-midwifery programmes throughout the USA to obtain either a Master's degree or a certificate, it is first necessary to be licensed as a registered nurse (RN). Some nurse-midwifery education programmes accept RNs with a diploma obtained through a hospital programme. Some education programmes offer a three-year plan in which nursing is studied during the first year, and a Master's degree and a nurse-midwifery certificate are obtained by finishing the rest of the programme.

Upon successful completion of a programme accredited by the American College of Nurse-Midwives (ACNM), the graduate is eligible to sit for the national examination conducted by the ACNM Certification Council, Inc. Further information on certification is available directly from the College.

Information on careers in midwifery is available from the midwifery college or association in your country; addresses for countries not listed below are available from the International Confederation of Midwives in London.

*American College of Nurse-Midwives:* 818 Connecticut Avenue, NW, Suite 900, Washington, DC 20006, USA (tel +1-202-728-9860; fax 202-728-9897; e-mail info@acnm.org Website www.acnm.org/).

*Royal College of Midwives:* 15 Mansfield Street, London W1M 0BE, UK (tel 020-7312 3535; fax 020-7312 3536).

*Australian College of Midwives Inc:* 1st Floor, 3 Bowen Crescent, Melbourne, VIC 3000, Australia.

*New Zealand College of Midwives Inc:* PO Box 21106, 906-908 Colombo Street, Edgeware, Christchurch, New Zealand (tel +64-3-377 2732; fax 03-377 5662; e-mail nzcom@clear.net.nx Website http://webnz.com/midwives/).

*International Confederation of Midwives:* Eisenhowerlaan 138, 2517 KN Den Haag, The Netherlands (tel +31-703-060520; fax 703-3555651; Website www.internationalmidwives.org).

## HOME CARE

Home care workers (or home care assistants) provide assistance to people in their homes that does not require specific nursing skills. They help with dressing and feeding, bathing and toileting, and changing clients' bed linen. Other tasks include talking with clients, helping them to maintain contact with family, friends and community, and assisting with their shopping and recreation. The aim is to achieve maximum independence and quality of life for the client. The care worker may also accompany them on trips that help them to remain part of the community.

In the UK the United Kingdom Homecare Association Ltd produces a handbook for care workers, which includes information on training. The Association represents independent organisations providing home care services, and is concerned with setting high standards of domiciliary care. Information on working in the public sector is available from the Local Government Management Board.

*United Kingdom Homecare Association Ltd:* 42b Banstead Road, Carshalton Beeches, Surrey SM5 3NW, UK (tel 020-8288 1551; fax 020-8288 1550; Website www.ukhca.co.uk).

*Local Government Management Board:* Layden House, 76-86 Turnmill Street, London EC1M 5QU, UK (tel 020-7296 6585; fax 020-7296 6666).

## PARAMEDICS/EMERGENCY MEDICAL TECHNICIANS

For many years ambulance drivers were simply that, they loaded and unloaded patients and had some first-aid skills but for many years they were essentially chauffers for emergency doctors. Nowadays with increasing dangers in modern life from bigger faster vehicles or criminal activity the risk of a fatality if treatment is dealyed has grown; rising pressures on staff now mean that a doctor can not always be spared to ride in an ambulance when that vehicle may be as likely to be dealing with a drunken partygoer as it is to be attending a major car crash. Therefore in Britain and America a new professional has entered the medical profession the Paramedic or Emergency Medical Technician, usually easy to spot in their green jumpsuits and quite common to many people through television's *ER* and *Casualty.*

In Britain there are several grades of paramedic and the training they recieve and help they can give to patients varies accordingly. The *British Association of Emergency Medical Technicians* lists six levels of skill: *First Responder, Emergency Medical Technician* (with three additional grades *D, I+I* and *Advanced*) and *Registered EMT Paramedic,* the first five can be awarded to those not in full-time paramedical employment.

A First Responder has taken the First Aid At Work four day course. The EM Technician is the entry level for professional pre-hospital carers and includes ambulance staff and nurses who have taken 60 hours of academic study and 250 hours hands-on training, this is also covered by accredited Ambulance Aid courses at Levels 1-3. An *EMT-D* has been trained in the use of defibrillators, and must obtain a certificate of competency annually, while the *EMT-I+I* has undergone training in cannulation, fluid therapy, endotracheal intubation and the management of traumatised patients. The practical training requirement is for the candidate to have carried out a minimum of 25 successful intubations and again an annual competency certificate is required. The *EMT-Advanced* must have obtained both previous skill levels. *Registered Paramedics* must hold all previous qualifications, an annual competency certificate and be in full-time paramedical employment. All paramedic staff are required to undergo regular retraining with an approved training officer or Doctor.

*National Association of Emergency Medical Technicians:* 408 Monroe Street, Clinton, MS 39056-4210, USA (tel +1-800 34 NAEMT; Website www.naemt.org).
*British Association of Emergency Medical Technicians:* Ty Cristion, Bodedern, Anglesey, LL65 3UB, UK (tel 01407-742222; e-mail admin@baemt.org.uk Website www.baemt.org.uk).

# Dentistry

## DENTIST

The dentist is the key health professional in the provision of dental care. Much of a dentist's work is highly technical and requires a great deal of manual dexterity. There is an increasing emphasis on preventive work, and the dentist is also expected to counsel and educate patients.

Approximately two-thirds of dentists in the UK work in general practice. From their earnings these dentists equip and maintain their surgery and pay their staff – for example, nurses and receptionists. Most young dentists start working as assistants or associates in a group practice; later they may become partners or set up a practice on their own. The clinical work undertaken in general practice is wide. Most dentists provide a complete range of treatment, although some refer more complicated cases to hospital.

Hospital dentists follow a similar career path to that of hospital doctors (see above), moving through training grades and postgraduate study towards their chosen specialisation. Four specialisations are recognised: orthodontics, oral surgery, restorative dentistry and paediatric dentistry. Oral surgeons may work in conjunction with medical specialists.

The Community Dental Service is concerned with special needs patients, public health education, research and treatment, usually in local clinics, and school inspections. Newly qualified dentists can enter the Service as dental public health officers.

There are 13 dental schools in the UK. The Bachelor of Dental Surgery course lasts 5 years (6 years for those who did not take science subjects at 'A' level). The course involves theoretical and practical training in all branches of dentistry. On completion of the course the dentist must register with the General Dental Council in order to practice in Britain. The main source of job advertisements is the *British Dental Journal*.

In the USA. dental education programmes are conducted at the post-college level. Basic dental education programmes last for a minimum of 4 years, and lead to one of two equivalent degrees: Doctor of Dental Surgery (DDS) or Doctor of Dental Medicine (DMD). Before a dentist can treat patients in the USA, his or her qualifications must be approved by a governmental agency so that the dentist can be awarded a license to practise. Licensure is carried out at state level. Licensure requirements vary from state to state, and a license awarded by a particular state board of dentistry permits the dentist to practise only in that state. The American Dental Asociation produce an informative booklet, *Information on Education and Licensure*, for those who wish to work or train as dentists in the USA.

**Note for US Dentists:** In some European countries, a US dentist may work as a 'dental assistant', where the term does not mean a paraprofessional as in the U.S. but a graduate dentist who practices under the supervision of a licensed dentist and receives a salary or a comensurate percentage.

## DENTAL HYGIENIST

Dental hygienists are largely concerned with preventing tooth and gum problems. While dentists are responsible for carrying out filling or extraction work, they may prescribe other treatment that can be given by the dental hygienist – for example, scaling and polishing, or painting with fluoride. In hospitals, dental hygienists care for the patient's mouth before and after oral surgery. They also provide dental health education before treatment, giving information to patients on how to maintain healthy teeth and gums. Dental hygienists work in hospitals, in community dental services, and in general practice (in the UK about 70% of dental hygienists work in this category).

As with dentists, dental hygienists find that their training places great emphasis on acquiring manual skills. Training in the UK involves a one-year course at a dental hospital, for which good GCSE passes and two A-levels or previous training as a dental nurse are required. In the USA, dental hygienists undertake an educational programme accredited by the Commission on Dental Education; such a programme is conducted at the post-secondary level and lasts for a minimum of 2 years. Licensure by the appropriate state board of dentistry is then necessary.

# DENTAL NURSE

The dental nurse assists the dentist in the clinical treatment of patients, and also cares for the patient before and after treatment. Clinical duties include mixing filling compounds or impression materials to the dentist's specification, helping to keep the patient's mouth clean during treatment, processing X-rays, completing record cards, sterilising instruments and equipment, and generally keeping the surgery in good order. The UK's 27,000 dental nurses are mostly employed in general practices but some work in dental hospitals, community dental services and even the armed forces. Working as a dental nurse may form a basis for studying to become a dental hygienist.

Various training options are available. In the UK it is possible to study for a National Certificate, either by combining 2 years' full-time surgery experience with evening classes, or by taking a full-time training course at a dental hospital or college of further education. In the USA formal education in dental assisting is available, although generally neither this nor licensure are required for employment (the exception is in those states where dental assistants are registered to perform intraoral functions).

# DENTAL THERAPIST

Dental therapists work exclusively within the community dental service and hospitals, providing dental care to children and expectant mothers. They generally carry out the same duties as the dental hygienist including cleaning and polishing the teeth, applying fluoride gels, and giving advice on dental health education. But the therapist is also able to undertake simple dental fillings and extract children's teeth, to the written prescription of the patients' dentist. Applicants need to have had experience as a dental nurse.

In the UK there are three training courses for dental therapists offering a Diploma in Dental Therapy, these are in London, Cardiff and Sheffield, with another in Liverpool for qualified dental hygienists. The educational requirements for these courses are 5 good GCSE passes and a nationally recognised dental nursing qualification, or two A-level passes. On successful completion of the diploma course and registration with the General Dental Council the therapist is free to practise, although their registration must be renewed annually.

# DENTAL TECHNICIAN

Dental technicians prepare dental applications for individual patients. They make dentures, crowns and bridges and prepare corrective braces for the teeth. Most specialise in a particular subdiscipline after training, in prosthetics, crowns and bridges, orthodontics or maxillo-facial technology. In larger hospitals, some technicians specialising in maxillo-facial work make appliances for patients suffering from facial disease or injury.

Much of the work is done by hand, producing each individual piece of work to exact specifications. From impressions of the patient's teeth and gums, the technician makes casts and moulds, and gradually assembles the device required, paying strict attention to facial shape and tooth colour, as well as ensuring a comfortable and effective fit in the patient's mouth. Technicians do not normally have direct contact with patients, but work in the laboratory to the dental surgeon's prescription. They work in hospital laboratories, in community dental services and in commercial laboratories.

Training as a dental technician can involve one of several routes, although all emphasise the importance of practical skills and developing the manual dexterity central to the work. Training places may be available in dental practice laboratories, hospital dental departments or commercial laboratories, involving part-time study at college. Full-time courses in dental technology are available at some colleges (lasting 3 years in the UK). In the USA formal education is typically not necessary for employment.

## FURTHER INFORMATION

Information on training, qualifications and careers is available from the dental association in your country, although some like the British Dental Association also produce information aimed at foreign dentists coming to the UK. There are also organisations representing the individual professions referred to above; these are listed by country in Part III or the national dental associations listed below will be able to provide you with details of these.

*American Dental Association:* 211 East Chicago Avenue, Chicago IL 60611, USA (tel +1-312-440 2500; Website www.ada.org).

*British Dental Association:* 64 Wimpole Street, London W1M 8AL, UK (tel 020-7935 0875; fax 020-7487 5232; e-mail Enquiries@bda-dentistry.org.uk Website www.bda-dentistry.org.uk).

*Australian Dental Association:* PO Box 520, St Leonards, NSW 1590, (75 Lithgow Street, St Leonards NSW 2065), Australia (tel 02-9906 4412; fax 02-9906 4917; e-mail adainc@ada.org.au Website www.ada.org.au).

*Canadian Dental Association:* 1815 Alta Vista Drive, Ottawa, Ontario K1G 3Y6, Canada (tel 613-523 1770; fax 613-523 7736; e-mail reception@cda-adc.ca Website www.cda-adc.ca).

*New Zealand Dental Association:* PO Box 28 084, Auckland 5, New Zealand (tel 09-524 2778; fax 09-520 5256; e-mail nzda@nzda.org.nz).

*World Dental Federation (FDI):* 7 Carlisle Street, London W1V 5RG, UK (tel 020-7935 7852; fax 020-7486 0183; Website www.fdi.org.uk).

# Supporting Medical Professions

In addition to the professions already discussed there are many areas of health work which are equally professional and specialised in their training and work but which in the UK are considered as having a supporting role to the main healthcare professions. These are described below and include, biomedical science, occupational therapy, physiotherapy, podiatry and radiography. Overseas professionals wishing to find out more about working in the UK can contact their equivalent professional body or the umbrella organisation for these professions, the Council for Professions Supplementary to Medicine, which is often responsible for arranging mutual recognition agreements.

*Council for Professions Supplementary to Medicine:* 184 Kennington Park Road, London, SE11 4BU, UK (tel 020-7582 0866).

## BIOMEDICAL SCIENCE

Investigations carried out by biomedical scientists play an important part in modern medical care. Their work is vital for the diagnosis of disease, the evaluation of the effectiveness of treatment, and research into the causes and cures of disease. Biomedical scientists are employed in all aspects of health care, including public and private sector hospitals, research laboratories and government departments. The major areas of specialisation are clinical chemistry, haematology, transfusion science, cellular pathology, medical microbiology, virology and immunology.

In the UK a degree in a relevant science subject is usually necessary to work in biomedical science. Anyone who wishes to be employed in a qualified grade in a pathology or biomedical laboratory in the NHS sector must be registered with the Council for Professions Supplementary to Medicine; this will involve obtaining a relevant degree, successfully completing 1 or 2 years' supervised laboratory experience, which includes filling a training logbook and passing an oral examination.

In the USA the equivalent career field is known as clinical laboratory science (CLS). Most CLS professionals complete a baccalaureate degree or an associate degree with laboratory work experience. Professional certification by a nationally recognised certifying body is a prerequisite for most positions in the field (one such organisation is the National Certification Agency (NCA) for Medical Laboratory Personnel). Certification criteria generally include graduation from an accredited CLS programme or accumulated work experience; experience in clinical chemistry, haematology, microbiology and blood banking is usually required. Some states require medical laboratory technologists to be licensed at the state level.

The Institute of Biomedical Science in London can provide information on training, qualifications and careers. The American Society for Clinical Laboratory Science is a similar source of information in the USA, and has a publication called *Opportunities in Medical Technology Careers* available that covers educational requirements, job opportunities and salary levels.

*American Society for Clinical Laboratory Science:* 7910 Woodmont Avenue, Suite 530, Bethesda, Maryland 20814, USA (tel +1-301-657-2768; fax 301-657-2909; Website www.ascls.org).

*Institute of Biomedical Science:* 12 Coldbath Square, London EC1R 5HL, UK (tel 020-7713 0214; fax 020-7436 4946; e-mail mail@ibms.org Website www.ibms.org).

*Australian Institute of Medical Scientists:* PO Box 1911, Milton, QLD 4064, Australia (tel +61-7-3876 2988; fax 07-3876 2999; e-mail aimsnat@medserv.com.au Website www.aims.org.au).

*Canadian Society for Medical Laboratory Science:* PO Box 2830 LCD1, Hamilton, Ontario L8N 3N8, Canada (tel +1-905-528 8642; fax 905-528 4968; Website www.csmls.org/).

*New Zealand Institute of Medical Laboratory Science:* PO Box 3270, Christchurch, New Zealand (tel +64-3-313 4761; fax 03-313 20989; e-mail nzimls@exevents.co.nz Website www.nzimls.org.nz).

# DIETETICS

Dietitians apply the science of nutrition to promoting health and treating and preventing disease. They work in both clinical and community settings. Their work involves increasing public awareness of the relationship between nutrition and health, and eliminating health hazards associated with food during production and distribution. Some dietitians specialise in particular areas, such as the treatment of children or people with particular medical conditions. A controlled diet is always necessary for diabetics, for example, and the dietitian provides appropriate support and advice to these patients. Others practise among a wide range of people needing dietary advice.

Whatever the reasons for a patient's referral, the dietitian identifies key areas in their eating habits and negotiates change where necessary. Dietitians therefore apply their knowledge to developing a diet plan appropriate to the patient's condition and lifestyle. Dietitians work with patients and their carers, taking into account food habits, cultural or religious customs, and social and financial position. They work as part of a multidisciplinary team with doctors, nurses, therapists and other staff. They have an important role in educating individual patients, other clinicians and the general public about nutrition in both sickness and health.

Dietitians may also specialise in areas such as oncology or gastroenterology; or they may choose to work within the community, with elderly people, or with people with mental health problems or learning disabilities. Research can be another important area for dietitians.

In the UK dietitians become qualified by completing either a four-year degree in nutrition or dietetics, or a two-year postgraduate diploma in dietetics after a first degree in a related subject such as physiology or biochemistry. The British Dietetic Association can supply general careers information and details of where recognised courses can be taken. In the USA information is available from the American Dietetic Association.

*American Dietetic Association:* 216 West Jackson Boulevard, Chicago, Illinois 60606-6995, USA (tel +1-312-899 0040; e-mail cdr@eatright.org Website www.eatright.org).

*British Dietetic Association:* 5th Floor, Elizabeth House, 22 Suffolk Street, Queensway, Birmingham B1 1LS, UK (tel 0121-616 4900; fax 0121-616 4901; Website www.bda.uk.com).

*Dietitians' Association of Australia:* 1/8 Phipps Close, Deakin ACT 2600, Australia (tel +61-2-6282 9555; fax 02-6282 9888; e-mail scassidy.daa@webone.com.au Website www.daa.com.au).

*Dietetians of Canada:* 480 University Avenue, Suite 604, Toronto, Ontario M5G 1V2, Canada (tel +1-416-596 0857; fax 416-596 0603; e-mail centralinfo@dietitians.ca Website www.dietitians.ca).

*New Zealand Dietetic Association Inc:* PO Box 5065, Wellington, New Zealand.

## OCCUPATIONAL THERAPY

Occupational therapy is the treatment of physical and psychiatric conditions using specially selected activities, in order to help people who are temporarily or permanently disabled to recover independence and cope with everyday life. It involves working in one of three main areas: with the physically disabled; with those with mental health problems; and with people who have learning difficulties.

Occupational therapists work in hospital and community settings, and also in people's homes. Treatment frequently focuses on helping people with everyday activities; for example, teaching new ways of managing basic personal care and home skills. It may also mean helping people manage in social or potentially difficult situations, and encouraging them to practise skills necessary for them to return to work. Providing support and advice to family carers is also an important aspect of the therapist's work.

Occupational therapists work in many specialities – for example, with people with spinal or head injuries, or with people who have had strokes, heart attacks or amputations. Some therapists work with disabled children, or in the rehabilitation of elderly people. Older people face problems ranging from stiff joints to the more serious effects of a stroke, heart condition or memory loss. Therapists aim to enable them to continue living at home, with as little dependence on relatives as possible. If people are in residential care, the therapist will visit them there, advising staff and recommending treatment.

All preregistration occupational therapy courses in the UK are BSc degree level (or above) and are validated by the College of Occupational Therapists, Council for Professions Suplementary to medicine (CPSM) and the awarding university. State registration with the CPSM is required in order to be able to practice in the UK, and successful completion of a validated course will confer eligibility for State registration.

To become an occupational therapist in the USA, you must complete an education programme accredited by the Accreditation Council for Occupational Therapy Education. Three routes are possible: a Bachelor's degree, a post-baccalaureate certificate programme, or a professional Master's degree programme; all of these include a period of supervised clinical experience. To become an occupational therapy assistant, it is necessary to complete either a two-year associate degree or one of a limited number of certificate programmes; these accredited programmes also include supervised clinical experience. Entrance requirements vary from school to school, but will typically require previous study in the biological and behavioural sciences, and often voluntary or paid work experience with disabled people.

The College of Occupational Therapists in the UK can provide career information and a list of places where occupational therapy can be studied. Similar information is available from the American Occupational Therapy Association in the USA.

*American Occupational Therapy Association Inc:* 4720 Montgomery Lane, PO Box 31220, Bethesda, Maryland 20824-1220, USA (tel +1-301-652 2682; fax +1-301-652 7711; e-mail accred@aota.org Website www.aota.org).

*College of Occupational Therapists:* 106-114 Borough High Street, London SE1 1LB, UK (tel 020-7357 6480; fax 020-7450 2299; Website www.cot.co.uk Careers Line 020-7450 2332).

*Australian Association of Occupational Therapists (AAOT):* 6 Spring Street, Fitzroy VIC 3065, Australia (tel +61-3-9416 1021; fax +61-3-9416 1421; e-mail otausnat@ozemail.com.au).

*Canadian Association of Occupational Therapists:* CTTC Building, Suite 3400, 1125 Colonel By Drive, Ottawa, Ontario K1S 5R1, Canada (tel +1-613-523-2268; toll free 800-434 2268; fax +1-613-523-2552; Website www.caot.ca).

*New Zealand Association of Occupational Therapists:* PO Box 12-506 (Royal Society of New Zealand Offices, 4 Halswell Street, Thorndon), Wellington 6001, New Zealand (tel +64-4-473 6510; fax +64-4-473 1841).

## ORTHOPTICS

Orthoptists diagnose and treat defects of vision and abnormalities of eye movement.

Most orthoptists are employed in the eye department of a hospital, and see patients referred to them by GPs or local consultants. Others work in the community, providing vision screening in schools, mobile units and health clinics. In some specialist units the orthoptist's work is closely related to that of the ophthalmic consultant.

Much of an orthoptist's time is spent assessing vision in young children with eye problems, such as squint. If surgery is required, the orthoptist is involved in monitoring progress after the operation. In older patients the problems vary from strokes to damage caused in accidents; orthoptists diagnose the problem, advise on the best course of treatment and monitor progress. In some clinics orthoptists assist the ophthalmic consultant in the diagnosis and management of glaucoma.

In the UK training is through a three-year degree course, successful completion of which leads to statutory State Registration. For further information on orthoptics in the UK contact the British Orthoptic Society.

*British Orthoptic Society:* Tavistock House North, Tavistock Square, London WC1H 9HX, UK.

*Optometrists Association Australia:* PO Box 185, Carlton South, VIC 3053, Australia (tel +61-3-9663 6833; fax 03-9663 7478; e-mail ausoptom@ozemail.com.au).

# PHARMACY

The pharmacist is an expert in the field of drugs and medicines. Pharmacists understand the properties of drugs and their effects on human physiology, in order to advise clinical staff when they should, or should not, be used. It is also the responsibility of the pharmacist to ensure that the strict legal controls on drugs are adhered to.

Once qualified, the pharmacist has a wide choice of career options, including working as a community pharmacist (the 'local chemist'), as a hospital pharmacist, or in the pharmaceutical industry. Some hospital pharmacists undertake research work, often in collaboration with medical staff or colleagues in the pharmaceutical industry.

Community pharmacists work from high street, local and rural pharmacies and ensure that medicines ordered on doctors' prescriptions or bought over the counter are correctly and safely supplied, with appropriate patient counselling on use and adverse side-effects.

Hospital pharmacists work with doctors, nurses and other health professionals to ensure that patients receive the most appropriate medicines and that those medicines are used in the most effective way. Other medical products, such as sterile preparations and intravenous feeds, are prepared in hospital pharmacies, by or under the supervision of the pharmacist. Pharmacists formulate medicines in the pharmacy when necessary. The pharmacist's job also entails a fair amount of contact with patients on the wards and in out-patient departments. Stock control and general administration and management of the pharmacy are among their other responsibilities.

Many pharmacists work in the pharmaceutical industry in research and product development; others undertake research in universities and hospitals. Areas of specialisation available to pharmacists include the use of radioactive materials and paediatric care.

Pharmacists in the UK complete a four-year degree course leading to a MPharm at one of 16 universities, followed by the Royal Pharmeceutical Society's one year pre-registration training in a pharmacy with competency based registration examination. The professional associations for pharmacists in the UK (and also the training, assessment, and registration authorities) are the Royal Pharmaceutical Society of Great Britain and the Pharmaceutical Society of Northern Ireland, which can supply more detailed career information and the addresses of schools of pharmacy.

In the USA competition for places in pharmacy school is intense. A minimum of 5 years of college is required for a Bachelor of Science degree in pharmacy. Many colleges require students to complete the first 2 years of pre-professional study before they are accepted onto the professional pharmacy programme. The profession has adopted plans to move towards a single-entry-level programme of study (PharmD), with a minimum of 6 years of study. Pharmacists are required to be licensed in all states, and to be eligible for a license candidates must be graduates of approved schools of pharmacy and successfully pass state licensing examinations. In most states candidates must also serve an internship period working under a practising pharmacist. Further careers information is available from the American Pharmaceutical Association.

British pharmacists considering working overseas can contact the Royal Pharmaceutical Society of Great Britain for information on the professional requirements for pharmacists in the country in which they wish to work.

*American Pharmaceutical Association:* 2215 Constitution Avenue, NW, Washington, DC 20037, USA (tel +1-202-628 4410; fax 202-783 2351; e-mail membership@mail.aphanet.org Website www.aphanet.org).

*Royal Pharmaceutical Society of Great Britain:* 1 Lambeth High Street, London SE1 7JN, UK (tel 020-7735 9141; fax 020-7735 7629; e-mail enquiries@ rpsgb.org.uk).

*Pharmaceutical Society of Northern Ireland:* 73 University Street, Belfast BT7 1HL, UK (tel 028-9032 6927).

*Pharmaceutical Society of Australia:* Pharmacy House, 44 Thesiger Court, Deakin ACT 2600, Australia (tel +61-2-6283 4777; fax 02-6285 2869; e-mail psa.nat@psa.org.au).

*Pharmacy Examining Board of Canada*: 123 Edward Street, Suite 603, Toronto, Ontario M5G 1E2, Canada (tel +1-416-979 2431; fax 416-599 9244; e-mail pebccdn@ibm.net).

*Pharmaceutical Society of New Zealand:* PO Box 11-640, Wellington, New Zealand (tel +64-4-802 0030; fax 04-382 9297; Website www.psnz.org.nz).

*International Pharmaceutical Federation:* PO Box 84200, 2508 AE The Hague, The Netherlands (tel +31-70-302 1970; fax 70-302 1999; Website www.fip.nl).

# PHYSIOTHERAPY

Physiotherapy involves the rehabilitation of people who have suffered loss of physical function or mobility through illness, injury or old age. Using their special skills in exercise, movement, electrotherapy and manual techniques such as massage, manipulation and mobilisation, physiotherapists help patients resume as active and independent a life as possible.

Physiotherapists work closely with other health professionals, including occupational therapists, GPs, health visitors and district nurses, as well as with the patient's relatives and carers.

Physiotherapists work in a variety of situations, including in the local community, in hospitals, in industry, in special schools and in private practice. In the community treatment and advice for patients and carers are given in their own homes, in residential and nursing homes or day centres, in schools and in health centres. In hospitals physiotherapists are needed in virtually every department, from general out-patients to intensive care. Hospitals also often have the facilities for more specialised therapy to be carried out. Physiotherapists are also involved with preventive medicine and health education, and some work with sportsmen and sportswomen to improve their performance and accelerate recovery from injury. As well as treating injuries, physiotherapists advise on eliminating the risks of injury by correct self-care and health education. Other areas in which physiotherapists can specialise include working in the community, orthopaedics, obstetrics, private practice and working with elderly people.

All physiotherapy courses in the UK lead to a BSc honours degree in physiotherapy, and last for 3 or 4 years full time. In addition to these there some part time courses available over a four year period. Approved qualifications are acceptable for membership of the Chartered Society of Physiotherapy and for State Registration; the Society can provide a list of recognised schools and further careers information. In the UK physiotherapists working for the NHS will work around 36 hours per week with some extra time on a rota to cover weekends and evenings; mostly this will be for additional pay or time off in lieu. Rates of pay at the time of writing were between £13655 and £33780 according to position and experience although new rates of pay are due to be agreed in March 2000.

In the USA training in physical therapy (as physiotherapy is known) is available in 176 institutions throughout the country – half at the baccalaureate and half at the Master's level. Physical therapists receive extensive training on accredited programmes and graduate with a Bachelor's degree or an advanced degree (Master's or Doctorate). The American Physical Therapy Association (APTA) encourages students pursuing a career in physical therapy to enter the profession with a post-baccalaureate degree; the majority of the colleges and universities are in the process of changing their programmes from Bachelor's to post-baccalaureate degrees; however, obtaining a degree at Bachelor's level allows full professional privileges and currently fulfils all licensure requirements. The *Where We Stand* and *International Issues* pages of APTA's website provide careers and related information for those wishing to work in the USA.

*American Physical Therapy Association:* 1111 North Fairfax Street, Alexandria, Virginia 22314, USA (tel +1-703-684-2782; fax 703-684-7343; Website www.apta.org).

*Chartered Society of Physiotherapy:* 14 Bedford Row, London WC1R 4ED, UK (tel 020-7306 6666; fax 020-7306 6611; e-mail general.csp@csphysio.org.uk Website csphysio.org.uk).

*Australian Physiotherapy Association:* PO Box 6465, Melbourne, Vic 3004, Australia (tel +61-3-9534 9400; fax 03-9534 9199; e-mail national.office@physiotherapy.asn.au Website www.physiotherapy.asn.au).

*Canadian Physiotherapy Association:* 2345 Yonge Street, Suite 410, Toronto, Ontario M4P 2E5, Canada (tel +1-416-932-1888; fax 416-932-9708; e-mail information@physiotherapy.ca Website www.physiotherapy.ca).

*New Zealand Society of Physiotherapists:* PO Box 27386, Wellington, New Zealand (tel +64-4-801 6500; fax 04-801 5571; e-mail nzsp@mail.netlink.co.nz).

*South African Society of Physiotherapy:* PO Box 92125, Norwood 2117, South Africa (tel +27-11-485 1467; fax 011-485 1613; Website saphysio.org.za).

*World Confederation for Physical Therapy:* 46 Grosvenor Gardens, London, SW1W 0EB, UK (tel 020-7881 9234; fax 020-7881 9239; e-mail wcpt@dial.pipex.com).

# PODIATRY/CHIROPODY

Podiatry (often known as chiropody in the UK, although the term 'podiatry' is gradually being adopted) is concerned with keeping the feet in healthy condition and with the treatment of foot-related problems and disabilities. It involves curative foot care and preventative services, and also the recognition of medical conditions that manifest themselves in the feet. Chiropodists work in a variety of places, including private practice, hospitals, community health centres, nursing homes, doctors' surgeries and industry.

Central to a podiatrist's clinical work is the assessment, diagnosis and treatment of diseases and abnormalities of the foot. A new patient's medical history will include details of any earlier foot problems. The podiatrist then makes a careful examination of the patient's feet; depending on the problem, this can involve analysis of how the patient walks and a biomechanical examination using specialised equipment. A plan of treatment is then drawn up.

The podiatrist's work can vary greatly from patient to patient, depending on their particular problems. The aim is not only to cure the patient's problem, but to prevent it recurring, or any new ones developing. Health promotion is another important aspect. Where problems can not be cured or prevented, the aim of the treatment is to keep the patient as free from pain as possible, to enable them to remain mobile, and to stop matters from getting worse.

Treatments carried out by podiatrists include removing corns and calluses; treating a wide range of nail conditions; using chemical treatments for verrucae and corns; prescribing a range of insoles (*orthoses*) for patients to wear in their shoes, to prevent their problem returning; and using specialised podiatric instruments and equipment.

Podiatrists are sometimes supported in their work by foot care assistants, who are trained to carry out some supportive tasks.

Specialisations available to podiatrists include treating patients with diabetes or rheumatoid arthritis, who are at greater risk of developing serious foot problems; sports medicine; surgical aspects of podiatry; and treating particular age groups, such as children or the elderly.

The recognised standard for the profession in the UK is State Registration, set by the Government through the Council for Professions Supplementary to Medicine. Only State Registered Chiropodists can work within the National Health Service. To reach this standard a podiatrist/chiropodist must complete a three-year course leading to a BSc in Podiatry. There are currently thirteen schools providing degree courses in the UK, details of which are available from the Society of Chiropodists and Podiatrists.

In the USA podiatrists need to have graduated from a college of podiatric medicine in the USA, and to have successfully completed a qualification examination. In addition, all states require podiatrists to pass state licensure examinations, and over two-thirds require an additional year of postgraduate training.

The Society of Chiropodists and Podiatrists in the UK can provide general advice about the profession, as well as addresses for relevant organisations and schools overseas. The American Podiatric Medical Association can provide information on the profession in the USA, and information on schools and state boards for examination and licensure.

*American Podiatric Medical Association:* 9312 Old Georgetown Road, Bethesda, Maryland 20814-1698, USA (tel +1-301-571-9200; e-mail askapma@apma.org Website www.apma.org).

*Society of Chiropodists and Podiatrists:* 53 Welbeck Street, London W1M, UK 7HE (tel 020-7486 3381; fax 020-7935 6359; e-mail eng@scpod.org Website www.feetforlife.org).

*Australian Podiatry Council:* 41 Derby Street, Collingwood, VIC 3066, Australia (tel +61-3-9416 3111; fax 03-9416 3188).

*Canadian Podiatric Medical Association:* 900-45 Sheppard Avenue E., Toronto, Ontario M2N 5W9, Canada (tel 416-927 9111; fax 416-733 2491; e-mail info@podiatrycanada.org Website www.podiatrycanada.org).

*New Zealand Society of Podiatrists Inc:* PO box 14697, Wellington, New Zealand (Website www.podiatry.org.nz).

## PSYCHOLOGY

Clinical psychologists work with people experiencing a variety of mental and physical problems. They draw on psychological knowledge and theory to assess these problems, recommend clinical interventions and evaluate the outcome. These problems may be emotional, related to addiction, psychosexual, social/interpersonal, psychosomatic, medical or due to various other causes.

A period of assessment always precedes treatment. In all cases, the psychologist tries to understand or change an essentially psychological problem of an individual, family or group. Much of the psychologist's work involves the clinical assessment of patients in relation to diagnosis, prognosis, suitability for treatment, guidance and rehabilitation techniques.

Clinical psychologists usually work in a clinic of some kind, many of which are attached to general or psychiatric hospitals, and in university psychology departments, general practices and community mental health centres. They work with various groups, including children and young people, the elderly, people with learning or physical disabilities, and people in the penal system.

In the UK an honours degree in psychology is normally needed to enter professional training in clinical psychology. This training takes at least 3 years, and can be achieved through university-based courses, in-service training or independent training. Further information is available from the British Psychological Society.

*American Psychological Association:* 750 First Street, NE, Washington DC 20002-4242, USA (tel +1-202-336 5500; e-mail education@apa.org Website www.apa.org).

*British Psychological Society:* St Andrew's House, 48 Princess Road East, Leicester LE1 7DR, UK (tel 0116-254 9568; e-mail mail@bps.org.uk Website www.bps.org.uk).

*Australian Pyschological Society:* 1 Grattan Street, Carlton, VIC 3053, Australia (tel +61-3-9663 6166; fax 03-9663 6177; e-mail membership@ psychsociety.com.au Website www.aps.pyschsociety.com.au).

*Canadian Pyschological Association/Societe Canadienne de Pyschologie:* 151 Slater Street, Suite 205, Ottawa, Ontario K1P 5H3, Canada (tel +1-613-237 2144).

*New Zealand Psychological Society Inc:* PO Box 4092, Wellington, New Zealand (tel +64-4-801 5414; fax 04-801 5366; e-mail office@pyschology.org.nz Website www.pyschology.org.nz).

# RADIOGRAPHY

In the UK radiography has two main branches: diagnostic and therapuetic radiography, while the different types of radiographer are known as radiologic technologists in the USA.

Diagnostic radiographers produce high-quality images that aid diagnosis of disease and the extent of injury. In a hospital diagnostic radiographers undertake a very wide range of work. A variety of imaging processes are used, and radiography equipment is becoming increasingly complex and computerised. Radiographers have to be computer literate, but the main tasks remain looking after patients and producing images. Diagnostic radiographers are responsible for ensuring that the patient is exposed only to the amount of radiation necessary to produce a diagnostic image. They are also involved in evaluating the final radiograph. As they learn to operate many different types of equipment, radiographers may specialise in an area such as ultrasound or magnetic resonance imaging. Some of the responsibilities of the diagnostic radiographer in the UK are assumed by separate professions in the USA. Ultrasound examinations, for example, are performed by the diagnostic medical sonographer, and work involving the use of radioactive materials is carried out by the nuclear medicine technologist.

Therapeutic radiographers plan and deliver prescribed treatments using x-radiation and other radiation sources. They contribute to a team effort, working with doctors, physicists and nurses to deliver care to patients suffering from cancer and some non-malignant tumours. The role of the therapuetic radiographer within the cancr care team is very specialised but they are able to develop their role to cover all aspects of the cancer patients care path.

All radiography qualifying courses in the UK are at undergarduate and postgraduate level. Undergraduate courses normally take 3 years to qualify (4 years in Northern Ireland), and half the time will involve clinical education within hospital departments. Successful graduates are eligible for State Registration by the Radiographers Board of the Council for Professions Supplementary to Medicine, which is essential for employment in the NHS. In the USA the educational requirements for the various radiographic fields differ: in some instances high school graduates may enter training programmes in hospitals; other programmes require work at community colleges or four-year degree programmes.

The College of Radiographers in the UK and the American Society of Radiologic Technologists can provide further information on courses and careers.

*American Society of Radiologic Technologists:* 15000 Central Avenue SE, Albuquerque, New Mexico 87123-3917, USA (tel +1-505-298-4500; fax 505-298-5063; Website www.asrt.org).

*College of Radiographers:* 2 Carriage Row, 183 Eversholt Street, London NW1 1BU, UK (tel 020-7391 4500).

*Australian Institute of Radiography (AIR):* PO box 1169, Collingwood VIC 3066, Australia (tel +61-3-9419 3336; fax 03-9416 0783).

*Canadian Association of Medical Radiation Technologists:* Suite 1510, 130 Albert Street, Ottawa, Ontario K1P 5G4, Canada (tel +1-613-234 0012; fax 613-234 1097; Website www.camrt.ca).

*New Zealand Institute of Medical Radiation Technology:* PO Box 25668, St Helier, Auckland, New Zealand (tel +64-9-528 1087).

*International Society of Radiographers and Radiological Technologists (ISRRT):* 170 The Donway West, Suite 404, Don Mills, Ontario M3B 1K8, Canada (tel +1-416-510-0805; fax 416-445 4268).

## SPEECH AND LANGUAGE THERAPY

Speech and language therapists work with people who have communication difficulties for a variety of reasons – physical, mental, social and emotional. After assessing the nature of the problem, therapists use their theoretical and practical skills to rehabilitate, educate and counsel patients and their families, with the aim of helping the patient to achieve as much independent communication as possible.

Patients treated range from children with delayed or disordered speech and language development to people with voice loss caused by damage either to the vocal cords or to the larynx, and from those who have suffered brain damage because of a head injury, stroke or progressive neurological disease to patients with mental health problems that have affected their ability to communicate.

The therapist's assessment of a patient's problem may lead to a course of therapy to improve the patient's own use of speech and language, or the therapist may suggest appropriate aids to communication.

Speech and language therapists normally work with either children or adults. Some specialise in just one area, such as patients with impaired hearing; others work with patients with a wide variety of problems, perhaps based in a hospital or health centre, or working within the community.

In the UK qualification is by a three or four-year course leading to an honours degree. Following graduation therapists obtain a licence to practise from the Royal College of Speech and Language Therapists – this is a requirement for employment in the National Health Service. The RCSLT has recently joined the Council for Professions Supplementary to Medicine and is discussing mutual recognition arrangements with professional bodies in Ireland, Australia, Canada and the USA.

*American Speech-Language Hearing Association:* 10801 Rockville Pike, Rockville, Maryland 20852, USA (tel +1-888-321 ASHA; Website www.asha.org).

*Royal College of Speech and Language Therapists:* 2/3 White Hart Yard, London SE1 1NX, UK (tel 020-7378 1200; fax 020-7403 7254; e-mail postmaster@rcslt.org Website www.rcslt.org).

*Speech Pathology Association of Australia:* 2nd Floor, 11-19 Bank Place, Melbourne VIC 3000, Australia (tel +61-3-9642 4899; fax +61-3-9642 4922; e-mail sppathau@vicnet.au Website http://home.vicnet.au/~sppathau/).

*Canadian Association of Speech-Language Pathologists and Audiologists:* 130 Albert Street, Ottawa, Ontario K1P 5G4, Canada (tel +1-613-567 9968; fax +1-613-567 2859; e-mail caslpa@caslpa.ca Website www.caslpa.ca).

*New Zealand Speech-Language Therapists Association:* Suite 369, 63 Remuera Road, Newmarket, Auckland (tel +64-3-235 8257; fax +64-3-235 8850 Website www.nzsta-speech.org.nz).

# Alternative Medicine

## INTRODUCTION

The various techniques included below are on the fringes of what is conventionally regarded as health care. None of them make use of modern drugs, and all of them place some emphasis on 'holistic' treatment – i.e. treating the patient 'as a whole'. These methods are generally divorced from the normal medical approach, which requires systematic understanding of the human body and the causes of illness, supported by clinical evidence in order to make a precise diagnosis and prescribe a course of treatment. It is for this reason that the various 'alternative' therapies often lack credibility in the eyes of the health establishment. Some of them are, however, becoming increasingly accepted, as explanations for their effectiveness are found, and to the extent that their credibility is increasing, they are losing their claim to be alternative in any meaningful sense.

All of them involve acquiring specialised skills of some kind, and various establishments offer appropriate training courses. Some degree of medical training is normally also required – this can be quite general, or can involve in-depth study of such subjects as physiology and anatomy. This is necessary as practitioners need to make medical diagnoses in order to determine what kind of treatment the patient needs, and in some cases embarking on alternative treatment without a sound medical understanding of a patients's condition can have disastrous consequences.

The numbers of practitioners in alternative medicine has increased significantly in the UK over the last decade, and there are now organisations representing standards for most of the techniques.

## ALTERNATIVE MEDICINE ABROAD

The degree to which these alternative techniques are recognised varies greatly from one country to the next. In general, however, there is official scepticism towards them and although acknowledgement of their value may be increasing, they remain on the periphery of what is usually accepted as health care. For any particular country in which you are interested you should try to make contact with the organisation representing your chosen technique in that country to find out about its status; if the address is not included in this book, the Ministry of Health may be able to help, and will at least be able to tell you whether the technique has state recognition.

## ACUPUNCTURE

Acupuncture is derived from ancient Chinese medicine. Today there are over 3 million practitioners worldwide, and although the majority of these practise in the East, over the last 50 years there has been an increasing number of people in the West training to become acupuncturists.

Treatment involves piercing the skin with needles at specific points – this is believed to restore the balance in flows of energy around the body. A range of conditions can be treated – including arthritis, high blood pressure and menstrual disorders – and the treatment can also be used to induce anaesthesia.

The theory underlying treatment is very involved and so detailed training is required. If you are interested in studying acupuncture, a list of accredited colleges and other training centres should be available from the acupuncture organisation in your country. These organisations will also be able to provide information on the extent to which acupuncture is an accepted form of treatment in your country; in the UK, for example, a growing number of traditional acupuncturists are practising in the National Health Service, and many registered doctors practise acupuncture in addition to their normal medical work. In the USA however, the acceptance of qualifications will vary by state, with some requiring herb or science training and the number of required hours spent in training ranging from 1300 to 2500.

*National Acupuncture and Oriental Medicine Alliance:* 14637 Starr Road SE, Olalla, Washington 98359, USA (tel +1-253-851 6896; fax 253-851 6883; Website www.AcuAll.org).

*British Acupuncture Council:* 63 Jeddo Road, London W12 9HQ, UK (tel 020-8735 0400; fax 020-8735 0404; e-mail info@acupuncture.org.uk Website www.acupuncture.org.uk).

*Australian Acupuncture and Traditional Chinese Medicine Association Ltd:* PO Box 5142, West End, QLD 4101, Australia.

*Acupuncture Foundation of Canada Institute:* Suite 204, 2131 Lawrence Avenue East, Scarborough, Ontario M1R 5G4, Canada (tel +1-416-752 3988; fax +1-416-752 4398; e-mail info@afcinstitute.com Website www.afcinstitute.com).

*New Zealand Register of Acupuncturists:* PO Box 9950, Wellington 6001, New Zealand (tel/fax +64-4-476 4866; e-mail nzra@acupuncture.org.nz Website www.acupuncture.org.nz).

*South African Chiropractic, Homeopathic and Allied Health Services Professional Council:* PO Box 17005, Groenkloof 0027, South Africa.

## CHIROPRACTIC

Chiropractic is a diagnostic, corrective and preventive therapy for mechanical disorders of the spine. Chiropractors focus on adjusting the vertebrae, but also work on the bones, joints, ligaments, tendons and muscles to effect improvements in the health of the person as a whole. Chiropractors use their hands for treatment; apart from X-rays for diagnosis, machinery and drugs are rarely used. Medical opinion is divided on chiropractic's benefits, but research has shown that it often succeeds where conventional methods fail.

In the UK, fully trained practitioners have 6 years' training and a BSc in chiropractic. At the time of writing a General Chiropractic Council is being established (following the passing of the Chiropractic Act in 1994), and once this is up and running only those practitioners registered with it will be entitled to describe themselves as chiropractors.

*American Chiropractic Association:* 1701 Clarendon Blvd, Arlington, VA 22209, USA (tel +1-800-986 4636; fax 703-243 2593; Website www.amerchiro.org/)

*British Chiropractic Association:* Blagrave House, 17 Blagrave Street, Reading RG1 0QB, UK (tel 0118-950 5950; fax 0118-958 8946; Website www.chiropractic-uk.co.uk).

*Canadian Chiropractic Assocation:* 1396 Eglinton Avenue West, Toronto, Ontario M6C 2E4, Canada (tel +1-416-781 5656; fax +1-416-781 7344; e-mail ccachiro@ccachiro.org).

*Chiropractors Association of Australia:* PO Box 241, Springwood, NSW 2777, or PO Box 6248, South Penrith DC, NSW 2750, Australia (tel +61-2-4751 5644; fax 02-4751 5856; e-mail caa_nat@pnc.com.au Website caa.com.au).

*New Zealand Chiropractors Association Inc:* PO Box 7144, Wellesly Street, Auckland, New Zealand.

*Chiropractic Association of South Africa:* 929 Pretorius Street, Arcadia, Gauteng, South Africa (tel +27-12-434832).

## HERBAL MEDICINE

This form of treatment is based on traditional methods involving a wide range of plants (and various parts of plants), including flowers, trees, and even seaweed. Herbalists prescribe a range of plant-based products in various forms – such as ointments, lotions and tablets – in the belief that these can assist healing, or maintain good health in an already healthy person. The prescription of herbal medicines is based on in-depth questioning about a patient's lifestyle, health and medical history.

Further information about training and working as a herbalist is available from the address below.

*National Institute of Medical Herbalists:* 56 Longbrook Street, Exeter EX4 6AH, UK.

## HOMEOPATHY

Homeopathy is 'treatment of the whole person'. Remedies are produced from animal, plant and mineral sources and are produced in a variety of forms. A central principle is that these extracts are provided as 'microdoses', which consequently are not supposed to produce side effects.

In the UK it is practised by medical doctors who have undertaken specialist training and who may practise homeopathy within the National Health Service, and by professional homeopaths who lack conventional medical training. The former are members of the Faculty of Homeopaths, while the lay homoeopaths are members of the Society of Homoeopaths. Training is available at a number of colleges throughout the country. In the USA a homeopath is also usually a medical doctor who has decided to specialise. Homeopathy is well established in Europe and in countries throughout the world; information on training and practice is available from the addresses below.

*National Center for Homeopathy:* 801 North Fairfax Street, Suite 306, Alexandria, Virginia 22314-1757, USA (tel +1-703-548-7790).

*Faculty of Homeopaths:* 15 Clerkenwell Close, London, EC12 0AA, UK (tel 020-7566 7810; Website www.trusthomeopathy.org)

*Society of Homoepaths:* 4a Artizan Road, Northampton, NN1 4HU, UK (tel 01604-621400; fax 01604-622622; Website www.homoeopathy.org.uk).

*Australian Federation of Homeopaths:* PO Box 806, Spit Junction NSW 2088, Australia.

*New Zealand Council of Homeopaths:* PO Box 51-195, Tawa, Wellington, New Zealand.

*Homeopathy Association of West Cape:* PO Box 426, Rondebosch, West Cape, South Africa (tel +27-21-689 5061).

## HYPNOTHERAPY

As its name suggests, hypnotherapy makes use of hypnosis to achieve therapeutic effects. Hypnosis is a state of altered consciousness during which the unconscious mind becomes receptive to suggestion. Hypnotherapy has proved particularly effective in the treatment of physical conditions where psychological factors are thought to be important; these include psychosomatic illnesses, and conditions caused or exacerbated by stress, such as migraines and eating disorders.

In the UK most hypnotherapists work on their own or in private practice. Further information on training is available from the address below.

*National Association of Counsellors, Hypnotherapists and Psychotherapists:* 145 Coleridge Road, Cambridge CB1 3PN, UK.

## OSTEOPATHY

Osteopathy is a system of diagnosing and treating patients by manipulating bones, muscles, ligaments and connective tissue. Osteopaths relieve pain and tension by applying precisely calculated and executed levels of touch, which range from gentle cranial work to vigorous manipulation.

Osteopathy is an increasingly respected form of 'alternative' therapy, and there is considerable evidence of its benefits. Especially as it was the first 'complementary health' profession to be accorded statutory recognition. Much of the treatment focuses on the manipulation of the spine, but it can have more extensive benefits than this would perhaps suggest, relieving the effects of a range of muscular and skeletal disorders.

Osteopathy involves a complex system of manipulation that requires a sound knowledge of anatomy. Before setting out on a course of osteopathic treatment, the osteopath makes a clinical examination of the patient's condition; this is an integral part of the procedure and vital in order to ensure that osteopathic manipulation is not performed on patients on whom it could inflict harm.

In the UK osteopathy is available on the National Health Service to a limited extent. From May 2000 the Osteopaths Act (1993) will be law and only those practitioners registered with the General Osteopathic Council will be entitled to call themselves osteopaths. Osteopaths can register under a Professional Portfolio and Profile scheme details of which can be obtained from the Council. Osteopathy has greater recognition in the USA where it is taught in medical schools. Further information on training and qualifications is available from the addresses below.

*American Osteopathic Association:* 142 E. Ontario Street, Chicago, Illinois 60611, USA (tel +1-312-202-8000; Website www.aoa-net.org).

*General Osteopathic Council:* 176 Tower Bridge Road, London, SE1 3LU, UK (tel 020-7357 6655; Website www.osteopathy.org.uk).

*Australian Osteopathic Association:* PO Box 242, Thornleigh, NSW 2130, Australia (tel +61-2-9980 8511; fax 02-9980 8466; e-mail aoa@tpgi.com.au Website www.osteopathic.com.au).

*Canadian College of Osteopathy:* 39 Alvin Avenue, Toronto, Ontario, Canada (e-mail ceo@ceo.edu Website www.ceo.edu/index).

# PART II

## Finding a Job Abroad

# INTRODUCTION

As is the case when looking for any kind of work, searching for a job in health care can involve a variety of different approaches. When looking for a position overseas, it is essential that you understand how the health sector is organised in the countries in which you are interested, so that you can focus your efforts appropriately. In some countries direct application may well bear fruit; in others you will need to scour the local press until suitable vacancies come up; in others you may have little choice but to apply through agencies or recruitment consultancies who specialise in dealing with the immigration and registration red tape for your profession in that particular country. If you are interested in working in the voluntary/NGO sector, you will need to know which organisations operate in the part(s) of the world where you are interested in working, and what their requirements are.

This section of the book includes advice on some of the main approaches to securing work overseas, and then provides extensive directories of organisations in both the paid and the voluntary/NGO sectors who can help you. To help you find your way around these directories, the Country Guides in Part III include summaries of the organisations working in the various countries and regions. These Guides also include overviews of how the health sectors are set up, and how opportunities can best be targeted.

As a first step you could contact First Point (tel 020-7724 9669; www.firstpointinter.com) who offer visa and other advice for those wanting to work abroad.

Part II concludes with a section outlining the preparations you need to make before leaving for a position abroad, including financial and administrative arrangements, and familiarising yourself with the language and culture in your destination country.

# THE PROS AND CONS OF WORKING ABROAD

**Pros:**
The opportunity for a new work experience.
The excitement of a new life in a new land.
Potentially better rates of pay for the same work.
Getting to work in a better climate.
The cost of living is often cheaper elsewhere, so your salary goes further.
Your job and home are in somebody else's expensive holiday resort

**Cons:**
You may have to retake exams to prove you can do a job you've done for years.
You may well have to learn a new way of working.
According to where you go, you may have to learn a new language.
Sometimes local salaries can be lower than those at home.
The salary might be good, but the exchange rate can reduce any savings when you return.
You have to create a whole new social life.

Of course if you don't like warm weather or barbecues then you may not immediately take to working in Australia, even if the lifestyle and countryside really attract you. But each to their own, most of the world will have hot weather periodically, and in a continent the size of Australia you would be hard put not to find somewhere that suited you and had a job going; the same is true of the USA and Canada. The most important point in travelling elsewhere to work is not to stay inside your own head, if you are prepared to leave your home behind as far as working and settling in go then you will have both a great time earning money and socialising with new friends. You will be living and experiencing a cultural phenomenon over a long period of time, somewhere that normally you would have to pay extraordinary amounts of money to see very briefly.

What you gain professionally from working abroad will depend on the nature of the work. At one end of the spectrum you may be working in a well equipped private-sector hospital, and earning a higher salary than you get in a similar post at home; depending on the local cost of living, your overall standard of living could be significantly higher. In addition you may be working in a better-funded health care environment than you are used to at home.

On the other hand working in the voluntary sector can be very rewarding, particularly in developing countries where the contribution an individual makes to improving the welfare of the community can be especially significant and conspicuous. Professionals working in such situations may receive only a small income or basic allowance – or even no income at all, just the provision of food and accomodation.

Whatever the circumstances, a placement of this kind is certain to provide new experience of some kind, and possibly also new skills that may prove valuable when looking for work in the future.

There are other reasons for wanting to work abroad – in order to develop your language skills, or a long-held desire to live in a particular country.

However, before you drop everything and rush down to your travel agent you need to think quite hard about where you want to go and if there will be or could be any work there for you. There is a brilliant opportunity available for you to enhance both your own experience of life and your CV, not to mention the fact that while you are overseas you may decide to settle permanently. But you should not expect to be able to wander off and find work straight away, the expatriate press is full of tales of woe from people who went unprepared. The information in this book should certainly give you a head start in planning a period of work outside of your homeland, and hopefully the information in the latter half of this chapter will prepare you for the any problems you encounter in your new home.

# Getting a Job

## ADVERTISEMENTS

Regularly looking through the advertisements for overseas job opportunities is an important way of finding out about what kinds of jobs are available, and about what the requirements are for those working in your field in the country (or countries) in which you are interested. Writing to the advertisers for more information about the jobs on offer is another useful source of information.

Looking through the journals relevant to your particular profession is often a principal way of finding out about the latest employment opportunities abroad. The Country Guides in Part III of this book include information on some of the key publications for the various professions. In the UK, for example, the weekly *British Medical Journal* and the *Nursing Times* regularly include overseas vacancies in their classified advertisement sections. Alternatively you can subscribe to or regularly consult the local newspapers for the country (or even the region or city) that you are interested in working in; the jobs pages of these newspapers can be another important source of information on vacancies for health professionals.

One advantage that looking through journals published in your own country has over searching through the overseas press is that jobs advertised in the former are placed there by overseas employers or recruitment agencies who are prepared to employ health professionals from the country where the journal is published, and probably to obtain work permits where required. Overseas newspapers are naturally aimed at their local readerships, most of whom will not need to worry about visas, work permits and other documentation. But you can make a direct application in response to an overseas advert, and if you want to subscribe to the foreign edition then you also get a head start on current trends within the profession in your destination country.

## Useful Addresses:
### Professional Journals

*BMJ Classified:* BMA House, Tavistock Square, London, WC1H 9JR, UK. A seperate issue from the British Medical Journal packed full of vacancy information.

*Deutches Arzteblatt:* Postfach 400243, Köln, Germany (tel +49-(0)2234-701 1120; fax 02234-701 1142; e-mail aerzteblatt@aerzteblatt.de). A weekly issue in German with vacancy listings.

*Irish Medical Times:* 15 Harcourt Street, Dublin 2, Ireland (tel +353-1-475 7461; fax 01-475 7467; e-mail medtimes@iol.ie Website www.imt.ie).

*Nature:* Macmillan Magazines Ltd, Porter's South, 4-6 Crinan Street, London, N1 9XW, UK (tel 020-7843 4985; fax 020-7843 4998; Website www.nature.com).

*Nature America:* P.O. Box 5055, Brentwood, TN 37024-5055, USA, (tel (USA only 800-524 0384) or +1-615-377 3322; Website www.nature.com).

*Nature:* (Australasia) Macmillan Magazines, Locked Bag 1400, South Yarra, VIC 3141, Australia (tel +61-3-9825 1188; e-mail aabbott@macmillan.com.au Website www.nature.com)

*Nursing Standard:* Nursing Standard House, 17-19 Peterborough Road, Harrow, HA1 2AX, UK (tel 020-8423 1066; e-mail nursing.standard@rcn.org.uk Website www.nursing-standard.co.uk).

*Nursing Times:* Greater London House, Hampstead Road, London, NW1 7EJ, UK (subscriptions tel 020-8956 3522; e-mail nt@healthcare.emap.co.uk).

### National Press

*El Pais:* Miguel Yuste 40, E-28037 Madrid, Spain, (tel +34-91-337 8200; fax 91-304 8766).

*Frankurter Allgemeine Zeitung:* Hellerhofstrasse 2-4, D-60327 Frankfurt am main, Germany (tel +49-69-75910; Website www.faz.de). Vacancy listings on Saturdays.

*The Guardian:* 119 Farringdon Road, London, EC1R 3ER, UK (tel 020-7278 2332; fax 020-7837 2114; Website www.guardian.co.uk).

*Hong Kong Standard:* 4/F Sing Tao Building, 1 Wang Kwong Road, Kowloon Bay, Kowloon, Hong Kong (subscriptions tel +852-2798 2859; e-mail circulate@hkstandard.com Website www.hkstandard.com).

*Irish Independent:* 90 Middle Abbey Street, Dublin 1, Ireland (tel +353-1-873 1333). Job adverts on Thursday and Saturday.

*Japan Times:* 5-4 Shibaura, 4-chome, Minato-ku, Tokyo 1080023, Japan (e-mail jtsales@japantimes.co.jp Website www.japantimes.co.jp). English Langugae Japanese news.

*Le Monde:* 21 bis, rue Claude Bernard, BP 218, F-75226 Paris Cedex 05, France (tel +33-1-42 17 39 00; fax 01-42 17 39 26).

*Mail & Guardian:* P.O. Box 32362, Braamfontein 2017, Johannesburg, South Africa (fax +27-11-727 7110; Website www.mg.co.za). A South African weekly, with an electronic daily version (*Daily Mail & Guardian*) which covers all of Africa.

*The New York Times:* 1120 Avenue of the Americas, New York, NY 10036, USA (tel 800-NYTIMES/698 4637; Website www.nytimes.com). Very useful jobs section, especially as it can often be found in major newsagents outside the USA.

*Søndag Aftenposten:* Akersgat 51, Boks 1178 Sentrum, N-0107 Oslo, Norway (e-mail aftenposten@aftenposten.no). Has a vacancies section *Jobb*. This Norwegian weekly is often available in academic libraries.

*The Straits Times:* 390 Kim Seng Road, Singapore 23945, Singapore (e-mail straits@cyberway.com.sg Website http://straitstimes.asia1.com). The oldest south-east Asian English Language daily.

*Svenska Dagbladet:* Görwellsgatan 28, S-105 17 Stockholm, Sweden (Website www.svd.se). Sweden's main daily.

*The Times:* P.O. Box 495, Virginia Street, London, E1 9XN, UK (tel 020-7782 5000; Website www.the-times.co.uk).

## Expatriate Press

There is a range of newspapers and magazines aimed at the expatriate worker already living in another country, and these often carry advertisements both for jobs back home and from agencies specialising in placing foreign staff. All of these magazines can also supply the would-be travelling health professional with information on migrating abroad and the contact details for agencies and health authorities.

In Britain the excellent *Overseas Jobs Express* is aimed at those seeking work abroad and expatriate workers of all nationalities, the paper's content is made up of job opportunities, news and articles about moving to other countries to work. *OJE* is produced twice a month and can only be obtained by subscription, although you can choose between three, six and twelve month subscriptions. In addition to this there are a number of magazines aimed at Australians and New Zealanders on holiday, such as *TNT, Australian Outlook, New Zealand News UK, Southern Cross*, and *New Zealand Outlook* all of which are intended to keep their readers in touch with home with the added bonus of carrying adverts from agencies which can place qualified staff in a number of 'temp' positions. The same is true of the newspaper produced for South Africans staying in Britain *The Star & SA Times*, this edition published in London carries at least four pages of job ads.

For Americans and Canadians living in Britain and Europe there are *The Canada Post*, and *The American*, both of which are produced with the benefit of expatriates in mind. *The Canada Post* is produced in Britain, for those Canadians living there, while *The American* is produced for Americans living overseas generally. Of course there is also the international American daily the *International Herald Tribune* which is produced at various locations around the world.

## Useful Addresses

*Australian Outlook:* Consyl Publishing & Publicity Ltd, 3 Buckhurst Road, Bexhill on Sea, Sussex, TN40 1QF; tel 01424-223111.

*Canada Employment Weekly:* 15 Madison Avenue, Toronto, Ontario M5R 2S2,

Canada; tel 416-964 6069; fax 416-964 3202. In the UK and Europe contact Barkers Worldwide Publications; tel 01483-776141. Canada's largest career weekly, the paper carries hundreds of job vacancies and useful advice.

*The Canada Post:* Top Floor, 6 Pembridge Road, Notting Hill Gate, London, W11 3HL; tel 020-7243 4243; fax 020-7243 4245; e-mail info@ canadapost.co.uk.

*The American:* 110 Mill Road, Westhampton Beach, New York 11978, USA; tel 516-288 4621; fax 516-288 6284. A colourful weekly tabloid (circulation 25,000) available at shops, news-stands and by subscription As well as news stories of interest to American expatriates it also carries classified adverts.

*International Herald Tribune:*
181 Avenue Charles de Gaulle, 92521 Neuilly Cedex, France; tel +33-1-41 43 93 00; fax 1-41 43 92 12; e-mail subs@iht.com.

Barbican City Gate, 40 Marsh Wall, London, E19 9TP; tel 020-7628511; fax 020-7628 5533.

850 Third Avenue, New York, NY 10022, USA; tel +1-212-752 3890; fax 212-755 8785; Website http://www.iht.com A daily broadsheet edited in Paris and distributed around the world with discounts of around 50-60% for new subscribers.

*The Irish Post:* Uxbridge House, 464 Uxbridge Road, Hayes, Middlesex, UB4 0SP; tel 020-8561 0059; fax 020-8561 3047.

*New Zealand News UK:* 3rd Floor, New Zealand House, Haymarket, London, SW1Y 4TE; tel 020-7747 9200; fax 020-7747 9223; e-mail nznlondon@aol.com

*New Zealand Outlook:* Consyl Publishing & Publicity Ltd, 3 Buckhurst Road, Bexhill on Sea, Sussex, TN40 1QF; tel 01424-223111.

*Overseas Jobs Express:* Premier House, Shoreham Airport, Sussex, BN43 5FF; tel 01273-440220; fax 01273-440229; e-mail editor@overseasjobs.com Website http://www.overseasjobs.com

*The Star & SA Times:* 3rd Floor, New Zealand House, Haymarket, London, SW1Y 4TE; tel 020-7747 9200; fax 020-7747 9223; e-mail satimes@aol.com

*Transitions Abroad:* PO Box 1300, Amherst, MA 01004-1300, USA; tel 413-256 3414; fax 413-256 0373. Is a bi-monthly magazine with articles on living and working abroad, and active involvement as a guest in the host community rather than as a tourist. An annual subscription presently costs $24.95 in the USA, $29.95 in Canada and $38 around the world.

*Union Jack:* PO Box 1823, La Mes, CA 91944-1823, USA; tel (toll free in USA: 800 262-7305) 619-466 3129; fax 619-466 1103; Website www.ujnews.com. America's only national paper aimed at Britons living in the States, it has a circulation of 200,000, and claims to have subscribers in every state.

*USA Today:* 1000 Wilson Boulevard, Arlington, VA 22229, USA; tel +1-703-273 3400; Website www.usatoday.com.

69 New Oxford Street, London, WC1A 1DG; tel 020-7559 5900. An American daily available across Europe and on-line, international circulation averages 70,000 annually. Friday is the publication day for the weekend edition and classified adverts are carried every Monday, Wednesday and Friday.

## THE INTERNET

Apart from the many places advertised in the print media or carried by the recruitment agencies listed later in this chapter there is the almost limitless potential of the internet as a way of finding a job. Traditional recruitment agencies with websites are waiting to help you into a job and there are also several websites dedicated solely to listing vacancies on-line, where you can surf for vacancies in the Bahamas, or post your cv for consideration by recruiters. Many of these also provide useful information for those who wish to find out about local conditions, red-tape, or to keep up to date with professional developments.

Below are some of the websites that may be of use to the surfing jobseeker, however, bear in mind that websites are not permanent fixtures; sites may disappear and URLs (addresses) can change without the site administrators setting up a forwarding page to carry you to the new address.

### Recruitment Sites

*http://www.appointments-plus.co.uk*
This is the electronic appointments section of the Internet edition of the Daily Telegraph.

*http://www.bestjobsusa.com*
The best jobs in the USA, but you will need a browser which can read frames.

*http://www.bacdubai.com*
Business Aid Centre, Dubai, UAE (fax +971-376 467). Medical and hospital administration personnel for the United Arab Emirates.

*http://www.bnauk.com*
The British Nursing Association has branches across the UK; addresses are available on their website. Appointments are available for short and long-term contracts in Europe, the Middle East and the USA.

*http://www.careermag.com*
The Career Magazine site, which claims to be where America looks for work. The site includes advice, job postings, employer profiles and a discussion forum.

*http://www.careerpath.com*
A major site for finding work on-line as it has job listings culled from the net and from 88 US newspapers.

*http://www.docjob.com*
Physician employment in the USA.

*http://www.dentjob.com.au*
Website of Dentist JobSearch Australia, listing employment options in Australia and New Zealand, for private, government clinic, locum or permanent work.

*http://www.e-h-l.com*
EHL Corporation, Edmonton, Canada (tel +1-780-413 9176, fax +1-780-413 9177). Professional medical search and placement services, with an emphasis on international relocation. Clients in Canada, USA, UAE, Qatar, Saudi Arabia, New Zealand, Australia, Singapore, UK, Belgium, Germany, South Africa, and Bermuda.

*http://www.employment.com.au*
Australian employment opportunities.

*http://www.grafton-group.com*
The homepage of Grafton Recruitment, Ireland's leading recruitment consultancy with offices around the world, they have a section devoted to nursing jobs.

*http://erol.users.netlink.co.uk/health.html*
Health Jobs Online, medical, nursing, and therapy jobs in the USA and internationally; as well as information on conferences and other links.

*http://www.intlmedicalplacement.com*
International Medical Placement, 100 Sylvan Parkway, Suite 200, Amherst, NY 14228, USA (tel +1-716-689 6000, fax +1-716-689 6187). Industry leader in

physician recruitment to the USA across all specialties.
*http://www.iscworld.com*
This is the website of International Staffing Consultants, and it carries vacancies from across the USA and around the world.
*http://www.joblink2usa.com*
Joblink International are specialists in the recruitment and placement of foreign staff within the USA.
*http://www.londoncareers.net*
The London Careers Net is home to the capital's leading recruitment magazines.
*http://www.medexplorer.com*
Medexplorer host a an employment centre on their site in addition to all the information, discussion forums and resources for medical professionals.
*http://www.michaelpage.com*
Michael Page International recruitment and placement agency, they also provide information on working and living abroad.
*http://www.monster.co.uk or http://www.monster.com*
The Monster Board is originally an American recruitment website, but now has sister sites in 8 other countries. They all carry job vacancies and useful information and several have a specific page for health jobs for example Australia has *http://healthcare.monster.com.au*
*http://www.muselik.com*
This is an information centre for travellers heading for the Czech Republic and includes job listings, these are often for jobs in the USA as much as Prague.
*http://www.heenan.net/nursejobs/index.shtml*
Nurse Jobs, another specialist nursing site, including nurse/researcher jobs in the UK and a useful information resource.
*http://www.nursing-portal.com*
The Nursing Portal an extensive and thorough site with jobs and information in the UK market.
*http://www.nzhealth.co.nz*
The website of the New Zealand Health also has vacancy listings and useful information.
*http://www.overseasjobs.com*
The site for travelling job hunters, operated by Overseas Jobs Express, it includes an International Job Finder.
*http://www.personnelnet.com*
Personnelnet Jobs in Health, the only UK Internet recruitment site that covers all jobs in the health industry: nursing, medical, administrative, managerial, and support positions, across the acute, community, mental, and independent health sectors.
*http://www.pohly.com*
Pam Pohly Associates, 2707 Woodrow Court, Suite 100, Hays, KS 67601, USA. Specialists in healthcare and executive jobsearch and placement, their website is a goldmine of useful information and links.
*http://www.candocs.com*
Susan Craig Associates Inc., 371 Berkeley Street, Toronto, ON M5A2X8, Canada (tel +1-888 289 2614, fax +1-416-960 6467). Specialises in placing Canadian doctors and nurses in the USA. Register on-line via their website.
*http://www.topjobs.co.nz*
The topjobs site is full of vacancies and information, on New Zealand and Britain; it has a sister site nzjobs.co.uk but some browsers seem to have trouble finding it, so it may have disappeared even though some advertisements still list it.
*http://www.villagedoctor.com*

The Village Doctor internet based service which places physicians with small communities in exotic locations around the world. Positions available in North and South America, the Caribbean, Africa, Nepal, Australia, and the South Pacific.
*http://dir.yahoo.com/health/employment*
Yahoo one of the biggest web-services providers has several pages of job information, including this area dedicated to health jobs.

## DIRECT APPLICATION

Direct application to public health authorities and hospitals – in countries where there is a large public sector involvement in the provision of health care – is an obvious approach to finding out about current vacancies. Up-to-date information on the general extent of such opportunities should be available from the appropriate medical, nursing and other professional associations, not to mention the hospitals themselves. Lists of public health care providers should be available from the same organisations, as well as from the Ministry or Department of Health in the country concerned. Often there are also associations representing private hospitals, clinics and other health care centres, and these may have similar lists available. The advent of the internet has in many cases made direct application easier as many health authorities and hospitals have websites which as well as providing information also list job opportunities, one such is the American hospital in Dubai *www.ahdubai.com.*

In all cases it is obviously better if you can find out something about each hospital that you are writing to, rather than sending the same standard letter to every address you can find; again, the professional organisations should be able to guide you to the information you need. When applying directly to potential employers doctors will probably improve their chances if they locate the institutes, medical schools, hospitals, etc. best known for their speciality and write to the head of the department.

## HOSPITAL MANAGEMENT ORGANISATIONS

Many countries have private health care sectors where health management organisations are significant operators. These organisations will usually be involved in establishing, operating and managing specific health care facilities. In some countries – for example, in the Middle East – recruitment of overseas health professionals to hospitals run by such organisations is usually through agencies specifically set up to ensure that these hospitals are staffed by well qualified and experienced personnel. Several of these agencies are included under *Recruitment Agencies and Consultants* below. In other cases these organisations recruit through advertisements or you can approach them through direct application, as described above.

## EMBASSIES

The amount of information on countries' health systems available from their Embassies, Consulates and High Commissions varies greatly. Some countries produce detailed publications describing how the system is structured, how many personnel are employed and how the system is likely to develop in the future – for example, in the light of changes in government health policy. This information is extremely useful for those investigating what kind of opportunities are (or are likely to become) available. For other countries it is much harder to obtain current information, and the embassy is likely to redirect your enquiry to the Ministry of

Health in the country itself, where you may not have much success unless you know the local language.

## WORD OF MOUTH

Knowing the right people is an important part of getting certain jobs. In some European countries, for example, recommendation by people who know you can be all-important. Getting yourself known can also be particularly important in the voluntary/NGO sector – positions are often filled without the vacancy being advertised, networks of contacts being used to identify suitably qualified and experienced people who are known to be looking for an overseas position of this kind.

# Recruitment Agencies and Consultants

## INTRODUCTION

Recruitment agencies provide health professionals with a very important means of accessing overseas jobs while still at home and with finding a new job in the destination country should temping or taking a working holiday be the plan. At the very least agencies should be able to bring to a professional's job-searching efforts their experience of the employment market in the country (or countries) in which they specialise, together with their expertise in matching applicants to the vacancies that are available and ensuring that the various administrative obstacles are overcome. Some agencies offer more and actually provide the main route by which professionals wanting to enter a particular job market or to work in a specific institution can find the work they are looking for; in this case the service they provide is obviously vital for the job-seekers concerned.

It will often be worthwhile to get in touch with several agencies to find out which can provide you with the service most likely to meet your requirements. Different agencies working in similar fields will often have very different amounts of experience to offer, and for the health professional looking to obtain the best position he or she can it obviously makes sense to deal with someone with as long a track record as possible in the country and/or the profession concerned, and preferably both. Some agencies employ consultants with huge amounts of experience in very specialised areas – for example, in a particular country or region (whether in the public or private sectors, or with NGOs and voluntary organisations), or in particular professions, such as radiology or occupational, speech and physiotherapy. It is in the potential applicant's interest to find out just how much experience any individual agency has available.

Other questions to ask yourself to help you differentiate between the various agencies operating in your field include:

– What links with professional organisations and the health care industry do the consultants dealing with you have?
– Do they have an extensive network of contacts, so that they are in touch with the latest developments in your profession in that country?
– How familiar are they with relevant legislation and registration requirements? How much information do they provide on subjects such as insurance, occupational health, training and career development?

– How extensive is their client base – do you get the impression that you are being presented with a selection of the best jobs available?

– Does the agency provide support to its candidates once they have been found a position – does the support they provide continue for the duration of the placement?

In many cases the recruitment procedures for the agencies listed below are very similar. The qualifications, experience and references of an applicant will be checked, and if these are in order an attempt will be made to match the applicant to a suitable vacancy. If a vacancy is found and the employer for whom the agency is acting makes the applicant a job offer, then a contract will be sent to the applicant (he or she may also be asked to undergo a medical). Necessary paperwork such as visas and work permits will then be obtained. Sometimes the order in which these steps take place may vary.

One piece of paper often required is a 'certificate of good standing' (or something similar) issued by the regulatory authority in the country where you are registered. This may be requested either by the relevant registering authority in your destination country or by the recruitment agency you are using.

Registration requirements for the various professions differ between different countries and part of the agency's job will often be to advise the applicant on the registration process – at its simplest this may involve having your qualifications verified, or it may mean taking an examination set by the relevant authority in the country concerned. Your agency will also provide you with 'orientation' information to assist you in adapting to the working culture and living conditions in the destination country – this is particularly important where there are pronounced cultural differences, as experienced by Westerners living and working in the Middle East, for example.

The number of vacancies that any particular agency has available, and in which areas of health care, can vary considerably with time – agencies are ultimately dependent on their clients providing them with details of vacancies, and they can not match health professionals to jobs that do not exist. Variability in the employment market is something to consider when trying to find a suitable position: see what work different agencies have on their books, and ask if the chances of finding what you are looking for vary at different times. Although most agencies always have some work available, flexibility in choosing where you work and at what time of year will improve the chances of a position being found that matches your qualifications, skills and experience, and your longer-term career aspirations.

Using an agency generally does not involve a cost for the applicant, as the agency will receive payment from each employer for whom an employee is found. Therefore there are no financial reasons why you should not shop around and evaluate different agencies' services.

## Further Information

Many British employment agencies dealing with overseas work are registered with the Federation of Recruitment and Employment Services Ltd (FRES: 36-38 Mortimer Street, London W1N 7RB; Website www.fres.co.uk) this is a professional body overseeing the activities of member recruitment agencies. Agencies which diplay the FRES logo have to abide by codes of professional conduct, so it is always safest to use one of their members. They also have a free jobseekers phoneline (0800-320588) on which jobseekers can purchase a list of agencies specialising in overseas placements.

# LIST OF AGENCIES

## Alliance Nurses Agency

59 Merrion Square, Dublin 2, Ireland (tel +353-1-678 7333; fax 01-678 7281).
Alliance specialise in the recruitment of nurses and carers for temporary and permanent places in the Greater Dublin area of Ireland. At the time of writing there was a significant shortage of nurses in all disciplines in Ireland, especially those specialising in Intensive Care and Coronary Care. As all applicants must obtain registration with the Irish Nursing Board (*An Bord Altranais*), before they can be placed, and non EU/EEA applicants need work permits, the agency provides asistance with these. There is also a relocation allowance.

## AMAQ Services

88 L'Estrange Terrace, Kelvin Grove (PO Box 123, Red Hill) Qld 4059, Australia (tel 07-3872 2222; fax 07-3856 5744; e-mail s.russet@amaq.com.au).
AMAQ (Australian Medical Association Queensland) Services places medical practitioners in full-time and part-time locum GP positions in Queensland. The majority of these positions are outside the state's metropolitan areas, and work is available in various locations and for various periods of time. As many of the locum positions are in rural areas, experience is desirable in one or more of the following areas: anaesthetics, obstetrics and emergency medicine. AMAQ Services sponsors its doctors so they can obtain a temporary working visa, and will provide an induction programme to provide familiarisation with Australian billing practices, access to services, government forms and protocols.

## AMA Locum Service (WA)

PO Box 133 (14 Stirling Highway), Nedlands WA 6009, Australia (08-9273 3000/3033; fax 08-9273 3073; e-mail amats@vianet.net.au).
The AMA Locum Service in Western Australia sponsors suitably qualified medical practitioners for short and long-term positions in general practice throughout the state. The demand in Western Australia – particularly in the rural areas – for locum support, exceeds the supply of available local practitioners. Registration with the Medical Board of Western Australia is required, and essentially allows only rural work – details are available. Placements are for a minimum of 3 months. All travel and accommodation within the state is provided. Permanent Residency options are also available for suitably qualified general practitioners.

## The Anaesthetists Agency

Little Meadow, Boldre Lane, Lymington, Hampshire SO41 8PD, UK (Freephone numbers (valid in the UK only): 0800-830 930, and 08080 OXYGEN. Standard numbers: tel +44-(0)1590-675111; fax 01590-675114; e-mail aalocums@dial.pipex.com).
This medical agency is the only one-specialty medical agency in the UK. Its main work involves providing locum anaesthetists to NHS hospitals throughout the UK mainland and its islands. Occasionally posts are filled in Australia. The agency is looking to recruit anaesthetists, whether currently resident in the UK or in other countries, who already have the right to work in the UK. Most will be coming to the UK for personal reasons; others will travel to the UK at their own expense in order to fill locum posts. All of the work arranged is temporary, but occasionally doctors take up full-time posts following on from a locum. Work is available at all grades, including consultant grade.
   Applicants will need to supply originals or photocopies of their passports,

degrees and diplomas, a current General Medical Council Medical Registration Annual Renewal Certificate, and evidence of immunity to hepatitis B.

# The Anaesthetists Agency

*safe locum anaesthesia, throughout the UK*

**Tel:**

**+ 44 (0) 1590 675 111**

**0800 830 930**  free UK only

**08080 699 436**  free UK only    FREEPOST (SO3417)

**08080 OXYGEN**  free UK only    Lymington

**Fax:**                           Hampshire

**+ 44 (0) 1590 675 114**          SO41 9ZY

**Angela Shaw Associates**
Montrose House, 412-416 Eastern Avenue, Ilford IG26 6NQ, UK (tel 020-8554 7691; fax 020-8554 9900).
Angela Shaw Associates is an agency specialising in finding locum positions for occupational therapists, physiotherapists, speech and language therapists, and qualified social workers in the UK. Placements can last from around 4 weeks to 6 months, and are usually in NHS hospitals, private hospitals, private practice and social services. The agency offers a wide choice of posts, free advice on UK entry and tax matters, plus help with accommodation and free indemnity insurance.

The agency advertises extensively in professional journals such as *Physiotherapy Frontline* and *Community Care*, and also in South African, Australian and New Zealand journals, in response to the many enquiries from these parts of the world from qualified occupational therapists and physiotherapists wanting to work in the UK. Applicants enquiring from overseas may reverse phone charges. Assistance can also be provided to travelling therapists and social workers looking for work outside the UK. Telephone the number given above for further advice.

**Arabian Careers Ltd**
Berkeley Square House, 7th Floor, Berkeley Square, London W1X 5LB, UK (tel 020-7495 3285; fax 020-7355 2562; fax & Voicemail 020-7681 2901; e-mail recruiter@arabiancareers.com).
Arabian Careers Ltd recruits qualified staff for various prestigious hospitals located

throughout Saudi Arabia.12 month contracts are offered with generous benefits. The following categories of hospital staff are recruited: doctors (GPs and consultants); dentists (general and specialist); nurses (RGN, RM, RSCN); allied health care professionals, and support services.

### AssignMED (Medical Staffing Assignment Bureau Pty Ltd)
P.O. Box 23735, Gezina 0031, Pretoria South Africa (tel +27-12-330 1202; fax 012-330 3369).
This agency places nurses in temporary work at hospitals across South Africa. The recruitment procedure is fairly simple, but includes a skills test to see if applicants require refresher courses before being placed.

### Auckland Medical Bureau
PO Box 37753 (Level 3, 232 Parnell Road), Parnell, Auckland, New Zealand (tel +64-9-377 5903; fax +64-9-377 5902; e-mail doctors/amb.nz@xtra.co.nz).
The Auckland Medical Bureau arranges posts for medical doctors in locum and permanent positions in general practice and hospitals throughout New Zealand. Positions in Australia and the Pacific Islands are also occasionally available. Assistantships and the sale of practices anywhere in the country can also be arranged.

The Bureau's register includes New Zealand and overseas graduates eligible for registration with the Medical Council of New Zealand – doctors from the UK, Ireland, Australia, Canada, South Africa and the USA are eligible for registration. Hospital placements include specialists and the full range of non-specialist doctors from junior house officers to senior registrars in most disciplines. General practice placements cover metropolitan, provincial and rural areas. Locum posts vary in length. Work is usually available all year.

The Bureau is able to clarify registration eligibility with the Medical Council and arrange appointments for registration with a Medical Council referee. It can also assist with work visas/permits.

### Australian Medicos Pty Ltd
PO Box 114 (Suite 4A, Royal Arcade, 401 New South Head Road), Double Bay NSW 2028, Australia (tel 02-9326 2233; fax 02-9362 3920).
This agency places doctors in private practice and hospital work throughout New South Wales, and has links with the Rural Doctors Resource Network, the major representative body for country doctors. It also places doctors in rural areas in other states such as Queensland, Tasmania, Western Australia and the Northern Territory. Doctors are placed in short and long-term positions, in assistantship with a view to associateship or partnership, and with institutions and government bodies such as the armed forces, the water board and mining companies.

### BML Medical Recruitment Consultants
Mylen House, 11 Wagon Lane, Sheldon, Birmingham, B26 3DU, UK (tel 0121-742 7524; fax 0121-742 3512; e-mail info@bmlmed.co.uk Website www.bmlmed.co.uk).
BML recruit across the spectrum of health care professions for posts in the Middle East and doctors of all grades for positions in the UK. Placements in the Middle East last between one and two years, while those in the UK vary from locum posts, lasting between a week and several months to permanent and consultant posts.

Recruitment is initially by submission of a CV followed by a screening process and interviews to identify areas of interest. BML also maintains an extensive database of candidates' details.

Candidates for posts in the Middle East are offered a full briefing on all aspects of living and working in the area. While the regional offices provide support for candidates across the UK.

**Capital Locum Recruitment**
34 South Molton Street, London, W1Y 2BP, UK (tel 020-7244 7755; fax 020-7370 2266; e-mail register@capitallocum.co.uk Website www.capitallocum.co.uk).
Capital Locum Recruitment provide a dedicated service for doctors in and around London. They have a variety of short and long-term placements in NHS and private hospitals. These are available for all specialities and grades. Candidates are requested to provide a current CV, proof of registration and qualifications, health declaration and Hepatitis B status.

**Centennial Nurses Agency**
34 Queens Park Road, Bondi Junction, Sydney, NSW 2000, Australia (tel +61-2-9369 4325; fax 02-9388 0016; e-mail joy@centennialnurses.com.au Website www.centennialnurses.com.au).
Centennial supply registered nurses to hospitals in Sydney and NSW, placements are advertised and arranged through their website, which is a mine of information. Although they only deal with nurses on working holiday visas or who hold Australian residency, at the time of writing they were planning to expand into placing Australian staff in the USA.

## Choice Personnel

P.O. Box 7108, Cloisters Square, Perth, WA 6850, Australia (tel +61-8-9321 2011; fax 08-9321 1113; e-mail kjones@choice.net.au Website www.choice.net.au).

This recruitment company covers all aspects of medical and allied health recruitment to Saudi Arabia, the United Arab Emirates and South East Asia. There is also scope for the recruitment of non-Australian staff for places in Australia.

Staff recruited include audiologists, dietitians, doctors, medical technicians, nurses, occupational therapists, pharmacists, physiotherapists, podiatrists, radiographers and medical secretaries. The only restriction is that candidates should hold qualifications from either: Britain, Australia, New Zealand, Canada, South Africa or the USA.

Placements are on a one year contract basis, with salaries varying according to qualifications and experience. For placements in the Middle East, candidates need to take an extensive medical and have a minimum of two years post qualification experience.

Benefits include transport, uniforms, free mid-year flights, salary bonus and furnished accommodation.

## Coast Health Care Ltd

PO Box 387, Greymouth, New Zealand (tel 03-768 0499; fax 03-768 2791; e-mail ekremer@coasthealth.co.nz).

Coast Health Care places staff in a range of professions in positions in New Zealand; these include physiotherapists, occupational therapists, radiographers nurses, and the following medical specialisations: psychiatrist, specialist anaesthetist, specialist obstetrician & gynaecologist, general surgeon, orthopaedic surgeon and specialist physician. Both short and long-term vacancies are available. Staff are recruited from South Africa and the UK in particular, and speculative applications are welcome.

## Direct Medical Services

76 Portswood Road, Southampton SO17 2FW, UK (tel 023-8039 3988; fax 023-8039 3908; Website www.direct-medical.com).

This agency places qualified, experienced locum doctors and dental personnel at all levels in NHS Trusts and private hospitals throughout the UK. Both short and long-term placements are available, and the agency accepts CVs via their website.

## DSI Staff RX Inc

601 Cleveland Street, Suite 350, Clearwater, Florida 33755, USA (tel 800-345 9642; fax 813-446-4609).

This medical temporary staffing agency concentrates on the fields of diagnostic imaging and radiation therapy – including X-ray, computerised tomography (CT), magnetic resonance imaging (MRI), special procedures, cardiac catheterisation and mammography, and also ultrasound, echocardiography, vascular sonography, nuclear medicine and radiation therapy. TeamStaff RX places staff throughout the USA, but staff have also been found for positions in Saudi Arabia, Germany and Australia.

## eNZed Paramedical

65 MacDonald Road, Glenview, Hamilton 2001, New Zealand (tel +64-7-843 0080; fax +64-7-843 0081; e-mail enzedpa@wave.co.nz).

This is a recruitment service which specialises in placing Occupational Therapists, Speech Language Therapists and physiotherapists in positions throughout New Zealand. They also receive occasional requests from employers for other allied health professionals. Contracts vary from short-term locum work to permanent

positions, although there is not the scope for short-term work in New Zealand that there is in other more densely populated countries. Advice on applying for professional registration and qualification recognition is provided as well as Work Visa applications. In addition to suitable qualifications, a high level of English language fluency is essential to gain professional registration. Employers prefer applicants with at least 2-3 years post graduate work experience in their own country prior to seeking work in New Zealand.

**Geneva Health International**
UK Head Office: 128-129 Cheapside, London, EC2V 6LL, UK (tel 020-7600 0859; fax 020-7600 0944).
NZ Head Office: Level 2, Hewlett Packard Building, 137-147 Quay Street, Box 106 339, Auckland, New Zealand (tel +64-9-916 0200; fax 09-916 0201).
Geneva Health International is an international company, specialising in sourcing and recruiting health professionals around the world. Placements are on a permanent, temporary and short-term contract basis within the following areas: clinical nursing, medical specialists, allied health, management consulting and community care. Their database of available positions and candidates extend throughout New Zealand, Australia, Canada and the United Kingdom.
Geneva Health International offer a comprehensive package to candidates. Assistance and support with immigration, obtaining registration with professional bodies, accommodation, banking and other identified needs that are expected from relocating internationally. Health professionals seeking a position that recognises expertise and experience should contact Geneva Health International as their aim is to bring the right people to the right organisation to ensure that the focus on care is maintained and enhanced.

**HCA International Ltd**
Southgate Office Village, Ground Floor, 284 Chase Road, Southgate, London N14 6HF, UK (tel 020-8882 6363; fax 020-8882 5266; e-mail hcauk@hcaintl.com).
HCA has more than 20 years' experience recruiting a wide variety of staff for the King Faisal Specialist Hospital & Research Centre in Riyadh, Saudi Arabia. The hospital, with 550 beds, primarily serves as a specialist referral centre for the Kingdom and also provides comprehensive care for certain VIP patients. It is internationally recognised as a pioneer in oncology, IVF, cardiovascular surgery programmes and kidney/bone marrow/liver transplant surgery. They also recruit medical personnel for the Shaikh Khalifa Medical Center in Abu Dhabi, posts there are on a one year renewable contract basis.
HCA are mainly seeking well qualified professionals in the following specialties: consultants, RGNs, RSCNs, radiographers, physiotherapists, medical secretaries, CSSD technicians and laboratory technologists. Most positions are for 2 years. The recruitment procedure normally takes 1-3 months, although for more senior staff it may take up to 6 months. Applicants are required to undergo a full physical examination once the contract has been offered.

**Initial Health Personnel**
Copenhagen House, 5-10 Bury Street, London, EC3A 5AT, UK (tel UK Southern Region 0207-645 5150; fax 020-7929 6476; UK Northern Region 0121-643 5675; fax 0121-643 9570; Website www.initialps.co.uk/health). In Canada (tel +1-905-803 8883; fax 905-803 8110; e-mail initial.health@rentokilinitial.com).
Initial Health Personnel is part of Rentokil Initial plc the world's largest business service organisation, with operations in every major market. Their recruitment

# Nurses '....it's the chance of a lifetime'

At Initial Health Personnel we currently have staff working successfully in the UK from Australia, New Zealand, USA, Canada and South Africa. With seven years' experience in international recruitment, our professional team give on-going support and advice to our overseas employees.

As Susan Stajan from Toronto who is currently working at on NHS Trust Hospital in Birmingham says:

*"The Canadian office was very helpful and friendly... They helped me arrange my visa and liaised with the UKCC, making the whole experience very easy and smooth . . . My contract is very flexible and I can come and go as I please . . . If you love a challenge and love to travel then it's a chance of a lifetime. The worst thing is the fear of the unknown, but Initial Health Personnel do everything they can to make you feel comfortable"*

We give free advice on:
- UK entry requirements
- Visas and work permits
- UKCC registration
- Accommodation
- Tax and Banking arrangements

We are currently recruiting General & Speciality Nurses, ODP's & Theatre Nurses and with over 500 clients throughout the UK, we have a wealth of opportunities from which to choose.

What's more, we encourage all of our staff to continue with their professional development through in-house training and by making funding available, for external courses. So when it's time to return home you have had a great experience and have an even better resumé!

**So why not broaden your horizons and join our growing International team? To find out more about these opportunities and to see if you are eligible to join, please contact Initial Health Personnel, Copenhagen House, 5-10 Bury Street, London EC3A 5AT.**

Tel: +44 20 7645 5150 Fax: +44 20 7929 6476
e-mail: initialhealth@initialps.co.uk
www.initialps.co.uk/health

services in the USA, Canada, Australia and South Africa are actively recruiting health personnel for positions throughout the UK. Professional teams provide assistance and advice on entry requirements and registration within the UK, plus ongoing support and professional development for all their overseas staff.

Initial offer a variety of contract options across all specialities of nursing and for other health professionals such as occupational therapists and physiotherapists. Initial Health Personnel offer full time permanent positions with guaranteed annual salaries and associated benefits. For working holidaymakers there are unprecedented options with good hourly rates.

There is an established branch network (Southern Region – London, Bristol and Southampton, Northern Region – Birmingham, Wellingborough, Leeds, Sheffield and Manchester) which offers the chance to work from diverse locations in a variety of specialities and environments during a stay in the UK.

For further information contact Initial Health Personnel using the details above.

**Jenrick Medical**
Jenrick House, 145 Frimley Road, Camberley, Surrey GU15 2PS, UK (tel 01276-676121; fax 01276-676050; e-mail medical@jen-med.demon.co.uk).
Jenrick Medical recruits internationally for medical staff, especially pharmacists, nurses, occupational therapists and physiotherapists. The company focuses on recruiting professionals for for permanent or contract work in the UK and they offer help with visas and work permits. Vacancies for suitably qualified professionals in the UK are always available, and in addition there are normally vacancies in Europe and throughout Australia and New Zealand. A variety of short-term, long-term, locum and permanent contracts are available, so that in the majority of cases an employee can be matched with a suitable position. The number of vacancies for different professions varies – at the time of writing the skill areas listed above were in particular demand.

**K & K Occupational Health Services**
280 Fulham Road, London, SW10 9EW, UK (tel 020-7-351 1987; fax 020-7351 1988; Website www.kandk.co.uk).
K & K was established in 1960 and has always specialised in providing Occupational Health Practitioners/Nurses. They have a prestigiuos client list, covering

a range of industries in the public and private sectors, and they are committed to providing the highest quality of service to customers. Based in London their team of recruitment and nursing professionals provide services to occupational health services to clients across the UK.

K & K's recruitment procedure includes interviews and checks on qualifications, skills and experience to ensure that they make suitable placements matching staff to clients.

Their website also provides information on their services and a registration point for candidates.

## Lifeline Personnel Ltd

28 South Molton Street, London W1Y 1DA, UK (tel 020-7499 7747; fax 020-7499 7767; e-mail lifeline@lifeline-personnel.com).

Lifeline is a specialist recruitment company that finds long and short-term jobs in the NHS, Private healthcare and non-profit organisations. Work is offered in all areas of London for secretarial and admisitration staff, including medical secretaries, PAs, medical administrators, ward and clinic clerks, medical records staff, finance staff and data entry personnel. Temporary and permanent placements can be arranged.

Candidates can contact Lifeline initially by telephone or fax to make an appointment to register. On registration they will be given a full briefing on the work offered and the rates of pay, they will also take a skills evaluation (typing and word-processing) and two previous employment references are required. Proof of eligibility to work in the UK is essential.

Successful candidates will be given help with opening bank accounts and obtaining a National Insurance number. Medical training for those who wish to cross-train can also be arranged at subsidised rates.

## LG International

The Locum Group, Clocktower House, 287-289 Cranbrook Road, Ilford, Essex IG1 4UA, UK (tel 020-8252 5000; fax 020-8252 5250; e-mail pr@locumgroup.com Website www.locumgroup.com).

LG International is the specialist overseas agency of the Locum Group. Its primary service is to recruit qualified and experienced professionals from the Medical, Health, Technical & Scientific, Care, Education and Housing professions for temporary and permanent work throughout the UK. Via a network of overseas agents and their own dedicated Head Office department LG International are able to provide a local service advising and helping candidates prepare for a working holiday in the UK. Their client base spans both the public and private sectors offering a wide choice of challenging assignments, in addition to which they offer competitive rates of pay, personal service and many other benefits.

## Locums (UK) Ltd

Botley Mill Business Centre, Botley, Southampton, SO30 2GB, UK (tel 01489-788772; fax 01489-788771; e-mail doctors@locums.co.uk Website www.locums.co.uk).

Locums (UK) provide a wide choice of quality placements either short or long-term throughout the UK, to private and NHS hospitals. They offer an assured professional and friendly service for doctors of all grades and specialities. To register with Locums (UK) please supply an updated CV, two recent references, proof of registration and qualifications and evidence of Hepatitis B status.

**Medacs Healthcare Services plc**
The Old Surgery, 49 Otley Street, Skipton, BD23 1ET, UK (tel within the UK) 0800-442200; (from outside the UK) +44-1756-703000; fax +44-1756-798196; e-mail registration@medacs.com Website www.medacs.com).

Medacs is one of the UK's leading healthcare recruitment agencies with offices throughout the country. It places doctors in all grades and specialities in jobs in the majority of British hospitals. It also has an office in Johannesburg and interviews for positions are regularly held in the Netherlands and Germany. Doctors are not placed in countries other than the UK.

Positions last from a few days or weeks to 6 months, or can even be on a permanent basis. The database of available work is continually updated and doctors are matched to jobs twice a day.

Separate departments provide help and advice to doctors from Australia and New Zealand, Ireland, Germany, the Netherlands, the Mediterranean and South Africa who wish to work in the UK. Medacs Kensington deals specifically with placing consultants in short-term, substantive and permanent positions. Medacs Private Healthcare Services Division works exclusively within the private sector and recruits RMOs for private hospitals and doctors to work on cruise ships.

Medacs is normally able to offer doctors travelling from abroad a selection of positions in their speciality. For overseas doctors looking to work in the UK for a reasonable period of time (3-6 months), special packages can be put together that may include return flights, payment of GMC registration fees, assistance with visas and other benefits depending on circumstances.

To register with Medacs you will need to supply an up-to-date CV, copies of certificates, proof of hepatitis B status and two references; also note the general conditions for working as a doctor in the UK described on page 159, and that there are also specific requirements that apply for doctors from particular countries.

### MediCall International

Barkat House, 116-118 Finchley Road, London NW3 5HT (tel 020-7435 8098; fax 020-7794 6284; e-mail intl@mcs-ltd.com).

This agency places Western health professionals in positions in hospitals in Bahrain, Qatar, Saudi Arabia, the UAE and Yemen. Applicants should have a minimum of 2 years' post-qualification experience. Positions are available for doctors, nursing staff, laboratory technicians, microbiologists, dental technicians, ECG technicians, X-ray technicians, physiotherapists and support services managers. CVs accepted as Word attachements by e-mail.

### Medical Staffing International Ltd

35 Kesteven Avenue, Glendowie, Auckland, New Zealand (tel +64-9-575 4258; fax 09-575 4259; e-mail Kirsten@medicalstaffing.co.nz Website www.medicalstaffing.co.nz).

Medical Staffing International Limited specialises in the short term and long-term placement of Occupational Therapists, Physiotherapists and Speech and Language Pathologists all over New Zealand. They provide a personalised service to both candidates and clients, this supportive involvement ensures successful placements for both parties.

Medical Staffing's advice to overseas applicants includes information on registration and visa processes, and they recommend that job seekers have at least one years experience. Their website has downloadable application forms and has several useful links for the would-be expatriate worker. As their recruitment staff motto is 'there are no silly questions only silly answers' they have been successfully providing solutions to many challenges for several years. The director of Medical Staffing International is a Licentiate Member of the Recruitment & Consulting Services Association.

### Montpellier Health Care

Montpellier House, 47 Rodney Road, Cheltenham, GL50 1HX, UK (tel 01242 221685; fax 01242-261854; Website www.montpellier-health.com).

Run by doctors for doctors, Montpellier Health Care is one of the largest providers of Resident Medical Officers to UK hospitals and recruits internationally for these positions. They also place doctors in General Practice and 'out of hours' deputy posts. The agency will organise work permits and offers a flexible benefits package.

### Morgan & Banks

Level 11, Grosvenor Place, 225 George Street, Sydney NSW 2000, Australia (tel 02-9256 3507; fax 02-9251 3975).

This agency recruits medical staff for positions throughout Australia. Applicants need to have a degree from the UK, Ireland, Singapore, Hong Kong or South Africa, and the following are particularly sought after: GP trainees; training registrars in emergency medicine, psychiatry and medicine (training is accredited in the UK); and consultants with extensive experience and recognised qualifications to work in designated 'areas of need'. Some clients reimburse airfares if doctors are committed to work for 12 months, and Morgan & Banks offer assistance with airfares, accommodation and visas.

### Network Overseas (Medical Division)

34 Mortimer Street, London, W1N 8JR, UK (tel 020-7580 5151; fax 020-7580 6242; e-mail medical@networkoverseas.cc Website www.networkoverseas.cc).

Network Overseas place health professionals in overseas placements for all aspects of health work (from secretarial to Chiefs of Medical Staff and from Biomedical Engineers to Hyperbaric Operatives). They recruit and process personnel for 40 hospitals in the Middle Eastern region and most placements are within Saudi Arabia, Abu Dhabi, Bahrain and Dubai. Occasional openings arise in Lebanon, Egypt, Kuwait and other Emirate States. Both locum (short term) and contract (one year or greater) work is offered but locums are likely to occur more in specialised medical professions than in nursing or technological posts.

Recruitment begins with the submission of an applicant's c.v. From this they will match offers and inform the applicant of relevant vacancies against which they are likely to receive offers. Where possible, job descriptions and information on the locality and facility are included at this point in the procedure. Once a candidate has expressed interest, the application is discussed with the client(s) concerned and interviews are arranged and further documentation in support of the applicant obtained.

Once the point of contracting has been reached, the agency will assist in the medical, visa issue, flight arrangements and mobilisation for the candidate. They also arrange for the candidate to be met at their destination and transported to their site of accommodation and work. The only costs incurred by the candidate is postage and, if they choose to use their own GP as opposed to Network Overseas' medical facilities, the cost of a medical. In Saudi Arabia and Kuwait, all candidates are required to have a full employment medical (including a HIV check) and a client visa invite. For the Emirates, the medical is performed on arrival.

### Nightingale Nursing Bureau Ltd
2 Tavistock Place, London WC1H 9RA, UK (tel 020-7833 3952; fax 020-7278 4067; e-mail enquiries@nightingale-uk.demon.co.uk).

This long-established agency places nurses, midwives and nursing auxiliaries from overseas particularly from Australia, New Zealand and South Africa in short and long-term nursing placements in the UK. The company also finds sponsorship opportunities for nurses and midwives wanting to take up permanent positions. Work is available in the National Health Service and independent sector including with individual patients at home. Nightingale Nursing also has a branch in Sydney, Australia, which places both native and overseas nurses in New South Wales. The company is particularly committed to maintaining high professional standards and to assisting nurses on its register to gain access to courses and study days.

For information and assistance for trips to the UK or Australia please call:
*In Australia:* Cathy Bouvy (tel 02-9964 9266; fax 02-9964 9449; e-mail nightingale-aust@bigpond.com).
*In New Zealand:* Holly Trillo (tel/fax 09-376 4223).
*In South Africa:* Viviane du Plessis (tel/fax 021-685 5898).

### Northern Clinical Training Network (NCTN)
Private Bag 92024, Auckland 1, New Zealand (tel +64-9-366 1623; fax 09-366 1635; e-mail crew@nctn.co.nz).

The NCTN is an organisation which recruits registrars and House Officers of all levels on behalf of all Hospital and Health Services in the Auckland area of New Zealand (Waitemata Health, South Auckland Health, Auckland Healthcare). The NCTN recruits in all disciplines for residents and monitors and facilitates the work of the various Vocational Training Committees which often are responsible for determining entry to a vocational training programme. This includes both temporary and permanent positions but does not include undergraduate clinical experience. Those seeking undergraduate clinical experience should contact the

New Zealand medical schools directly. Positions are advertised annually in the *BMJ, Australian Medical Journal*, on the website www.nzjobs.co.nz and in the local New Zealand newspapers for the next year's annual intake, the latter two also carry advertising for any unexpected vacancies.

## Nursing Management Services
*UK Office:* 2 Doncastle Court, Arcadia Avenue, Finchley, London N3 2JU, UK (tel 020-8349 2282; fax 020-8349 2218; Website www.gonms.com).
*US Office:* 2400 Herodian Way, Suite 110, Smyrna, Atlanta, Georgia 30086, USA (tel 770-956-0500; fax 770-956-1894).
*Australia Office:* Walker House, 61 Walker Street, North Sydney, NSW 2060, Australia (tel 02-9956 7533; fax 02-9956 7833).
*South Africa:* PO Box 3571, Rivonia 2128, 1st Floor, Syringa Buildings, Homestead Road, Rivonia, South Africa (tel 011-803 1234; fax 011-803 1345)
Nursing Management Services (NMS) is an agency specialising in placing nurses in the USA and the UK. Placements in the USA last from 13 to 54 weeks, and are in facilities ranging from the smallest community hospitals to county-operated facilities with over 2000 beds. Benefits included in the package include assistance with professional licensing and endorsement, medical and liability insurance, furnished accommodation, assistance with airfares and relocation, an education allowance, visa processing (if required) and orientation. Nurses are recruited from both the USA and other English-speaking countries, and will need to have at least 2 years' postgraduate experience. Nurses will also need to have a current TB screening and be immunised against rubella and hepatitis B.

Opportunities in the UK are available for nurses with at least 12 months' post-registration experience. Placements last for between 12 and 52 weeks and can be in a variety of settings, ranging from small privately run units to busy teaching hospitals. Free fully furnished accommodation, end-of-contract bonuses and excellent rates can be expected for all UK contracts.

## Panacea Healthcare
PO Box 33750, Auckland, New Zealand (tel 09-489 5159); PO Box 19147, Hamilton, New Zealand (07-838 2332).
Panacea Healthcare provides nursing and carer services in clinical and community settings in the Auckland and Hamilton regions of New Zealand. Placements can be found for registered and enrolled nurses, hospital aides and carers. Panacea's main focus is on placing staff on temporary assignments, although a permanent placement service exists – staff expressing an interest in permanent employment can usually be placed, depending on their skills, experience and flexibility.

Applicants are advised to contact Panacea before they arrive in New Zealand so that they can begin the process of gaining registration or certification with the relevant professional body (for nurses this is the New Zealand Nursing Council, and registration can take some months to process). Once in New Zealand the applicant arranges an interview with Panacea, where the necessary documents are checked and further information provided.

## Paterson Healthcare
2 Littlegate Street, Oxford, OX1 1QT, UK (tel 01865-203511; fax 01865-723910).
Paterson Healthcare is an agency offering locum positions and agency work to healthcare staff throughout the UK. Whatever your profession or clinical area of interest, their team of experienced recruitment consultants will find you the position you are looking for. Advice is given on UKCC registration and they can

help with opening bank accounts. Accommodation is usually available and they offer weekly pay at excellent rates and four weeks holiday pay pro rata. Locum placements are usually for 3-6 months. Continous work is available with immediate start. A record of the professional experience gained is presented to staff when they move on to another country.

**Pulse**
80 High Holborn, London WC1V 6LS (tel 020-7959 1000; fax 020-7959 1001). Pulse provides nursing staff to UK hospitals that are experiencing staffing shortfalls. It works closely with its parent company Match Healthcare Services. Flexibility in choosing placements and continuous assignments are available, and advice on registration, accommodation and professional development is also offered.

**Recruitment International**
International House, PO Box 300, Harrogate. North Yorkshire HG1 5XL, UK (tel 01423-530533; fax 01423-530558; e-mail ri_group@compuserve.com).
Recruitment International has been established since 1981 and throughout this time it has been closely associated with the recruitment of Medical Staff to the Middle East and in particular to Saudi Aramco in Saudi Arabia. In order to support the demands of Saudi Aramco for healthcare professionals of all types, Recruitment International has a large amount of experience recruiting across many disciplines. These include Nursing Staff, Doctors, Pharmacists, Occupational and Physiotherapists, MLSO and Radiological Staff. Applicants looking to work in the Middle East can rely on full briefings before assignment and can look forward to some of the finest packages available

**Richmond Medical Agency Ltd**
RMA House, 157 Stanwell Road, Ashford, Middlesex, TW15 3QN, UK (tel +44 (0)1784-422300; fax +44 (0)1784-422318; e-mail rmalocums@aol.com).
Richmond Medical Agency is an established company with over 15 years of medical recruitment experience, covering all specialities nation-wide. Their experienced consultants offer prompt and efficient service, ensuring that the maximum effort is made to meet your requirements. They are inundated with locum requirements on a daily basis, necessitating a constant demand for doctors. To register with Richmond Medical you will need to supply the following; a current copy of your CV including the names of two referees; certificates of all medical qualifications, your current General Medical Council Certificate; evidence of immunity to hepatitis B (no more than two years from date of vaccination); a radiation protection certificate; and proof of eligibility to work within the UK. For further details contact Richmond Medical at the above address.

### RICHMOND MEDICAL AGENCY LTD

## LOCUM VACANCIES THROUGHOUT THE UK

If you seek a change in location we can offer a wealth of opportunities. With locum vacancies readily available throughout the UK you will be guaranteed a fast, efficient and professional service to meet your needs. If you hold a valid work permit and GMC registration call our experienced consultants today for excellent rates, prompt payments and quality assignments nationwide.

Recruitment &
Employment
Confederation

**Tel: ++44 (0) 1784 422300**
Fax: ++44 (0) 1784 422318
Email: rmalocums@aol.com

Recruitment &
Employment
Confederation

Richmond Medical Agency Ltd
RMA House, 157 Stanwell Road, Ashford, Middlesex, TW15 3QN, UK

## Robert Coleman Associates

2 London Wall Buildings, London Wall, London EC2M 5UU
Tel: 020 7628 5001 · Fax: 020 7628 5002 · Email: info@robertcoleman.com
Please see our Website at http://www.robertcoleman.com/
We are always looking for qualified people in the following areas:

**Biomedical Scientists**

Medical Laboratory Scientific Officers (MLSOs) - Candidates registered overseas or Medical Laboratory Assistants (MLAs)
- Microbiologists  – Immunologists  – Biochemists/Clinical Chemists  – Endochronologists
- Histologists  – Virologists  – Haematologists (Blood Transfusion)  – Cytoscreeners

**Occupational Therapists**   **Audiologists**   **Cardiographers**
**Physiotherapists**   **Radiographers**   **Operating Dept. Assts.**

Pharmacists - Pharmacy Technicians and Pharmaceutical Sales
Social Workers   Speech Therapists

## Robert Coleman Associates

2, London Wall Buildings, London Wall, London EC2M 5UU, UK
(tel 020-7628 5001; fax 020-7628 5002; e-mail info@robertcoleman.com).
The core activities of Robert Coleman Associates are centred round the recruitment of professionals, locum and permanent, who are active in the areas supplementary to medicine, in UK, Australia and South Africa. Additionally, the agency supplies contract nurses to and from both Australia and South Africa. Biomedical scientists, medical laboratory assistants, occupational therapists, physiotherapists, radiographers, audiologists, pharmacists, speech therapists and social workers are all catered for. RCA are keen to retain their reputation for looking after those professionals they recruit from overseas so applicants can expect a comprehensive service during their stay in UK, including guidance with registration, accommodation, tax and banking.

## R. S. Locums Ltd

Kensway House, 388 High Road, Ilford, IG1 1TL, UK (tel 020-8478 8219; fax 020-8514 4313; e-mail Doctors@rslocums.co.uk).

RS Locums is an agency which specialises in the provision of locum doctors on a temporary or permanent basis nationwide. Their client base has included HM Prison Service, the Ministry of Defence and the pharmeceutical industry. RS Locums offer a range of opportunities to doctors throughout the UK. Those using the agency need to supply an up-to-date CV, references and evidence of registration with the Medical Council. RS Locums will also help and give advice on visa and PLAB requirements.

## Slade Consulting Group (Qld) Pty Ltd

PO Box 10348, Brisbane Qld 4000, Australia (tel 07-3869 1993; fax 07-3869 1557).

Slade Consulting group is Queensland health's only quality assured official recruitment representative and has represented the public hospitals of Queensland for over a decade. They specialise in the temporary placement of doctors from the UK, Ireland and South Africa who have completed their undergraduate training in those countries in public hospitals in Queensland. Slade has a streamlined programme and facilitates the immigration and medical registration process. Employment under this programme is within an 'area of need' and for a specified period of 52 or 53 weeks, and appropriately qualified applicants are considered for 'registration with conditions', which means that the applicant does not need to sit the Australian Medical Council examination. Suitable qualifications include qualifications from specified universities in New Zealand, the UK, Ireland and South Africa. Employment packages in two different locations in Queensland may be available, and the cost of air travel to Australia is reimbursed.

## Stateside Nursing Ltd

82 Brixham Crescent, Ruislip, HA4 8TX, UK (tel 01895-622101; e-mail stateside@vossnet.co.uk).

Stateside Nursing has spent the last 6 years sending UK and other foreign qualified nurses to temporary and permanent posts in the USA. This includes extensive research into the licensing and administrative processes which apply to nurses entering the USA to work. Their information pack includes information on the NCLEX RN examination, study aids including sample questions, details of the services of a notary to authenticate documents and information on obtaining a green card (Resident Alien permit).

Nurses who use Stateside can sign up for a preparatory course for the NCLEX exam and through them obtain places within hopsitals and agencies in the US. A sample package includes round-trip airfare, green card sponsorship, and free housing.

They also act on behalf of hospitals in the UK seeking to employ staff from Australia, Canada, New Zealand and the US amongst others. This scheme also enables them to provide work to staff awaiting the processing of their green card.

## Strand Nurses Bureau

Brettenham House, 1 Lancaster Place, London, WC2E 7RN, UK (tel 020-7836 6397; fax 020-7240 6324).

In business since 1974, Strand Nurses Bureau place all grades of nurse and nurse specialists in agency or short and long term placements. These placements can include private clients in their own homes, NHS or private hospitals, GP Practices, industry, nursing homes, and aeromedical placements. For placements in private homes they recruit for 5 levels of care ranging from carers who provide domestic support and companionship to general and high dependency registered nurses.

Strand deals predominantly with staff from Australia, New Zealand and South Africa coming to the UK on working holiday or ancestry visas and those who hold British/EEC passports. Although they mainly place candidates in London and the rest of the UK they also place staff in vacancies in Australia and the Middle East.

Their recruitment procedure involves interviews and document checks. Candidates must provide two recent professional references, proof of eligibility to work in the UK, proof of up to date immunisations and police checks, especially if they are going to work with children. In return candidates are given help with bank accounts and accommodation. Other benefits include pay bonuses on completion of a certain number of hours, 4 weeks pro rata holiday pay, a free uniform, and assistance with finding placements on their return home.

**Time & Place Associates (TAP)**
Enterprise House, 113-115 George Lane, South Woodford, Lonodn, E18 1AB, UK (tel 020-8530 8555; fax 020-8530 7888; Website www.tap-locums.com).
Time & Place Associate recruit occupational therapists, physiotherapists, speech & language therapists and social workers for private and NHS hospitals, clinics and social services departments across the UK.

TAP deals extensively with overseas health professionals coming to work in the UK, although at least 6 months experience is recommended. Their placements cover specialisations within outpatient care, special needs, and paediatrics. Assignments last from one to six months and in some instances two years.

Advice on visas, banking, tax and accommodation is provided as well as a mail forwarding service. Further details can be obtained from the above address.

**Technic Services Medical**
The Clock Tower, Bridge Street, Walton-on-Thames, Surrey, KT12 1AY, UK (tel 01932-247600; fax 01932-247501).
Technic Services Medical specialises in the recruitment of occupational therapists and physiotherapists for jobs throughout England, Scotland and Wales. Positions are available in NHS hospitals, the community and the private sector, and the agency offers a variety of employment options including locum work, short-term contracts and permanent posts, as well as positions under the work permit scheme.

The agency is managed by a medically qualified recruitment consultant with first-hand experience of coming to Britain on a working holiday. Assistance with state registration and arranged accommodation are provided. Benefits for locum staff include a payroll every weekday and free professional indemnity insurance cover.

**United Medical Enterprises Ltd**
c/o Saudi Medicare Company, PO Box 25639, Riyadh 11466, Saudi Arabia (tel 9661-454 0387; fax 9661-456 1231; e-mail billquinlqn@hotmail.com).
This organisation is principally involved in the recruitment of staff for hospitals managed by Saudi Medicare in Saudi Arabia and by Allied Medical in Abu Dhabi and Dubai in the United Arab Emirates. Recruitment is mainly for senior hospital medical staff, GPs, dentists, registered general nurses in most specialities, and the full range of paramedical staff. Senior hospital managers and support staff are also recruited, and occasionally health care staff for other locations worldwide.

Most contracts are for 2 or 3 years, although occasionally one-year or shorter contracts can be arranged. Speculative CVs are accepted but candidates are advised to telephone first to discuss the possibility of vacancies arising. The recruitment procedure takes from 2 to 6 months, depending on the category of staff required. While the company did have a London office in the last edition of this book, recruitment is now carried out entirely from the offices in Saudi Arabia.

### United Medical Recruitment
Sun Alliance House, 166-167 St Helens Road, Swansea, SA1 4DQ, UK (tel 01792-472525; fax 01792-472535; e-mail info@united-medical.co.uk).
This agency places hospital and general practice doctors in posts throughout the UK, USA and the Middle East. Locum and substantive positions are available in all specialities.

### Worldwide Healthcare Exchange
The Colonnades, Beaconsfield Close, Hatfield, Hertfordshire AL10 8YD, UK (tel 01707-259233; fax 01707-259223; e-mail wheuk.co.com Website www.whe.co.uk).
Worldwide Healthcare Exchange (WHE) is a network of healthcare recruitment companies that specialises in placing English-speaking nurses in suitable posts throughout the world. Placements range in length from 3 months to a year. WHE has its own offices in Sydney, Melbourne and New Zealand, they also work with BNA (British Nursing Association) in the UK, IMR (International Medical Recruitment) in Australia and New Zealand, MPSS in Germany, Wightman International in Spain, MTA in South Africa and IPNS in Hong Kong. As a result, WHE has a wide range of jobs in all these countries and can provide support and advice both in the nurse's home country and in the country they plan to visit. The package offered by WHE includes professional advice on the work opportunities available, help with registration and work permit applications, preferential airfares, and a 24-hour telephone helpline. WHE also provides a 'career passport', enabling nurses to record the professional experience they gain while travelling.

# Non-Governmental and Voluntary Organisations

## INTRODUCTION
Health professionals are needed by a variety of non-governmental and voluntary organisations throughout the world, and especially in developing countries. The contributions of these workers support a range of initiatives, from community-oriented primary health care programmes to projects at the Ministry of Health level. There is also a growing need for experienced personnel for emergency and relief work, as indicated by the number of organisations described below specialising in this area.

The availability of skills is improving in many developing countries; some charities do not send expatriates if local personnel are available and more appropriate, and those people that they do send from the UK are encouraged to hand over operational work to local agencies as soon as possible.

Working in health in a developing country means working in partnership with local people. Providing training and helping to develop more efficient, effective methods are often important aspects of such projects, working towards the goal of a health care system that can be sustained once the overseas agency has moved on. Health professionals may find themselves working as part of a multi-disciplinary team of development workers, and may need to liaise with a range of people and organisations, including local and international voluntary agencies and government bodies.

Working on these kinds of projects can be a very demanding experience, and a range of skills other than formal qualifications is usually required. The ability to adapt to a foreign culture is essential – this is often not a simple process, and can involve adjusting to the local conditions, work practices, availability of resources, food and lifestyle. An ability to get on with people, and to operate in often difficult circumstances, is also likely to be vital – the local health infrastructure may often lack money, staff and medical supplies.

Many of the organisations listed below require their staff or volunteers to have several years' experience in developing countries or working for similar organisations. In all cases, good communication and interpersonal skills and the ability to work well in a team are also important, and ability in languages other than English may also be desirable, particularly in countries where English is not the main European language; French, Spanish and Portuguese are all useful in different parts of Latin America, Africa and Asia.

Different organisations provide different arrangements for their staff/volunteers, and it is important to find out what these are for any organisation in which you are interested. You may be provided with a salary at the local rate, accommodation and board, social security contributions at home for the duration of the placement, a return flight, training and insurance, but the support provided varies greatly.

In many cases vacancies with these organisations will not necessarily be filled through advertising, but perhaps through co-operation with similar organisations – by 'word of mouth' or by circulating CVs. Similarly looking for a position may involve sending in your details to be kept on file and then waiting whatever length of time it takes for the organisation to be informed of a suitable vacancy; in such a situation it is as well to bear in mind that the prime concern of most of these agencies is to provide staff to meet specific requirements, not to cater for the aspirations of individual health professionals, and so considerable patience may be needed until a position for which you are the best candidate available comes along. International Health Exchange (described below) provides an excellent means of keeping up-to-date with the latest opportunities.

Health professionals with little or no experience of working in developing countries will find courses and workshops aimed at providing an insight into what is involved invaluable. Many of the organisations listed below will be able to provide advice on suitable courses; in particular, International Health Exchange is an excellent source of information, produces a summary sheet of short courses in the UK and overseas, and itself runs a number of courses and workshops.

# LIST OF AGENCIES

### Action against Hunger
1 Catton Street, London WC1R 4AB, UK (tel 020-7831 5858; fax 020-7831 4259; e-mail clc@acf.imaginet.fr Website www.aah-uk.org).

Action Against Hunger is an international emergency relief and development organisation with offices in London, Paris, Madrid and New York. It intervenes in over 35 countries in Africa, Asia, Central America, Eastern Europe and the Caucasus, providing emergency relief in the following areas: nutrition, health, food security and water.

Action Against Hunger employs doctors, nurses, nutritionists, midwives and health educators on an on-going basis. Contracts are for a minimum of one year and include a basic salary paid in the UK plus all travel, accommodation, insurances, and an in-country living allowance.

Applicants must be qualified health professionals with at least two years professional work experience. Conatct Cathy Lennox-Cook at the above address for more details.

### Action Health

The Gate House, 25 Gwydir Street, Cambridge CB1 2LG, UK (tel 01223-460853; fax 01223-461787; e-mail actionhealth@compuserve.com).

Action Health is concerned with the promotion of appropriate health care in developing countries, and operates in India, Tanzania and Uganda. Its primary health care and training programmes focus on skills transfer and developing self-reliance in the communities where it works. It recruits fully qualified health professionals with a minimum of two years' post-qualification experience to work as health trainers. Contracts range in length from one to two years. Applications are welcome from doctors, physiotherapists, midwives, health visitors, occupational therapists, and speech and language therapists, and Action Health considers applications from individuals, couples, families, mature individuals and those with no previous experience of working overseas.

All of Action Health's health trainers fundraise before going overseas. The volunteer package includes round-trip airfare and local transport costs, accommodation and food, a monthly allowance, in-country support, paid leave, National Insurance VDW Class II cover, and health and baggage insurance.

### Australian Volunteers International

71 Argyle Street, PO Box 350, Fitzroy, Victoria 3065, Australia (tel +61-3-9279 1788; fax 03-9419 4280; e-mail ozvol@ozvol.org.au Website www.ozvol.org.au).

Australian Volunteers International is one of the largest voluntary technical assistance agencies, sending Australian volunteers to live and work in developing communities in some 50 countries throughout Asia, Africa, Latin America and the Pacific, and in remote Aboriginal communities within Australia. The largest proportion of placements are taken by health personnel and teachers, but other skill areas are also recruited.

All volunteers, minimum age 20, must have at least two years' work experience or a tertiary or trade qualification in their chosen area of assignment. Applicants must be of Australian nationality or hold permanent residency status in Australia. Placements are usually for 2 years although this time period may vary.

Volunteers are paid roughly the same as the local salary for the position held in the host country. Conditions vary from one place to another. This salary/allowance should cover basic living costs, expenses over and above this amount should be funded by the volunteer. Health insurance and airfares will be provided. Accommodation will be arranged either free of charge or charged at a percentage of the volunteer's salary.

AVI produces several publications available from AVI's Media & Public Affairs Unit free of charge: an annual report; *Interaction*, a quarterly newsletter for friends and supporters; *Out There*, a quarterly newsletter for volunteers in the field; various returned volunteer newsletters (different ones published by each state office); and various promotional brochures outlining the organisation and its services.

### British Red Cross

9 Grosvenor Crescent, London SW1X 7EJ, UK (tel 020-7235 5454; fax 020-7245 6315; e-mail information@redcross.org.uk).

The British Red Cross (BRC) works as part of the International Red Cross and Red Crescent Movement, protecting and assisting victims of conflicts and natural disasters, with neutrality and impartiality, in the UK and overseas. British Red Cross volunteers not only provide a trained and skilled response to emergencies, but also care for people in crisis, by offering vital services in the local community.

The BRC maintains a register of suitably qualified doctors and nurses who are available to work overseas. This work is organised in liaison with one of the two main constituent bodies of the International Red Cross: the International Committee of the Red Cross (ICRC) and the International Federation of the Red Cross and Red Crescent Societies ('the Federation'); both of these bodies have their headquarters in Geneva. The Federation represents the national Red Cross and Red Crescent Societies internationally. On occasion medical personnel may be required to work directly for the BRC on bilateral programmes.

The ICRC is mainly concerned with medical and humanitarian activity in or close to areas of armed conflict, and the work concentrates on the care of the victims of war – both military and civilian. Surgical hospitals are either run or supported by the ICRC. Personnel working in these situations inevitably have to accept an element of personal risk.

Surgeons and anaesthetists accepted to work in ICRC hospitals need to be broadly trained and competent to act without supervision across a wide surgical spectrum. Because of these requirements candidates must have a higher degree and be at senior registrar/junior consultant level. A knowledge of the management of war wounds is clearly advisable. The BRC may invite surgeons to attend an ICRC surgical workshop near Geneva, which takes place once a year. Nurses must be experienced in surgical/operating theatre nursing, and a knowledge of intensive care/accident and emergency nursing is advantageous. In addition considerable maturity is needed when working in conflict situations.

The Federation undertakes longer-term projects in developing countries, focusing on community health. The emphasis of the Federation's work is on contributing to community development without encouraging dependency on outside assistance. In addition to these projects the Federation also has many emergency relief and rehabilitation programmes, generally in response to natural disasters. There are also rare occasions when a doctor with previous overseas experience is required to execute a needs analysis.

Doctors accepted to work for the Federation must have an extensive knowledge of community/primary health care. Nurses working in development programmes for the Federation must have experience in community health and tropical diseases, and have a degree in public health. A midwifery qualification is an advantage in many situations. Nurses are also needed for relief and refugee programmes run by the Federation. The training and supervision of local staff is a key aspect of many missions.

Other staff requirements may include prosthetists, particularly in conflict situations or in places where conflicts have taken place (for example, where landmines may still be active); and occasionally physiotherapists and laboratory technicians.

The often heavy workload and sometimes difficult working and living conditions mean that it is necessary to be physically fit and mentally robust, and there is a need to be resilient and adaptable to fit in well as a member of an often multinational team. Candidates must be over 25 years of age, and considering the requirements mentioned the preferred upper age limit for a first overseas mission is 50 years of age.

The length of overseas posts is very flexible; in the case of relief work posts typically last for 6 months, but can be extended; for posts in development, posts usually last for 1 year, which can be extended to 2 years. Positions are salaried, and come with a local allowance, flights, transport and insurance, and other benefits. Doctors must hold full registration with the British General Medical Council and be resident in the UK. Nurses must be RGNs with the UKCC and have a minimum of 3 years' postgraduate experience. It is preferable to have some overseas experience, particularly in areas of deprivation or disaster. Furthermore delegates need to have the maturity to operate in sometimes politically sensitive situations, and diplomatic skills can be an important asset, particularly in terms of ensuring that the neutrality of the ICRC/Federation is protected.

Previous experience of working in similar posts is preferable for overseas positions arranged through the BRC; recruitment for positions through Geneva often requires previous International Red Cross experience. Requests for staff from the ICRC and the Federation arrive at the BRC, which then decides which positions it will recruit for. Positions can be anywhere in the world, reflecting the fact that there is a national Red Cross and Red Crescent Society in almost every country in the world. The BRC has a large number of personnel on file, and potentially suitable delegates are contacted and the details of the post discussed with them. The final choice of applicant is made in Geneva by either the ICRC or the Federation, which may be choosing from more than one candidate, depending on the response from other Red Cross/Red Crescent Societies.

Once accepted, delegates attend briefings, a medical examination, and if possible a one-week basic training course attended by representatives of the ICRC and the Federation, and by previous delegates. Once in the field delegates work for the ICRC or the Federation, rather than the national Society, although the latter will be involved in looking after arrangements at home.

The BRC mostly fills its vacancies by word of mouth. It does advertise in the International Health Exchange's magazine (see page 78), and occasionally places advertisements for specialist positions in national newspapers and technical magazines. If you meet the requirements specified above, send a full CV to the Overseas Personnel Officer at the above address. Nationals from outside the UK should contact their own national society; addresses for several of these are included below:

*International Committee of the Red Cross:* 19 Avenue de la Paix, CH-1202 Geneva, Switzerland, (tel +41-22-734 6001; fax 22-733 2057; e-mail dc_com_cip@icrc.org Website (English) www.icrc.org (French & Spanish) www.cicr.org).

*American Red Cross:* Office of the President, 17th and D Streets, NW, Washington, DC 20006, USA (tel 202-728-6600; fax 202-775-0733).

*Australian Red Cross:* P.O. Box 196, Carlton South, VIC 3053, Australia (tel 03-9345 1800; fax 03-9348 2513; e-mail redcross@nat.redcross.org.au Website www.redcross.org.au).

*Canadian Red Cross:* 1800 Alta Vista Drive, Ottawa, Ontario K1G 4J5, Canada (tel 613-739-3000; fax 613-731-1411).

*New Zealand Red Cross:* Red Cross House, 14 Hill Street, Wellington 1, PO Box 12-140, New Zealand (tel 04-472 3750; fax 04-473 0315).

*South African Red Cross Society:* 21 Broad Road,Wynberg 7800, South Africa (tel +27-21-797 8602; fax +27-21-797 9147; e-mail Redxnatgadija@ cybertrade.co.za).

**CARE International UK**
Tower House, 8-14 Southampton Street, London WC2E 7HA, UK (tel 020-7379 5247; fax 020-7379 0543; Website www.careinternational.org.uk).

CARE is one of the world's largest relief and development charities, working in Africa, Asia, Latin America and eastern Europe.

CARE International UK employs only professionals with extensive experience in their field, preferably gained with an organisation similar to CARE. For overseas posts, several years' experience of working in a developing country are also required. Medical specialists are needed in areas relevant to CARE's health-related projects and programmes; GPs, nurses and others with a clinical background and/or no overseas experience do not normally meet CARE's requirements. Areas in which CARE employs staff include water supply and sanitation, family planning, reproductive health, immunisation programmes, HIV and AIDS, nutrition, midwifery and childcare. Many of CARE's health professionals have a Masters degree in public health or another relevant subject, such as tropical medicine and hygiene.

Staff are recruited through advertisements in the London-based *Guardian* on Thursdays, the *Guardian Weekly* and specialist publications. In addition CARE maintains a database of suitable candidates, drawn from unsolicited applications and short-listed applicants for specific vacancies – this database is searched when vacancies arise. Wherever possible skilled local staff are preferred as this encourages local ownership of the project – overseas staff need to be adaptable, receptive and sympathetic to local plans and aspirations, in addition to having the necessary qualifications, skills and experience.

Applicants need to have a first or second degree and/or an equivalent professional qualification in a field of study relevant to CARE's programmes; approximately 3 years' professional experience in a developing country; a proven ability to live and work with different cultures; English-speaking ability and fluency in at least one other language (preferably French, Spanish or Portuguese); and a reasonable standard of computer literacy.

## Concern Worldwide
52-55 Camden Street, Dublin 2, Ireland (tel +353-1-475 4162; fax 01-475 4649; e-mail hrenquiries@concern.ie Website www.concern.ie).

Concern Worldwide is a voluntary organisation devoted to the relief, assistance and advancement of people in 21 of the world's poorest countries including Angola, Afghanistan, Burundi, Bangaladesh, Cambodia, Democratic Republic of Congo, East Timor, Ethiopia, Haiti, Honduras, India, Kosovo, Laos, Liberia, Mozambique, North Korea, Rwanda, Sierra Leone, Somalia, Tanzania and Uganda. As well as providing emergency relief, Concern works alongside people to provide long-term support for development. Its operations are based on a network of about 120 skilled expatriate staff who work closely with around 2000 national staff. Concern's programmes cover health, nutrition, community development, natural resources, education and engineering.

Concern Worldwide personnel are skilled professionals from various backgrounds each has a range of responsibilities, including providing guidance and training for local staff as well as project administration.

Concern recruits personnel on 2 year contracts as well as short-term (3-6 months) contracts in emergency situations. Applicants must be over 21 with a minium of 18 months post qualification work experience. For further information about Concern Worldwide operates, contact the HR department at the above address.

## CUSO
400-2255 Carling Avenue, Ottawa, Ontario K2B 1A6, Canada (tel 613-829-7445; fax 613-829-7996; e-mail Linda.henderson@cuso.ca Website www.cuso.org).

CUSO is a Canadian development organisation that recruits and places Canadians overseas to share their skills, generally for two-year terms. There are currently about 300 CUSO volunteers working in the field, in placements co-developed by local CUSO staff and the host country partner. CUSO works in Africa, Asia, the South Pacific, Latin America and the Caribbean, and also provides funds to locally controlled projects in Canada.

During the 1970s and 1980s CUSO sent a large number of health professionals overseas, mostly in the area of primary health care. Since then, however, the number of medical postings has declined; current health positions might deal with specific issues such as AIDS or disabilities, or more generally with community health, health policy and/or health administration.

During their placement, 'cooperants' receive a local salary to cover overseas living costs. Benefits also include airfare, medical/dental/life/disability insurance, a settling-in allowance, orientation, language training if required and Can$9200 in cash benefits to assist with departure, resettlement and other costs.

Applicants should send a copy of their résumé to the CUSO office nearest to them (a list is available from the above address); those residing outside Canada should send their résumé to the Ottawa address. Due to CUSO's funding arrangement with the Canadian government, CUSO can only accept applications from Canadian citizens or Canadians with landed immigrant status.

## Emmanuel Hospital Association
808/92 Deepali Building, Nehru Place, North Delhi – 19, India (tel +91-11-643 2055/646 1487; fax 11-643 2055) and P.O. Box 43, Sutton, SM2 5WL, UK (tel 020-8770 9717; fax 020-8770 9747; e-mail enquiries@eha.org.uk Website www.eha.org.uk).

Emmanuel Hospital Association (EHA) is a federation of hospitals and community health and development projects that provides affordable health care services to over 7 million people across Northern India. There are partner offices in the UK, USA and Canada; the UK office has recently been refounded as EHA-UK a charity which recently sent medical teams to Albania to assist refugees from Kosovo.

The EHA community health and development projects in India provide preventive services, integrating health with development and trains local people as health care givers to make it sustainable, it also mobilises the community to further help themselves by organising them into self-help groups through micro enterprise programmes. Sanitation, adult literacy and income generation are also integrated into these health programmes.

The Association recruits: trained doctors – obstetricians/gynaecologists, surgeons, opthalmologists, physicians, ENT specialists, orthopaedics, plastic surgeons; nurses; dentists; health workers; technical professionals e.g. engineers, IT specialists, architects, builders, evaluators; those with educational qualifications – literacy experts, school teachers, trainers; professional videographers, photography technicians, creative writers; business experts – microenterprise and credit scheme professionals, financial managers, and accountants. Relevant qualifications are required of the individual roles. Knowledge of English is essential, any other language (Hindi, Marathi) skills very desirable and in some cases necessary. A stipend is paid to cover basic board and lodging for volunteers when in India; any other expenses (airfare, insurance, etc.) to be met by the volunteer. Placements from 6 months to two years arranged all year round.

## Health Projects Abroad
PO Box 24, Bakewell, Derby DE45 1ZW, UK (tel 01629-640051; fax 01629-640054; e-mail info@hpauk.org).

Health Projects Abroad has been working with communities and health authorities in Tanzania, East Africa since 1991, supporting small village-led, construction projects and Community Based Health Care programmes. A similar programme has just been launched in Cameroon. Complementing the development work, HPA organise a volunteer programme, offering young people aged 18-28 the chance to live in an african village and take part in a community project. Volunteers help with basic building work on schools and health dispensaries alongside local people.

Each group of 10 volunteers has with them a Medical Professional Volunteer – an RGN (or equivalent) with experience of A&E and (preferably) tropical medicine, a good sense of humour and a calm responsible disposition. There is no age limit for Professional Volunteers and although their remit is the health of the volunteers and to participate in the group project work, there is usually scope to learn a lot about the local health system.

All volunteers contribute towards the cost of taking part. Medics raise £1600 to cover flights, food, language tuition, all pre-departure training and travel insurance. Full back up and training is provided both in the UK and in-country. A large proportion of the funding for the development work comes from money raised by volunteers. Advice on training and fundraising is provided; HPA is a National Training Award winner.

Full information on HPAs's work and volunteering can be obtained from the address above..

**Health Unlimited**
Prince Consort House, 27-29 Albert Embankment, London SE1 7TS, UK (tel 020-7582 5999; fax 020-7582 5900; e-mail general@healthunlimited.org Website www.healthunlimited.org).

Health Unlimited is a British Charity working in 12 countries in Africa, Asia and Latin America. It is particularly concerned with the most excluded and vulnerable people – indigenous people threatened with political and economic instability and communities affected by long term conflict. Projects are currently being undertaken in Brazil, Burma, Cambodia, China, El Salvador, Guatemala, Laos, Namibia, Nicaragua, Peru, the Somali speaking Horn of Africa and the African Great Lakes Region.

Working in partnership with local people, community organisations, representative bodies and governments, their long term programmes focus on training health workers, promoting community action for disease prevention, improving access to state health services and building local capacity to sustain the programmes after their teams leave. Health Unlimited also has Well Women Media Projects which use the media, especially radio, to disseminate health awareness messages to large numbers of people.

The majority of overseas staff working for Health Unlimited are local to the area or country in which they work, recruitment is only done internationally when the necessary skills are not available nationally or regionally.

Overseas staff must be qualified in the required discipline and have experience of working overseas in a development context. A background in either community health, health training, community development or development management is essential. Vacancies for doctors and nurses whose main experience is in a clinical practice are rare as Health Unlimited is not involved in curative health.

Recruitment is through the international *Guardian Weekly* and specialist magazines (such as International Health Exchange's *The Health Exchange* and *Vacatureblad*, a Dutch publication). Health Unlimited do not keep a register of possible applicants.

Contracts are usually for two years, often extendable. Salaries (at a non-taxed rate) start at around £10,000 for health workers and at around £12,000 for managers. In addition accommodation and living allowance are paid, with an annual home leave and flights. Most Health Unlimited posts are unaccompanied. Further details are available from Madeleine Hammond at the address above.

**Health Volunteers Overseas**
c/o Washington Station, PO Box 65157, Washington DC 20035-5157, USA (tel +1-202-296 0928; fax 202-296 8018; e-mail info@hvousa.org Website www.hvousa.org).
HVO is a private non-profit organisation committed to improving health care in developing countries through training and education. HVO currently recruits 300 fully trained and qualified medical professionals per year to participate in programmes in the following specialities; anesthesia, dentistry, nursing, oral and maxillofacial surgery, orthopaedics, pediatrics, internal medicine and physical therapy. A nursing division is being developed for 2001. Programme sites are in Africa, Asia, the Caribbean and South America.

Although each programme is different in goals and content, the principal concept remains the same – that volunteers should teach rather than provide service. Applicants of any nationality are accepted; most programmes require Board Certified or Board Eligible physicians, dentists, oral surgeons or physical therapists, RNs and CRNAs. Volunteer requirements vary according to programme site. Usual length of placement is two to four weeks. Most sites provide housing for volunteers, but at other sites housing arrangements are made for the volunteers but the volunteers absorb the cost. A one month assignment costs a volunteer on average $3,000 (for transportation, room, board etc) in personal expense.

Those interested should contact Barbara Edwards at the above address.

**Institute for International Cooperation and Development (IICD)**
PO Box 520, Williamstown, Massachusetts 01267, USA (tel 413-458-9828; fax 413-458-3323; e-mail iicdinfo@berkshire.net Website www.iicd-volunteer.org).
The IICD is a non-profit organisation committed to 'promoting global understanding and international solidarity'. As part of its activities in India, Africa and Latin America, the IICD organises volunteer projects in Zimbabwe, Zambia, Brazil, Honduras, Guatemala, El Salvador and Nicaragua involving community health programmes and health education. Programmes generally last for 6 to 18 months, including preparation and follow-up periods in the USA. Volunteers must be at least 18 years of age, and there are no specific academic or skill requirements. In order to take part in the programme volunteers need to pay a fee; this will be in the range of US$3800-5500, and covers training, accommodation, board, insurance and flights.

For more information contact the Administrative Director at the above address.

**International Cooperation for Development (ICD)**
Unit 3, Canonbury Yard, 190a New North Road, London N1 7BJ, UK (tel 020-7354 0883; fax 020-7359 0017; e-mail ciirlon@gn.apc.org or jobs@ciir.org Website www.ciir.org).
ICD is a department of the Catholic Institute for International Relations. It recruits people to work in development projects in the developing world, where they share their skills with local communities in order to work against poverty and promote self-reliance. It has 120 people working in development projects in Central and South America, the Caribbean, Africa and the Middle East, of whom approximately 40% are health workers. Health professionals working with ICD include midwives, doctors, health visitors, pharmacists, and occupational, speech and physiotherapists.

All ICD workers have a qualification relevant to the work that they are undertaking, a minimum of 2 years' work experience, and often a background in formal or informal training. Each person is recruited for 2 years. For more information contact the ICD at the above address.

**International Health Exchange**
134 Lower Marsh Road, London SE1 7AE, UK (tel 020-7620 3333; fax 020-7620 2277; e-mail info@ihe.org.uk).
International Health Exchange supports the work of international aid agencies by helping to recruit and train health personnel working in relief and development programmes. It provides information, support and advice to a broad spectrum of health professionals – from anaesthetists to occupational therapists – and lobbies national health services to release staff for overseas contracts, and to look favourably on the international experience gained.

IHE maintains a central register of health personnel available for international work. Through this – and its extensive network of contacts – IHE identifies candidates for overseas posts on behalf of operational relief and development agencies. Its training courses, such as 'Humanitarian Principles and Practices' and 'Health Care in Emergencies', provide health workers with a better understanding of the context of health programmes in the South.

IHE's two popular magazines, *The Health Exchange* and *Job Supplement*, appear alternately every month. They report on practical approaches to health development, include features written by practitioners in the field, and contain all the latest job listings. For further information, contact IHE at the above address.

**International Medical Corps**
*US Office:* Human Resources Department, 11500 West Olympic Boulevard, Suite 506, Los Angeles, California 90064-1524, USA (tel 310-826-7800; fax 310-442-6622; e-mail imc@imc-la.org Website www.imc-la.org).
*UK Representative:* Ivan Tomlin, 3 Anselm Road, Hatch End, Pinner, HA5 4LH UK (tel/fax 020-8428 4025; e-mail ivan-tomlin@freeuk.com)
The International Medical Corps (IMC) is a non-profit humanitarian organisation established in 1984 by American physicians and nurses. IMC's doctors, nurses, medical and support personnel provide emergency medical services, health care training and humanitarian assistance to populations throughout the world affected by war, poverty and disaster. IMC maintains a database of health personnel for its programmes. It provides competitive salary and health insurance packages, with room and board and round trip airfare included. Contact one of the above addresses for details of current programmes.

**International Service (formerly known as UNAIS)**
Suite 3a, Hunter House, 57 Goodramgate, York YO1 7FX, UK (tel 01904-647799; e-mail unais-uk@ges2.poptel.org.uk Website www.oneworld.org/is).
International Service works in partnership with organisations in Latin America, western Africa and the Middle East. It promotes long-term development by providing skills and experienced personnel to collaborate with locally organised initiatives. Applications are welcome throughout the year from doctors, nurses, therapists and health educators to work in its health programmes.

Contracts are for a minimum of 2 years, and the package includes a living allowance, accommodation, NI and medical insurance, language training, flights and various grants. For further information contact the recruitment administrator at the above address.

**Médecins Sans Frontières**
*International Office:* Rue de la Tourelle 39, B-1040 Brussels, Belgium (tel 02-280 1881; fax 02-280 0173).
*US Office:* 6 East 39th Street, 8th Floor, New York, NY 10016, USA (tel 212-679-6800; fax 212-679-7016; e-mail dwb@newyork.msf.org).
*UK Office:* 124-132 Clerkenwell Road, London, EC1R 5DL, UK (tel 020-7713 5600; fax 020-7713 5004; e-mail office@london.msf.org).
*Australian Office:* PO Box 847, Broadway, NSW 2007, Australia (tel 02-9552 4933; fax 02-9552 6539; e-mail office@sydney.msf.org).
*Canadian Office:* 720 Spadina Avenue, Suite 402, Toronto, Ontario M5S 2T9 Canada (tel 416-964 0619; fax 416-963 8707; e-mail msfcan@passport.ca)
Every year Médecins Sans Frontières (MSF) sends out over 2000 volunteers to some 80 countries throughout the world affected by war, famine or natural disaster. MSF is the world's largest independent aid agency of its kind, and has developed a detailed understanding of the best ways to bring effective relief to the victims of conflicts and natural disasters, constantly improving its methods of providing emergency aid.

MSF needs qualified doctors, nurses (RGNs), anaesthetists, midwives, laboratory technicians and surgeons with 2 years' post-qualification experience. A diploma in tropical medicine is preferable. For all categories of staff previous travel and work experience in developing countries is highly valuable.

The selection process involves a number of interviews, tests and pre-departure courses, and takes some time. Volunteers are contracted for 9 months, but some take on longer assignments – MSF is not able to accept people wanting to work on short placements. For further information applicants should contact their nearest office – please note that the UK office is unable to accept applications from non-UK residents.

**Medical Aid for Palestinians**
33a Islington Park Street, London N1 1QB, UK (tel 020-7226 4114; fax 020-7226 0880; e-mail admin@map-uk.demon.co.uk).
This charity works to develop Palestinian health services in the Middle East, mainly in the West Bank, the Gaza Strip and Lebanon. It works in partnership with local health organisations to provide emergency relief, training and long-term development programmes. It is involved in all areas of health care and recruits experienced doctors, nurses and health workers to share their skills with local staff. Placements are for 6 months (and are renewable), and the package includes flights, accommodation, health insurance, a living allowance and various grants.

**MERLIN (Medical Emergency Relief International)**
14 David Mews, Porter Street, London W1M 1HW, UK (tel 020-7487 2505; fax 020-7487 4042; e-mail hq@merlin.org.uk Website www.merlin.org.uk).
MERLIN believes that access to health care is a fundamental human right. To uphold this right, they provide medical relief to people suffering as a result of conflict, natural disaster or epidemic disease anywhere in the world, regardless of race, religion or political affiliation. It is currently working in Albania, Democratic Republic of Congo, Kenya, Liberia, Russia, Sierra Leone and Tajikistan.
MERLIN sends teams of medical and support staff to areas where local health infrastructures have collapsed and people are at their most vulnerable. Merlin teams stay in the field until the situation has stabilised, typically for 6-12 months. After the crisis they provide medical expertise, training and supplies, in order to regenerate local health services for the future. Their aim is to leave behind a sustainable healthcare service.
Merlin recruits doctors and nurses to join its register of medical staff available for work overseas. Further qualifications and or experience in tropical medicine, epidemiology, vector control, public health, community health or nutrition are useful. Previous overseas work experience is highly desirable.
MERLIN offers a comprehensive overseas package that includes 6-12 month contracts, comprehensive insurance cover, a monthly allowance, one return flight and all daily living expenses in the field. If you are interested in volunteering for Merlin, please contact the Recruitment Team at the above address.

**Operation Crossroads Africa**
475 Riverside Drive, Suite 1366, New York, New York 10115, USA (tel +1-212 870 2106; fax 212-870 2644; e-mail oca@igc.apc.org Website www.igc.org/oca).
Operation Crossroads Africa sends pre-med, pre-nursing and medical and nursing students to work on community health/medical projects in 10-12 African countries and Brazil, each summer. They also recruit volunteers for annual community health/medical and education/training (which includes women's development) projects in Ghana, Kenya and South Africa.
Volunteers work 5-6 hours a day. Projects are six weeks long and are in rural villages. The work groups (8-10 volunteers per group) then travel for one week in the host country. All groups work with local counterparts. The programmes run from mid-June to mid-August.
Volunteers are aged between 17 and 35. Knowledge of French is preferred for francophone countries and Portugese for Brazil and Guinea Bissau. Applicants of any nationality are welcomed. Participants must attend a 3 day orientation in New York prior to departure paying their own way to New York and all other expenses. There is also a participation fee of $3,500, but help is given with fundraising.
A free brochure, programme application and annual report are available from the above address.

## PCEA Tumutumu Hospital

Private Bag, Karatina, Kenya (e-mail Tumutumu@AfricaOnline.co.ke).

PCEA Tumutumu Hospital is a 200 bed prebyterian church hospital providing medical, surgical, paediatric and maternity care. There are also active community health, and nurse training departments.

Doctors, pharmacists and nurse tutors are also required for a minimum period of two years (doctors can arrange one year stays). 20 elective places are available for 8 week stays, plus up to 6 other volunteers are needed annually. Fluency in English as well as respect for the Christian tradition of the hospital is imperative. No smoking or alcohol is allowed in the hospital compound, including the student accommodation block. A housing and maintenance allowance is provided to long-term volunteers. All other volunteers get board and lodging free but no expenses. Church members can also apply to the Church of Scotland for sponsorship, although this requires a 4 year stay.

Applications to the Medical Superintendent at the above address.

## Save the Children Fund (SCF)

17 Grove Lane, London SE5 8RD, UK (tel 020-7703 5400; fax 020-7793 7614; Website www.savethechildrenfund.org.uk).

Although SCF has a long tradition of emergency relief work, the principal emphasis of its overseas activity is on long term programmes concerned with health, nutrition, food security, community development and welfare, helping to establish schemes that governments and local organisations will be able to sustain. SCF recruits staff locally within each country whenever possible and training is a key element of all its overseas programmes. Over 3500 locally appointed staff are currently employed in over 70 countries.

Salaried posts in various health disciplines are occasionally available with SCF. These will include health advisors, managers, co-ordinators, PHC and MCH specialists and nutritionists.

Applicants must be qualified medical personnel and/or hold postgraduate qualifications in community/public health/human nutrition and have a minimum of 2 years relevant overseas development/emergency experience.

For details of current vacancies contact the Overseas Personnel Section at the above address. Salaries vary according to the post and grade and SCF has a competitive benefits package including accommodation and flights.

## Skillshare Africa

126 New Walk, Leicester LE1 7JA, UK (tel 0116-254 1862; fax 0116-254 2614; e-mail skillshare-uk@geo2.poptel.org.uk Website www.skillshare.org).

Skillshare Africa is a charity that sends skilled and qualified development workers to work in support of development projects in Botswana, Lesotho, Mozambique, Namibia, South Africa and Swaziland. As the charity's name suggests, its work emphasises the sharing of skills and the promotion of self-reliance in communities.

Many Skillshare Africa projects involve health and health care facilities – for example, the renovation of Lichinga hospital in Mozambique and the provision of a medical team and new equipment. Development workers are recruited in response to specific requests from governments, organisations and communities in the countries concerned, and need to have relevant qualifications and at least 2 years' post-qualification experience. Most placements last for 2 years.

For more information on what being a development worker involves and on how Skillshare Africa operates, contact the above address.

**United Nations Volunteers**
Postfach 260 111, D-53153 Bonn, Germany (tel +49-228-815-2000; fax +49-228-815-2001; e-mail hq@unv.org Website www.unv.org).
United Nations Volunteers (UNVs) work in some 148 countries, 75 per cent of them in countries designated as least developed. Many of the 2,300 UNVs currently serving are health professionals – doctors, nurses and midwives. The major areas of work are in helping the development of comprehensive health services, disease prevention and control and the treatment and prevention of HIV/AIDS. The average assignment is for a period of two years.

Potential volunteers need to have university-level (and often postgraduate) qualifications in the discipline concerned, together with several years' work experience. Some 70 percent of UNVs are from developing countries.

Health professionals who would like to be considered for a position as a UN Volunteer should send a curriculum vitae to United Nations Volunteers Offshore Processing Centre, P.O. Box 25711, 1311 NICOSIA, Cyprus, e-mail enquiry@unv.org. For comprehensive application information, visit the UNV Internet web site www.unv.org/unvols/index.htm.

**Voluntary Service Overseas (VSO)**
317 Putney Bridge Road, London SW15 2PN, UK (tel 020-8780 7500; fax 020-8780 7207; e-mail enquiry@vso.org.uk).
VSO the largest independent volunteer sending agency in the world, places Health Professionals in a variety of positions throughout Africa, Asia, the Pacific Islands and Eastern Europe. Qualified, experienced health workers from a range of skills are needed including, Doctors, Nurses, Midwifes, Health Educators, Occupational Therapists, Speech Therapists, Physiotherapists, Pharmacists, MLSO's, Radiographers and Dieticians.

All posts require a relevant qualification and a minimum of 2 years post qualification experience. Positions are for 2 years (12 months in some Ea t European placements) and volunteers receive return flights, accommodation, a living allowance, a series of grants plus other benefits.

**WaterAid**
Prince Consort House, 27-29 Albert Embankment, London SE1 7UB, UK (tel 020-7793 4500; fax 020-7793 4545; e-mail information@wateraid.org.uk Website www.wateraid.org.uk).
WaterAid is a charity that works to help poor people in developing countries achieve lasting and sustainable improvements to their domestic water supplies, sanitation and hygiene practices. It works through partner organisations and the beneficiaries of its work are actively involved in the planning, implementation and management of the project. Technologies appropriate to the local conditions are used and the work is planned so that the benefits are sustainable by the local community without long-term external support.

The only specialism in the health field that WaterAid is involved in is hygiene promotion, although improvements in health in the broadest sense are relevant in all the work it funds. It focuses its efforts in Africa and Asia; at the time of writing there were staff working in Bangladesh, Ethiopia, Ghana, India, Malawi, Madagascar, Mozambique, Nepal, Nigeria, Tanzania, Uganda and Zambia. Approximately one third of these staff have a health education/community development background.

Voluntary placements are not available with WaterAid; posts are full-time and contracts are for a fixed period (normally 2-3 years). Positions are advertised in newspapers such as *The Guardian* and *The Guardian Weekly*, and WaterAid normally requires candidates to possess a postgraduate qualification in a field relevant to the post, together with experience of working in a developing country.

---

### The International Directory of Voluntary Work

New edition contains over 750 organisations looking for voluntary help from all types of people for all kinds of work. Covers short, medium and long term residential opportunities in Europe and around the world in addition to non-residential oppoprtunities in the United Kingdom and the USA.

£10.99 softback ISBN 1-85458-237-2

Available from Vacation Work Publications, 9 Park End Street, Oxford OX1 1HJ (Tel 01865-241978; Fax 01865-790885; Website www.vacationwork.co.uk).

---

# Denominational Organisations

## INTRODUCTION

The organisations listed in this section carry out similar development and relief work to the voluntary agencies and NGOs described in the previous section, much of which involves health care projects. The vital difference with the agencies described below is that their contribution to the welfare of developing countries takes place within a religious context, and often with specifically missionary objectives, so health professionals considering working for such organisations need to be committed to these aims. The working environment – for example, in a mission hospital – will often combine health care with the dissemination of evangelical doctrine.

A useful source of information for Christians wanting to work overseas are the directories published by Christian Vocations These are *The Short-term Service Directory* (£4.95) for placements lasting one week to two years, and *Jobs Abroad* (£4.25) for places lasting more than two years, each book includes details of numerous vacancies with Christian organisations around the world, including opportunities for medical and other health care personnel.

*Christian Vocations:* Holloway Street West, Lower Gornal, Dudley DY3 2DZ, UK (tel 01902-882836; fax 01902-881099; e-mail info@christianvocations.org Website www.christianvocations.org).

## LIST OF AGENCIES

### Action Partners Ministries

Bawtry Hall, Bawtry, Doncaster DN10 6JH, UK (tel 01302-710750; fax 01302-719399; e-mail info@actionpartners.org.uk Website www.actionpartners.org.uk).

Action Partners is a small Christian organisation with links with a number of churches and missionary societies in Africa, including Cameroon, Chad, Egypt, Kenya, Ghana, Nigeria, Sudan and Congo. Only a few of its 50 overseas workers are involved in health, although there are a number of vacancies in hospitals and are involved in health, although there are a number of vacancies in hospitals and health projects that could be filled by suitable workers.

Specific projects include Vom Christian hospital in northern Nigeria where there is a need for specialists in obstetrics/gynaecology, surgery and paediatrics. The focus of the Mangu Leprosy and Rehabilitation Centre is on people suffering from leprosy, but also on children who have suffered from rickets or polio, so orthopaedic surgery is needed and staff for the very busy physiotherapy department as well as general medical work. Doctors and nurses are also needed for a small hospital in northern Cameroon with which Action Partners has links. Apart from these institutional projects, most of the organisation's work is in rural extension medical work, health training, immunisation programmes and child welfare.

Most openings are for relatively long-term projects, although staff are also recruited for temporary vacancies in emergencies.

## Baptist Missionary Society

PO Box 49, Baptist House, 129 Broadway, Dicot, OX11 8XA, UK (tel 01235-517700; fax 01235-517601; e-mail mail@bms.org.uk Website www.rpc.ox.ac.uk/bms).

Baptist Missionary Society has opportunites for people of all ages to work in teams or individually, across Asia, Europe, Africa, Central and South America. There are year out schemes, summer teams (2-6 weeks), and placements for those with a work skill (medics, teachers, administrators) for four weeks to two years. Volunteers are required for nursing and other medical work, administration and teaching.

Applications with CV to the Volunteer Co-ordinator at the above address.

## Catholic Medical Mission Board

10 West 17th Street, New York, New York 10011-5765, USA (tel 212-242-7757; fax 212-807-9161; e-mail RdeCostanzo@CMMB.org Website www.cmmb.org).

This organisation places licensed and certified US and Canadian doctors and registered nurses in independently operated Catholic medical mission hospitals and clinics in Africa, the Caribbean, Eastern Europe, Central and South America, India and Papua New Guinea. The length of service depends on current mission needs; tours of service lasting 1 month, 6 months or 1-2 years may be available. Potential applicants can contact the Co-ordinator, Programme Services at the above address for further information.

Non-US/Canadian personnel interested in working with one of the Mission's affiliated facilities should send a stamped, self-addressed envelope to the above address and ask for a list of contact details.

## Christians Abroad

1 Stockwell Green, London SW9 9HP, UK (tel 020-7734 5956; fax 020-7346 5955; Website cabroad.org.uk; World Service Enquiry tel 020-7346 5950; e-mail wse@cabroad.org.uk Website wse.org.uk).

This charity operates a number of initiatives useful to those thinking of working in overseas development. These include World Service Enquiry, which provides information and advice to people of any faith or none about working overseas; 'One to One' guidance interviews with trained careers advisors; and *Opportunities Abroad*, a monthly listing of vacancies through around 60 aid, development and mission agencies – around 150 health posts are advertised in each issue (please call one of the above numbers for details of subscription rates). A database of skilled personnel seeking work overseas is also kept and searched on behalf of agencies with vacancies.

Projects provides an ecumenical recruitment service on behalf of Christians Abroad's overseas partners. Qualified Christian medical staff are recruited as required, mainly for sub-Saharan Africa – in the past these have included doctors, nurses, physiotherapists and laboratory technicians.

For more information on these various services contact the address or visit the websites listed above.

### Christoffel Blindenmission

Nibelungstrasse 124, D-64625 Bensheim, Germany (tel 062-51 131 241; fax 062-51 131 165; e-mail communication@com-i.org Website www.cbmi.de).

Christoffel Blindenmission (CBM) is an inter-denominational Christian mission organisation. It assists national churches, international missions and other overseas agencies by providing funds, expert personnel and professional advice, with the aim of preventing and curing blindness, educating and rehabilitating blind and physically disabled people, treating the sick and helping the poor. CBM supports approximately 1000 projects in nearly 100 countries in Africa, Asia and Latin America. Ophthalmologists, orthopaedic surgeons and physiotherapists are needed, and two or four-year extendible contracts are available. Contact the Overseas Personnel department at the above address for more details.

### CORD (Christian Outreach - Relief and Development)

1 New Street, Leamington Spa, CV31 1HP, UK (tel 01926-315301; fax 01926-885786; e-mail CORD_UK@compuserve.com).

CORD is a relief and development agency committed to helping refugees, children and marginalised people both during crises and in the aftermath of emergencies. Wherever possible it works alongside other organisations (such as government health departments and the United Nations), and its role is largely supervisory, encouraging local initiatives and community involvement.

Most of CORD's expatriate staff are recruited for work in Cambodia, Mozambique, Albania, Rwanda and Tanzania. In Tanzania the work is currently concerned with providing health services for refugee camps in the north-west of the country; staff include a doctor, a nurse and a health visitor. In Cambodia the health work is more longer-term and developmental, and involves an experienced health co-ordinator and a midwife training health workers and researching how health services in a particular province may be improved. In Mozambique the work is very similar.

All team members are committed Christians. Most contracts are for a minimum of 1 year. All expenses are paid, and there is a local allowance. A sliding scale of home allowance is paid for those with overseas experience. Previous overseas experience is useful but not always essential. For more information contact the Personnel Officer at the above address.

### Edinburgh Medical Missionary Society

7 Washington Lane, Edinburgh EH11 2HA, UK (tel 0131-313 3828; fax 0131-313 4662).

This Christian society is interdenominational and is engaged in a range of overseas missionary projects. One of these is the Nazareth Hospital in Israel, which the Society owns, and which although integrated into the Israeli Ministry of Health system as a district general hospital still thrives as a Christian missionary centre.

The hospital provides a wide range of services, and has departments for general medicine, surgery, renal dialysis, maternity services, palliative care, X-ray services, physiotherapy, pharmacy and neo-natal intensive care. Provision of nursing training is also an important activity. The hospital has 136 beds, and approximately

98% of the staff are from the local community, with the remaining 2% coming from overseas.

There are limited opportunities for the employment of overseas staff in the hospital. Applications should be sent to the Chief Executive Officer, Nazareth Hospital Emaus, P.O. Box 11, 16100 Nazareth, Israel.

## HCJB World Radio

*US Office:* PO Box 39800, Colorado Springs, CO 80949-9800, USA.

*UK Office:* 131 Grattan Road, Bradford BD1 2HS, UK (tel 01274-721810; fax 01274-741302; e-mail bcooke@hcjb.org.uk Website hcjb.org).

This organisation is involved in a range of evangelical activities, including radio broadcasting (HCJB stands for 'heralding Christ Jesus' blessings). Its health care projects include two general hospitals in Ecuador, one in Quito and one in Shell. The 72-bed Quito hospital has an international staff and offers preventive and curative medicine, teaching and training in medicine and other health disciplines to Latin Americans, and mobile clinics serving the surrounding rural areas. The mission also has 7 clinics around the city giving good quality basic medical and dental care. It also carries out research into Ecuador's health needs. The hospital in Shell has 35 beds and provides a 24-hour emergency service, out-patient clinics, in-patient medical and surgical care, and teaching seminars for the local medical community.

Short-term placements are available lasting up to 3 months, and full-time missionary service for 3 years and over. Medical missionaries are required to speak fluent Spanish. Missionaries raise their own financial support through supporting churches and friends, and are 'born again' Christians. Contact one of the above addresses for current information on the organisation's health professional requirements.

## International Nepal Fellowship (INF)

*UK Office:* 69 Wentworth Road, Birmingham B17 9SS, UK (tel 0121-427 8833; fax 0121-428 3110; e-mail ukoffice@inf.org.uk).

*Mission Headquarters:* INF, PO Box 5, Pokhara, Nepal (tel 61-20111; fax 61-20430)

INF is a Christian organisation involved in a range of health initiatives in Nepal. These projects include hospital-based curative work, leprosy and TB control programmes, rural community health programmes, community-based rehabilitation, and drugs and AIDS-related programmes. Short and long-term positions are available.

Opportunities are available for various professions, depending on the particular project. INF's TB Project requires nurses, doctors, administrators, managers and training officers, all to specialise in TB, or to work in TB combined with leprosy control work. INF members need to be sufficiently experienced and qualified to supervise Nepalis, and previous training in public health is desirable, although in-service training can be provided. INF's involvement with the Western Regional Hospital in Pokhara requires experienced and specialised doctors, surgeons and nursing sisters, and also pharmacists, physiotherapists and sister tutors.

INF requires candidates to have an active Christian faith with church involvement in the UK. Workers contribute to INF's work on a voluntary basis and are responsible for raising their own financial support.

## The Jerusalem Princess Basma Centre for Disabled Children

P.O. Box 19764, Jerusalem 91197, Israel, (tel +972-2-626 4536; fax 02-627 4449). This charitable NGO looks after disabled children up to 15 years old, providing recreational therapy and hydrotherapy. They have places for volunteers who wish to undertake a period of practical training as part of their course, but also require staff skilled in occupational therapy and physiotherapy.

Applicants should forward enquires with references and be prepares to stay at least 3 months, places are available all year round. Accomodation can be arranged in shared rooms in the centre or nearby for male staff (who are not allowed to sleep in the centre for cultural reasons). Pocket money of $50 per month is payable to qualified volunteer staff.

**Latin Link UK**
175 Tower Bridge Road, London SE1 2AB, UK (tel 020-7939 9000; fax 020-7939 9015; e-mail ukoffice@latinlink.org Website www.latinlink.org).
Latin Link works with churches in Latin America in a wide range of activities; these include preventative medicine and community development. Latin Link currently places staff in Ecuador, Peru, Bolivia, Brazil, Argentina, Costa Rica and Nicaragua, although these are not necessarily medical staff. The main focus is to match individuals with long-term projects. Latin Link currently has three doctors working in Peru and nurses working in Peru and Ecuador. They work individually, mainly in very poor rural and urban areas. At the time of writing medical staff are needed for an orpahange in Ecuador, where the orphan's parents have died of AIDS. Approximately 3 medical students are also sent on electives each year and in the future the same may be available for nurses, paramedics and dentists.

Opportunities exist for committed Christians to contribute to this work. Suitably qualified applicants can undertake a period of service lasting for a minimum of 3 years. Shorter periods of service (1-2 years) are also available. All applicants are self-funded. A reasonable knowledge of Spanish (Portuguese for Brazil) is required but can be learned 'in situ'.

**The Leprosy Mission**
*UK Office:* Goldhay Way, Orton Goldhay, Peterborough PE2 5GZ, UK (tel 01733-370505; fax 01733-370960; e-mail post@tlmew.org.uk).
*International Office:* 80 Windmill Road, Brentford, Middlesex TW8 0QH, UK (tel 020-8569 7292; fax 020-8569 7808; e-mail friends@tlmint.org Website www.leprosymission.org)
The Leprosy Mission is an international, interdenominational Christian organisation working with leprosy patients in over 30 countries, mainly in Africa, and southern and south-east Asia. The Mission works with patients both directly, through its own hospitals and clinics, and in co-operation with many churches, governments and voluntary groups. The Mission aims to meet the physical, spiritual, social and psychological needs of people affected by leprosy, and to work towards the eradication of the disease.

The Mission's overseas staff include occupational therapists, doctors (both physicians and surgeons), physiotherapists and some administrators and other professionals. The main role of all overseas personnel is to train local staff. Candidates should have at least 2 years' post-qualification experience, be committed and practising Christians of any Protestant or Reformed denomination, be of sound physical and mental health, have an aptitude for languages, and be willing to adapt to tropical living conditions.

For long-term salaried posts, a minimum period of service of 4 years is usually required. It is preferable if candidates have had some training at Bible college. All candidates undergo specialist training in the treatment and management of leprosy, and language training is usually arranged. Short-term consultancy posts generally require more professional experience, have other terms and conditions, and are usually on a shared-funding basis.

The Leprosy Mission has 25 national offices around the world, for more information contact Mrs Chris Crawford in the UK office, or Miss Vanessa Lillington-Price at the international office.

**Medical Missionary Association/Christian Medical Fellowship**
157 Waterloo Road, London SE1 8XN, UK (tel 020-7928 4694; fax 020-7620 2453; e-mail 106173.333@compuserve.com Website www.healthserve.org).
The Medical Missionary Association (MMA) is a Protestant, interdenominational organisation that seeks to support and promote Christian 'healthcare-with-mission' in the developing world. It provides advice and information to Christian health professionals concerning opportunities for both short and long-term work, and produces magazines and newsletters which are aimed at anyone interested in Christian health care work in developing countries. The magazines include an extensive summary of vacancies overseas.

The Christian Medical Fellowship has 4500 doctors in its membership and supports the work of members who are overseas in Christian hospitals and medical posts. The Fellowship works in partnership with the MMA. Neither organisation recruits staff or volunteers, but both seek to help health professionals, including elective students, who wish to work overseas, particularly in positions that are mission or church-related. Contact the above address for further information and details of their publications.

**Mennonite Central Committee**
21 South 12th Street, PO Box 500, Akron, Pennsylvania 17501-0500, USA (tel 717-859-1151; fax 717-859-2171; e-mail mailbox@mcc.org Website www.mcc.org).
The Mennonite Central Committee (MCC) is the relief, service and development agency of the Mennonite and Brethren in Christ churches of North America. Health care forms an important part of its activities, with health personnel working in clinical and community health settings in approximately 20 countries around the world, including Africa, Central and South America, Asia, and the USA and Canada. At the time of writing nurses were needed for various positions in North America, in public health clinics and inner-city hospitals; these positions require at least a degree in nursing, health education and/or nutrition, and previous work experience is sometimes needed. Overseas staff needed include community development and health workers.

MCC workers need to be active Christians and committed to nonviolent peacemaking. All overseas and most North American assignments are volunteer positions. MCC provides living support and pays each worker a monthly stipend of US$50. Workers serve two-year terms in North America and three-year terms in overseas assignments.

**Mid-Africa Ministry**
157 Waterloo Road, London SE1 8UU, UK (tel 020-7261 1370; fax 020-7401 2910; e-mail mid_africa_ministry@compuserve.com Website www.go.to/mam).
Mid-Africa Ministry is a small Anglican mission working in Rwanda, Burundi, Uganda and D.R. Congo. The Ministry sends skilled medical personel to work under the authority of African bishops and in partnership with African and expatriate colleagues. The work is in rural district hospitals, clinics and health centres seeking to respond to the need for quality health care in these countries. All personnel must be committed Christians.

Health workers are required in a range of disciplines. Doctors with GP training, casualty and general surgery experience are needed, as are nurses with general nursing training and midwifery skills; a diploma in tropical medicine and nursing is required for some countries, but is not essential for short-term work. Specialist disciplines in which professionals are required include physio and occupational therapy, ophthalmology and nursing tuition.

The Ministry pays allowances, travel costs, and health and school expenses for those going overseas for periods of 3 years or more. Selection involves a number of interviews, medicals and references, with training in Bible college, a tropical medicine course and language training. Short-term workers are also sent overseas, and they follow a shorter recruitment procedure.

**Nepal Leprosy Trust**
15 Duncan Road, Richmond, Surrey TW9 2JD, UK (tel 020-8332 9023; fax 020-8948 2703; e-mail nlt@dial.pipex.com).
Nepal Leprosy Trust exists to empower both people affected by leprosy and those other marginalised group to particpate with equality and dignity in their own communities. NLT has been serving the people of Nepal since 1972 and now manages a number of leprosy services, rehabilitation, income generation and social welfare projects. Lalgadh Leprosy Services Centre, in south east Nepal, provides examination and diagnostic services, in-patient and out-patient services, training and education and a self-care training unit. A pioneering community-based empowwerment and rehabilitation project will commence in 2000.

Enquiries concerning permanent and short-term vacancies should be addressed to the General Administrator at the above address.

**SAO Cambodia (formerly known as Southeast Asian Outreach)**
Bawtry Hall, Bawtry, Doncaster, DN10 6JH, UK (tel 01302-714004; Website www.sao-cambodia.org).
SAO Cambodia is a Christian mission working solely in Cambodia. It is involved in four sustainable development projects in the country, one of which includes healthcare. Both short and long-term opportunities are available for suitably qualified professionals, who possess full church endorsement.

**TearFund**
100 Church Road, Teddington, Middlesex TW11 8QE, UK (tel: 0845-355 8355; fax: 020-8943 3594; e-mail enquiry@tearfund.org Website: www.tearfund.org).
Tearfund is a evangelical Christian relief and development charity that works in partnership with churches and Christian groups in over 90 countries. The emphasis of Tearfund's work is on promoting community-based health development.

Skilled personnel are seconded to work for varying lengths of contract as community health advisors, facilitators, public health specialists, and community-based rehabilitation co-ordinators. For these salaried posts applicants require a relevant qualification plus previous overseas experience. All staff are involved in training national colleagues.

Applicants for placements need to be committed Christians For positions in relief or development workers are employed by Tearfund, and normally seconded to Tearfund's partner organisation in the host country. Salary, orientation, travel and agreed assignment costs are paid by Tearfund.

**Volunteer Missionary Movement**
The University Chaplaincy Building, Mount Pleasant, Liverpool, L3 5TQ, UK (tel 0151-709 7676; e-mail Alice@vmmuk.freeserve.co.uk).

The Voluntary Missionary Movement (VMM) recruits, prepares and sends mature committed people, with professional/technical skills, to work in development projects in Africa and Central America. Volunteers usually serve for two years.

**WEC International**
Bulstrode, Oxford Road, Gerrards Cross, Bucks, SL9 8SZ, UK (tel 01753-884631; fax 01753-882470; e-mail em.bulstrode@talk21.com Website www.wec-int.org or www.cin.co.uk/wec).
WEC International (Worldwide Evangelisation for Christ) is an evangelical, interdenominational faith mission working in over 60 countries. It has a strong commitment to reaching the remaining 'unevangelised' peoples of the world, and an increasing emphasis in 'creative access nations' where mission endeavour has previously been minimal. Medical work is only secondary to WEC International's main objective of caring for the spiritual needs of the people with whom it is working

There are medical openings currently available in the Middle East, Gambia, Guinea Bissau, Ghana, Chad, Congo and Central Asia. These are for doctors, nurses, midwives, anaesthetists, physiotherapists and child pyschologists (for children in crisis ministries). At the time of writing there is an urgent need for female midwives and gynaecologists for a maternity centre.

The volunteer recruitment procedure involves application forms, references and a residential induction, the duration of which depends on the length of time you wish to volunteer for. Successful applicants will become part of a team offereing pastoral care and support. Financial support is the responsibility of the individual volunteer.

Contact the UK headquarters at the above address for further details.

# Governmental and Intergovernmental Organisations

## INTRODUCTION
A great number of overseas health and related development programmes, especially in developing countries and countries affected by war and disaster, are funded at the governmental and intergovernmental levels. This funding often reaches those working on the ground through the voluntary and aid organisations described in detail in the previous section, but governmental agencies also often have a visible role. The following pages describe some organisations intimately involved in overseas health programmes.

## LIST OF ORGANISATIONS

**Department for International Development**
Abercrombie House, Eaglesham Road, East Kilbride, Glasgow G75 8EA, UK (tel 01355-844000; fax 01355-844099).
The Department for International Development (DFID) is the Government Department responsible for administering the United Kingdom's international development programme. DFID works to develop strategies which aim to ensure that the UK is able to make an effective contribution to improving health in

developing countries such as in Africa, Asia, Latin America and the Caribbean. Initially, the aim is to educate poorer countries in eliminating poverty and decreasing the risk of ill health.

Assistance for the Health and Population sector in developing countries is moving away from support for General Practitioner, Registrar and Nursing assignments and is now moving towards 4 key areas: Health Sector Planning, Management and Financing; Population Programmes, including Family Planning; Sexually transmitted diseases, including HIV and AIDS and Communicable Disease Control.

Examples of the specialists employed in the Health and Population sector are Economists, Planners and Field and Hospital Managers.

Long and Short Term Consultants are required from time to time. Further information on consultant opportunities, can be obtained via e-mail (sh-thompson@dfid.gov.uk), by telephone (01355-844000 ext. 3390) or by writing to CBISS, Room AH369 at the above address.

Technical Co-operation Officers are also required, recruitment is dealt with by Recruitment Personnel and Management Branch (RPMB). Vacancies are generally advertised and require candidates to have a good degree and very often a second degree. It is useful for candidates to have substantial post-graduate experience gained in a developing country and in the UK and also to have experience in training, management and policy development.

Vacancies are generally long-term, (ie 2 or 3 years) but occasionally they can be short-term (ie up to 4 months). A Guide to overseas Terms and Conditions of employment is available on request. This and further information can be obtained via e-mail (recruitment-enqs@dfid.gov.uk), by telephone (01355-844000 ext. 3193/3288) or by writing to General Enquiries Section, AH303 at the above address.

The nationality criteria is normally that candidates should be either citizens of the European Economic Area or British Commonwealth citizens who have a right of abode and the right to work in the UK.

Information can also be obtained on the internet www.dfid.gov.uk.

**World Health Organisation**
Avenue Appia 20, 1211 Geneva 27, Switzerland (tel 22-791 2111; fax 22-791 0746).

The World Health Organisation (WHO) is an agency of the United Nations. It has a staff of 4600, including 1500 internationally recruited professionals and 3100 locally recruited general staff. Approximately 1450 staff work at the WHO headquarters in Geneva; 1400 work in the regional offices in Alexandria, Brazzaville (Congo), Copenhagen, Manila, New Delhi and Washington DC; and 1750 work in some 190 country projects in field stations.

The WHO recruits professionals in various categories, including medical officers specialising in epidemiology, health education, health planning, statistics, malariology, maternal and child health (including family planning), nutrition, public health administration, and research promotion and development; public health nurses and nurse educators; pharmacists working in drug quality control; scientists working in entomology, human reproduction, microbiology, parasitology, pharmacology, tropical diseases and toxicology; and sanitary engineers working in environmental health, water supply, sanitation and waste disposal. Professionals also work in administrative support services, health information support, and programme development and management. Doctors without specialisation and experience in public health administration will not normally be recruited.

The organisation's recruitment criteria emphasise the importance of maintaining an appropriately international balance in the nationalities of its staff, the filling of vacancies by internal promotion where possible, and increasing the proportion of female professional staff.

When a vacancy occurs at headquarters or in a regional office, the post is advertised throughout all UN agencies and the details are distributed to potential recruitment sources outside the UN, including Ministries of Health, universities, professional associations and NGOs. An advertisement may also be placed in some internationally reputed newspapers and professional journals. Recruitment for field project posts is normally made from applications kept on file at headquarters or in the regional offices.

The minimum qualifications for a fixed-term professional post are normally a degree, a postgraduate specialisation and 5 years' experience relevant to the post, very often in developing countries. Depending on the location of the post, applicants will need to have excellent knowledge of either English or French; at least a working knowledge of English is needed for most assignments. Competition for the limited number of professional vacancies each year is intense. Professional staff normally work on a two-year contract, including a one-year probationary period.

Professionals whose qualifications enable them to undertake a specific task for a particular WHO programme may also be recruited on a short-term basis for periods normally ranging from a few weeks to 6 months.

Applicants interested in field positions (which are not normally advertised), in short-term employment and in general employment opportunities should write to the Personnel Officer (MPR) at the address given above. Their details will be evaluated and, if suitable, will be kept on file for consideration in the future.

# Before You Leave

As has been stated earlier, in addition to arranging your travel, immunisations and resettlement documents, you can find out a lot about your potential new home while still at the planning stage, through its embassy. Another helpful source of information will be the national tourist office concerned, the Internet or even the various books and travel guides available such as Vacation Work's 'Travellers' Survival Kit' and 'Live & Work' series of books (see page 256). Admittedly travel guides are aimed at the tourist reader who is seeking information on what to see and how to get to it, but they will still give you a flavour for the country. The 'Live & Work' series of books are aimed specifically at the migrant worker and cover all aspects of either a temporary or permanent move elsewhere. Other sources of information are the expatriate newspapers and magazines, mentioned at the beginning of this chapter, which while aimed at keeping travellers and expats in touch also provide the would-be traveller with inside information on how attractive the country is, some of these are listed earlier on page 42.

If you'd rather know something about the work and social culture of a country before planning a move, then as well as the 'Live & Work' books you might find the books in Kuperard's 'Culture Shock' series helpful. They can be obtained from good bookshops or you can contact the publisher's distributors (Bailey's Distribution Ltd: Unit 1a/1b Mountfield Industrial Estate, New Romney, Kent, TN28 8XU; tel 01797-369966.) to order them directly. The 41 titles in the series have been written by expatriates living in the countries concerned and are a helpful down-to-earth source of information on what it's really like to live there. For a more tongue in cheek look at your destination Oval Books (c/o Ravette Publishing,

P.O. Box 296, Horsham, RH13 8FH, UK; tel +44(0)1403-711443; fax 01403-711554) produce a series of *'Xenophobe's Guides'* which are irreverant studies of national foibles, but also a useful preparatory tool. There are currently 24 titles in the series covering Europe, Australasia, Asia and America.

# RED TAPE

When planning a move to a new job in another country it is always important to get in touch with the nearest embassy, high commission or consulate of the country in which you are interested in working. The staff there will be able to tell you the current situation concerning visas, work permits and immigration requirements. While we have tried to provide condensed information on these subjects in Part III the *Country Guide*, regulations may change over a very short period. Unfortunately not many embassies have staff who are able to provide specialist advice relevant to particular aspects of the employment market in their country; more probably they will give you the contact addresses for government departments specifically dealing with staffing in the health sector and the verification of qualifications from overseas professionals looking for work in the country; many of these addresses are included in Part III of this book. These contacts should be able to provide you with the latest information on the organisation of the health service, any specialisations where there are currently staff shortages, whether your qualifications will be recognised (or what kind of approval procedure exists), and perhaps also the practice of your particular profession. Bear in mind that irrespective of how well qualified you are, you will be subject to the normal immigration and man-power requirements for the country in which you want to work.

Finding out about the red tape for your profession in your chosen destination country is vitally important – often the issuing of the required paperwork by the immigration authorities will depend on you supplying documentary proof that there is work waiting for you, and your eligibility for employment may in turn depend on whether your qualifications and experience are acceptable to the appropriate registration authority. If you are attempting to find work through one of the agencies described earlier in this part of the book, then these matters will probably be taken care of for you. If you are looking for work independently, you will need to negotiate these obstacles yourself, and the appropriate country section(s) in Part III of this book will help.

Your professional organisation in your home country may also have useful information available for those of its members considering working abroad; at the very least they will be able to provide you with contact details for the equivalent organisation in your destination country. Nurses in the UK, for example, can obtain detailed information on nursing overseas from the Royal College of Nursing, and their leaflet *General Information on Working Abroad* includes detailed information on what nurses need to consider before they leave the country, including a step-by-step checklist of things to keep in mind when signing a contract.

## Medical Indemnity Insurance

It is essential that you check the status of your indemnity insurance before heading overseas. While many practitioners within the UK are covered by the NHS, which would include those coming from overseas to take up a NHS post, this cover does not include 'good samaritan' or general practice work. So its best to take out some form of cover with one of the medical defence organisations, or to check that your current organisation will cover you or has some arrangements with organisations in your destination country. Many professional associations, e.g. the Royal College of Nursing, provide indemnity cover, in fact the RCN's scheme will cover student and qualified nurse members working overseas for up to £3 million (£1 million in the USA).

**Useful Addresses:**
*Royal College of Nursing:* 20 Cavendish Square, London, W1M 0AB, UK (tel
+44-20-7647 3456; Website www.rcn.org.uk).
*The Medical Defence Union Ltd:* 3 Devonshire Place, Lonodn, W1N 2EA, UK (tel
020-7486 6181; membership services 0161-428 1234). Can offer cover for
'good samaritan' work around the world, and short-term cover in some
countries. If this is not available they can suggest suitable agencies for
indemnity cover to members who wish to work outside the UK.
*The Medical Protection Society:* 33 Cavendish Square, London, W1M 0PS, UK
(tel 020-7637 0541; e-mail info@mps.org.uk Website www.mps.org.uk). Is a
non-profit mutual association with offices around the world.
*The Medical and Dental Defence Union of Scotland:* Mackintosh House, 120
Blythswood Street, Glasgow, G2 4EA, UK (tel 0141-221 5858; e-mail
info@mddus.com Website www.mddus.com). Offers cover across the UK.

# LEARNING THE LANGUAGE

If you are considering working in any country where the national language is not
your own then you obviously need to consider how you are going to negotiate the
potential language barrier. English speakers are in the privileged position of having
their language spoken very widely internationally, but even so knowledge of the
local language can be very important even in countries where English seems to be
almost universally understood.

The question of language is particularly important for health professionals, who
need to communicate with both their patients and their colleagues clearly and
effectively. Patients, in particular, will expect to be able to communicate with you
in their own language, often in testing conditions, and they may find it hard to
place their trust in you if you appear to be struggling to understand them.
Depending on the nature of your work, you may be dealing with children, elderly
people and patients in pain or other kinds of distress, and your ability in the
language will need to be up to the task of handling such situations. If possible, you
should be able to speak and write the language well enough to be able to perform
your job as effectively as you do in your home country when you are using your
own language – for example, when writing reports, liaising with colleagues and
dealing with people on the telephone.

Another thing to bear in mind is that in other English-speaking countries the
vocabulary used may vary, and in some cases the same words may have different
meanings – a potential source of confusion or misunderstanding that you should be
aware of.

Learning the language before you go is obviously the best idea, and in some
cases may be a prerequisite to obtaining a visa/work permit and/or registration.
Where this is not possible it may be acceptable to take a course in the country
while you are working, depending on the level of proficiency you are required to
possess.

## Self-Study Courses

The advantage of self-study courses is that they allow the student to absorb
material at their convenience and own learning pace, thus you can fit in some study
while working rather than having to arrange your life around a course timetable.
The disadvantages are, that a lot of self-motivation is required and it is not possible
to practice spontaneous conversation and your pronunciation may suffer. However,

these methods are popular, relatively cheap and would not still be available if they were ineffective. Almost all self study courses are available from bookshops and most include tapes to help you train your ear for the sound of the language.

In Britain the BBC offers learning language materials for adults in fifteen languages and these range from simple survival guides to comprehensive courses. This range includes phrase-books, tapes, grammar guides and travel packs which are available in all good bookshops or direct from the BBC, with prices ranging from £2.99 to £12.99. These packs often tie in with the language courses broadcast by the BBC in the 'Learning Zone' on BBC Two, between 2am and 7am on weekdays and 2am-5am on weekends. Further details about the BBC's language courses can be obtained from the BBC (BBC Information, P.O. Box 1116, Belfast, BT2 7AJ; tel 0870-0100222; e-mail edinfo@bbc.co.uk; Website www.bbc.co.uk/education).

You can also study languages on the Internet, one example is Peter Schröder's German language sites which have sections devoted to all aspects of the language and includes sound files to illustrate pronunciation: *http://www.geocities.com/ CollegePark/Hall/1238/intro.html* is the online edition while *http:// members.icanect.net/peters1/intro.htm* gives details of the cd-rom edition for study at home off-line.

The alternative to self-study is the full or part-time taught course. The former, while expensive, can give you a good grip on the language very quickly, and in some cases while on holiday in the country. This is useful as you can get some groundwork out of the way while you learn the language, and with the benefit of first hand experience decide if the place really is what you're looking for. Part-time courses in languages can usually be fitted in to busy work and social lives, and are often organised at local education centres. These can vary between courses for complete beginners through to degree level fluency, and can be held in libraries, schools, and colleges.

### Self-study
*BBC Books:* Book Service By Post Ltd, PO Box 29, Douglas, Isle of Man, IM99 1BQ; tel 01624-675137; fax 01624-670923. Books and tapes can be ordered direct. Overseas readers can order through the BBC Shop in Newcastle, (tel 0191-222 0381; fax 0191-261 9902), however the shop does not offer an enquiry service.

*Linguaphone:* Carlton Plaza, 111 Upper Richmond Road, London SW15 2TJ; tel 020-8333 4898; fax 020-8333 4897. 610 Fifth Avenue, New York, NY 10020, USA; tel 212-581 8810. Website www.linguaphone.co.uk Provide a range of self-study courses in over 30 languages to suit different language learning needs. Travel Packs are available from WH Smith, AA Travel Shops and all good bookshops and they cover simple holiday vocabulary. Full Language Courses aim to teach between 1,500-3,000 words of vocabulary. The Full Courses are available as books, cassettes, CDs and videos, and include a special Business Course.

### Language Courses
*Berlitz (U.K.) Limited:* 321 Oxford Street, London W1A 3BZ; tel 020-7408 2474; fax 020-7493 4429. Princeton Berlitz International Inc., 400 Alexandra Park, Princeton, NJ 08540-6306, USA; tel 609-514 3400; fax 609-514 3405; Website www.berlitz.com. Another international organisation, Berlitz offers language courses which can then be continued at any of its 330 centres around the world. The Berlitz method involves tailoring the course to the individual's requirements as far as the level and course intensity is required. The cost varies

depending on these factors. Further details may be obtained from the above address.

*CESA Languages Abroad:* Western House, Malpas, Truro, Cornwall, TR1 1SQ; tel 01872-225300; fax 01872-225400; e-mail languages@cesa.freeserve.co.uk Website www.cesalanguages.com. Arrange courses in European languages at sites in the countries concerned, and through partnerships they can arrange Chinese or Japanese tuition.

*EF International Language Schools:* Kensington Cloisters, 5 Kensington Church Street, London, W8 4LD; tel 020-7878 3550; fax 020-7795 6625; e-mail languages.gb@ef.com Website www.ef.com. EF Center Boston, 1 Education Street, Cambridge, MA 02141, USA; tel 617-619 1000. EF Education Pty Ltd, Suite 2, Level 3, 44 Miller Street, Sydney, NSW 2060, Australia; tel 02-995-74699. Probably the most well known of the European language schools, EF is actually the world's largest private educational organisation. Their instructors provide intensive language tuition at a variety of levels for students, adult learners and businesses.

*Euro-academy Limited:* 77a George Street, Croydon, CR0 1LD; tel 020-8686 2363; fax 020-8681 8850; e-mail euroacademy@btinternet.com. Crash, Intensive and Business courses are available all year and last from two to four weeks. Requests for their brochures 'Learn the Language on Location' and 'Business Class' can be obtained freepost in the UK from the above address if the post code CR9 9ER is used.

*Eurolingua Institute:* Eurolingua House, 61 Bollin Drive, Altrincham, WA14 5QW; tel/fax 0161-972 0225; Website www.eurolingua.com Provides unique opportunities for people of all ages to learn languages in the country where they are spoken. Combined language learning, study, activity and holiday programmes are offered including one-to-one homestay programmes.

## ADAPTING TO LOCAL CULTURE

How difficult you find it to adapt to the local conditions in a foreign country will be influenced by your particular circumstances – for example, if you are placed in one of the modern Western-style hospitals in Saudi Arabia with accommodation and all mod cons readily available, you are likely to feel more secure than if you are thrust into a disaster situation in a remote region of Africa. However although the degree of 'culture shock' experienced by health professionals using recruitment agencies may be less than for staff and volunteers sent out by relief and development organisations, it is important for all health professionals to realise that there will inevitably be differences in working practice and cultural changes to adjust to.

It is particularly important to be aware of cultural differences, as a lack of sensitivity to the norms of a different society can easily cause great offence, or even break the law. Women, for example, are not allowed to drive in Saudi Arabia, a law that would be unthinkable in the West, and there are also specific dress codes that particularly affect women. As a general rule professionals should bear in mind that it is up to them to adapt to the culture of their host country, and not the other way round.

If possible get in touch with fellow professionals who have spent some time working in the same country. They will be able to provide first-hand advice on what to expect. If you are finding a position through an agency, it will be able to put you in touch with people who have been through an experience similar to the one you are about to embark upon. Furthermore, many professional organisations are able to offer similar services to their members.

Even workers moving between such similar cultures as Britain and the USA, will find that they will suffer some form of culture shock, or personal dislocation in the first few weeks there. While the language of another country will initially prove a barrier to all but the fluent (and even they may suffer some problems at the hands of dialects), this can be overcome relatively easily.

Different lifestyles and cultural attitudes may however, prove a problem for longer. In Germany it may take some time before the expatriate feels that they have been accepted by their co-workers, and even then they will still be referred to by their title not their first or even nickname. In Australia, the Briton may find themselves the butt of office jokes for a few weeks while they settle in to their new environment, where life can be very relaxed if you work hard, but the urban wildlife can be dangerous to the unwary. So it is wise to make sure that you are fully prepared and aware of the different cultural niceties, such as cakes for co-workers on your birthday, before you go.

With these problems in mind several companies have been set up by entrepreneurs aware of the shock that some places can give the unwary. These are often run by expats and the courses they provide are based on first hand experience, and are very likely to be given by recently returned expats who can give you current information.

One example of such a company is the Centre for International Briefing, which can provide customised residential briefings for any country, these are suitable for businessmen or their families. The programmes provide in-depth information about the country, including politics, economics and social issues. Practical advice on the business and working environments are given by recently returned businessmen or expatriates, allowing the trainee to prepare their communication and negotiation skills for the new workplace. An alternative is to dig out information about recruitment agencies, as some of them, such as Michael Page, arrange seminars on a regular basis on the topic of working in another country.

**Useful Addresses**
*The Centre for International Briefing:* Farnham Castle, Farnham, Surrey, GU9 0AG, UK (tel 01252-720416; fax 01252-719277; e-mail marketing@ cibfarnham.com ;Website www.cibfarnham.com).
*Corona Worldwide (The Women's Corona Society):* The Commonwealth Institute, Kensington High Street, London W8 6NQ, UK (tel 020-7610 4407; fax 020-7602 7374; Website www.commerce.co.uk/coronaww). A voluntary organisation with branches in the UK and overseas providing, among other services, postal or personal briefings for women and men about to live or work abroad. Membership of the society is free to any woman who has attended a meeting; men can join as associate members.
*Michael Page International:* Savannah House, 11 Charles Street, London, SW1Y 4QZ; tel 020-7831 2000; 020-7839 8086; Website www.michaelpage.com

# EXPATRIATE CLUBS

A good source of information, both for your planning and to avoid cultural pitfalls while you are there, are the cultural exchange or expatriate clubs and societies. In addition to help they can provide before you go and once 'in country', they can also provide you with a touch of home should you feel homesick. While some expatriates are employed on their return by companies specialising in briefing people on foreign cultures, as mentioned earlier, a cheaper option closer to home is to contact local groups of exchange clubs. This can be done usually through the telephone directory, local library society information files or by contacting the information department of the relevant embassy. Once overseas your own embassy and consulate network should be able to give you contact details for the expat groups. Vacation Work's 'Live & Work' books previously mentioned list expatriate social clubs, so you can make contact in advance and benefit from their 'inside' knowledge. Or you can just carry on surfing your information on-line, as several expatriate organisations now have websites.

**Useful Expat Websites:**

http://www.aca.ch

The American Citizens Abroad website, organised by this expat organisation to keep US expats informed on issues back home, they also carry some influence on Capitol Hill on behalf of expats. This site also has a range of useful information and links to other sites for non-US citizens.

*http://www.expatexchange.com*

This site is the result of a link up between two other US expat sites, it deals mainly with self-help and expat experiences.

*http:expatnetwork.co.uk*

*http://www.cs.cmu.edu/dellaert/belgians/long.html*

Run by an expatriate Belgian based in America.

## FINANCIAL CONSIDERATIONS

Before going abroad to work it is important to spend time carefully planning your financial arrangements, as there will inevitably be costs involved before you actually start work. These costs will include flights, the costs of registering with the relevant authority for your profession, and medical insurance. You should also allow yourself sufficient funds on which to live until you receive your first wages.

Opening a bank account in your destination country before you go makes sense if you can arrange it, as then it will be ready and waiting to receive your salary. Depending on the country, you may find it useful to bring with you a letter from your bank manager at home, confirming that you are a good customer.

Anyone working overseas should be fully aware of their tax liabilities in the host country. Look into this before you start earning, as it is not unknown for employers to inadvertently tax their overseas professionals at too low a rate, thereby rendering them liable for substantial tax bills at some point in the future (perhaps even once they have left the country). Enquire at the main tax office in your destination country for information.

## OTHER ARRANGEMENTS

Before leaving your home country you will need to explore how your time overseas will affect whatever social security schemes you are part of. For example, if you work in the National Health Service in the UK you should contact the NHS Pensions Agency or the Scottish Office Pensions Agency for information on the options available – such as transferring your membership of the NHS Pensions Scheme to your new employment overseas, or maintaining your membership of the Scheme while you are abroad. British health professionals should also contact the Contributions Agency to discuss arrangements with their National Insurance contributions while they are overseas; the Agency also produces a helpful leaflet called *Social Security Abroad* (N138). Special arrangements exist for EU countries and countries that have social security agreements with the UK. Information on taxation is available from the Inland Revenue Claims Branch (International) or from your tax office; ask for leaflet IR58, *Going to Work Abroad?*

You will need to make sure that you have indemnity insurance – this will ensure that you are financially protected if legal action is taken against you concerning your professional practice. Indemnity insurance is known as malpractice insurance in the USA. Contact your professional association for advice in this area. In the UK, for example, the Royal College of Nursing provides its members with worldwide indemnity insurance, although the level of cover is significantly less for the USA and Canada and members taking up work in these countries are advised to take out a separate malpractice insurance policy locally.

*Contributions Agency:* Longbenton, Newcastle-upon-Tyne NE98 1YX, UK (tel 0191-225 7975; fax 0191-225 4215).

*Inland Revenue Claims Branch (International):* St John's House, Merton Road, Bootle L69 9BB, UK (tel 0151-472 6206; fax 0151-472 6003).

*NHS Pensions Agency:* Hesketh House, 200-220 Broadway, Fleetwood, Lancashire FY7 8LG, UK (tel 01253-774774; fax 01253-774597).

*Scottish Office Pensions Agency:* St Margarets House, 151 London Road, Edinburgh EH8 7TG, UK (tel 0131-244 3283; fax 0131-244 3334).

## KEEPING IN TOUCH

Although you may be having the time of your life in your new job, there will be times when you miss your old home, or you may just wish to keep up to date with life at home. In which case you can subscribe to newspapers or magazines aimed at expatriates 'in-country', some of these have been mentioned earlier (on page 42), or you can arrange an overseas subscription to many home papers, or surf their websites, that of *The Times* is updated on a daily basis to carry the stories printed that day in London.

Those professionals working overseas on a temporary basis may also wish to keep up to date with professional matters too, so its worth arranging subscriptions to your professional journals, in addition to those for 'local' journals in your new home.

### Useful Addresses:

**Professional Journals:**
*BMA News Review:* BMA House, Tavistock Square, London, WC1H 9JP, UK (tel 0207-383 6122; fax 020-7383 6566).

*British Journal of General Practice:* 14 Prince's Gate, Hyde Park, London, SW7 1PU, UK (tel 020-7581 3232; fax 020-7 584 6716; Website www.rcgp.org.uk).

*British Medical Journal:* BMA House, Tavistock Square, London, WC1H 9JR, UK (tel 020-7383 6270; fax 020-7383 6402; e-mail subscriptions@bmj.com Website www.bmj.com).

*Community Care:* Quadrant House, The Quadrant, Sutton, SM2 5AS, UK (tel 020-8652 4861).

*Dental Update:* Unit 2, Riverview Business Park, Walnut Tree Close, Guildford, GU1 4UX, UK (tel 01483-304944; Website www.gwarman.co.uk/dupdate/).

*Deutches Arzteblatt:* Postfach 400243, Köln, Germany (tel +49-(0)2234-701 1120; fax 02234-701 1142; e-mail aerzteblatt@aerzteblatt.de).

*Disability Now:* 6 Market Road, London, N7 9PW, UK (tel 020-7619 7323; Website www.disabilitynow.org.uk).

*Hospital Doctor:* Reed Healthcare Publishing, Quadrant House, The Quadrant, Sutton, SM2 5AS, UK (tel 020-8652 8745).

*Hong Kong Medical Journal:* Pearson Professional (Hong Kong) Ltd, Suite 108, Asian House, 1 Hennessy Road, Wan Chai, Hong Kong (tel +852-2863 2655; Website www.hkmj.org.hk).

*Irish Journal of Medical Science:* Royal Academy of Medicine, 6 Kildare Street, Dublin 2, Ireland (tel +353-(0)1676 7650; Website www.iol.ie/rami/).

*Irish Medical Journal:* IMO House, 10 Fitzwilliam Place, Dublin 2, Ireland (tel 01-676 7273; fax 01-662 2818; Website www.imj.ie).

*Irish Medical Times:* 15 Harcourt Street, Dublin 2, Ireland (tel 01-475 7461; fax 01-475 7467; e-mail medtimes@iol.ie Website www.imt.ie).

*Journal of Alternative and Complementary Medicine:* 9 Rickett Street, London, SW6 1RU, UK (tel 020-7385 0012; fax 020-7385 4566).

*Journal of the American Medical Association:* American Medical Association, PO Box 10945, Chicago, IL 60610, USA (tel freephone in USA 800-AMA-2350; +1-312-670 7827; Website www.ama-assn.org).

*Lancet:* 84 Theobalds Road, London, WC1X 8RR, UK (tel 020-7611 4100; Website www.thelancet.com) and 655 Avenue of the Americas, New York, NY 10010, USA (tel +1-212-633 3800; fax 212-633 3850; subscriptions 800-462 6198).

*The Medical Journal of Australia:* Private Bag 901, North Sydney, NSW 2059, Australia (tel +61-2-9954 8666; fax 02-9954 8699; e-mail mja@ampco.com.au Website www.mja.com.au).

*Nature:* Macmillan Magazines Ltd, Porter's South, 4-6 Crinan Street, London, N1 9XW, UK (tel +44020-7843 4985; fax 020-7843 4998; Website www.nature.com).

*Nature America:* P.O. Box 5055, Brentwood, TN 37024-5055, USA, (tel (USA only) 800-524 0384 or +1-615-377 3322; Website www.nature.com).

*Nature:* (Australasia) Macmillan Magazines, Locked Bag 1400, South Yarra, VIC 3141, Australia (tel +61-3-9825 1188; e-mail aabbott@macmillan.com.au Website www.nature.com)

*New England Journal of Medicine:* 860 Winter Street, Waltham, MA 02451-1413, USA (tel +1-718-893 3800; fax 718-893 0413; Website www.nejm.org). Available in 10 national editions.

*Nursing Standard:* Nursing Standard House, 17-19 Peterborough Road, Harrow, HA1 2AX, UK (tel 0208-423 1066; e-mail nursing.standard@rcn.org.uk Website www.nursing-standard.co.uk).

*Nursing Times:* EMAP Healthcare, Greater London House, Hampstead Road, London, NW1 7EJ, UK (subscriptions tel 0208-956 3522; e-mail nt@healthcare.emap.co.uk).

*Occupational Health:* Quadrant House, The Quadrant, Sutton, SM2 5AS, UK (tel 020-8652 4669; fax 020-8652 8805).

*The Pharmaceutical Journal:* 1 Lambeth High Street, London, SE1 7JN, UK (tel 020-7735 9141; fax 020-7582 7327).

*Postgraduate Doctor (Africa, Caribbean, Middle East):* PMH Publications, PO Box 100, Chichester, PO18 8HD, UK (tel 01243-576444; Website www.pmh.uk.com). A series of titles published six times a year with each title containing articles aimed at the specific region.

*Practising Midwife:* 174a Ashley Road, Hale, Cheshire, WA15 9SF, UK (tel 0161-929 0190; fax 0161-929 1818).

*Professional Nurse:* EMAP Healthcare, Greater London House, Hampstead Road, London, NW1 7EJ, UK (tel 020-7874 0384; e-mail pn@healthcare.emap.co.uk).

*Southern Medical Journal:* Southern Medical Association, 35 Lakeshore drive, Birmingham, AL 35209, USA (tel +1-205-945 1840; fax 205-945 4992; Website www.sma.org).

*Therapy Weekly:* EMAP Healthcare, Greater London House, Hampstead Road, London, NW1 7EJ, UK (tel 020-7874 0360; fax 020-7874 0368).

**The Internet:**
In addition to the websites and online editions of the journals mentioned on page 41 and above, such as the *Medical Journal of Australia*'s *eMJA*, *The Lancet Interactive*, or the *Irish Medical Times*, there are also several professional journals availble only in an electronic form. Some of these are listed below:

*http://www.cinahl.com*
The homepage of Cinahl Information Systems which has comprehensive database of journals across the world.
*http://www.hsj.co.uk*
The *Health Service Journal*, a major professional journal with an on-line edition.
*http://www.medexplorer.com*
Medexplorer host a very useful site for contacting other professionals, keeping up to date and finding a new job.
*http://www.priory.com/med.htm*
*Medicine On-Line* an independent peer review free journal also has seperate sections for different disciplines.
*http://omj.med.jhu.edu/*
The Osler Medical Journal is an internet publication created by the medical staff of Johns Hopkins Hospital.
*http://www.usyd.edu.au/su/anaes/VAT/VAT.html*
*The Virtual Anaesthetic Textbook* an online resource for anaesthetists.
*http://www.gretmar.com/webdoctor*
WebDoctor is an internet resource page for physicians that has links to various on-line journals, where the entire text of articles are available.
*http://webmedlit.silverplatter.com/*
WebMedLit provides a daily updated access point to the best on-line medical journals.

**Newspapers and Magazines**
*The Times:* 1 Pennington Street, London, E1 9XN, UK (tel 020-7782 5000; Website www.the-times.co.uk).
*London Review of Books:* 28-30 Little Russel Street, London, WC1A 2HN, UK (subscriptions tel 020-7209 1141; e-mail subs@lrb.co.uk; Website http://www.lrb.co.uk). For the literary minded this fortnightly magazine is full of essays, book reviews, letters and poems, and will keep the expat up to date on the latest publications in the UK.

# INTERNATIONAL ORGANISATIONS

In addition to the various professional bodies operating at national or regional levels, there are many international organisations. These are often committed to the same purposes as national bodies (to provide a professional standard of training and work) but many also aim to enhance the working conditions of health professionals, or to lobby governmental bodies for improvements in healthcare, training and provision. Some have been recognised by the United Nations, while others are used as consultative bodies in order to devlop new health systems. Their global nature also makes them amply suited to providing professional information on possible destinations. Membership will often enhance professional standing, but also allows professionals far from their original professional association a chance to keep up to date with new trends in theory and practice.

**Useful Addresses:**

*Commonwealth Medical Association:* BMA House, Tavistock Square, London, WC1H 9JP, UK (tel +44-20-7-383 6095; fax 020-7383 6195; e-mail com-med-assn@compuserve.com Website www.cma.co.za).

*International Chiropractors Association:* 1110 N. Glebe Road, Suite 1000, Arlington VA 22201, USA (tel 703-528 5000; fax 703-528 5023; e-mail chiro@chiropractic.org Website www.chiropractic.org).

*International Confederation of Midwives:* Eisenhowerlaan 138, NL-2517 KN Den Haag, The Netherlands (tel +31-703-060520; fax 703-3555651; Website www.internationalmidwives.org).

*International Council of Nurses:* 3 place Jean-Marteau, CH-1201 Geneva, Switzerland (tel +41-22-908 0100; fax 022-908 0101; e-mail webmaster@icn.ch Website www.icn.ch). Has a website in English, French and Spanish.

*International Pharmaceutical Federation:* PO Box 84200, 2508 AE The Hague, The Netherlands (tel+31-70-302 1970; fax 70-302 1999; Website www.fip.nl).

*International Society of Radiographers and Radiological Technologists (ISRRT):* 170 The Donway West – Suite 404, Don Mills, Ontario M3B 1K8, Canada (tel +1-416-510-0805; fax 416-445 4268; e-mail isrrt@compuserve.com Website www.isrrt.org).

*World Confederation for Physical Therapy:* 46-48 Grosvenor Gardens, London, SW1W 0EB, UK (tel 020-7881 9234; fax 020-7881 9239; e-mail wcpt@dial.pipex.com).

*World Dental Federation (FDI):* 7 Carlisle Street, London W1V 5RG, UK (tel 020-7935 7852; fax 020-7486 0183; Website www.fdi.org.uk).

*World Medical Association:* BP 63, F-01212 Ferney-Voltaire Cedex, France (tel +33-50 40 75 75; fax 50 40 59 37; info@wma.net Website www.wma.net).

# COMING HOME

Even while you are fully occupied with your work overseas, you will need to keep in mind that at some point you will be returning home. It is therefore important that you plan ahead and so avoid returning without a position to go to. How you keep abreast of opportunities back home is up to you, but subscribing to professional journals is always useful, especially those best known for job vacancies and their coverage of employment issues. Subscribing to a journal will also allow you to keep abreast of developments in your field, which will be important for when you return to look for work. Also keep in touch with colleagues still working in your home country – they will be useful sources of information on the employment situation, and especially so in relation to vacancies not advertised but filled internally or through professional networks. You can also use your home leave for job interviews and maintaining professional contacts.

Another important consideration is maintaining your registration in your home country; this is likely to make resuming your career easier when you return. Keeping up your membership of your professional organisation will also be a good means of keeping up-to-date with developments in your profession – keep them informed of your whereabouts and they will be able to supply you with newsletters, updates and other useful sources of information.

Although it may be clear to you how your experience overseas has enhanced your professional skills, it is likely that you will need to give some thought to how you can best present this experience to employers, both in interview situations and when revising your CV or résumé. Many of the recruitment agencies described earlier in Part II are keen to promote the advantages of gaining experience in overseas positions, and will provide written confirmation of the experience you have gained; some are also keen to encourage health professionals finding work through them to take additional courses and improve their skills, further increasing the benefits that working overseas can provide.

# PART III

## Country Guide

# WESTERN EUROPE

Since the first edition of this book was written Europe has become more integrated as a workplace than ever before. The free-trade and freedom of movement regulations of the EU (European Union) have been added to by the arrival of the world's newest currency unit the Euro (see below). So that if one has rights of residency and work within one of the 18 EU/EEA countries, one can move to work in any one of the others, and eventually without having to convert your wages into different currencies. However, those freedoms may be subject to minor variations in national regulations regarding training and registration. At the time of writing the EU consists of 15 countries: Austria, Belgium, Denmark, Finland, France, Germany, Greece, Ireland, Italy, Luxembourg, the Netherlands, Portugal, Spain, Sweden and the United Kingdom. A further 3 countries form the EU/EEA (European Economic Area) Iceland, Liechtenstein and Norway, an economic, geographic and social appendix to the EU, where the countries have chosen to have close ties with the EU without joining yet. The EU/EEA states have harmonised many regulations to cover entry and work, while it is not yet a superstate this cooperation has important repercussions for health professionals seeking to move across, or to come and work in western Europe. This is an area to watch especially closely as the EU may soon expand to include many eastern European nations.

One of the benefits of the EU is the restrictions on working hours; prior to the adoption of these regulations in the UK junior doctors might find themselves working 80-90 hour weeks, often going 24 hours without sleep. This has now changed for the better with 'safe hours' and 'working time' regulations ensuring that doctors should be able to expect 8 hours rest in a 32 hour period of duty, and to work no more than 56 hours in a week. A summary of working hours can be found on the website of the Australian Medical Association (http://domino.ama.co.au/)

## The Euro

On 1 January 1999, eleven member states of the EU effectively replaced their national currencies with the new currency the 'euro'. This is a single currency for Europe, and it has been created as a keystone in the transition towards Economic and Monetary Union (EMU), with participating countries forming the 'euro-zone'. The eleven countries of the euro-zone are Austria, Belgium, Finland, France, Germany, the Republic of Ireland, Italy, Luxembourg, the Netherlands, Portugal and Spain. The UK, Denmark, Greece and Sweden have decided not to join EMU at this stage. Britons and observers of the UK national press will know that the joining of the euro-zone by the UK is a political hot-potato.

Throughout the euro-zone the euro is currently a notional currency, there will not be any euro coins or bank notes in circulation until 2002. Electronic transactions, however, are already being handled in the new currency, and it is now common to see prices quoted both in the national currency and in the euro in shops and supermarkets. From 1 July 2002, the *only* notes and coins used in countries participating in EMU will be euros.

The value of the euro fluctuates like that of any other currency, but euro-zone countries now share a single foreign-exchange rate policy and a single interest rate. The euro will be divided into 100 cents, and there will be seven bank notes in denominations of 5, 10, 20, 50, 100, 200, and 500 euro. Coinage will consist of 1, 2, 5, 10, 20, and 50 cent coins and 1 and 2 euro. At the time of writing, the euro is floating close to parity with the US$1 on the international money markets.

Any payments you receive in euros when working in euro-zone countries can be converted to your national currency (such as pounds sterling), and it is also possible to open a euro bank account. You should also remember that once the full changeover is effected in the euro-zone, you will only have a limited time in which to exchange any national bank notes you may be holding.

The British government has a euro information website site at www.euro.gov.uk.

## Recognition of Qualifications within the EU

### EU Medical Directives
In 1975, the European Union (then named the European Economic Community) issued two Directives concerning medical qualifications and training. The first concerned mutual recognition of primary medical qualifications and specialist medical qualifications within the EU. The second covered the minimum standards of training required in order to be awarded such qualifications. Both Directives have been superseded by the consolidated Directive 93/16, regarding primary medical qualifications, which requires that all EEA member states must recognise each other's primary medical qualifications. A list of these qualifications can be found on page 155

## OPPORTUNITIES

In terms of looking for work, health professionals now find themselves in a stronger position than before as a result of the Directives, as they are better able to approach employers in an EU/EEA country as members of the profession in that country, having made good any gaps in their education and training. It is therefore much easier for employers to judge the suitability of an applicant's qualifications, and this is likely to be particularly significant in professions where there is a shortage of qualified staff. Recruitment and retention of staff may become easier for employers in some cases – for example, in any professions where there is a surplus of trained staff in other EU/EEA states. It may, however, be more difficult in other cases because of the likely increase in competition for professionals.

In the following country guides contact addresses have been included for Ministries of Health and equivalent government organisations, and these should be able to provide you with general information on employment in the health sector. Professional organisations are also important sources of information, and you should contact the one appropriate to your field as soon as possible; they will be able to direct you to where information on current opportunities is available, be it the national or local press, agencies, the hospitals and clinics themselves, or specialist journals.

One of the most effective means of finding out about the current employment situation is contacting the regional health authorities for the areas in which you are interested in working; the Ministry of Health should be able to provide you with addresses. Nationals of an EU/EEA member state are entitled to make use of the employment service in all other EU/EEA countries, and it may be worth visiting the employment office in the region where you are looking for work for advice on opportunities in the health sector.

One of the key considerations for anyone considering entering the European job market is language. While fluency in one of the major languages such as English, French or German will help you in several countries, work in health care in many places may well not be available to you unless you speak the national language – be it Danish, Portuguese or Italian. Where competition for jobs is greatest (and even in countries where it is not a major problem), knowing the language may well be a decisive asset, if not a prerequisite.

Bear in mind that many of the countries in this section have quite small populations, and therefore their need for overseas health professionals may be correspondingly small. To avail yourself of the largest number of opportunities, therefore, it may be worthwhile not to restrict yourself in your search to just one country. Which languages you speak will affect your options in this respect; for example, if you speak German, you have the choice of looking for a position in Germany, Austria, Switzerland, Luxembourg and certain regions of several other countries, such as Belgium and the Czech Republic.

A great deal of additional information on employment regulations, working conditions and overcoming red tape is available for most of the EU/EEA countries in the *Live and Work in...* series of books, published by Vacation Work (see page 256).

**Note for US Dentists:** In some European countries, a US dentist may work as a 'dental assistant' where the term refers not to a paraprofessional as in the USA but to a graduate dentist who practices under the supervision of a licensed dentist and receives a salary or a comensurate percentage.

# Austria

*Austrian Embassy:* 3524 International Court, NW, Washington, DC 20008, USA (tel 202-895-6700; fax 202-895-6750).
*Austrian Embassy:* 18 Belgrave Mews West, London SW1X 8HU (tel 020-7235 3731; fax 020-7235 8025).
*Austrian Embassy:* 445 Wilbrod Street, Ottawa, Ontario K1N 6M7, Canada (tel 613-789-1444; fax 613-789-3431).
*Currency:* Austrian Schilling (AS)
*Exchange rate:* £1 = AS 22; $1 = AS13.7
*Capital:* Vienna
*International Telephone Code:* +43
*Population:* 7,812,000
*Area:* 84,000 sq. km
*Language:* German

Historically Austria has always been at the centre of Europe, although after the Second World War it found itself instead on the fringes of the western half of the continent, bordering the Iron Curtain. It is a modern, prosperous republic, and joined the European Union in 1995. Although an attractive country with a high standard of living, it is also an expensive place to live.

## SKILLS AND QUALIFICATIONS

As described on page 107, the recognition of professional qualifications throughout the EU/EEA is covered by Directive 93/16. For detailed enquiries on these matters in Austria, contact the Federal Ministry for Health and Consumer Protection.

### Medicine

Doctors who are EU/EEA nationals and who completed their training in an EU/EEA member state should direct their application for registration to practise to the Austrian Medical Association (Österreichische Ärztekammer). Those who have successfully completed a course of study in medicine or specialist training outside the EU/EEA, or who are not EU/EEA nationals and are looking for professional experience in Austria, should contact the Federal Ministry for Health and Consumer Protection (Bundesministerium für Gesundheit und Konsumentenschutz, Abteilung II/D/13).

## VISAS AND WORK PERMITS

Visas are not normally required in order to visit Austria, provided the length of stay is less than 6 months (3 months for US nationals); consult your nearest Austrian Embassy for full requirements. EU/EEA nationals do not need work permits to take up employment, but non-EEA nationals will need their employers to obtain a work permit (*Arbeitsbewilligung*) on their behalf. Within three months of living in Austria an identity card with photograph must be obtained from the aliens' police or *Bezirkshauptmannschaft*, this will entitle the holder to five years residence.

## JOB OPPORTUNITIES

The federal states (*Bundesländer*) are responsible for the recruitment of health professionals, as well as for their contracts and salaries, and so enquiries should be made at the state level. Contact addresses are available from the Federal Ministry for Health and Consumer Protection.

Several possibilities are available to doctors and medical specialists who want to gain professional experience in Austria; these include medical positions for study purposes in hospitals and similar institutions, as long as the training of Austrian doctors is not thereby threatened; independent professional experience in general medicine or medical specialisations, as long as the demand exists; and professional experience gained on a freelance basis, again as long as there is a demand. Further information on the full range of health professions is available from the Federal Ministry for Health and Consumer Protection, but note that the information is produced only in German.

## PROFESSIONAL ORGANISATIONS

*Austrian Association of Dietitians:* Raaber Bahngasse 3/2/8, A-1100 Vienna, Austria (tel 0222-6269 984).

*Austrian Association of Medical Laboratory Technologists:* Rennweg 79-81/316, A-1030 Vienna, Austria.

*Austrian Physiotherapy Association:* Koestlergasse 1/29, A-1060 Vienna, Austria (tel/fax 01-587 99 5130; e-mail physio.opv@physio.at Website www.physio.at/physio).

*Österreichische Ärztekammer:* (Austrian Medical Association) Weihburggasse 10-12, A-1011 Vienna, Austria (tel 01-51501/403; fax 01-51501/410).

*Österreichischer Krankenpflegeverband:* (Austrian Nurses' Association) Mollgasse 3a, A-1180 Vienna, Austria (tel 01-478 6387; fax 01-478 2710).

*Österreichisches Dentistenkammer:* (dentists) Kohlmarkt, A-1014 Vienna, Austria (tel 01-533 70640; fax 01-533 0758; Website www.oedk.at/).

*Verband der Diplomierten Ergotherapeuten Österreichs:* (occupational therapists) Sperrgasse 8-10, A-1150 Vienna, Austria (tel 0222-892 9380).

*Verband der Diplomierten, Radiologisch-Technischen, Assistentinnen und Assistenten österreichs:* (radiographers/radiological technologists) Simmeringer Hauptstrasse 34-40/1/1/VI, A-1110 Vienna, Austria

## USEFUL ADDRESSES

*Bundesministerium für Arbeit, Gesundheit und Soziales:* (Federal Ministry for Labour, health and Social Affairs) Stubenring 1, A-1011 Vienna, Austria (tel 01-711000; Website www.bmags,gv,at).

*Bundesministerium für Gesundheit und Konsumentenschutz:* (Federal Ministry for Health and Consumer Protection) Radetzkystrasse 2, A-1031 Vienna, Austria (tel 0222-711 72).

*Bundesministerium für wirtschaftliche Angelegenheiten:* (Federal Ministry for Economic Affairs) Referat X/A/1a, Stubenring 1, A-1011 Vienna, Austria (tel 01-71100-2109; fax 01-7142722).

# Belgium

*Belgian Embassy:* 3330 Garfield Street, NW, Washington, DC 20008, USA (tel 202-333-6900; fax 202-333-3079).

*Belgian Embassy:* 103-105 Eaton Square, London SW1W 9AB (tel 020-7470 3700; fax 020-7259 6213).

*Belgian Embassy:* 4th Floor, 80 Elgin Street, Ottawa, Ontario K1P 1B7, Canada (tel 613-236-7267; fax 613-236-7882).

*Currency:* Belgian Franc (BF; BF1 = 100 centimes).

*Exchange rate:* £1 = BF64.76; $1 = BF40.19.

*Capital:* Brussels.

*International Telephone Code:* +32

*Population:* 9,978,000.

*Area:* 31,000 sq. km.

*Languages:* Dutch (57%) French (42%), German (1%)

As the seat of both the European Commission and the European Council of Ministers, Belgium is probably uniquely qualified among the countries of the European Union to describe itself as being 'at the heart of Europe'. It is a constitutional monarchy, and a committed advocate of the vision of Europe as an integrated union of co-operating countries.

Belgium itself provides a model of the problems of federal integration between different peoples, as the nation is made up of Dutch and French-speaking communities which are split on roughly equal geographical terms, and the country's government is partially regionalised to reflect this division in the population.

## HEALTH SERVICES

The health care services in Belgium are of a very high standard and are funded by public or private sickness funds/insurance schemes. The public sickness funds *mutualitié/ziekenfonds* reimburse 75% of the costs of treatment and medicines to individual patients; these funds being supported by social insurance deductions from wages. 83% of doctors and dentists work in practices which are linked to the sickness fund system, this is indicated by the term *conventionné/gekonventioneerd* the remainder work as entirely private practitioners. There is a variety of hospital services supplied by the public and private sectors, with the hospitals and (*hôpital/ziekenhuis*) especially the university hospitals providing a wider range of services than the generally private clinics (*clinique/kliniek*).

## SKILLS AND QUALIFICATIONS

As described on page 107, the recognition of professional qualifications throughout the EU/EEA is covered by Directive 93/16. For detailed enquiries on these matters in Belgium, contact the Director at the Ministère de l'Education (French-speaking) or the Ministerie van Onderwijs (Dutch-speaking). Belgian medical training lasts seven years with specialists training for a further five years.

## VISAS AND WORK PERMITS

European citizens will not need a visa, work or residence permit to enter or work in Belgium, although if they wish to stay for more than three months they must register at the local town hall within eight days of arrival. This will gain them an 'Aliens' Card Model B, the 'Mauve Card' which is valid for up to one year. If you plan to stay longer then you should apply for the 'Blue Card' or EU Residence Card, which is valid for five years. For either of these you will need proof of employment or sufficient funds to support yourself. Non European citizens do not need visas for stays of up to three months but if they plan to stay longer they should apply for an 'Authorisation of Provisional Sojourn' prior to entry and then the Model A 'Orange Card'. They will also need work permits arranged through the embassy in their homeland, there are three types A, B and C, although C is rarely issued these days. Non-EU citizens will not be able to obtain a residence permit without a work permit.

Unfortunately due to the recent high levels of unemployment in Belgium it is increasingly difficult for these applicants to obtain work permits, and they must prove that there is no local source of labour (i.e. from within the EU/EEA) to fill the vacancy. In order to obtain an identity card, non-EEA nationals must demonstrate that they are in a position to support themselves financially.

## JOB OPPORTUNITIES

The best sources of job advertisements are the national dailies and often the weekend editions. Of the Belgian newspapers, the French-language *Le Soir* carries a good selection of vacancies, and you may also want to look in the English-language weekly *The Bulletin*.

Focus Career Services is a Brussels-based non-profit association providing services to people of all nationalities looking for new employment opportunities. It can offer information on job opportunities and advice on searching for a job in Belgium, and also publishes a bi-monthly newsletter.

## PROFESSIONAL ORGANISATIONS

*Association Belge des Syndicats Médicaux:* (medical association) Chaussée de Boondael 6 bte 4, B-1050 Brussels, Belgium (tel 02-644 1288; fax 02-644 1527).

*Association Belge des Technologues de Laboratoire:* (medical laboratory technologists) Stenenmolenstraat 64, B-2800 Mechelen, Belgium.

*Association Dentaire Belge:* (dentists) 40 rue Washington bte 22, B-1050 Brussels, Belgium.

*Association des Kinesitherapeutes de Belgique:* (physiotherapists) H Henneaulaan 69, B-1930 Zaventum, Belgium (tel 02-725 2777; fax 02-725 3076).

*Fédération Nationale Neutre des Infirmier(ière)s de Belgique* (Belgian Nurses' Association) rue de la Source 18, B-1060 Brussels (tel 02-537 0193; fax 02-143 3453).

*Heymans Institute for Pharmacology:* Medical School, University of Ghent, De Pintelaan 185, B-9000 Ghent, Belgium (tel 09-240 3374).

*La Société de Médecine Dentaire:* Avenue De Fré 191, B-1188 Brussels, Belgium (tel 02-375 8175; fax 02-375 8612; e-mail smd@mail.belgavillage.be Website www.belgavillage.be/smd).

*Nationale Belgishe Federation von Ergotherapeuten/Fédération Nationale Belge des Ergotherapeutes:* (occupational therapists) 87 rue de Percke, B-1180 Brussels, Belgium

## USEFUL ADDRESSES

*Dienst Gelijkwaardigheid, Ministerie van Onderwijs:* Bestuur van het Hoger Onderwijs en wettenschappelijk Onderzoek, Koningsstraat 136, B-1000 Brussels, Belgium (tel 02-211 4211; fax 02-211 4250).

*Equivalences de l'Enseignement supérieur, Ministère de l'Education & de la Recherche scientifique de la Communauté française:* Quartier des Arcades, 6ème étage, 204 rue Royale, B-1010 Brussels, Belgium (tel 02-210 5577; fax 02-210 5992).

*Focus Career Services:* 23 rue Lesbroussart, B-1050 Brussels, Belgium (tel 02-646 6530).

*NARIC-Vlaanderen:* Hendrik Consceincegebouw, Koning Albert II-laan 15, B-1210 Brussels, Belgium (tel 02-553 9817); for professional recognition of qualifications.

# Denmark

*Royal Danish Embassy:* 3200 Whitehaven Street, NW, Washington, DC 20008, USA (tel 202-234-4300; fax 202-328-1470; Website www.denmarkemb.org).

*Royal Danish Embassy:* 55 Sloane Street, London SW1X 9SR (tel 020-7333 0200; fax 020-7333 0270).

*Royal Danish Embassy:* Suite 450, 47 Clarence Street, Ottawa, Ontario K1N 9K1, Canada (tel 613-234-0704; fax 613-234-7368).

*Currency:* Danish Krone (Kr).

*Exchange rate:* £1 = Kr11.95; $1 = Kr7.41.

*Capital:* Copenhagen.

*International Telephone Code:* +45

*Population:* 5,162,000.
*Area:* 44,000 sq. km.
*Language:* Danish; English often spoken

Denmark is a constitutional monarchy (the present monarch is Queen Margrethe II). It joined the European Union in 1973, and is now considered to be one of the Union's strongest economies. Culturally it is closely related to the other Nordic countries. A quarter of the country's population live in the Copenhagen area.

## HEALTH SERVICES

Virtually all health care services in Denmark are financed, planned and operated by public authorities at the regional and local levels. The services are paid for mainly through general taxation. Total health care expenditure is 6.3% of GDP, which is quite low compared to other developed countries. Everyone in Denmark is entitled to almost all health care services free of charge. There are 2.78 doctors per 1000 inhabitants.

As in many other developed countries, increasing health care costs and changing health patterns have led to changes in the country's health policy. This is particularly notable in the emphasis on disease prevention rather than curative medicine. In recent years there has been a general trend of distributing tasks from the hospital sector to the primary health sector. More services have been made available at community level and the services of the primary health sector have been expanded.

The Ministry of Health coordinates Danish health policy at the national level. The counties are responsible for running and planning the main health care services, i.e. hospitals and primary health care. The local authorities at district level are responsible for home nursing services and a number of preventive programmes, including public health nurses, school health and dental services for children.

Virtually all hospitals are owned and run by the counties. There are over 115 hospitals in Denmark. Of these 10 are large specialised hospitals with national or regional functions that centralise specific treatments. There are a further 18 large specialised hospitals to provide specialists for each county. There are nearly 70 local general hospitals and 15 specialised psychiatric hospitals. The hospital sector employs 98,000 people, including nearly 9000 doctors and 23,000 nurses. In recent years there have been major changes in the way hospitals function; they have been increasingly directed at out-patient treatment, thereby relieving the pressure on in-patient facilities.

Denmark has approximately 3200 GPs. GPs can refer patients to specialists in primary health care or hospitals, and also to social services, health visitors and home nurses. There are about 800 full-time practising specialists in Denmark, and a similar number have other positions, usually within the hospital system, and carry on their own private practices on a part-time basis. The largest groups of specialists in primary health care are ear, nose and throat and eye specialists.

There are 3400 practising dentists, the majority of whom have private practices. Physiotherapists are allowed to set up in private practice. It is usual for municipalities to employ physiotherapists – for instance, in nursing homes. All pharmacists are authorised by the state, which decides their number and location.

As is the case in most EU countries Denmark has a large proportion of elderly citizens. Denmark has developed a policy of caring for the elderly in their own homes for as long as is practicable. This is achieved by supplying, at the state's expense, a network of visiting nurses, 24-hour emergency call-out systems, home helpers, meals on wheels and cleaners. This auxiliary sector of health care employs

28,000 personnel. With rising health care costs the Danish government is looking at ways of contracting out such services.

## SKILLS AND QUALIFICATIONS

As described on page 107, the recognition of professional qualifications throughout the EU/EEA is covered by Directive 93/16. For detailed enquiries on these matters in Denmark, contact the Erhvervsministeriet at the address below.

In order to obtain authorisation to practise as a doctor in Denmark, the National Board of Health has to be contacted after an offer of a job is received, but before it is taken up. The regulations governing applications from foreign doctors to work in Denmark are given in the leaflet *Guidelines for the Registration of Doctors of Medicine with a Degree from Abroad*, available from the National Board of Health (Sundhedsstyrelsen) at the address below.

## VISAS AND WORK PERMITS

If you are a citizen of Finland, Iceland, Norway or Sweden you may enter, stay and work in Denmark without a work and residence permit. If you are an EU/EEA national you do not need a work permit, and may stay in Denmark for up to 3 months from the date of arrival without a residence permit. If you intend to stay for more than 3 months you must apply for a residence permit no later than 15 days before the end of the 3 months; you will be granted the permit if you have paid employment or sufficient funds to support yourself. You will also need to contact the nearest Municipal Registry for registration as a temporary tax-payer.

If you are not an EU/EEA national you must apply for a work and residence permit before coming to Denmark; contact the Danish consular representative in your country for information.

## JOB OPPORTUNITIES

The National Board of Health emphasises the general difficulty of finding work in Danish hospitals, particularly without a good knowledge of Danish. Furthermore there is likely to be a surplus of doctors for some years to come.

For information on working in the health service at the regional and district levels contact the Association of County Councils and the National Association of Local Authorities, respectively (addresses below). Qualified medical staff who are interested in working in Denmark can consult the weekly journal of the Danish Medical Association, in which vacancies are advertised, the journal can be obtained directly from the DMA (address below). In addition to this, recent changes to advertsising restrictions now allow training and employment advertisements for doctors to appear in any Danish publication.

A complete list of hospitals and other medical institutions can be obtained from the Danish Medical Association. Nurses can consult the journal *Sygeplejersken*, available from the Danish Nurses' Organisation.

The Sunday edition of the newspaper *Berlingske Tidende* and also *Politiken* are worth consulting for job vacancies.

## PROFESSIONAL ORGANISATIONS

*Danish Association of Occupational Therapists:* Norre Voldgade 90, DK-1358 Copenhagen K, Denmark (fax 33 14 44 37).
*Danish Dietetic Association:* Norre Voldgade 90, DK-1358 Copenhagen K, Denmark (tel 33 13 82 11).

*Danish Medical Association/Dan Almindelige Danske Laegeforening:*
Trondhjemsgade 9, DK-2100 Copenhagen Ø, Denmark (tel 35 44 85 00; fax
35-44 85 05; e-mail dma-international@dadl.dk Website www.dadl.dk).

*Danish Nurses' Organisation:* Postboks 1084, DK-1008 Copenhagen K, Denmark
(tel 33 15 15 55; fax 33 15 24 55).

*Dansk Tandlaegeforening:* (dentists) Amaliegade 17, DK-1256 Copenhagen K,
Denmark (tel 7025 7711; Website www.dtf-dk.dk).

*Danske Fysioterapeuter:* (physiotherapists) Norre Voldgade 90, DK-1358
Copenhagen K, Denmark (tel 33 13 82 11; fax 33 93 82 14; e-mail df@fysio.dk
Website www.fysio.dk).

*Faglig Sammenslutning af Rontgensygeplejersker:* (radiographers/radiological
technologists) Kanslergade 5, 3rd Floor TH, DK-2100 Copenhagen O,
Denmark.

*Landssammenslutningen af Hospitalslaboranter:* (medical laboratory
technologists) Norre Voldgade 90, DK-1358 Copenhagen K, Denmark

## USEFUL ADDRESSES

*Erhvervs – og Selskabsstyrelsen:* Erhvervsministeriet, Kampmannsgade 1, DK-
1780 Copenhagen, Denmark (tel 33 12 42 80; fax 33 32 44 80).

*Ministry of Health:* Herluf Trolles Gade 11, DK-1052 Copenhagen K, Denmark
(tel 33 92 33 60; fax 33 93 15 63).

*National Association of Local Authorities:* Gyldenløvesgade 11, DK-1603
Copenhagen V, Denmark (tel 33 12 27 88; fax 33 12 23 50).

*National Board of Health:* Amaliegade 13, Postboks 2020, DK-1012 Copenhagen
K, Denmark (tel 33 91 16 01; fax 33 93 16 36).

*Udlaendingestyrelsen:* (Aliens' Department) Ryesgade 53, DK-2100 Copenhagen
Ø, Denmark, (tel 31-39 31 00; fax 31-39 45 20).

# Finland

*Finnish Embassy:* 3301 Massachusetts Avenue, NW, Washington, DC 20008, USA
(tel +1-202-298-5800; fax 202-298-6030: Website www.finland.org).

*Finnish Embassy:* 38 Chesham Place, London SW1X 8HW (tel 020-7235 9531;
fax 020-7235 3680).

*Finnish Embassy:* Suite 850, 55 Metcalfe Street, Ottawa, Ontario K1P 6L5,
Canada (tel 613-236-2389; fax 613-238-1474).

*Currency:* Markka (FIM).

*Exchange rate:* £1 = FIM9.5; $1 = FIM5.92.

*Capital:* Helsinki.

*International Telephone Code:* +358

*Population:* 5,029,000.

*Area:* 338,000 sq. km.

*Languages:* Finnish, Swedish (6%); English often spoken

Finland is a sparsely populated country on the eastern side of the Baltic. It has been
a republic since 1919, when it finally broke free from the Russian sphere of
influence, and joined the European Union in 1995. It is a well developed country
with excellent communications and transport, and low environmental pollution. It
experienced a severe economic recession in the early 1990s, and its economy is

undergoing a period of gradual recovery, with unemployment high in certain sectors of the economy.

## HEALTH SERVICES

The Finnish health care system is of a high standard and available to all. It is largely decentralised, and is paid for mainly through local taxes and state support, although there is a significant private sector. A national sickness insurance scheme covers most health care costs, although private treatment is more expensive. Health care in Finland places particular emphasis on health promotion, disease prevention and primary medical care.

A nationwide hospital network was established from the 1950s to the 1970s. In the early 1970s a comprehensive system of primary health care services was finalised, relying on municipal health centres. These centres employ doctors, nurses, physiotherapists and other health professionals. If necessary patients attending a health centre are referred to a hospital or its polyclinic (out-patients department).

There are 21 hospital districts in Finland and the municipal governments within each district are responsible for their central hospital(s). To supplement the main hospitals there are smaller local hospitals that provide treatment in specialist fields. Supplementary hospitals are maintained by the local authorities. In all there are 430 hospitals in Finland.

The 455 municipalities organise the health services needed by elderly people, including home care and a range of auxiliary services.

The National Research and Development Centre for Welfare and Health (STAKES) is an agency of the Ministry of Social Affairs and Health which compiles and maintains databases, registers and statistics to oversee the health services in Finland.

### Dentistry & Oral Health

Within Finland oral health services are provided by public and private practices in an almost equal division (41% public, 47% private). Public sector services are relatively new and are mainly provided by municipalities at local health centres. Student, University and Military healthcare form a subdivision of public dental services. Dentists in public practice receive a salary, with 20-30% of their remuneration coming from serrvice fees. Specialist oral healthcare is mostly provided by private practitioners, but treatments requiring hospitalisation are provided by central or university hospitals.

At present there are around 4,800 dentists working in Finland, with around 1200 dental hygienists and 6500 dental assistants. A dentist's training lasts 5 years, with graduates taking a further 6 months of vocational training before being licensed to practice independently.

### Salaries

The following sample salaries are average monthly incomes taken from employers' statistics for 1997:.

| | |
|---|---|
| Assistant nurse | FIM86,208. |
| Registered nurse | FIM114,204. |
| Dentist (municipal health centre) | FIM206,220. |
| Assistant physician | FIM221,100. |
| Consultant physician | FIM251,892. |
| Physician (municipal health centre) | FIM286,200. |

## SKILLS AND QUALIFICATIONS

In Finland the right to practise health professions is granted by the *Terveydenhoullonoikeusturvakeskus* TEO (National Board of Medico-Legal Affairs) which can also supply a useful guide to the Finnish healthcare system to those who wish to work there. TEO itself is subordinate to the Ministry of Social Affairs and Health, but is responsible for registering health professionals, monitoring their work, recognising any education and qualifications gained outside of Finland and *Terhikki* the Central Register of Health Professionals. Terhikki is maintained by *Stakes* the National Research and Development Centre for Welfare and Health, and contains professional and personal details of 200,000 health professionals working in Finland.

Further information on working in Finland is also available from the Ministry of Education or individual professional bodies. Applications from EU nationals to practice a profession should be submitted in Finnish, Swedish or English, including proof of nationality, degree certificates, certfication of your right to practise in your homeland and certification that your education complied with EU directives. To obtain a decision on the right to practice in Finland from TEO costs the applicant FIM400. Local authorities may also expect applicants to show some fluency in Finnish or Swedish, although this is not a requirement for licensing.

Within the Finnish health system the varying educational backgrounds of the different types of health professional are covered by a registration system which divides professionals into those who are 'licensed', and those who are entitled to a 'protected occupational title'. In essence the TEO grants either a licence to practice, or the right to use a professional title within a health care environment.

**Licensed Professions** include: dentist, dental/oral hygienist, dental technician, dietitian, medical doctor, medical laboratory technologist, midwife, occupational therapist, optician, pharmacist, physiotherapist, pyschologist, public health nurse, radiographer, registered nurse, speech therapist.

**Protected Occupational Title** covers the following professions: assistant nurse, chiropodist, dental assistant, children's nurse, physiotherapy assistant, mental nurse, pyschiatric nurse, psychotherapist, trained chiropractor, trained osteopath.

### Physicians

Under the terms of the EU Directives on qualifications (93/16/EEC) Finland will allow those applicants from EU/EEA states who were practising medicine before 1995 to have the corresponding right in Finland. Those who qualified after 1995 can gain the right to practise as a licensed physican, where they are supervised for two years. Or they can practise as an independent general practitioner on completion of a two year additional training period.

### Dentists

Foreign dentists can practice in Finland once they have been licenced by the TEO, pre-requisites are that they hold a degree in dentistry and the right to practice in their homeland. They should also have completed a period of supplementary training. This is administered by the University of Turku, Faculty of Dentistry, to ensure that their training meets the level required of Finnish dentists, it also checks the immigrant's qualifications (in theory and practice) and gives them the chance to familiarise themselves with local legislation and administrative practice. On completion of the supplementary training they are granted a *preliminary licence* to work in a community health centre (provided that they have an offer of work from one), after six months they can apply for an *extended licence*. Dentists holding extended licences can work in public or private practices.

Physicians and Dentists that wish to work in public practise will also need to obtain a sickness insurance number (SV) from the Social Insurance Institution (*Kansaneläkelaitos* or *Kela*), this allows them to prescribe medicines, and be paid for work carried out under the social insurance scheme, full details on how to apply can be obtained from TEO.

### Students

Healthcare students wishing to study in Finland have a choice for a range of degree and non-degree courses at universities and polytechnics, details of these can be obtained from the Centre for International Mobility.

### Nordic Nations

Generally the rules above apply to all EU/EEA nationals, but as the system of education in Nordic nations is so similar, the Joint Nordic Labour Market agreement of 1994 allows individuals licenced to practice in one Nordic country to obtain corresponding rights in another Nordic country. In Finland this covers: chiropodists, chiropractors, dentists, dental assistants, dental hygienists, doctors, medical laboratory technicians, midwives, occupational therapists, opticians, pharmacists, physiotherapists, mental nurses, practical nurses, pyschologists, public health nurses, radiographers, registered nurses and speech therapists.

## VISAS AND WORK PERMITS

Citizens of Nordic countries do not need visas, residence or work permits to enter live or work in Finland. Citizens of EU/EEA countries are entitled to live, look for work and work in Finland without residence permits, as long as the work does not last for more than 3 months. If it lasts more than 3 months, then they must obtain residence permits. Work permits are not required. A residence permit normally lasts for 5 years; if your job is for less than 1 year, a residence permit will be granted for that period.

If you are not an EU/EEA national you will need both a residence and a work permit. To obtain the latter you will need to have been offered a job in Finland, and your employer will need to check that the local employment office will support a foreign worker being taken on – the main reason for them not supporting you will be if there is already a suitable candidate for the post in Finland. Unless you hold a valid Finnish residence permit, applications for work permits must be made from outside Finland, via the embassy or consulate nearest to to you. If you have rights of residence in Finland then you can make your work permit application through the local police, permits cost FIM400 from outside Finland or FIM800 if applying in Finland.

Although health professionals running a practice count as self-employed the work and residence permit regulations apply to them also. The National Board of Medico-Legal Affairs can provide information on the permits needed to practise a particular profession in Finland. For queries concerning visas and immigration you can contact either the Finnish Embassy in your own country or the *Ulkomaalaisvirasto* (Directorate of Immigration) in Helsinki.

## JOB OPPORTUNITIES

In general terms there is currently no particular demand for overseas health care professionals in Finland. To find out specific information on the parts of Finland in which you are interested in working, you should contact the local employment office; addresses and contact numbers are available from the Ministry of Labour (the details for the employment office in Helsinki are included below). Information on salary levels is available from Kunnallinen työmarkkinalaitos in Helsinki.

## PROFESSIONAL ORGANISATIONS

*Association for Dental Assistants and Dental Hygienists:* Asemamiehenkatu 4, FIN-00520 Helsinki, Finland (tel 09-155 2770).

*Association for Dental Technicians:* Ratamestarinkatu 11 A, FIN-00520 Helsinki, Finland (tel 09-278 7850).

*Finnish Association of Physiotherapists:* Asemamiehenkatu 4, FIN-00520 Helsinki, Finland (tel 90-149 6817; fax 90-148 3054; e-mail fiomisto@fysioterapeuttiliitto.fi Website www.health.fi/fysioterapeutit).

*Finnish Dietetic Association:* Neljas Linja 17-19E, FIN-00530 Helsinki, Finland.

*Finnish Dental Society:* Bulevardi 30 B-5, FIN-00120 Helsinki, Finland (tel 09-680 3120; fax 09-646263).

*Finnish Federation for Dental Hygienists:* Kauppiaankatu 7 G, FIN-00160 Helsinki, Finland (tel 09-631641).

*Finnish Federation for Denturists:* Ratamestarinkatu 11 A, FIN-00520 Helsinki, Finland (tel 09-149 6306; fax 09-149 6300).

*Society of Radiographers in Finland:* c/o Tehy, Asemamiehenkatu 4, FIN-00520 Helsinki, Finland.

*Suomen Hammaslääkäriliitto:* (Finnish Dental Association) Fabianinkatu 9 B, FIN-00130 Helsinki, Finland (tel 09-622 0250; fax 09-622 3050; e-mail hamma@fimnet.fi Website www.hammasll.fi).

*Suomen Lääkäriliitto:* (Finnish Medical Association) PL 49, FIN-00501 Helsinki, Finland (tel 90-393091; fax 90-3930794).

*Suomen Laboratoriohoitajaliitto Slaby ry:* (medical laboratory technologists) Asemamiehenkatu 4, FIN-00520 Helsinki, Finland.

*Suomen Toimintaterapeuttiliitto ry:* (Finnish Association of Occupational Therapists) Rautatielaisenkatu 6, FIN-00520 Helsinki, Finland (tel/fax 09-144360; e-mail toimisto.toimintaterapeuttiliitto@co.inet.fi).

*Terveyden – ja sosiaalihuoltoalan ammattijärjestä Tehy ry:* (Finnish Federation of Nurses) Asemamiehenkatu 4, FIN-00520 Helsinki, Finland (tel 90-229 0020; fax 90-148 1840)

## VOLUNTARY ORGANISATIONS

Information on voluntary health care organisations is available from the following organisation, which produces a directory in English specifically on the subject:.

*Sosiaali – ja terveysjärjestöjen yhteistyöyhdistys YTY ry:* Ilkantie 4, FIN-00400 Helsinki, Finland (tel 90-580 3360)

## USEFUL ADDRESSES

*Association of Finnish Local Authorities:* 2 linja 14, FIN-00530 Helsinki, Finland (tel 09-77 11).

*Centre for International Mobility (CIMO):* PO Box 343, FIN-00531 Helsinki, Finland (tel 09-7747 7033; Website www.cimo.fi); for information for medical students wishing to study in Finland.

*Kunnallinen työmarkkinalaitos:* Toinen linja 14, FIN-00530 Helsinki, Finland (information on salary levels).

*Employment Office (International Service):* Haapaniemenkatu 4A 2krs, FIN-00530 Helsinki, Finland (tel 09-7021).

*Ministry of Education:* Meritullinkatu 10, FIN-00170 Helsinki, Finland (tel 09-13 41 71).

*Ministry of Labour:* PL 524, FIN-00101 Helsinki, Finland (tel 09-185 61).

*Ministry of Social Affairs and Health:* PO Box 267, FIN-00171 Helsinki, Finland (tel 09-1601; fax 09-160 5763).

*National Board of Medico-Legal Affairs:* Siltasaarenkatu 18C, FIN-00531 Helsinki, Finland (tel 09-3967 280; fax 09-3967 2842).

*Opetushallitus:* (Recognition of Qualifications) PL 380, FIN-00531 Helsinki, Finland (Website www.oph.fi/english/tutkintojentunnustaminen/).

STAKES: PO Box 220, FIN-00531 Helsinki, Finland (tel 09-36671; fax 09-761307; Website ww.stakes.fi).

*Tehy:* (The Union of Health and Social Care Services) PO Box 10, FIN-00060 Tehy, Finland (tel 09-155 2762; fax 09-148 3038; e-mail tehy.international@tehy.fi).

*Ulkomaalaisvirasto (UVI):* (Directorate of Immigration) PO Box 92, FIN-00531 Helsinki, Finland (tel 09-476 5500; fax 09-476 5858; Website www.uvi.fi).

# France

*French Embassy:* 4101 Reservoir Road, NW, Washington, DC 20007, USA (tel 202-944-6000; fax 202-944-6072).

*French Embassy:* 58 Knightsbridge, London SW1X 7JT (tel 020-7201 1000; fax 020-7201 1004).

*French Embassy:* 42 Sussex Drive, Ottawa, Ontario K1M 2C9, Canada (tel 613-789-1795; fax 613-562-3704).

*Currency:* Franc (F; F1 = 100 centimes).

*Exchange rate:* £1 = F10.49; $1 = F6.5.

*Capital:* Paris.

*International Telephone Code:* +33

*Population:* 57,049,000.

*Area:* 544,000.

*Language:* French

France is one of the leading countries in the European Union and one of its most powerful economies. France is one of the key countries in favour of closer European integration, but even so non-francophones will not find a job easily.

## HEALTH SERVICES

The French health system is based on the principles of free choice for the patient and equal access to health care for all. Most hospitals are in the public sector (this includes both public hospitals and private hospitals working within the public health service). There are approximately 550,000 beds, of which 65% are in the public sector, 19.3% in the profit-making private sector, and 15.7% in the not-for-profit sector. The cost of these hospitals is covered by compulsory and supplementary insurance schemes. The public sector also includes the majority of preventive medicine institutions (mother and child protection centres, school health services, occupational medicine, social disease clinics). Private practice provides the bulk of outside practitioner care and a proportion of hospital care in the form of private clinics. Alongside salaried doctors practising in the public sector, private practitioners enter into agreements with the sickness insurance schemes. The patient has a free choice of doctor and has direct access to all categories of practitioner. In general patients pay for any treatment and are reimbursed by sickness insurance schemes, and Friendly Societies or private insurance companies.

The French health service is characterised by compulsory sickness insurance (financed by social contributions) covering virtually the whole population and a variety of types of practice, producing a fragmentation of methods of organisation and funding. The state is involved in setting tariffs and investments but not the volume of services delivered by the private sector, which has seen a rapid and uncontrolled escalation in expenditure.

It is widely believed that there are too many doctors working in France. Up to 1997 there were 184,516 doctors working in the country, a density of 3.17 per 1000 inhabitants.

## SKILLS AND QUALIFICATIONS

As described on page 107, the recognition of professional qualifications throughout the EU/EEA is covered by Directive 93/16. For detailed enquiries on these matters in France, contact the Ministère de l'Education.

## VISAS AND WORK PERMITS

EU/EEA nationals do not need visas to enter the country, and are entitled to do so to look for work. Non-EEA nationals should consult their nearest French Embassy for information. Once a job is found you will need to apply for a residence permit (*carte de séjour*) either from the local *Commissariat de Police* or if in Paris from the *Préfecture de Police*. EU/EEA nationals do not need work permits; non-EEA nationals will need their prospective employer to apply for one on their behalf, and also need to find a position that can not be filled by an EU/EEA national.

## JOB OPPORTUNITIES

As in some other European countries, private employment agencies are prohibited as such and operate only as temporary employment bureaus (*agences de travail temporaire*). EU/EEA nationals are entitled to use the French National Employment Service (Agence Nationale pour l'Emploi (ANPE)), which has offices throughout the country. A list of ANPEs is available from the main office (address below).

There is a very uneven distribution of doctors in France, especially in general practice. *Départements* experiencing shortages are mainly to the north of the country. Disparities in the distribution of specialists are less pronounced. The Association Médicale Française may be able to provide information on where demand for doctors is greatest.

## PROFESSIONAL ORGANISATIONS

*Association Dentaire Française:* 7 rue Mariotte, F-75017 Paris, France (tel 01-58 22 17 10; fax 01-58 22 17 40; Website www.adf.asso.fr)..

*Association des Dieteticiens de Langue Française:* 35 Allee Vivaldi, F-75012 Paris, France (tel 01-40 02 03 02). `

*Association Française du Personnel Paramedic d'Electroradiologie:* (radiographers/radiological technologists) Boîte Postale 9, F-75622 Paris, Cedex 13, France.

*Association Médicale Française:* Secrétariat administratif, 37 rue de Bellefond, F-75441 Paris Cedex 09, France (tel 01-45 96 34 52; fax 01-45 96 34 50).

*Association Nationale Française des Ergothérapeutes:* (occupational therapists) 38 rue Eugène Oudine, F-75013 Paris, France (tel 01-45 83 50 38; fax 01-45 86 81 71; Website www.anfe.asso.fr).

*Federation Française des Masseurs Kinesitherapeutes Reeducateurs:* (physiotherapists) 24 rue des Petits Hotels, F-75010 Paris, France (tel 01-44 83 46 00; fax 01-44 83 46 01; e-mail ffmkr@kinephysio.com Website www.ffmkr.com)

## USEFUL ADDRESSES

*Agence Nationale pour l'Emploi (ANPE):* Le Galilée, 4 rue Galilée, F-93198 Noisy-le-Grande (tel 1-49 31 74 00).

*American Hospital:* 63 boulevard Victor Hugo, Neuilly-sur-Seine, Paris, France (tel 01-46 41 25 25).

*English Medical Centre:* 8 bis rue Quinhault, F-78100 St German-en-Laye, France (tel001-30 61 25 61).

*Federation Hospitaliere de France:* 33 Avenue d'Italie, F-75013 Paris, France.

*Hertford British Hospital:* 3 rue Barbès, F-92300 Levallois-Perret, Paris, France (tel 01-46 39 22 22).

*Ministère de l'Education nationale et de la Culture DAGIC 7:* rue de Grenelle 110, F-75007 Paris, France (tel 1-40 65 65 90; fax 1-45 44 57 87).

*Ordre National des Médecins:* 180 boulevard Haussmann, F-75389 Paris Cedex 08, France (tel 1-53 89 32 00; fax 1-53 89 32 01).

# Germany

*Embassy of the Federal Republic of Germany:* 4645 Reservoir Road, NW, Washington, DC 20007, USA (tel 202-298-4000; fax 202-298-4249).

*Embassy of the Federal Republic of Germany:* 23 Belgrave Square, London SW1X 8PZ (tel 020-7824 1300; fax 020-7824 1435).

*Embassy of the Federal Republic of Germany:* PO Box 379, Postal Station 'A', 14th Floor, 275 Slater Street, Ottawa, Ontario K1P 5H9, Canada (tel 613-232-1101; fax 613-594-9330).

*Currency:* Deutschmark (DM1 = 100 Pfennig).
*Exchange rate:* £1 = DM3.12; $1 = DM1.94.
*Capital:* Berlin.
*International Telephone Code:* +49
*Population:* 80,980,000.
*Area:* 357,000 sq. km.
*Language:* German; English widely spoken professionally

Germany is a federal republic composed of 13 states (*Länder*) and three city states – Berlin, Bremen and Hamburg. The country is one of Europe's largest nations and one of the leading economic powers. Although the absorption of East Germany during the 1990s lead to an economic downturn the situation is slowly improving, however, the western half of the nation still has a significantly higher standard of living than those *Länder* of the former East German Republic. As in Britain a new socialist government has tried to find a 'third way', to improve the economy.

## HEALTH SERVICES

The German health service dates back to the middle of the nineteenth century, it is still one of the most well equipped free health services in the world. The provision of health care in Germany is funded by a national statutory contribution system to insure that healthcare is available to everybody. Private healthcare is an option for those who wish to opt out of the national system. Important aspects of health policy come under the areas of influence of the *Länder*, and the districts and local authorities into which they subdivide. A host of governmental and non-governmental organisations are involved in public health care. According to recent statistics there are over 610,000 beds in around 2300 hospitals in Germany, and 1370 centres of preventive medical care/rehabilitation.

Most of the hospitals are general hospitals, but about 10% specialise in the treatment of long-term illness. Public hospitals provide 863 of the total number of hospitals. Churches and non-profit-making organisations such as the German Red Cross run another 845 charitable hospitals, and thereby provide a significant proportion of the beds available. Private hospitals are usually comparatively small, and make a less significant contribution to the system running only 373 hospitals.

Germany has a high ratio of doctors to patients. According to recent figures there are 279,000 doctors practising in the country. Increasingly doctors are obtaining supplementary qualifications in specialist branches of medicine, and also forming joint surgeries and medical partnerships, alongside the more conventional one-doctor surgeries. There are presently over 56,000 practising dentists; the majority of those in the former West Germany have set up their own surgeries. There are over 42,000 pharmacists, mainly working in pharmacies but also in the pharmaceutical industry. There are over 390,000 nurses working in general hospitals.

Almost 90% of the population is insured with a statutory health insurance fund, these average a deduction at source of about 13% from an individual's wages. Out-patient services are largely provided by independent doctors and dentists working under contract to the statutory health insurance system, and almost all doctors and dentists practise in this way, working on a freelance basis in their own surgeries. According to a recent survey there were over 77,000 independent doctors and over 35,000 independent dentists practising in this way.

Many members of paramedical professions such as physiotherapists and midwives are self-employed. There are also 14,000 'non-medical practitioners' working in Germany; this mainly involves treatment using natural remedies.

There are about 4500 centres providing homecare services to the ill, disabled and elderly, employing large numbers of nurses. In addition home helps provide help with simple nursing tasks and household chores. There has been a recent expansion in this type of care in the former East Germany, funded by the federal government.

German doctors in practices close to the borders with Belgium and the Netherlands have recently developed a system in agreement with Belgian and Dutch insurers whereby patients can obtain treatment across the border. Foreign patients wil recieve a 'treatment pass' which will allow them to gain access to a full range of treatments and make up for a lack of specialist services.

**Salaries**
The following figures are taken from a recent survey of average pre-tax earnings within some of the medical specialisations and professions:

| | |
|---|---|
| Dentist | DM196,600 |
| Non-Specialist Doctor | DM115,800 |
| Dermatologist | DM196,800 |
| Ear, Nose & Throat Specialist | DM250,800 |
| Gynaecologist | DM203,500 |
| Neurologist | DM178,400 |
| Opthamologist | DM223,100 |
| Orthopaedic Specialist | DM229,100 |
| Paediatrician | DM174,300 |
| Radiologist | DM232,600 |
| Surgeon | DM172,600 |
| Urologist | DM200,300 |

On average a doctor running a practice will have a turnover of around DM470,00, but after tax and operating costs this leaves a take home salary of DM185,00.

## SKILLS AND QUALIFICATIONS

As described on page 107, the recognition of professional qualifications throughout the EU/EEA is covered by Directive 93/16. The federal nature of the German state means that each Land has to register a new health professional and recognise their qualifications if gained elsewhere, under the terms of various directives. Within Germany one body, the Ständigen Konferenz der Kultusminister der Länder (Standing Conference of Ministers of Education and Cultural Affairs of the Lander) acts as an umbrella organisation for the Länder ministers of education. This has a secretariat branch part of which, the Zentralstelle für Ausländisches Bildungswesen (Central Office for Foreign Education) acts as an advisory body to *Länder* health authorities on the recognition of foreign qualifications. Qualifications gained outside the EU/EEA are recognised if they are equivalent to the corresponding German qualification.

The national professional associations will also be able to provide information on registration procedures and obtaining licenses to practise at the level of the individual *Länder*.

### Physicians

Medical training in Germany consists of pre-clinical and clinical training, in a similar fashion to that of the UK and USA. Medical students take four semesters of pre-clinical study concentrating on the sciences, before the *physicum* examination, at some point during this period medical students must also undertake a period of nursing work to ensure that they understand all aspects of health provision. This is followed by two semesters of clinical training (1st Clinical) ending in the *1st Staatsexam*. A further 4 semesters (2nd Clinical) continues their training including practical lectures and teaching about the administration of the health system. The *2nd Staatsexam* is followed by a one year period of practical work in a clinic, after passing the *3rd Staatsexam* the qualification *Arzt in Prakticum* is granted. AiPs are doctors in all but name as they carry out all the work of a medical doctor during an eighteen month period of supervised work, in either a hospital or practice under a suitably qualified supervisor.

Medical specialisations require the completion of further training with the training period *fach arzt* varying in length according to the subject; surgery (*chiurgie*) requires six years while anaesthesia is only four years.

**Non-Medical Practitioners**
These practitioners are not subject to a mandatory curriculum, but do need to take an examination conducted by the Health Office.

## VISAS AND WORK PERMITS

Visas are not required by EU/EEA nationals and citizens of Australia, Canada, New Zealand and the USA for visits of up to 3 months. EU/EEA nationals do not require a work permit to take up employment in Germany, but must apply for a residence permit (*Aufenthaltserlaubnis-EG*) if intending to stay and work for more than 3 months. These are obtained from local civic authorities (*Einwhonermeldeamt*) and last for five years. The process can take about two weeks. Non-EEA nationals need both residence permits and work permits.

## JOB OPPORTUNITIES

**Physicians**
At present Germany has rather too many doctors and recent medical graduates, 12,000 graduate every year and in 1999 11,000 doctors were unemployed. This together with the *AiP* system of supervision for newly qualified doctors (which has an unfortunate potential for bullying) means that there are few opportunities and many German staff are looking for work abroad, notably in the UK where the GMC has over 2,000 German doctors on its lists.

The weekly medical journal *Deutsches Ärzteblatt* contains a large section of advertisements for doctors and others working in the medical field; details of rates and subscriptions are available from the publisher, Deutscher Ärzte-Verlag (address below).

Agencies for permanent employment are a government monopoly in Germany and the contact organisation is Zentralstelle für Arbeitsvermittlung. This office handles enquiries for all types of work, and can also supply a list of local offices throughout the country.

**Nurses**
There has been an expansion in the numbers of nursing staff since reunification, especially in the new *Länder*. Nurses should consult the journals *Deutsche Krankenpflegezeitschrift* and *Krankenpflege* – the latter is published by the DBfK, the German Nurses' Association. Nursing jobs may also be found in the local press.

Several international agencies deal with nursing opportunities in Germany. *Jenrick* (see page 56) can place nurses in positions throughout the country; *O'Grady-Peyton International* sometimes have vacancies for nurses in Germany and they also have a local office placing staff in other countries. In all cases, ability in the German language is an advantage, and sometimes a prerequisite.

## PROFESSIONAL ORGANISATIONS

*Bundesärztekammer:* (German Medical Association) Herbert-Lewin-Strasse 1, D-50931 Cologne, Germany (tel 0221-4004 209; fax 0221-4004 380).
*Bundeszahnärztekammer:* (German Dental Association) Postfach 410168, D-50861 Cologne, Germany.
*Deutscher Berufsverband für Pflegeberufe (DBfK):* (German Nurses' Association)

Hauptstrasse 392, D-65760 Eschborn, Germany (tel 06173-65086; fax 06173-61644).

*Deutscher Verband der Diatassistenten:* (dietitians) Bismarckstrasse 96, Postfach 105112, D-40042 Düsseldorf, Germany (tel 0211-162175).

*Deutscher Verband der Ergotherapeuten:* (occupational therapists) Postfach 2208, D-76303 Karlsbad, Germany.

*Deutscher Verband für Physiotherapie:* Deutzer Freiheit 72-74, D-50679 Cologne, Germany (tel 0221-9810270; fax 0221-98102725; e-mail info@zvk.org Website www.zvk.org).

*Deutscher Verband Technischer Assistenten in der Medizin:* (medical laboratory technologists/radiographers/radiological technologists) Spaldingstrasse 110B, D-20097 Hamburg, Germany.

*German Opthamological Society:*Berliner Strasse 14, D-69120 Heidelberg, Germany (tel 6221-411787; fax 6221-484616; e-mail DOG-HD@t-online.de Website www.dog.org/

*Institut der Deutschen Zahnärzte (IDZ):* Universitätsstrasse 71-73, D-50931 Köln, Germany (tel 0221-40010; fax 0221-404886; e-mail idz@kzbv.de Website www.idz-koeln.de).

## USEFUL ADDRESSES

*Deutsche Krankenhausgesellschaft:* Tersteegenstrasse 9, Düsseldorf, Germany.

*Deutsches Ärzteblatt:* (German Medical Journal) Ottostrasse 12, D-50859 Cologne, Germany (tel 02234-701 1120; fax 02234-701 1142; e-mail aerzteblatt@aerzteblatt.de; Website wwwaerzteblatt.de).

*Zentralstelle für ausländisches Bildungswesen im Sekretariat der Ständigen Konferenz der Kulturminister der Länder in der BRD (KMK):* (Central Office for Foreign Education) Lennéstrasse 6, D-53113 Bonn, Germany (tel 0228-501200; fax 0228-501229; e-mail zab@kmk.org).

*O'Grady-Peyton International* 332 Congress Street, Boston, Massachusetts 02210, USA, (tel +1-617-422 0300; fax 617-422 0399; Website www.opginc.com).

*Zentralstelle für Arbeitsvermittlung:* Auslandsabteilung, Feuerbachstrasse 42-46, D-60325 Frankfurt am Main, Germany (tel 069-7111-0).

---

# Greece

---

*Greek Embassy:* 2221 Massachusetts Avenue, NW, Washington, DC 20008, USA (tel 202-939-5800; fax 202-939-5824).

*Greek Embassy:* 1a Holland Park, London W11 3TP (tel 020-7221 6467; fax 020-7243 3202).

*Greek Embassy:* 76-80 MacLaren Street, Ottawa, Ontario K2P 0K6, Canada (tel 613-238-6271; fax 613-238-5676).

*Currency:* Drachma (Dr).

*Exchange rate:* £1 = Dr527; $1 = Dr328.

*Capital:* Athens.

*International Telephone Code:* +30

*Population:* 10,269,000.

*Area:* 132,000 sq. km.

*Language:* Greek

Although an integral part of the European Union, Greece is one of its less developed member states and has a relatively weak economy. As a result opportunities for overseas nationals are relatively few.

## HEALTH SERVICES

The Greek national health system is run by the Idrima Kinonikon Asfalisseon (IKA). All hospitals in Greece are under the supervision of the state. Private clinics have been permitted in Greece only as recently as 1990, and doctors are obliged to work either in the public sector (i.e. the national health system) or the private sector – doctors who practise in both simultaneously face permanent discharge.

Provincial health centres form an important part of the health system. They provide emergency and first aid care, special treatment, dentistry and preventive care. They also function as information centres in matters of family planning and social welfare. Every doctor is obliged to work in the provinces for one year, which helps to strengthen the role of the health centres.

Treatment from doctors and in hospitals within the Greek national health system is free. Some remote parts of the country are not covered by the IKA and only private medical treatment is available.

## SKILLS AND QUALIFICATIONS

As described on page 107, the recognition of professional qualifications throughout the EU/EEA is covered by Directive 93/16. For detailed enquiries on these matters in Greece, contact the Inter-University Centre for the Recognition of Foreign Educational Qualifications (DIKATSA).

Information on what supporting documents are necessary to obtain a work permit for practising in a particular profession is available from the Ministry of Health, Welfare and Social Security. Evidence of an adequate knowledge of Greek is likely to be important.

## VISAS AND WORK PERMITS

EU nationals are free to enter Greece for up to 3 months to look for work. If you intend to stay longer than 3 months then a residence permit is needed. A temporary permit is issued in the case of employment lasting for between 3 and 12 months. Permits are issued for 6 months in the first instance, and then renewed for a five-year period. Permits are obtained by applying within eight days of arrival to the local foreign residents department (*Ypiresia Allodapon*) or the local police station. Applications must be supported by a declaration of employment authenticated by the Labour Inspectorate, a valid passport and a medical certificate stating that you are not carrying any threats to public health.

Non-EEA nationals wanting to take up employment in Greece will first need to find work. The employer will then apply for work and residence permits on their behalf.

## JOB OPPORTUNITIES

EEA nationals have free access to the services of the Greek employment service. The Greek equivalent of a British Jobcentre is an office of the Manpower Employment Organisation. With a few exceptions, private employment agencies are forbidden by law in Greece.

Major newspapers such as *Ta Nea Eleftheros Typos*, *Eleftherotypia* and *Apogevmatini* all carry advertisements for jobs. The English-language *Athens News* also carries vacancies.

At the time of writing the opportunities for work in some professions were limited; the Hellenic Dietetic Association reported that there are few opportunities even for Greek dietians.

## PROFESSIONAL ORGANISATIONS

*Athens Medical Association:* Themistokleous 34, GR-10678 Athens, Greece (fax 01-384 1234).

*Hellenic Association of Ergotherapists:* (occupational therapists) Aristidou Street 8, GR-10559 Athens (tel 01-322 8979; fax 01-323 9776).

*Hellenic Dental Association:* Themistokleous 38, GR-10678 Athens, Greece.

*Hellenic Dietetic Association:* Erythrou Stavrou 8-10, GR-11526 Athens, Greece (fax 01-698 4400).

*Hellenic National Graduate Nurses Association:* Athens Tower (C Building) GR-11527 Athens, Greece (tel 01-770 2861; fax 01-779 0360).

*Medical Association of Greece:* Stadiou Street 29, Athens, Greece.

*Panhellenic Association of Medical Laboratory Technologists:*: Victor Hugo Street 14, GR-10438 Athens, Greece.

*Panhellenic Physical Therapy Association:* (physiotherapists) Gilfordou 12, GR-104 Athens, Greece (tel 01-821 3905; fax 01-771 1821).

*Panhellenic Society of Radiotechnologists:* Sokratous 73, GR-10432 Athens, Greece (fax 01-459 2666)

## USEFUL ADDRESSES

*Athens News:* Lekka Street 23-25, GR-10562 Athens, Greece (tel 01-322 4253).

*DIKATSA:* Leoforos Sygrou 112, GR-11741 Athens, Greece (tel 01-922 2526; fax 01-921 8052).

*Greek Red Cross:* Lykavettos Street 1, GR-10672 Athens, Greece.

*Ministry of Health, Welfare and Social Security:* Aristotelous Street 17, GR-10187 Athens, Greece (tel 01-523 2821; fax 01-524 8325).

---

# Ireland

---

*Irish Embassy:* 2234 Massachusetts Avenue, NW, Washington, DC 20008, USA (tel 202-462-3939; fax 202-232-5993).

*Irish Embassy:* 17 Grosvenor Place, London SW1X 7HR (tel 020-7235 2171; fax 020-7245 6961).

*Irish Embassy:* 170 Metcalfe Street, Ottawa, Ontario K2P 1P3, Canada (tel 613-233-6281; fax 613-233-5835).

*Currency:* Punt (IR£).

*Exchange rate:* £1 = IR£1.20; $1 = IR£0.78.

*Capital:* Dublin.

*International Telephone Code:* +353.

*Population:* 3,523,000.

*Area:* 70,000 sq. km.

*Languages:* Irish, English

The Republic of Ireland is one of the poorer countries of the European Union, but is currently experiencing considerable economic growth. It is seen as an attractive place to live by many foreigners, both for its landscape and the welcoming nature of the Irish.

## SKILLS AND QUALIFICATIONS

### Medicine & Dentistry
All doctors wishing to practise in Ireland must register with the Medical Council, the regulatory body for doctors. Qualifications obtained in the member states of the EU are recognised by the Council, but all other qualifications must be assessed by the Council before it will decide whether to grant temporary registration status. Information concerning eligibility for registration can be obtained from the Registrar of the Medical Council. Dentists are likewise required to register with the Dental Council.

### Nursing
*An Bord Altranais* (the Nursing Board) is responsible for the regulation of nurse training and registration. The qualifications of general nurses and midwives trained in member states of the EU are recognised on the basis of EU Directives. Applications for registration from nurses trained outside the EU are considered on an individual basis, and in these cases the Board may require additional clinical experience or theoretical instruction, or may prescribe a short period of orientation prior to registration.

### Medical Laboratory Science
Medical Laboratory Technologist/Scientists can only work in Ireland if they can provide written evidence of eligibility for membership of the Irish Academy of Medical Laboratory Science. Applications forms for the academy can be obtained by post with details of the necessary fees, and the eligibilty assessment and membership process takes approximately three months.

### Professions Supplementary to Medicine
With the exception of Pharmacists, Physiotherapists and those professions mentioned above all health professions will have to have their qualifications validated by the Department of Health and Children. Pharmacists and Physiologists will have to register and be validated by The Pharmaceutical Society of Ireland and the Irish Society of Chartered Physiotherapists. These bodies may charge a fee for validation.  For Speech and Language therapists there is a reciprocal recognition agreement covering graduates of the training course taught at Trinity College, Dublin and courses recognised by the UK's Royal College of Speech and Language Therapists.

## VISAS AND WORK PERMITS

EEA nationals do not need visas to enter Ireland, but they should obtain residence permits. Within Dublin these should be obtained from the Department of Justice, Equality and Law Reform, or the Aliens Registration Office, elsewhere they can be obtained from local police stations.

EEA citizens also do not need to apply for a work permit to be able to take up employment in Ireland, detailed information on the free movement of professionals is available from the Department of Enterprise Trade and Employment.

Most non-EEA nationals require visas and work permits,. Visas should be obtained from the applicant's nearest embassy or consulate, or the Department of Foreign Affairs in Dublin if there are no diplomatic missions in the applicant's country. For work permits the prospective employer must apply for a permit on behalf of the would-be employee; strict eligibility criteria apply and the permit and visa must be obtained in advance of entry.

## JOB OPPORTUNITIES

Appointments in the Irish Health Service are made by regional health boards, hospitals and the Local Appointments Commission. Information on the prospects for employment in your profession in Ireland can be requested from the Department of Health in Dublin.

There are several publications including advertisements for medical positions. The *Irish Medical Times* and the *Irish Medical News* are both weekly medical newspapers, and the Thursday edition of the *Irish Independent* and the Friday edition of the *Irish Times* are also useful. *The New World of Irish Nursing* is a journal published by the Irish Nurses' Organisation that nurses looking for work may find useful.

There are numerous recruitment agencies operating in Ireland, many of which operate in the health field. All agencies have under Irish law to have a trading premises and be licensed and registered, a list of licensed agencies is available from the Employment Agencies Section of the Department of Enterprise and Employment. Another useful organisation is FAS, the national training and employment agency, which may be able to direct you to information on current opportunities. The American agency *O'Grady-Peyton International* often have vacancies for Registered Nurses in Ireland.

At the time of writing Ireland is an exporter of health professionals, however, this historical trend is likely to reverse in the next year or so.

### Medicine

There are very few opportunities for doctors at the higher levels of the profession in Ireland, though there are some opportunities at the lower end – i.e. senior house officers and registrars – as many Irish graduates leave the country at this stage in their careers to gain experience abroad. Opportunities for senior registrars and consultants are extremely limited. Most non-EU nationals find that the only opportunities for them are in small hospitals that may not be recognised for further training by the Royal College of Physicians of Ireland or the Royal College of Surgeons of Ireland, these positions being less attractive for Irish graduates.

Once registered with the Medical Council, it is relatively easy to set up as a GP in private practice, but it is extremely difficult to get a General Medical Services list (GMS is the public health scheme), which is a security most doctors would like. Therefore this route may not be a very realistic option.

### Salaries

The following figures show the pay scales for consultants based on the revised common contract of 1998:

**Category I Consultants**

All Consultants in Palliative Care, Geriatricians and Psychiatrists
    in Midland, North Western & Western Health Boards       IR£83824
Consultants in Mid-Western, North-Eastern, South-Eastern
    and Southern Health Boards       IR£79605
Consultants in Eastern Health Board       IR£75614

**Category II Consultants**
All Consultants in Palliative Care, Geriatricians and Pyschiatrists
   in Midland, North Western & Western Health Boards     IR£74817
Consultants in Mid-Western, North-Eastern, South-Eastern and
   Southern Health Boards     IR£71054
Consultants in Eastern Health Board     IR£67520

The following figures are based on the 1999 Consolidated Salary Scales of the Department of Health & Children:

| Medical & Dental Grade | Minimum | Maximum |
|---|---|---|
| Area Medical Officer | IR£32011 | IR£41109 |
| Community Opthalmic Physician | IR£41109 | |
| Hospital Medical Officer (1) | IR£11897 | IR£17341 |
| Hopsital Medical Officer (2) | IR£10028 | IR£14644 |
| House Officer | IR£19189 | IR£27202 |
| Registrar | IR£25103 | IR£30003 |
| Senior Registrar | IR£31380 | IR£38429 |
| Psychiatrist | IR£25960 | IR£31247 |
| Dental Surgeon (Grade I-II) | IR£24200 | IR£38481 |
| Dental Surgeon (Principal) | IR£36738 | IR£43671 |
| Pyschiatric Nurse | IR£15664 | IR£22487 |
| Nursing Officer | IR£20171 | IR£24583 |
| Nurse Tutor | IR£25551 | IR£27659 |
| Staff Nurse (3) | IR£15300 | IR£22339 |
| Dual Qualified Nurse | IR£17305 | IR£23101 |
| Sister (Ward) | IR£20187 | IR£25020 |
| Sister (Theatre/Clinical) | IR£21137 | IR£25502 |

(1) Medical Officer for a District Hospital between <25 and >81 beds.
(2) Medical Officer for a County Home between <200 and >350 beds.
(3) Including Registered Midwife.

**Paramedical Grades**

| | | |
|---|---|---|
| Dietitian | IR£18880 | IR£24554 |
| Dietitian (Senior/Principal) | IR£21716 | IR£30687 |
| Dental Hygienist | IR£18039 | IR£23746 |
| Medical Labratory Technician | IR£18365 | IR£40933 |
| Occupational Therapist | IR£17982 | IR£29337 |
| Pharmacist | IR£17668 | IR£41909 |
| Physiotherapist | IR£17904 | IR£31928 |
| Radiographer | IR£17862 | IR£31911 |
| Speech & Language Therapist | IR£18588 | IR£30687 |

**Students**
University College Dublin's Faculty of Medicine has links under the EU's *Socrates* programme with medical schools in Belgium, France and Germany, students can therefore arrange to spend some of their study time in Ireland and obtain course credits under the European Credit Transfer System (ECTS).

# PROFESSIONAL ORGANISATIONS
*Academy of Medical Laboratory Science:* 31 Old Kilmainham Road, Dublin 8, Ireland (tel 01-677 5602; fax 01-677 5652).

*Association of Clinical Biochemists in Ireland:* c/o Our Lady's Hospital for Sick Children, Crumlin, Dublin 12, Ireland.

*Association of Occupational Therapists of Ireland:* 5 Breffni Terrace Mews, Sandycove, Co Dublin, Ireland.

*Association of Optometrists of Ireland:* 10 Merrion Square, Dublin 2, Ireland (tel 01-616933).

*Association of Physical Scientists in Medicine:* c/o X-Ray Department, Mater Hospital, Dublin 7, Ireland.

*Irish Association of Orthoptists:* c/o Mater Hospital, Dublin 7, Ireland.

*Irish Association of Speech Therapists:* PO Box 1344, Dublin 4, Ireland.

*The Irish College of General Practitioners:* Corrigna House, Fenian Street, Dublin 2, Ireland (tel 01-676 3705; fax 01-676 5850).

*Irish Dental Association:* 'Boyne', 10 Richview Office Park, Clonskeagh Road, Dublin 14, Ireland.

*Irish Medical Organisation:* 10 Fitzwilliam Place, Dublin 2, Ireland (tel 01-676 7273; fax 01-661 2758; e-mail imo@iol.ie Website www.imo.ie).

*Irish Nurses' Organisation:* 11 Fitzwilliam Place, Dublin 2, Ireland (tel 01-676 0137/0138; fax 01-661 0466).

*Irish Nutrition and Dietetic Institute:* Terenure Enterprise Centre, 17 Rathfarnham Road, Dublin 6W, Ireland (tel 01-283 9444).

*Irish Society of Chartered Physiotherapists:* c/o Royal College of Surgeons, 123 St Stephen's Green, Dublin 2, Ireland (tel 01-402 2148; fax 01-402 2160; e-mail iscp@indigo.ie Website www.iscp.ie).

*Psychology Society of Ireland:* 13 Adelaide Road, Dublin 2, Ireland.

*Royal College of Physicians of Ireland:* 6 Kildare Street, Dublin 2, Ireland (tel 01-661 6677; fax 01-676 3989).

*Royal College of Surgeons in Ireland:* 123 St Stephen's Green, Dublin 2, Ireland (tel 01-402 2100; fax 01-478 2649; e-mail info@rcsi.ie Website www.rcsi.ie).

*Society of Radiographers of the Republic of Ireland:* School of Radiography, St Vincents Hospital, Elm Park, Dublin 4, Ireland

*The Pharmaceutical Society of Ireland:* 37 Northumberland Road, Dublin 4, Ireland.

## USEFUL ADDRESSES

*An Bord Altranais:* (Nursing Board) 31-32 Fitzwilliam Square, Dublin 2, Ireland (tel 01-676 0226; fax 01-676 3348; Website www.nursingboard.ie).

*The Dental Council:* 57 Merrion Square, Dublin 2, Ireland.

*Department of Education and Science:* Marlborough Street, Dublin 1, Ireland.

*Department of Enterprise, Trade and Employment:* Kildare Street, Dublin 2, Ireland (tel 01-661 4444; fax 01-676 2654).

*Department of Foreign Affairs:* 80 St Stephen's Green, Dublin 2, Ireland (tel 01-478 0822; fax 01-478 1484).

*Department of Health and Children:* Hawkins House, Dublin 2 (tel 01-635 4000; fax 01-635 4001).

Department of Justice, Equality and Law Reform: 72 St Stephen's Green, Dublin 2, Ireland.

*FAS:* Baggot Court, 27-33 Upper Baggot Street, Dublin 4, Ireland (tel 01-668 5777; fax 01-668 2691).

*Higher Education Authority:* 21 Fitzwilliam Square, Dublin 2, Ireland (tel 01-612748; fax 01-610492).

*Irish Medical Journal:* 10 Fitzwilliam Place, Dublin 2, Ireland (tel 01-676 7273; fax 01-662 2818; e-mail admin@imo.ie; Website www.imj.ie).

*Irish Medical Times:* 15 Harcourt Street, Dublin 2, Ireland (tel 01-475 7461; fax 01-475 7467; e-mail medtimes@iol.ie).

*The Local Appointments Commission:* 1 Lower Grand Canal Street, Dublin 2, Ireland.

*Nursing Careers Centre:* PO Box 6703; Dublin 2, Ireland (tel 01-676 0226).

*Opticians Board:* 18 Fitzwilliam Square, Dublin 2, Ireland.

*Registrar of the Medical Council:* Portobello Court, Lr Rathmines Road, Dublin 6, Ireland.

*School of Clinical Speech and Language Studies:* Trinity College, 183-6 Pearse Street, Dublin, Ireland (tel 01-608 1496; fax 01-671 2152; Website www.tcd.ie/Clinical—Speech/).

*University of Dublin, Faculty of Medicine:* Admissions Office, Michael Tierney Building, University College Dublin, Bellfield, Dublin 4, Ireland (tel 01-706 1425; fax 01-706 1070; Website www.ucd.ie/medicine.html)

## REGIONAL HEALTH BOARDS

*Eastern Health Board:* Dr Steevens's Hospital, Dr Steeven's Lane, Dublin 8, Ireland.

*Midland Health Board:* Arden Road, Tullamore, Co Offlay, Ireland.

*Mid-Western Health Board:* 31-33 Catherine Street, Limerick, Ireland.

*North-Eastern Health Board:* Kells, Co Meath, Ireland.

*North-Western Health Board:* Manorhamilton, Co Leitrim, Ireland.

*South-Eastern Health Board:* Lacken,Dublin Road, Kilkenny, Ireland.

*Southern Health Board:* Cork Farm Centre, Dennehey's Cross, Cork, Ireland.

*Western Health Board:* Merlin Park Regional Hospital, Galway, Ireland.

## VOLUNTARY HOSPITALS

*Adelaide & Meath Hospital:* Tallaght, Dublin 24, Ireland (tel 01-414 2095; fax 01-459 6810).

*Beaumont Hospital;* PO Box 1297, Beaumont Road, Dublin 9, Ireland (tel 01-837 7755; fax 01-837 6982).

*The Children's Hospital:* Temple Street, Dublin 1, Ireland (tel 01-874 8763; fax 01-874 8355).

*Coombe Maternity Hospital:* Dolphin's Barn, Dublin 8, Ireland (tel 01-453 7561; fax 01-453 6033).

*Incorporated Orthopaedic Hospital:* Castle Avenue, Clontarf, Dublin 3, Ireland.

*Mater Hospital:* Eccles Street, Dublin 7, Ireland.

*Mercy Hopsital:* Grenville Place, Cork, Ireland.

*National Maternity Hospital:* Holles Street, Dublin 2, Ireland.

*National Rehabilitation Board:* Rochestown Avenue, Dun Laoire, Co Dublin, Ireland.

*Our Lady's Hospital for Sick Children:* Crumlin, Dublin 12, Ireland.

*Peamount Hospital:* Newcastle, Co Dublin, Ireland.

*Portincula Hospital:* Ballinasloe, Co Galway, Ireland.

*Rotunda Hospital:* Parnell Street, Dublin 1, Ireland (tel 01-873 0700; fax 01-872 6523).

*Royal Hospital:* Donnybrook, Dublin 4, Ireland.

*Royal Victoria Eye & Ear:* Adelaide Road, Dublin 2, Ireland.

*St James' Hospital:* James' Street, Dublin 8, Ireland (tel 01-453 7941).

*St John's Hopsital:* Limerick, Ireland.

*St Luke's Hospital:* Highfield Road, Rathgar, Dublin 6, Ireland (tel 01-497 4552).

*St Michael's Hospital:* Lower Georges Street, Dun Laoghaire, Co Dublin, Ireland

(tel 01-280 6901; fax 01-284 4651).
*St Mary's Orthopaedic Hospital:* Cappagh, Dublin 11, Ireland.
*St Mary's Hospital:* College Street, Baldoyle, Dublin 13, Ireland (tel 01-832 3056; fax 01-839 3718).
*St Vincent's Hospital:* Elm Park, Dublin 4, Ireland (tel 01-269 4533).
*South Infirmary/Victoria Hospital:* Old Blackrock Road, Cork, Ireland (tel 021-964333; fax 021-310153).

## OTHER AGENCIES

The following agencies may be able to help you in your job search:.

*Belgrave Nurses Bureau:* 47 Osprey Drive, Templeogue, Dublin 6W, Ireland (tel 01-450 3640).
*Fingal Nursing Agency:* 9 Newton Parks, Skerries, Co Dublin Ireland (tel 01-849 2189).
*Grafton Recruitment:* 1 Wellington Quay, Dublin, Ireland (tel 01-670 4564; fax 01-670 4694; e-mail grafton@iol.ie Website www.grafton-group.com).
*Healthcare Recruitment:* 15 College Green, Dublin 2, Ireland (tel 01-679 3561; fax 01-679 3717; e-mail agency@iol.ie). Specialists in placing health care staff of any specialisation in placements in Ireland, especially senior nurses and managerial level staff. They also train staff for new careers in pharmaceutical sales.
*Irish Pyschiatric Nurse Agency:* 9-10 Victoria Terrace, Dundrum, Dublin 14, Ireland (tel 01-298 0310; e-mail nurses@psychiatricnursesagency.ie). Specialists in pyschiatric and mental health nurse placements.
*Nurse on Call:* 59 Ranelagh, Dublin 6, Ireland (tel 01-496 5199; Website www.nurseoncall.ie).
*Nurses for Nursing Homes:* 31 Orlagh Wood, Scholarstown Road, Dublin 16, Ireland (tel 01-493 4829).
*O'Grady-Peyton International* 332 Congress Street, Boston, Massachusetts 02210, USA, (tel +1-617-422 0300; fax 617-422 0399; Website www.opginc.com).
*Professional Connections:* 5 City Gate, Bridge Street Lower, Dublin 8, Ireland (tel 01-679 2277; fax 01-679 2396; e-mail profconn@iol.ie Website www.profco.com). Place nurses in Ireland, England and the Gulf states.

# Italy

*Italian Embassy:* 1601 Fuller Street, NW, Washington, DC 20009, USA (tel 202-328-5500; fax 202-483-2187).
*Italian Embassy:* 14 Three Kings Yard, London W1Y 2EH, UK (tel 020-7312 2200; 020-7312 2230).
*Italian Embassy:* 21st Floor, 275 Slater Street, Ottawa, Ontario K1P 5H9, Canada (tel 613-232-2401; fax 613-233-1484).
*Currency:* Lira (L).
*Exchange rate:* £1 = L3098; $1 = L1929.
*Capital:* Rome.
*International Telephone Code:* +39
*Population:* 57,746,000.
*Area:* 301,000 sq. km.
*Language:* Italian

Italy has been a republic since 1946, and is regarded as one of the more politically turbulent countries of the European Union. The industrialised, more prosperous north of the country contrasts strongly with the poorer south. Italy is divided into 20 regions, which are further divided into provinces; it is at this level that health services are administered.

## HEALTH SERVICES

The Italian national health service provides free hospital accommodation and medical treatment to those who make social security payments, receive a state pension, are unemployed or are under 18 years of age. The system takes up considerable government expenditure but delivers what is generally regarded as a poor standard of service. Out-patients are normally treated at GPs' surgeries.

In addition to the state health service Italy has a very expensive, but very efficient, private sector with some excellent private clinics and hospitals. Many of the best private hospitals are run by the Church. Private medical insurance is popular in Italy in order to cover costs incurred in private health care.

Italy has an over-supply of doctors and produces more medical practitioners than any other European country, although in many cases their training is lacking in practical experience.

## SKILLS AND QUALIFICATIONS

As described on page 107, the recognition of professional qualifications throughout the EU/EEA is covered by Directive 93/16. For detailed enquiries on these matters in Italy, contact the Presidenza Consiglio del Ministri at the Ministerio Coordinamento, Politiche Communitarie, Via Giardino Theodoli 65, 00186 Rome, Italy (tel 06-69 98 373; fax 06-69 91 668).

## VISAS AND WORK PERMITS

On arrival EU/EEA nationals with a pre-arranged job should register with the nearest police station (*questura*) to obtain a residence permit (*Permesso di Soggiorno*). *These are issued free of charge, initially for three months and then in periods of two or five years. You may also be required to obtain a work registration card (libretto di lavoro)*. In addition to the residence permit you will also need to obtain a certificate (*certificato di residenza*), although this may seem like bureaucracy gone mad, this last document entitles the holder to claim health care and open a bank account amongst other things.

Citizens of Australia and New Zealand, can enter Italy without visas for 90 days, although they will then have to apply for a longer stay visa, they can do this in Italy. Other nationals will require visas before entering and work permits will only be issued in their homeland if the employer can show that no Italian can do the job.

## JOB OPPORTUNITIES

The state-run Ufficio di Collocaménto Manodòpera is the only employment and recruitment agency that is officially allowed to operate in Italy. Private employment agencies may only legally function as temporary employment bureaux, and will be listed in the Italian yellow pages. Proficiency in Italian is likely to be an essential skill.

For applying directly to potential employers, you will need their contact details. A list of health centres and hospitals for the region(s) in which you are interested in working should be available from the local health authority (again, consult the yellow pages).

## PROFESSIONAL ORGANISATIONS

*Associazione Italiana di Dietetica & Nutrizionie Clinica:* Via Lucilio 29, Rome I-00136, Italy.

*Associazione Italiana Technici di Laboratorio Biomedico:* (medical laboratory technologists) Via C Farini 70, I-20159 Milan, Italy.

*Associazione Italiana di Terapia Occupazionale:* (occupational therapists) Via Peralba 9, I-00141 Rome, Italy.

*Associazione Italiana Terapisti della Rehabilitazione:* (physiotherapists) Via Claterna 18, I-00183 Rome, Italy (tel/fax 06-772 01020; e-mail aitrn@mclink.it Website www.aitr.it).

*Associazione Nazionale Dentisti Italiani::* Via Savoia 78, I-00198 Rome, Italy.

*Consociazione Nazionale delle Associazioni Infermieri ed altri Operatori, Sanitario-Sociali:* (nurses' association) Via Arno 62, I-00198 Rome, Italy (tel/fax 06-884 0654).

*Federazione Nazionale Collegi Professional Technici Sanitari di Radiologia Medica:* (radiographers/radiological technologists) Via Ravenna 24, I-00161 Rome, Italy.

*Società Italiana di Medicina Generale (SIMG):* (medical association) Via Il Prato 66, I-50123 Firenze, Italy (Website www.smig.it).

*Società Optometrica Italiana:* (optometrists) Via G. Ancillotto 3, I-33170 Pordenone, Italy (tel 0434-532735; fax 0434-27610; Website www.freeweb.org/salute/optometria-sopti/).

# Luxembourg

*Embassy of the Grand Duchy of Luxembourg:* 2200 Massachusetts Avenue, NW, Washington, DC 20008, USA (tel 202-265-4171/2; fax 202-328-8270).

*Embassy of the Grand Duchy of Luxembourg:* 27 Wilton Crescent, London SW1X 8SD (tel 020-7235 6961; fax 020-7235 9734).

*Currency:* Luxembourg Franc (LF).

*Exchange rate:* £1 = LF64.5; $1 = LF40.19.

*Capital:* Luxembourg-Ville.

*International Telephone Code:* +352

*Population:* 390,000.

*Area:* 3000 sq. km.

*Languages:* German, French, Luxembourgish

This very small country has the lowest land area of all the European Union countries (although it is by no means the smallest state in Europe). Nestled between Germany, France and Belgium and the mixture of languages spoken reflects its location. The Grand Duchy is a constitutional monarchy, and is divided into 3 districts (Luxembourg, Diekirch and Grevenmacher), which subdivide into 12 cantons and 118 municipalities.

## HEALTH SERVICES

According to the most recent statistics available, there are 316 GPs, 532 specialists and 203 dentists in Luxembourg. The ratio of physicians per 1000 inhabitants in 1997 was 2.1 and there are 34 hospitals. The health system is funded by eight public and private funding schemes, the public schemes are: the Sickness Fund for Officials and Employees, the Sickness Fund for Officials and Employees of Local Authortities, the Sickness Fund for ARBED Workers and the Sickness Fund for ARBED Employees. In the private sector the funds are: the Sickness Fund for Workers, the Sickness Fund for Workers in the Private Sector, the Sickness Fund fro Self-Employed and the Agricultural Sickness Fund. In the four private schemes payments are made to different funds according to the area the individual works in. The funding schemes then reimburse the costs of healthcare (medical fees, prescription and convalesence charges). Each public fund is organised as a seperate financial and administrative entity, but the Union of Sickness Funds (*Union des Caisses de Maladie*) oversees the relationships between the funds and service providers. All the public funds come under the overall supervision of the Ministry of Social Security.

## SKILLS AND QUALIFICATIONS

As described on page 107, the recognition of professional qualifications throughout the EU/EEA is covered by Directive 93/16. For detailed enquiries on these matters in Luxembourg, contact the Ministère de l'Education.

## VISAS AND WORK PERMITS

EEA nationals can freely enter Luxembourg and look for work. A work permit is not required. EU/EEA nationals wanting to stay in Luxembourg for more than 3 months need to obtain an identity card.

Non-EEA nationals should apply to the Luxembourg Embassy in their home country for a visa, which will not however allow the applicant to seek employment in Luxembourg. These nationals will need to try to find employment by correspondence with potential employers, responding to advertisements in the Luxembourg press or communicating with the Administration de l'Emploi (Department of Employment). Having obtained employment, these nationals must apply for a work permit at the Ministère de la Justice; a *déclaration patronale* (employer's reference) will be needed to support the application. They will also need to apply for an identity card, which, if issued, serves as a residence permit and is valid for 5 years.

## JOB OPPORTUNITIES

Information on employment opportunities for foreign health care staff should be available from the Association des médecins et médecins-dentistes. Alternatively try the Ministère de la Santé or the Administration de l'Emploi.

German and French are languages very commonly used in Luxembourg, in addition to the national language, Luxembourgish, and knowledge of these languages is important for anyone looking for work.

## PROFESSIONAL ORGANISATIONS

*Association Luxembourgeoise des Assistants(ies) Techniques Medicaux de Radiology:* (radiographers/radiological technologists) 13 rue A Reding, L-5874 Hespereance, Luxembourg.

*Association Luxembourgeoise des Ergotherapeutes Diplomes:* (occupational therapists) Boîte Postale 1176, L-1011 Luxembourg.

*Association Luxembourgeoise des Kinesitherapeutes Diplomes:* (physiotherapists) Boîte Postale 645, L-2016 Luxembourg (tel 448039; fax 333904; e-mail gthommes@cmdnet.lu).

*Association des Médecins et Médecins-Dentistes:* (doctors and dentists) 29 rue de Vianden, L-2680 Luxembourg (tel 44 40 33; fax 45 83 49).

*Association Nationale des Dieteticien(ne)s du Luxembourg:* (dietitians) Postbus 62, L-7201 Walferdange, Luxembourg.

*Association Nationale des Infirmier(e)s Luxembourgeois(es):* (Luxembourg Nurses' Association) Boîte Postale 1184, L-1011 Luxembourg (tel 49 58 09; fax 40 85 85).

*Association Nationale des Laborantins Diplomes:* (medical laboratory technologists) Boîte Postale 1102, L-1011 Luxembourg

## USEFUL ADDRESSES

*Association d'Assurance Contre les Accidents:* 125 route d'Esch, L-1471 Luxembourg.

*Controle Medical de la Securite Sociale:* 125 route d'Esch, L1471 Luxembourg.

*Ministère de l'Education Nationale:* 29 rue Aldringen, L-2926 Luxembourg (tel 47 85 127; fax 47 85 130).

*Ministère de la Justice:* 16 boulevard Royal, L-2934 Luxembourg (tel 478 4510/4520; fax 227661).

*Ministère de la Santé:* (Ministry of Health) 57 et 90 boulevard de la Pétrusse, L-2320 Luxembourg (tel 4781; fax 484903).

*Ministere de la Securite Sociale:* 26 rue Ste Zith, L-2763 Luxembourg.

*Union des Caisses de Maladie:* 125 route d'Esch, L-1471 Luxembourg.

# The Netherlands

*Royal Netherlands Embassy:* 4200 Wisconsin Avenue, NW, Washington, DC 20016, USA (tel 202-244-5300; fax 202-537-5124).

*Royal Netherlands Embassy:* 38 Hyde Park Gate, London SW7 5DP (tel 020-7584 5040; fax 020-7581 3458).

*Royal Netherlands Embassy:* Suite 2020, 350 Albert Street, Ottawa, Ontario K1R 1A4, Canada (tel 613-237-5030; fax 613-237-6471).

*Currency:* Guilder (Dfl).
*Exchange rate:* £1 = Dfl3.5; $1 = Dfl2.19.
*Capital:* Amsterdam.
*International Telephone Code:* +31
*Population:* 15,200,000.
*Area:* 34,000 sq. km.
*Language:* Dutch; English widely understood

The Netherlands is a constitutional monarchy, and a key advocate of closer European integration – the town of Maastricht, famous for its treaty, is in the south of the country.

The Netherlands is a small country and has reclaimed large amounts of land from the sea for its increasingly cramped population. It also has a successful economy and the Dutch enjoy a high standard of living.

# HEALTH SERVICES

The Netherlands has an excellent two-tier health care system. The health service operates through its GPs, who authorise hospital admittance and the use of specialists. The majority of curative care is provided by private organisations but the state provides some of the curative and most of the preventative care; such as health education, school health and screening programmes and medical research.

Health care is largely funded through a system of public and private insurance schemes. The funding of health care is a mix of social security, social insurance, private insurance, out-of-pocket payments and government subsidies. However, the deductions for public health provision have a financial cut-off point, if an individual earns more than this then they will have to take out private insurance. A distinction is made between what are seen as normal medical expenses and the exceptional costs associated with long-term or high-cost treatment, where the risk is such that it can not be borne by individuals or adequately covered by private insurance. Such cover is provided by a compulsory national insurance scheme under the Exceptional Medical Expenses Act; with a few exceptions, everyone living in the country is covered. The cost of insurance under this Act is covered by a percentage of taxable income, flat-rate contributions and government funds.

The provision of health care takes up 8.9% of Dutch GDP, the money coming from allocations under the Exceptional Medical Expenses Act (42%), the Health Insurance Act (31%), private insurance (15%), government subsidies (5%) and other sources (7%).

### Salaries
According to the Ministry of Health, Welfare and Sport, salaries for general practitioners are generally in the range Dfl144,000–151,000, and for medical specialists Dfl186,000–200,000.

## SKILLS AND QUALIFICATIONS

As described on page 107, the recognition of professional qualifications throughout the EU/EEA is covered by Directive 93/16. For detailed enquiries on these matters in the Netherlands, contact NUFFIC. In the Netherlands most health professions are regulated by law, including doctors, dentists, pharmacists, nurses, midwives, dietitians, occupational therapists, physiotherapists, speech therapists, dental hygienists, orthoptists, podotherapists and radiographers.

In order to be allowed to practise in the Netherlands foreign professionals should write to the Ministerie van Volksgezondheid, Welzijn en Sport (Ministry of Health, Welfare and Sport).

## VISAS AND WORK PERMITS

EEA nationals and citizens of Australia, Canada, New Zealand and the USA do not need a visa to enter the Netherlands. Nationals of these countries need residence permits for stays of more than 3 months; other nationals need to apply to their nearest Dutch Embassy for permission to visit. Work permits are not needed by EU/EEA nationals; non-EEA nationals need to obtain work permits before they enter the country.

## JOB OPPORTUNITIES

The Ministry of Health, Welfare and Sport advises that generally speaking there is no particular need for overseas health professionals – the demand for and the supply of medical and most paramedical professions are more or less in balance. However there are some vacancies for GPs in the inner cities, and also in some medical specialisations – at the time of writing these included cardiology, ophthalmology, orthopaedics, paediatrics and rehabilitation. The Royal Dutch Medical Association may be able to provide up-to-date guidance on where the vacancies are.

There are numerous employment agencies (*uitzendbureaux*) in large towns throughout the country, and these may be worth approaching for temporary work in the health sector; consult the regional *Gouden Gids* (yellow pages) for addresses. One organisation that has information on temporary vacancies for doctors is Stichting Werkgelegenheid Geneeskundigen (Physicians Employment Foundation). Addresses of hospitals and medical organisations can be found in the *Geneeskundig Adresboek* (*Medical Address Book*), published yearly by Nijgh Periodieken te Schiedam. The government operates the Centraal Bureau voor de Arbeidsvoorziening (Central Bureau for the Supply of Labour), which may also be worth approaching for short-term positions.

There are also provisions for trained doctors, dentists and pharmacists to come to the Netherlands to work within the framework of an exchange programme between the Netherlands and a country outside the European Union, or for the benefit of international cultural relations. The employer submits an application for a temporary licence to the Ministry of Health. Foreign professionals applying in this way can work for a maximum of 2 years in the Netherlands to gain experience, if the training they received abroad is equivalent to that in the Netherlands. Further details are available from the Ministry of Health, Welfare and Sport.

## PROFESSIONAL ORGANISATIONS

*Koninklijk Nederlands Genootschap Fysiotherapie:* (physiotherapists) Postbus 248, NL-3800 AE Amersfoort, Van Hogendorplaan 8, The Netherlands (tel 033-467 2900; fax 033-467 2999; e-mail kngf@medilink.nl).

*Nederlandsche Maatschappij tot Bevordering der Tandheelkunde:* (dentists) Geelgors 1, Postbus 2000, NL-3430 CA Nieuwegein, The Netherlands (tel 030-607 6276; fax 030-604 8994; Website www.nmt.nl).

*Nederlandse Vereniging van Dietisten:* (dietitians) Secretariat EFAD, Boterstraat 1a, Postbus 341, NL-5340 AH Oss, The Netherlands (tel 04120-24543).

*Nederlandse Vereniging van Radiologisch Laboranten:* (radiographers/radiological technologists) Catharijnesingel 73, NL-3511 GM Utrecht, The Netherlands.

*Nederlandse Vereniging van Ergotherapie:* (occupational therapists) Kaap Hoorndreef 48B, NL-3536 AV Utrecht, The Netherlands.

*Nieuwe Unie '91:* (nurses' association) Leidseweg 83, Postbus 6001, NL-3503 PA Utrecht, The Netherlands (tel 030-964144; fax 030-963904).

*Royal Dutch Medical Association::* Postbus 20051, NL-2501 LB Utrecht, The Netherlands (tel 030-823911; fax 030-823326).

*Vereniging van Medische Analisten:* (medical laboratory technologists) Wilhelminapark 52, NL-3581 NM Utrecht, The Netherlands

## USEFUL ADDRESSES

*Centraal Bureau voor de Arbeidsvoorziening:* Postbus 437, NL-2280 AK Rijswijk, The Netherlands (tel 070-313 0228).

*Dutch Working Group on Nuclear Cardiology and Cardiovascular MRI:* Polikliniek Cardiologie, Gelreziekenhuizen, Postbox 9014, NL-7300 DS Apeldoorn, The Netherlands (tel 055-581 1319; fax 055-581 1331; Website www.nuclcard.nl).

*Ministerie van Justitie:* (Ministry of Justice) Postbus 20301, NL-2500 EH The Hague, The Netherlands; for residence permit applications.

*Ministerie van Sociale Zaken en Werkgelegenheid:* (Ministry of Social Affairs and Employment) Postbus 90801, NL-2509 LV The Hague, The Netherlands; for work permit applications.

*Ministerie van Volksgezondheid, Welzijn en Sport:* (Ministry of Health, Welfare and Sport) Postbus 5406, NL-2280 HK Rijswijk, The Netherlands (tel 070-340 6954/349 7409/340 7188).

*Nederlandse Zorgfederatie:* Postbus 9696, NL-3506 GR Utrecht, The Netherlands.

*Netherlands School of Public Health:* Admiraal Helfrichlaan 1, NL-3527 KV Utrecht, The Netherlands (tel 030-2913232; 030-2913242).

*NUFFIC:* Kortenaerkade 11, NL-2518 AX The Hague (tel 070-426 0260; fax 070-426 0395).

*Stichting Werkgelegenheid Geneeskundigen:* (Physicians Employment Foundation) Postbus 20058, NL-3502 LB Utrecht, The Netherlands.

---

# Norway

---

*Royal Norwegian Embassy:* 2720 34th Street, NW, Washington, DC 20008, USA (tel 202-333-6000; fax 202-337-0870; Website www.norway.org).

*Royal Norwegian Embassy:* 25 Belgrave Square, London SW1X 8QD (tel 020-7235 7151; fax 020-7245 6993).

*Royal Norwegian Embassy:* Suite 532, Royal Bank Centre, 90 Sparks Street, Ottawa, Ontario K1P 5B4, Canada (tel 613-238-6571; fax 613-238-2765).

*Currency:* Krone (Kr).

*Exchange rate:* £1 = Kr12.9; $1 = Kr8.07.

*Capital:* Oslo.

*International Telephone Code:* +47

*Population:* 4,274,000.

*Area:* 324,000 sq. km.

*Language:* Norwegian; English widely spoken

Norway is a beautiful country on the northern edge of Europe. It is a constitutional monarchy, with a form of government similar to that in the UK. North Sea oil has brought considerable prosperity to the country, and it now rates as one of Europe's wealthiest nations. Of the four countries considering joining the European Union in 1995, only Norway asserted its desire for independence and rejected membership.

## HEALTH SERVICES

There is a well developed health system in Norway and a very high standard of public health. Health care is essentially state-funded, though with the public sector complemented by a rising number of private hospitals and clinics. Most hospitals are in the public sector, and the majority of Norwegian doctors work in hospitals. Hospital treatment is free.

There is a compulsory national health insurance scheme for all residents.

## SKILLS AND QUALIFICATIONS

As described on page 107, the recognition of professional qualifications throughout the EU/EEA is covered by Directive 93/16. For detailed enquiries on these matters in Norway, contact the Ministry of Education.

There are 15 health care professions for which the Chief County Health Officer in Oslo provides authorisation or temporary licences to practise. These are: medical practitioner; dentist; dental hygienist; nurse; midwife; laboratory technician; auxiliary nurse; optometrist; psychologist; physiotherapist; chiropodist; chiropractor; occupational therapist; radiographer; and professional health worker for the mentally retarded. As Norway is a Nordic country, some health professionals benefit from the Joint Nordic Labour Market agreement of 1994 which allows individuals licenced to practice in one Nordic country to obtain corresponding rights in another Nordic country. Applicants from non-Nordic nations will have to provide a certain amount of documentation for the County Health Office to licence them. These applications can be sent in English, Danish, Norwegian or Swedish, contact the Officer at the address below for application details.

### Medicine

Several bodies participate in different ways in the registration of doctors: the universities evaluate the academic content of overseas qualifications, the public health authorities are responsible for official registration, and the Norwegian Medical Association is responsible for granting authorisation for specialist practice. The system is quite complex and a booklet entitled *Registration of Medical Practitioners in Norway* is essential reading for those interested; it is available from the Norwegian Board of Health or the Norwegian Medical Association.

Enquiries about how to obtain permission to practise as a specialist should be forwarded to the Norwegian Medical Association (address below).

### Physiotherapy

Physiotherapists from the EU and Nordic countries need to supply certified documentation of their education, registration, a copy of a valid passport, a certficate of good standing from a health authority and work experience documentation. Those from outside the EU will need to supply all the above plus details of the full programme of their training. One exception is that physiotherapists from Germany are treated seperately undergoing a nine-month trial period, as their curriculum seems to lack some of the training expected of a Norwegian physiotherapist.

## VISAS AND WORK PERMITS

Passport holders from Nordic and EU/EEA nations, the USA, Australia, Canada, New Zealand, and 57 other countries (contact the Directorate of Immigration for full details) can enter Norway without a visa.

If you are a national of an EU/EEA country, you are entitled to stay in Norway and look for work for a three-month period without having to obtain a work or residence permit, as long as you can support yourself. If you find work within the three-month period, you must apply for a residence permit, for which you will need a certificate of employment and a valid passport, residence permits are usually valid for 5 years. The permit can be obtained from the local police, or if you are taking up a post from outside Norway through the nearest embassy or consulate. Applications in Norway must be supported by proof of employment, if taking over a private practice then accounts and financial statements are required as well as permission from the relevant authorities. EU/EEA nationals will find further information in the booklets *Residence Permits in Norway* available from the Directorate of Immigration and *Looking for Work in Norway:* available from the Directorate of Labour. Those taking over a practice should obtain and read the pamphlet *For Immigrants Who Wish to Run a Business in Norway* available from the Ministry of Trade and Industry.

Nationals of non-EEA countries are very unlikely to be allowed in to Norway to work, unless they have special skills that local job applicants do not possess. If you have received an offer of employment in Norway due to the demand for your qualifications, you must apply for a work and residence permit through the Norwegian Embassy in your country.

All foreign nationals must undertake a medical examination for tuberculosis, this is free and should be arranged with the nearest health authority in Norway.

## JOB OPPORTUNITIES

In general Norway has adequate numbers of health care staff, so that there is no great need for overseas personnel. There are a few notable areas of need, however. Norway is experiencing a shortage of medical practitioners, and in particular in certain specialist areas: anaesthetics, morbid anatomy and histopathology, radiology, paediatric surgery and psychiatry. This shortage is mainly in northern and rural parts of the country. There is also an overall shortage of nurses, partly due to many Norwegian nurses working only part-time, and others not working at all. There also appears to be an increasing number of nurses working in non-nursing-related jobs.

Physiotherapists can find vacancies in the professional journal *Fysoterapeuten* which has 14 issues per year. The job market in this profession is healthy with no unemployment and physiotherapists in public employment have a minimum wage of Kr180,000 per annum, while those in private practice can earn up to Kr420,000.

Norway has a state-funded recruitment agency that can provide help to foreign applicants wanting to work in Norway – contact the Directorate of Labour for information. They should be able to provide information on jobs available for foreign health professionals. Alternatively the professional organisations listed below might be able to provide guidance.

Although English is widely understood in Norway, particularly among the professions, a sound knowledge of Norwegian is usually needed as you will be competing with Norwegian job-seekers for the available positions.

## PROFESSIONAL ORGANISATIONS

*Norges Apotekerforening:* (pharmacists) Slemsdalsvn 1, Postboks 5070 Maj, N-0301 Oslo, Norway (tel 22-69 60 40; fax 22-60 81 73; e-mail apotekerforeningen@apotek.no Website www.apotek.no).

*Norsk Bioingeniøforbund:* (medical laboratory technologists) Boks 9057, Grönland *obs:* 9057, N-0133 Oslo, Norway.

*Norsk Ergoterapeut Forbund:* (Norwegian Occupational Therapists' Association) Lakkegaten 19-21, N-0187 Oslo 1, Norway.

*Norsk Forening for Ernaering og Dietetikk:* (dietitians) Postboks 9202, Vaterland, N-0134 Oslo, Norway.

*Norske Fysioterapeuters Forbund:* (Norwegian Physiotherapists Association) Postboks 2704, St Hanshaugen, N-0131 Oslo, Norway (tel 22 93 30 50; fax 22 56 58 25; e-mail nff@fysio.no Website www.fysio.no).

*Norsk Psykologforening:* (Norwegian Psychological Association) Storgt. 10a, N-0155 Oslo, Norway.

*Norsk Radiografforbund:* (radiographers/radiological technologists) Lakkegate 19-

21, N-0187 Oslo, Norway.

*Norsk Sykepleierforbund:* (Norwegian Nurses' Association) Boks 2633, St Hanshaugen, N-0131 Oslo 1, Norway (tel 22 04 33 04; fax 22 71 60 96).

*Norske Fysioterapeutes Forbund:* (Norwegian Physiotherapists' Association) Postboks 7009, Majorstua, N-0306 Oslo, Norway (tel 22 69 78 00; fax 22 56 58 25).

*Norske Laegeforening:* (Norwegian Medical Association) Postboks 1152 sentrum, N-0107 Oslo, Norway (tel 23 10 90 00; fax 23 10 90 10; e-mail legeforeningen@legeforeningen.no Website www.legeforeningen.no).

*Norske Tannlaegeforening:* (Norwegian Dental Association) Frederik Stangs gt 20, N-0264 Oslo, Norway (tel 22-54 74 00; fax 22-55 11 09; e-mail tannlegeforeningen@tannlegeforeningen.no).

## USEFUL ADDRESSES

*Arbeidsdirektoratet:* (Directorate of Labour) Arbeidsmarkedsavdelingen (Labour Market Department) Postboks 8127 Dep., N-0032 Oslo, Norway (tel 22 94 24 00).

*Foetaksregisteret:* (Register of Business Enterprises) Postboks 1400, N-8901 Brønnøysund, Norway (tel 75 00 75 00).

*Fylkeslegen i Oslo:* (County Health Officer – Oslo) Postboks 8041 Dep, N-0031 Oslo, Norway (tel 22 00 39 00; fax 22 00 39 10).

*Fysioterapeuten:* PO Box 7009, Majorstua, N-0306 Oslo, Norway. Journal of the Norwegian Physiotherapists Association.

*Kirke- utdannings og forskningsdepartementet:* (Ministry of Education, Research and Church Affairs) Postboks 8119, N-0032 Oslo, Norway (tel 22 34 77 36; fax 22 34 27 33).

*Naerings-og Handelsdep:* (Ministry of Trade and Industry) Postboks 8014 Dep, N-0030 Oslo, Norway (tel 22 24 90 90).

*Rikstrygdeverket:* (National Insurance Administration) Drammensveien 60, N-0241 Oslo, Norway (tel 22 92 70 00; fax 22 55 70 88).

*Skattedirektoratet:* (Directorate of Taxes) Postboks 6300, Etterstad, N-0603 Oslo, Norway (tel 22 07 70 00).

*Sosial- og helsedepartementet:* (Ministry of Health and Social Affairs) Postboks 8011 Dep., N-0030 Oslo, Norway (tel 22 24 90 90).

*Statens helsetilsyn:* (Norwegian Board of Health) Postboks 8128 Dep, N-0032 Oslo, Norway (tel 22 24 88 88; fax 22 24 95 90).

*Utlendingsdirektoratet:* (Directorate of Immigration) Postboks 8108 Dep., N-0032 Oslo, Norway (tel 67 53 08 90; Website www.udi.no in French and English).

# Portugal

*Portuguese Embassy:* 2125 Kalorama Road, NW, Washington, DC 20008, USA (tel 202-328-8610; fax 202-462-3726).

*Portuguese Embassy:* 11 Belgrave Square, London SW1X 8PP (tel 020-7235 5331/4; fax 020-7245 1287).

*Portuguese Embassy:* 645 Island Park Drive, Ottawa, Ontario K1Y 0B8, Canada (tel 613-729-0883; fax 613-729-4236).

*Currency:* Escudo ($).

*Exchange rate:* £1 = 321$; $1 = 199$.

*Capital:* Lisbon.

*International Telephone Code:* +351

*Population:* 9,858,000.
*Area:* 92,000 sq. km.
*Language:* Portuguese

Portugal is a republic, and has been a member of the European Union since 1986. Membership has accelerated the process of modernisation in the country, although Portugal is still relatively under-developed compared to most countries in western Europe. Portugal has strong links with Britain, going back to the 14th century, making it a hospitable place for UK citizens.

## HEALTH SERVICES

Health care in Portugal is partly state-funded and partly private. The state system is run by the Ministério da Saúde. Standards of care in the public health service are not as high as in some other countries in western Europe, and while treatment in public hospitals and essential medicines are free, waiting times for an appointment or treatment often outweigh this benefit. The majority of Portuguese therefore take out private health insurance to ensure access to the private clinics and health centres. In the Algarve and other developed areas of Portugal there is an increasing number of private medical and dental clinics, these are staffed by Portuguese who have come over from the public sector or by foreigners. the clinics often specialise in just one area of medicine.

There are British hospitals in Lisbon and Porto. The Lisbon hospital is small and non-profit making, these hospitals also run out-patient services.

## SKILLS AND QUALIFICATIONS

As described on page 107, the recognition of professional qualifications throughout the EU/EEA is covered by Directive 93/16. For detailed enquiries on these matters in Portugal, contact the Ministry of Education.

## VISAS AND WORK PERMITS

Even though EU/EEA nationals can enter and work freely, they should still obtain a residence permit before entering the country as this will help them avoid the worst of the bureaucracy. This *Autorização de Residencia* which will help you to obtain a job, can be applied for from outside Portugal from the Foreigners' Department of the Ministry of Internal Affairs (*Serviço de Estrangeiros e Fronteiras*), although this may prove time-consuming. Within six months of settling, the expatriate should also obtain an Identity Card (*Arquivo de Identificação*). Other nationalities will need to obtain a residence visa and then the permit, although Americans, Canadians and Australians can enter without a visa for up to 60 days (90 for Australians). Europeans do not need work permits, only their *residencia* and Identity Card, but those wishing to work in Portugal should arrange a work permit at the same time as they arrange for a residence visa, to obtain this you will need the contract from your employer and approval from the Ministry of Labour.

## JOB OPPORTUNITIES

Most Portuguese newspapers feature job advertisements each day. The *Diário de Notícias* and *Público* feature the most jobs in the Lisbon area, while *Jornal de Notícias* is better for vacancies in Porto. English-language newspapers such as the *Anglo-Portuguese News Portugal Post* and *Algarve News* also advertise vacancies.

The Portuguese equivalent of a British Jobcentre is a *Centro do Emprego*, and it may be worth contacting the *Centro* in your region for information on health opportunities. The majority of employment agencies are based in Lisbon and Porto. They are listed in the *Páginas Amarelas* (yellow pages), and you can contact them to find any that operate in the health sector.

## PROFESSIONAL ORGANISATIONS

*Associaçao Nacional dos Dentistas Portugueses* (dentists) Rua Pascoal de Melo 15B – 2nd Piso, P-1100 Lisbon, Portugal.

*Associaçao Portuguesa de Enfermeiros* (Portuguese Nurses' Association) Rua Duque de Palmela No 27-4⁰ D, P-1200 Lisbon, Portugal (tel/fax 21-353 55 43).

*Associaçao dos Tecnicos de Radiologia de Portugal* (radiographers/radiological technologists) Travessa das Almas 32, c/v Esq, P-1200 Lisbon, Portugal.

*Associaçao Portuguesa de Fisioterapeutas* (physiotherapists) Ave Alvares Cabral 1A-2⁰, P-1250 Lisbon, Portugal (tel/fax 21-386 1344; e-mail apfisio@mail.telepac.pt).

*Ordem dos Farmacêuticos:* (Portuguese Pharamcists Association) Rua da Sociedade Farmacêutica 18, P-1000 Lisbon, Portugal (tel 21-319 1399; fax 21-319 1370).

*Ordem dos Médicos* (Portuguese Medical Association) Av Almirante Gago Coutinho 151, P-1749-084 Lisbon, Portugal (tel 21-8427100; fax 21-8427101).

## USEFUL ADDRESSES

*Foreigners' Department (Ministry of Internal Affairs), Serviço de Estrangeiros e Fronteiras:* Avenida Antonio Augusto Aguiar 20, Lisbon, Portugal.

*Ministry of Employment and Social Security, Mininstério do Emprego e Segurança Social:* Praça de Londres, 1000 Lisbon, Portugal. This ministry is in charge of all the employment service offices, Centros Emprego.

*Ministério da Educação:* Av. 5 Outubro 107, P-1069-018 Lisbon, Portugal (tel 21-793 1603; fax 21-796 4119).

*Ministério da Saúde:* Av João Crisóstomo 9, P-1000 Lisbon, Portugal (tel 21-354 4560; fax 21-314 2861)

## VOLUNTARY ORGANISATIONS

*Cruz Vermelha Portuguesa* (Portuguese Red Cross) Jardim 9 de Abril 1/5, P-1200 Lisbon, Portugal (tel 21-605571; fax 21-395 1045)

## BRITISH HOSPITALS

*British Hospital:* Rua Saraiva de Carvalho 49, P-1200 Lisbon, Portugal (tel 21-602020).

*British Hospital:* Rua da Bandeirinha 12, Porto, Portugal.

# Spain

*Spanish Embassy:* 2375 Pennsylvania Avenue, NW, Washington, DC 20037, USA (tel 202-452-0100/728 2340; fax 202-833-5670).

*Spanish Embassy:* 24 Belgrave Square, London SW1X 8SB, UK (tel 020-7235 5555/6/7; fax 020-7235 9905).

*Spanish Embassy:* Suite 802, 350 Sparks Street, Ottawa, Ontario K1R 7S8, Canada (tel 613-237 2193/4; fax 613-236-9246).
*Currency:* Peseta (Pta).
*Exchange rate:* £1 = Pta 266; $1 = Pta165.
*Capital:* Madrid.
*International Telephone Code:* +34
*Population:* 38,872,000.
*Area:* 505,000 sq. km.
*Language:* Spanish

Spain has been a democratic state since the death of Franco in 1975, and joined the European Union in 1986. As well as being an extremely popular destination with tourists from the UK, there is a large British expatriate population in the country, increasing Spain's appeal for UK citizens considering living there.

## HEALTH SERVICES

The Spanish health system is based on providing universal access to health care, with the addition of private healthcare for those who wish to pay for it. Public health care covers 98% of the Spanish population, provides two-thirds of the health sector, and is paid for principally through tax revenues and social security contributions. The body responsible for the national health service is the Instituto Nacional de la Salud (INSALUD) – the National Health Institute. About 8% of the population has some type of private health insurance.

The public health system is increasingly based on 'primary assistance units', which provide the population with integrated health care services. In addition 'support units' cover maternal and child health care, women's health, mental health (out-patients and community care) and physiotherapy.

However, for all the improvements to the system (in the 1980s only 86% of the population were eligible for public healthcare) there are still incidences of easily preventable illnesses such as TB, tetanus and diptheria in poorer areas. This is due to a concentration on curative rather than preventative care, and problems in the administration and distribution of resources. This is changing, but free treatment is still only available in a limited number of hospitals.

There are 799 hospitals in Spain. In terms of capacity, the public hospitals are the most important; private hospitals account for 58% of the hospitals, but for only 31% of the number of beds.

According to recent statistics the number of registered doctors is approximately 154,000, dentists 11,500, nurses 162,000, midwives 6500 and physiotherapists 2000. The number of health professionals has notably increased in recent years. Approximately 78% of health professionals work in the public health sector.

## SKILLS AND QUALIFICATIONS

As described on page 107, the recognition of professional qualifications throughout the EU/EEA is covered by Directive 93/16. For detailed enquiries on these matters in Spain, contact the Ministerio de Educación y Ciencia at the address below.

## VISAS AND WORK PERMITS

EEA nationals have to apply for a residence card if they wish to stay in Spain for over 3 months. If the stay is for less than a year, a temporary residence card will be issued; otherwise a five-year residence card will be granted.

If you are not an EU/EEA national you will need a residence visa. If you have been offered employment in Spain, both a visa and a work permit must be obtained before you arrive. Your prospective employer must draw up a formal offer of employment, which you will then need to produce when you apply for your residence visa in Spain. To obtain a work permit you will need to produce your employment contract and the visa. Work permits may be restricted to a specific area, type of work and employer.

## JOB OPPORTUNITIES

There are no private employment agencies in Spain. To find out about employment opportunities, therefore, you will need to contact the job centre(s) (*Oficinas de Empleo*) in the region(s) in which you are interested, study the local press or personally approach prospective employers. Addresses of hospitals and other health care services in the public sector should be available from INSALUD.

Spain has a surplus of professionals in medicine, and any demand that exists for foreign professionals is likely to be in providing health services for expatriates in certain parts of the country. The large British expatriate community in the country means that there may be employment opportunities for UK nationals in Spain that do not exist in other European countries. The medical field is one area where such opportunities might arise, and INSALUD or your professional association in Spain may be able to provide further information. However, as there is no central planning of staffing levels, the extent of any demand will probably only be discovered by making enquiries at the local level.

### PROFESSIONAL ORGANISATIONS

*Asociacion Espanola de Fisioterapeutas* (physiotherapists) Conde de Penalver, 38-2°, E-28006 Madrid, Spain (tel 91-401 11 36; fax 91-401 27 49).

*Asociacion Espanola de Microcirugia:* (microsurgeons) Santa Isabel 51, E-28012 Madrid, Spain (fax 91-804 44 11; e-mail informa@microcirugia.org Website http://microcirugia.org).

*Asociacion Espanola de Técnicos de Laboratorio* (medical laboratory technologists) c/o Mayor 6;1, E-28013 Madrid, Spain.

*Asociacion Professional Espanola de Terapia Ocupacional* (occupational therapists) c/o Modesto Lafuente 63 3°C, E-28002 Madrid, Spain.

*Consejo General de Colegios, Oficiales de Médicos* (doctors) Villanueva 11, E-28001 Madrid, Spain (tel 91-431 7236; fax 91-575 9548/576 4388).

*Organización Colegial de Enfermería* (nurses' association) Consejo General, C/. Don Ramón de la Cruz 67, E-28001 Madrid, Spain (tel 91-401 1200; fax 91-309 3049).

*Spanish Dietetic Association:* Avda Vallvidrera 73, Edificio Cruz Roja, E-08017 Barcelona, Spain

### USEFUL ADDRESSES

*Instituto Nacional de la Salud (INSALUD):* Alcalán 56, E-28071 Madrid, Spain.

*Ministerio de Educación y Ciencia:* Subdirección de Titulos, Convalidaciones y

Homologaciones, P. del Prado, 28-5a planta, E-28014 Madrid, Spain (tel 91-420 1625/3660; fax 91-420 3325).

# Sweden

*Royal Swedish Embassy:* 1501 M Street, NW, Washington, DC 20005, USA (tel 202-467-2600; fax 202-467-2699).
*Royal Swedish Embassy:* 11 Montagu Place, London W1H 2AL, UK (tel 020-7917 6400; fax 020-7724 4174).
*Royal Swedish Embassy:* Mercury Court, 377 Dalhousie Street, Ottawa, Ontario K1N 9N8, Canada (tel 613-241-8553; fax 613-241-2277).
*Currency:* Krona (Kr).
*Exchange rate:* £1 = Kr13.75; $1 = Kr8.57.
*Capital:* Stockholm.
*International Telephone Code:* +46
*Population:* 8,692,000.
*Area:* 441,000 sq. km.
*Language:* Swedish; English widely spoken

Sweden is a prosperous, modern country with a high standard of living and a famously comprehensive welfare system. It is a constitutional monarchy, and has recently come more into the mainstream of western European life through its joining the European Union in 1995.

## HEALTH SERVICES

About 9% of the Swedish GDP goes on health care, and health services in Sweden are generally of a very high standard. All Swedes are covered by the national health insurance system, which provides medical care, medicine, hospitalisation and most dental services either free of charge or at a small cost. The national insurance system is operated by a government agency, the National Social Insurance Board (*Riksförsäkringsverket*) which has local offices (*Försäkringskassan*) for payment of pensions and benefits.

Sweden has a decentralised health care system, with the county councils almost totally responsible for the funding and operation of services. The councils have considerable autonomy and the power to raise money through taxation. Together they run 90 hospitals and over 900 community-based health care centres. Medical care in Sweden has traditionally been hospital-oriented, with a high number of hospital beds by international standards, but in recent years primary care has been expanded and the number of hospital beds considerably reduced.

About 90% of all physicians in Sweden are employed in the county council sector; the remainder work as university teachers, private practitioners, and in occupational health and the pharmaceutical industry.

GPs in Sweden are usually salaried employees, and are qualified as specialists in family medicine. Similarly training posts for junior doctors are salaried positions with the county councils.

### Oral Healthcare

Swedish dentists have to work under an ethical code set by the Swedish Dental Association, private dentists have a similar code enforced by their association, and the Dental Act, states that all Swedish citizens are entitled to good quality Dental care. Free dental care for under 19s is provided by the Public Dental Service (NDS) within the framework of local government health centres. Adults can get subsidised care within the NDS, or on a fee per item basis at private dental practices, with care being subsidised at higher levels. For example where dental work costs less than Kr700 the patient will bear the entire cost, but above that the patient will bear 65% of the cost, dropping to 30% if treatment costs more than Kr13500. However, this system only covers dental work carried out by dentists who are affiliated to the social insurance system, and treatments like crowns and bridges have to be approved by the local insurance office in advance. Currently around 1% of Swedes have private dental insurance, mostly to cover expensive dental treatment.

At present around 99% of dentists in Sweden are employed or affiliated to the public dental service, the Swedish dental system is therefore similar to that of the UK where dentists club together to form a practice group, which then carries out subsidised or private dental treatment. However, such practices are referred to as 'private practices', the term 'general practice' indicating to a Swede that you have not specialised. Only 1% of Swedish dentists carry out entirely private treatment.

Private dental treatment is available in Sweden, in two schemes: *Praktikertjänst* where doctors or dentists form a collective company and that available from the Swedish Association of Private Dental Practitioners (PTL).

As with the NHS system in the UK for doctors, dentists in public practice are insured for liability by the social insurance system. Those in private practice have access to scheme run by the PTL, which costs around Kr1600 per annum.

## SKILLS AND QUALIFICATIONS

Information on registration requirements for foreign doctors and nurses is available from the National Board of Health and Welfare (address below). The following health care professionals should contact the Board for authorisation to practise in Sweden: doctors, dentists, dental hygienists, nurses, midwives, physiotherapists, chiropractors, opticians, pharmacists, psychologists, psychotherapists and speech therapists. When you contact the Board you will be sent a form that you need to complete and return, together with proof of your qualifications. A work and residence permit granted by the Board of Immigration is also required (though note that a permit granted on the basis of an offer of employment is not acceptable).

In the case of specialists and those with considerable medical experience, the compulsory 'complementary training' comprises a probationary period of 6 months in a Swedish hospital; others are required to pass a written and oral examination at Swedish graduation level. If the results of the medical examination/probationary appointment are satisfactory, then the Board will prescribe the requirements for registration for the particular applicant; these very often comprise the Swedish pre-registration period (*allmäntjänstgöring*), which lasts 21 months, and the applicant's educational background and experience will be taken into account. In addition a course in Swedish medical legislation is compulsory. Applicants also need to learn Swedish, and a compulsory language test must be passed before a medical appointment will be granted.

### Dentistry

In order to practise in Sweden, dentists must have been granted a licence and registered by the National Board for Health and Welfare, Division for Qualifications and Training. At present there are around 1200 dentists in 8 specialities, with an expected shortfall of 30% by 2006.

Dental Hygienists are licensed by the same body as for dentists, and while they may work independently most work within dental practices. A second dental assistant is the Orthodontic Auxilliary, these work under the direction of an orthodontist, undertaking one year of training and eventually they can carry out basic examinations, do bonding and simple arch work, so in this respect they are similar to dental therapists.

## VISAS AND WORK PERMITS

EEA, US and Canadian nationals do not need a visa for a visit to Sweden of up to 3 months; residence permits are required for longer stays. EU/EEA nationals do not need work permits; other nationals can apply for one from their nearest Swedish Embassy, once they have an offer of employment and they should obtain a residence permit in order to apply for professional registration.

## JOB OPPORTUNITIES

According to the National Board of Health and Welfare, opportunities for foreign medical personnel to be granted permission to practise are very limited, largely due to the lack of resources available to provide the compulsory complementary training (see above).

In recent years the number of Swedish physicians has steadily increased – from 1970 to 1995 the figure almost trebled, so that now there is one doctor for every 330 inhabitants. Two-thirds of these are specialists (including specialists in family medicine).

In addition to the doctors that graduate each year from the country's medical faculties, there is a yearly influx of some 200 doctors from non-EU countries, who are granted residence permits for political, humanitarian or family reasons. At the time of writing there is a surplus of physicians, with nearly 1000 doctors registered as looking for work – this figure includes many foreigners. There is strong competition for training posts, and particularly for specialist training.

Financial difficulties experienced by the county councils since the early 1990s mean that expansion in the provision of health services has ceased. The labour market for doctors is likely to remain fairly static for the forseeable future, though with some surplus likely. In the longer term, there may be increased demand for trained specialists in the early decades of next century.

Posts for physicians are advertised in the Swedish Medical Journal (*Läkartidningen*); usually physicians are employed in a position for an indefinite period, though there are exceptions – in the university hospitals, for example, where a contract period of 6 years is common. The physiotherapists' association magazine *Sjukgymnasten* carries vacancy listings and can give a good idea of the work situation in Sweden.

With dentistry training taking 5 years, the wastage rate through retirement of dental practitioners has been predicted as leading to a shortage of around 30%, although this will affect some specialisations more tham others.

## PROFESSIONAL ORGANISATIONS

*Institutet för Biomedicinsk Laboratorievetenskap* (medical laboratory technologists) Adolf Fredriks Kyrkogata 11, S-11137 Stockholm, Sweden.
*Legitimerade Sjukgymnasters Riksförbund* (Swedish Association of Registered Physiotherapists) PO Box 3196, S-103 63 Stockholm, Sweden (tel 08-696 97 45; fax 08-696 97 54; e-mail kansli@lsr.se Website www.lsr.se).
*Svensk Dietistforening (SDF)* (dietitians) S:t Eriksgatan 26, Box 12069, S-10222

Stockholm, Sweden.

*Sveriges Läkarförbund* (Swedish Medical Association) Villagatan 5, PO Box 5610, S-11486 Stockholm, Sweden (tel 08-790 33 00; fax 08-20 57 18; Website www.slf.se/).

*Svierges Privattandläkarförening:* (Swedish Association of Private Dental Practitioners) tel 08-666 1500; fax 08-661 2761; e-mail info@ptl.se.

*Svierges Tandläkarförbund:* (Swedish Dental Association) Box 5843, S-10248 Stockholm, Sweden (tel 08-666 1500; fax 08-662 5842; e-mail info@tandlakarforbundet.se Website www.tandlakarforbundet.se).

*Swedish Association of Health Officers* (contact for nurses) PO Box 3260, S-10365 Stockholm, Sweden (tel 08-14 77 00; fax 08-411 56 37).

*Swedish Association of Occupational Therapists:* PO Box 760, S-13124 Nacka, Sweden.

*Swedish Association of Ophthamologists:* Website www.svls.se.

## USEFUL ADDRESSES

*Läkartidningen (Swedish Medical Journal):* PO Box 5603, S-11486 Stockholm, Sweden (tel 08-790 33 00; fax 08-20 76 19).

*Landstingsförbundet (Federation of Swedish County Councils):* PO Box 70491, S-10726 Stockholm, Sweden (tel 08-702 43 00; fax 08-702 45 90).

*National Agency for Higher Education:* PO Box 7851, S-10333 Stockholm, Sweden (tel 08-453 70 00; fax 08-453 71 40).

*Socialstyrelsen (National Board of Health and Welfare):* BU-enheten, S-10630 Stockholm, Sweden; visiting address Linnégatan 87 (tel 08-783 30 00; fax 08-783 34 20).

*Svenska Dgabladet:* (newspaper) Gjörwellsgatan 28, S-10517 Stockholm, Sweden (tel 08-135000; Website www.svd.se).

*Svenska Läkaresällskapet* (Swedish Society of Medicine) PO Box 738, S-10135 Stockholm (tel 08-440 88 60; 08-440 88 99).

*Swedish Dental Journal & Tandläkartiidningen (Journal of the Swedish Dental Association):* PO Box 5843, S-10248 Stockholm, Sweden (tel 08-666 1542; fax 08-662 5842).

# United Kingdom

*Embassy of the United Kingdom:* 3100 Massachusetts Avenue, NW, Washington, DC 20008, USA (tel 202-462-1340; fax 202-898-4255).

*British High Commission:* 80 Elgin Street, Ottawa, Ontario K1P 5K7, Canada (tel 613-237-1530; fax 613-237-7980).

*Currency:* Pound (£).
*Exchange rate:* $1 = £0.62.
*Capital:* London.
*International Telephone Code:* +44
*Population:* 58,191,000.
*Area:* 242,000 sq. km.
*Language:* English

The United Kingdom is a popular destination for overseas health professionals, especially those from the other major English-speaking countries. Not only do these workers find British life relatively easy to adapt to, but there is a considerable availability of work. The UK is also a fascinating country to visit – London remains one of the world's most dynamic and economically important cities, and in the Scottish Highlands the UK has some of Europe's most outstanding scenery.

## HEALTH SERVICES

Most health care in the UK is provided by the National Health Service (NHS), which was founded in 1948 with the aim of providing health care to all, regardless of their means. Only 11% of the UK population has private health insurance. But for all its importance to the health of the nation the NHS recieves less money per capita than health services in many other nations; the USA spends £1,195 per person in its public system, Germany £1,146, while the UK trickles in at £740.

In the last decade the NHS has experienced a period of dramatic restructuring and the current Labour government has pledged to improve waiting times and the retainment and recruitment of staff. Staffing levels are at the heart of most problems in the NHS, there may be many beds in hospitals but if there are no staff to nurse the patient in them then they will not be used and stand idle. The problems of staff morale and retention are directly related to the shortage of staff, in a vicious circle of falling staff numbers. This has lead some NHS Trusts to discuss staff retention strategies with major supermarket chains in a bid to find out what will work best. One result of this is to offer flexible hours and retraining to entice staff who have left back into the health job market. Another approach is job-sharing in a bid to win back those nurses and physiotherapists who have left to raise families, while the government recently stepped in with a large boost to pay across all levels of nursing. The solution most often applied has been to recruit staff from overseas from places as far apart as Finland and Australia.

However, the government is faced with a long and politically embarrasing struggle which may not be resolved even by the next election. One attempt to improve funding has been to direct £300 million of tax revenues raised on tobacco directly into the NHS' coffers.

According to the latest management model, 'providing' is the responsibility of hospitals and community health services, who deliver the services, and 'purchasing' is the responsibility of the health authorities and fundholding GPs, who assess the health needs of their local populations and purchase the services to meet those needs. Purchasers buy in health care from self-governing NHS Trusts or privately run hospitals. Whether the consequent competition between providers and the risk of Trusts being driven out of business is in the best interests of long-term health care planning has yet to be seen.

Staff are now employed by the NHS Trusts rather than by the health authorities, as before. NHS GPs are self-employed and have contracts with the local health authorities, whereas doctors in the hospital service, public health medicine and community health are NHS employees. Over 10,000 GPs in over 2600 practices in England are now fundholders, providing services for 41% of the population. The money these GPs are allotted is used to purchase hospital treatment, drugs, medicines and other medical services for their patients and to pay for their staff. Most doctors in the UK practise in the NHS. The ratio of doctors to every 1000 people is 1.5.

## SKILLS AND QUALIFICATIONS

Professionals of any nation who wish to work in the UK can of course contact professional organisations for information on having their qualifications recognised, but they can also contact the National Advice Centre for Postgraduate Medical Education (NACPME). This is an information and advice centre for overseas-qualified doctors who wish to undertake medical training in the UK, operated by the British Council on behalf of the Department of Health. NACPME aims to provide doctors with as much information as they need either before coming to the UK or during their stay here.

NACPME provides information in the following areas: General Medical Council registration; the Professional and Linguistic Assessments Board (PLAB) test, and Categories of Exemption; International English Language Testing System (IELTS) as well as general information on immigration, employment, postgraduate courses and Royal College examinations. NACPME information can be found on the Internet as well as being available by post.

Doctors who are overseas should contact the British Council in their own country as they will be able to supply information on NACPME; overseas doctors in the UK and overseas doctors who do not have a British Council office in their own country should contact NACPME in Manchester or visit the Information Centre in London.

Another organisation offering help with studies for the UK registration and postgraduate medical and dental exams is UEPI, (Mounters Lane, Chawton, Alton, GU34 1RE, UK; tel/fax +44-1420-84184). Their correspondence courses to help prepare for the theory papers have been offered to UK and overseas medical and dental graduates since the last century. Examples of courses are PLAB/Dental Statutory, MRCP/MRCPCH, MRCOG, FRCS (General Surgery, ENT and Ophthalmology) and FDS.

## Dentistry

Dentists in the UK need to have a dental degree and to register with the General Dental Council (GDC) in order to practise. They can work in general practice seeing private or NHS patients or a mixture of the two, or they can work in hospitals. Those who wish to work in NHS general practice as associates or in their own practice must have their name entered on the local Health Authority's (Health Board in Scotland and Northern Ireland) Dental List. Dentists qualifying from UK dental schools must undertake a one-year vocational training period in practice, dentists from other EU dental schools are free to enter a NHS list without doing so. Information on practising in the UK can also be found on the British Dental Association's website www.bda-dentistry.org.uk/dentist/education/uk, as well as in the association's handbook 'Practising Dentistry in the UK' which can be posted to overseas dentists.

Dentists who obtained qualifications in the EU/EEA are eligible for registration as are those holding qualifications from Australia, Hong Kong, Malaysia (if obtained between 1950-1962), Malta (if obtained before 1978), New Zealand, Singapore and South Africa. Dentists from other countries are required to pass the GDC Statutory Examination, which allows non-EU dentists to gain UK registration without having to retrain. The exams are held twice a year and comprise written and clinical components. Information on this exam, which will be the International Qualifying Examination from 2000 onwards, can be obtained from the GDC.

Temporary registration is possible for those wishing to undertake clinical postgraduate training in the UK. Information on courses can be obtained from the National Advice Centre for Postgraduate Dental Education (Faculty of Dental Surgery, The Royal College of Surgeons of England, 35-43 Lincoln's Inn Fields, London, WC2A 3PN, UK; tel 020-7973 2181; fax 020-7973 2183).

## Biomedical Science

A degree in a relevant science subject is usually necessary to work in biomedical science. There is a register for medical laboratory scientific officers administered by the appropriate board of the Council for Professions Supplementary to Medicine, and registration is essential for officers working in the NHS and some related fields.

## Medicine

To work as a doctor in the UK it is necessary to register with the General Medical Council – for this you will need your original degree certificates, a current certificate of registration from your country and a letter of good standing from your medical council. In addition all UK hospitals now stipulate that doctors must be immunised against hepatitis B, so current status or proof of immunisation is required in all cases. No work or training involving direct contact with patients should take place until the doctor has applied for and obtained the appropriate registration certificate.

There are two levels of registration; full and limited, awarded by the GMC according to your qualifications and where they were gained. Doctors with EU/EEA citizenship and an EU/EEA primary medical qualification can obtain full registration. EU/EEA citizens who qualified outside the EEA may be eligible according to which medical school they qualified from. The regulations governing doctors from non-EEA countries are more complicated than those applying to doctors from the EU/EEA. Graduates of medical schools in Australia, Hong Kong, New Zealand, Singapore, South Africa and the West Indies may apply for full registration. Doctors whose qualifications are on the WHO list of approved courses are eligible to apply for registration with the GMC. Non-EEA doctors may qualify for full registration, or be eligible for limited registration. These doctors will need to produce evidence that they have appropriate knowledge and skills in medicine for working in the UK. Limited registration may be granted only for employment supervised by a fully registered medical practitioner, in training predominantly based in approved hospital posts. Limited registration lasts only twelve months, but it can be applied for on a consecutive basis up to total of five years. Doctors seeking limited registration must first pass, or be exempt from, the GMC's PLAB test, the Professional and Linguistic Assessments Board (PLAB) test assesses medical competence and English language proficiency. However, GMC registration does not in itself permit entry to the UK and seperate enquiries should be made to the Home Office in this regard.

## Primary Medical Qualifications

In accordance with Directive 93/16 all EEA member states must recognise each other's primary medical qualifications. The principal qualifications granted in EEA countries which, when held by an EEA national, are recognised for full registration by the General Medical Council (GMC) are:

**Austria:** *Doctor der gesamten Heilkunde and Diplom über die Spezifische Ausbildung in der Allgemeinmedizin /Facharzt diplom.*

**Belgium:** *Diplome- legal de docteur en medecine, chirurgie et accouchements/Wettelijk diploma van doctor in de genees-heel-en verloskunde/ Academische graad van doctor in de genees-, heel-en verloskunde/Academische graad van arts*

**Denmark:** *Bevis for bestaet laeagevidenskabelig embedseksamen and Dokumentation for gennemfort praktisk uddannelse.*

**Finland:** *Todistus lääketieteen lisensiaatin tutkinnosta/bevis om medicine licentiate examen and Paatos laakarin lailistamisesta.*

**France:** *Diplome d'Etat de docteur en medecine or Diplome d'universite de docteur en medecine.*

**Germany:** *Zeugnis über die arztliche Staatsprüfung and Approbation/Bestellung als Arzt.*

**Greece:** *Ptychio Iatrikes.*

**Iceland:** *Prof i laeknadeild Haskola Islands* and a certificate of practical training.

**Ireland:** Degrees of Bachelor of Medicine and of Surgery/Licentiate in Medicine and Obstetrics and Licentiate in Surgery and Obstetrics.

**Italy:** *Diploma di Laurea in medicina e chirurgia and Diploma di abilitazione all'esercizo della medicina e chirurgia.*

**Luxembourg:** *Diplome d'Etat de docteur en medecine, chirurgie et accouchements and Certificat de stage.*

**Netherlands:** *Universitair getuigschrift van arts.*

**Norway:** *Bevis for bestatt medisinsk embetseksamen* and a certificate of practical training.

**Portugal:** *Carta de curso de licenciatura em medicina and Diploma comprovativo da conclusa do internato geral.*

**Spain:** *Titulo de Licenciado en Medicina y Cirugia.*

**Sweden:** *Läkarexamen Licentiatexamen* and a certificate of practical training *Bevis om Legitimation.*

**United Kingdom:** Degrees of Bachelor of Medicine and of Surgery/Licentiate in Medicine and Licentiate in Surgery.

Certain other qualifications may also be accepted by the GMC and enquiries should be made to them direct. General advice and information about coming to the UK is available to overseas doctors from NACPME and the International Department of the BMA. An invaluable source of information on careers in medicine in the UK is *Medical Careers – A General Guide* published by the BMA (see page 254).

## Nursing

Nurses or midwives who have completed their training and gained registration outside the UK must apply to the UK Central Council for Nursing, Midwifery and Health Visiting (UKCC) for admission to the Professional Register maintained by the UKCC. Applications are dealt with on an individual basis. Those applicants with non-EU qualifications may be required to complete a period of supervised experience and assessment.

Registration of first level general nurses who trained in the EU is governed by EC Directive 77/452/EC. Midwives are required to meet the requirements of EC Midwives Directives 80/154/EC and 80/155/EC covering training and practice prior to UK registration.

Enrolled nurses trained outside the UK cannot be admitted to the UKCC Professional Register, to be admitted they must undertake a pre-registration diploma or degree programme.

## Speech and Language Therapy

Overseas Trained Speech and Language Therapists (OTSLTs) can contact the Royal College of Speech and Language Therapists (RCSLT) for information regarding the acceptance of their qualifications in the UK, as this is the body with statutory responsibility for recognition of qualifications. At the time of writing mutual recognition agreements were being discussed with the professional bodies of Australia, Canada, Ireland and the USA. As yet none exist and all OTSLTs must have a certificate to practise or letter of approval from the RCSLT before they can work in the UK. With the exception of EU qualified therapists, OTSLTs can gain approval if they are fully qualified in their home country and have a minimum of one-year's post-qualifying experience eg candidates from the USA must have their ASHA Certificate of Clinical Competence before coming to the UK. With the exception of EU candidates all OSLTs must have English as their first language or have obtained a Grade 8 on the British Council International English Language Testing System.

## Psychology

Under the terms of its Royal Charter (1965) amended in 1987 the British Psychological Society is required to maintain a public Register of Chartered Pyschologists, this lists 9,000 chartered pyschologists in the UK. Registration requires that the candidate should: be a member of the BPS, have an approved first qualification in pyschology, have undertaken further training in a specific area of pyschology and to have been judged fit to practise unsupervised. The British Psychological Society's Committee for the Scrutiny of Individual Clinical Qualifications (CSICQ) identifies what further training or experience is needed by those who have qualified abroad, in order to qualify in the UK. Those qualified as clinical psychologists in an EU country might be required to obtain further supervised experience, but will not normally be asked to sit more exams, although some written work may need to be submitted. Those needing a work permit to work in the UK should find that a CSICQ statement of their training or supervisory requirements speeds up the processing of their application.

## Professions Supplementary to Medicine

Overseas members of these professions – defined as chiropody, dietetics, occupational therapy, orthoptics and radiography – should contact the Council for Professions Supplementary to Medicine (CPSM) for information on how to obtain State Registration. State Registration is a prerequisite for employment in these professions in the NHS, and many professionals working in private practice also register. Overseas professionals should ensure that they obtain State Registration before they depart for the UK.

The CPSM is a statutory body that includes boards dealing with each profession. These boards are also the designated authorities for the recognition of qualifications within the EU/EEA.

## Physiotherapy

Physiotherapists wishing to obtain UK State Registration will need to apply to the CPSM, the application process itself can take up to three months. Applicants from EU/EEA states fall within the general directive 89/48/EEC on the acceptance of qualifications if they have had three years of training, while those with two years of training are covered by the supplemental directive 92/51/EEC. Non-EU/EEA applicants whose training corresponds to the UK's BSc degree are also eligible for registration. If the applicants training differs widely from that in the UK, then they will have to undertake an aptitude test or complete an adaption period (which can last up to three years).

## Homeopathy

In the UK homeopathy is practised by medical doctors who have undertaken specialist training and who may practise homeopathy within the National Health Service, and by lay homeopaths who lack medical training but who may practise as homeopaths with the proviso that they do not use the term 'doctor'. The medically trained homeopaths are members of the Faculty of Homeopaths, which has had statutory recognition since 1950, and thus maintains a register of medically trained homeopaths. Lay homoeopaths are allowed to practise under common law, and at the time of writing negotiations for recognition were ingoing.

### Osteopathy

The Osteopathy Act (1993) means that statutory registration will become law in May 2000, after this date anyone wishing to practice Osteopathy in the UK must be registered with the General Osteopathic Council through their Professional Portfolio and Profile scheme. Full details can be obtained from the Council's registration department (address below telephone extension 233).

## VISAS AND WORK PERMITS

Information on immigration to the UK is available from your nearest British Embassy, High Commission or Consulate, or from the Home Office, Immigration and Nationality Directorate. EU/EEA nationals do not have to comply with any immigration formalities, but they are advised to apply to the Home Office for a residence permit within 6 months of their arrival in the UK to help confirm their status. Generally speaking nationals of Commonwealth countries and the USA do not require an entry visa, although there are variations on this rule and it is wisest to check.

Work permits are granted for named individuals to undertake a specified post with a specified employer who is responsible for obtaining the permit; they are not transferable and are issued for a period of up to 4 years.

Doctors wishing to enter the UK for hospital-training-grade posts may be admitted for a maximum aggregate period of 4 years under postgraduate-training status (permit-free).

Dentists entering to set up their own practices are self-employed and so require leave to enter as business persons.

Doctors and dentists eligible to apply for NHS non-training posts will be subject to work permit provisions, and the prospective employer will have to apply to the Department for Education and Employment for a work permit. Work permits are granted for named individuals to undertake a specified post with a specified employer; they are not transferable and are issued for a period of up to 4 years.

Working Holiday Visas, valid for 2 years, are available to those under 27 years of age from Commonwealth nations (most commonly these are from Canada, Australia and New Zealand), these are used for example, by nurses arriving in London to take up some of the enormous amount of short-term work that is available.

## PRACTICAL INFORMATION

Overseas health professionals intending to work in the UK must register with the Department of Social Security (DSS) to obtain a National Insurance number. If in doubt contact your nearest DSS office for information. You will also need to obtain a tax coding from the Inland Revenue. If you are finding work through an agency, they will help you with these steps; otherwise your employer will be able to tell you what to do.

## JOB OPPORTUNITIES

In addition to the specialist publications mentioned in Part II and below, health vacancies are also advertised in national newspapers – for example, in *The Guardian* on Wednesdays.

## Biomedical Science

At present the NHS is chronically short of biomedical scientists, a recent survey carried out by the Institute of Biomedical Science found that 88% of NHS laboratories were understaffed. Given that the NHS laboratories deal with around 100 million pathology tests per year, there is obviously scope for overseas trained scientists to find employment.

## Dentistry

At the time of writing two thirds of the UK's health authorities are reporting a shortage of dentists. Chronic understaffing is again the problem, patients are complaining that they can not get onto a practice list because the dentists are overworked and dentists are complaining that they are short staffed and can not find new staff. Some health authorities have even tried advertising in Scandinavian papers in the hope of attracting professionals from an area with a perceived surplus of dentists.

Dental practitioners who wish to come to Britain and set up a practice recieve fees per item of treatment for NHS and private work, and for each NHS patient on their list they will recieve NHS capitation and continuing care payments. Although they will have to meet their own practice costs; staff, buildings, tools and materials. The latest Inland Revenue figures for dental income give average NHS nett earnings as £39,840 and average earnings from all sources as £55,025, while recently announced new pay levels should bring the base figure up to £46,730-£48,905 . Dentists working in hospitals, universities and the community sector receive a salary depending on their grade, these range from £16,710 (house officer) to £61,605 (consultant).

## Medicine

There is a serious shortage of doctors in the UK, current figures estimate that there are 4,000 consultant or specialist vacancies and 1,000 for general practitioners. There are large numbers of vacancies for GPs in inner cities throughout the country, and the problem is spreading to other areas as well. This shortage in the inner cities is partly a result of a huge amount of recruitment of doctors from such countries as Pakistan and India in the 1960s and 1970s, and these doctors are now beginning to retire as a group. Despite this reliance on immigrant doctors, Britain has done little to produce enough doctors to fill the gap. Much of the blame for this would appear to rest with decisions to cut the number of student places in the 1980s. There is also a serious shortage of junior doctors in the hospitals. This is partly because of the reduction in their working hours, which has created an extra 2500 senior house officer posts, although there are not enough medical graduates to fill them. There has also been inadequate planning for the increase in demand, and the situation is worsened by the very high drop-out rate among newly qualified doctors who can not cope with the working conditions.

The shortage of doctors is increasingly driving British hospitals to recruit in Europe, Australia, South Africa and the USA. Of 110,000 doctors working in the NHS in 1999, 25,000 were from outside the UK. As the qualifications of those trained in the EU are automatically recognised for practice in Britain, recruitment from Europe has obvious appeal as a short-term solution. Many German doctors are coming to Britain either to complete their medical training in specialisations or to find work in hospitals and general practices, driven by cuts in public spending and high unemployment in Germany. In 1990 138 Germans were registered with the General Medical Council; in 1999 that figure was 2,024.

Recently there has been a significant increase in the use of recruitment agencies and consultancies to fill NHS posts. In particular demand for senior staff far outstrips supply, and most trusts and hospitals are experiencing difficulty in attracting consultants and other grades of doctor. These recruitment problems are being felt in every speciality – for example, in accident and emergency, psychiatry, paediatrics and anaesthesia. Although specialists are now being produced after a shorter, more intensive training period, the continuing shortfall in the number of medical students and the high drop-out rate among newly qualified doctors mean that these recruitment difficulties are set to continue. Specialist agencies are therefore being brought in to address the problem.

A large number of vacancies appear in specialist medical publications. The weekly *British Medical Journal* (widely known as simply the *BMJ*) includes a substantial supplement of classified job advertisements, including both NHS Trusts and recruitment agencies looking for staff. *The Lancet* is another highly respected journal, but has far fewer vacancies in its classified section.

Detailed information on salary levels for doctors and medical staffing in the UK is included in the supplements available with the BMA publication *Medical Careers – A General Guide* (see page 254). At present the annual salary figures are:

| | |
|---|---|
| House Officer | £17,260 |
| Senior House Officer | £21,535 |
| Registrar | £24,070–£35,080 |
| Consultant | £48,905–£63,640 |
| General Practitioner | £50,760–£54,220 |

Consultants can also earn up to five discretionary points boosting their NHS pay to £73,925. On top of this all consultants can do private work outside of their NHS commitments; if they are 'full-time' this can only account for 10% of their annual income but 'maximum part-timers' can do as much private work as they wish and thus earn substantial sums.

### Agencies

Because of their recruitment problems, NHS Trusts are now making more use of agencies. The Trusts themselves often do not have the resources or the expertise to deal with the enquiries of applicants, and so an increasing proportion of the jobs available in the NHS are advertised through agencies.

The section on *Recruitment Agencies and Consultants* gives details of a number of agencies operating in various fields that place applicants with appropriate qualifications in positions throughout the British Isles: see the *List of Agencies* on pages 48-68.

### Nursing & Midwifery

There is a chronic shortage of nurses in the UK, (at the time of writing there were 17,000 nursing vacancies) a situation that is likely to continue for the forseeable future. Reasons for this have been the underfunding of some areas, simple mismanagement and a reduction of student numbers in the 1980s. All of which means that there is abundant work in the country for suitably qualified overseas nurses – particularly from countries where professional standards are high and nurses are up-to-date with the latest clinical methods.

Some NHS Trusts have been spending considerable sums of money recruiting nurses from European Union countries – such as Germany, Finland, the Netherlands and Sweden – to fill vacant posts. In 1999 Oxford's John Radcliffe hospital was recruiting nursing staff from as far afield as Australia in order to cope with its nursing shortage. Fifty Finnish nurses work in one London hospital alone, earning about £200 more per month than they would at home and recently nurses from Moscow have been offered free flights. NHS Trusts advertise in such publications as the *Nursing Times*, which has a substantial recruitment section each week. Alternatively as noted earlier many Trusts recruit through specialist agencies, which is often seen as a more effective way of tapping into overseas labour markets.

Many Trusts are receptive to the idea of helping nurses from overseas to continue their professional development, which is clearly useful for nurses wanting to be able to demonstrate to potential employers back in their own country that they have gained valuable experience from working in the UK. Access to courses, training and other methods of improving your employment potential are things to bear in mind when considering registering with a recruitment agency.

Before you can find work through an agency, you will need to obtain UKCC registration (see above). As well as documentation to confirm your nursing training and postgraduate qualifications/experience, the following paperwork will prove useful: documented proof of all immunisations and your antibody levels for hepatitis B and rubella; details of your last chest X-ray and Mantoux test results; details of your last lifting and handling course; and details of your IV therapy and CPR assessment. In certain circumstances where you may have access to children and other vulnerable members of the community – and especially if you wish to work as a Registered Sick Children's Nurse – you may need to provide a police check from your home country; this is most easily obtained before you leave for the UK.

## Salaries

The latest round of pay rises announced by the Government in a bid to recruit and retain staff have lead to the following pay figures:

| Grade | Min | Max |
| --- | --- | --- |
| C | £12,135 | £14,890 |
| D | £14,890 | £16,445 |
| E | £15,920 | £19,220 |
| F | £17,655 | £22,860 |
| G | £20,830 | £24,515 |
| H | £23,270 | £27,910 |
| I | £25,770 | £30,490 |

(Grade C: Enrolled Nurses; Grade E: Staff Nurses; Grade F-G: Ward Sisters; Grade H-I Clinical Experts & Managers. Nurses working in London recieve an aditional £1,570-£2,205 plus 5% of grade salary (up to £750) in London weighting.)

The latest rates of pay for Midwives range from £15,395 for newly qualified staff rising to £28,240 for the most senior staff.

## Agencies

*Strand Nurses Bureau* in London specialises in placing nurses in short and long term placements in London and the rest of the UK. *Nursing Management Services* is an agency specialising in placing nurses in the UK, in settings ranging from small privately run units to busy teaching hospitals. *O'Grady-Peyton International* sometimes have vacancies for nurses in the UK and they also have a local office placing staff in other countries. *Worldwide Healthcare Exchange (WHE)* is a network of healthcare recruitment companies that places English-speaking nurses in posts in the UK.

## Physiotherapy

Physiotherapists are currently classed as a 'shortage profession' by the Department of Education and Employment, at the time of writing there was a 10% shortfall, in other words there are 1000 unfilled vacancies for trained physiotherapists. This need for staff has been reflected in the removal of the requirement for vacancies to be advertised first within the EU/EEA, thus making it easier for non-European physiotherapists to find jobs and have work permit applications approved. Although the absence of recognition agreements can lengthen the registration process physiotherapists from Commonwealth nations can also enter to work on the Working Holiday visa scheme.

Current salaries for physiotherapists are as follows: Physiotherapist £13,420-15785; Senior II £15,510-18,755; Senior I £18,430-£21,485; Superintendent I-IV £18,430-£28,390; District £27,900-32,520; Principal £27,780-33,780.

## Speech and Language Therapists

The Working Holiday scheme can be used by Speech and Language Therapists from Commonwealth nations to come and work for two years in the UK. The only restriction within this scheme is an emphasis on casual work with low levels of responsibility. At the time of writing the number of overseas therapists working in Britain was 115, with over half coming from Australia, the remainder coming from Canada, India, New Zealand, South Africa and the USA. The latest figures for NHS salaries for Speech and Language Therapists are as follows: Grade 1 £13,822-£14,375; Grade 2 £14,375-24,861; Grade 3 £24,891-£35,426.

## Other Professions

Numerous agencies recruit overseas staff for positions in therapy, pharmacy and the supplementary professions. In particular there is a strong demand for qualified occupational therapists in the NHS and in social services departments, and there is a wide range of opportunities available to physiotherapists. The Institute of Biomedical Science's monthly publication *Biomedical Scientist* contains job advertisements for biomedical scientists, and can be obtained from the Institute. Some osteopaths secure contract work with the local Primary Care Group, but generally osteopaths work in private practices setting their own fees, these range from £20-£30 per session.

### Agencies

*Technic Services Medical* recruits occupational therapists and physiotherapists for UK positions. *Jenrick Medical* recruits overseas occupational and physiotherapists, pharmacists, specialist technicians and paramedical staff. *Angela Shaw Associates* is an agency specialising in finding locum positions for occupational therapists, physiotherapists, and speech and language therapists wishing to work in this country.

In addition the *Locum Group* recruits overseas therapists, pharmacists and residential and domiciliary care staff.

## PROFESSIONAL ORGANISATIONS

*Association of Anaesthetists:* 9 Bedford Square, London WC1B 3RA, UK (tel 020-7631 1650; fax 020-7631 4352; e-mail aagbi@compuserve.com; Website www.ncl.ac.uk/~nassocal).
*Association of Medical Secretaries, Practice Managers, Administrators and*

*Receptionists:* Tavistock House North, Tavistock Square, London WC1H 9LNH, UK (tel 020-7387 6005; fax 020-7387 2648; e-mail amspar@atlas.co.uk).

*British Association of Dental Nurses:* 11 Pharos Street, Fleetwood, FY7 6BG, UK (tel 01253-778631; fax 01253-773266).

*British Association of Dental Therapists:* 180 North Road, Pontywan, Cross Keys, Gwent, Wales.

*British Association of Emergency Medical Technicians:* Ty Cristion, Bodedern, Anglesey, LL65 3UB, UK (tel 01407-742222; e-mail admin@baemt.org.uk Website www.baemt.org.uk).

*British Association of Medical Managers:* 3rd Floor, Petersgate House, St Petersgate, Stockport, SK1 1YE, UK (tel 0161-474 1141; fax 0161-474 7167; Website www.bamm.co.uk).

*British Association of Occupational Therapists:* 6-8 Marshalsea Road, London SE1 1HL, UK (tel 020-7357 6480; fax 020-7378 1353).

*British Chiropractic Association:* Blagrave House, 17 Blagrave Street, Reading RG1 0QB, UK (tel 0118-950 5950; fax 0118-958 8946; Website www.chiropractic-uk.co.uk).

*British Dental Association:* 64 Wimpole Street, London W1M 8AL, UK (tel 020-7935 0875; fax 020-7487 5232; e-mail Enquiries@bda-dentistry.org.uk Website www.bda-dentistry.org.uk).

*British Dental Hygienists Association:* 13 The Ridge, Yatton, Bristol, BS19 4DQ, UK (tel 01934-876389).

*British Dietetic Association:* 5th Floor, Elizabeth House, 22 Suffolk Street, Queensway, Birmingham B1 1LS, UK (tel 0121-616 4900; fax 0121-616 4901; Website www.bda.uk.com).

*British Homoeopathic Association:* 27A Devonshire Street, London W1N 1RJ, UK (tel 020-7935 2163; Website www.nhsconfed.net/bha).

*British Medical Acupuncture Society:* Newton House, Newton Lane, Whitley, Cheshire, WA4 4JA, UK (tel 01925-730727; fax 01925-730492 e-mail Bmasadmin@aol.com Website www.medical-acupuncture.co.uk).

*British Medical Association:* BMA House, Tavistock Square, London WC1H 9JP, UK (tel 020-7387 4499; fax 020-7383 6454).

*British Nuclear Medicine Society:* 1 Wimpole Street, London, W1M 8AE, UK (tel 020-8291 7800; fax 020-8699 2227; e-mail office@bnms.org.uk Website www.bnms.org.uk).

*British Orthoptic Society:* Tavistock House North, Tavistock Square, London WC1H 9HX, UK.

*British Osteopathic Association:* Langham House East, Luton, LU1 2NA, UK (tel 01582-488455; fax 01582-481533; e-mail enquiries@osteopathy.org).

*British Psychological Society:* St Andrew's House, 48 Princess Road East, Leicester LE1 7DR, UK (tel 0116-254 9568; e-mail mail@bps.org.uk Website www.bps.org.uk).

*Carers' National Association:* 20-25 Glasshouse Yard, London EC1A 4JS, UK (tel 020-7490 8818; fax 020-7490 8824; Website www.carersuk.demon.co.uk).

*Chartered Society of Physiotherapy:* 14 Bedford Row, London WC1R 4ED, UK (tel 020-7306 6666; fax 020-7306 6611; e-mail general.csp@csphysio.org.uk Website csphysio.org.uk).

*College of Occupational Therapists:* 106-114 Borough High Street, London SE1 1LB, UK (tel 020-7357 6480; fax 020-7450 2299; Website www.cot.co.uk Careers Line 020-7450 2332).

*Faculty of Homeopaths:* 15 Clerkenwell Close, London, EC12 0AA, UK (tel 020-7566 7810; Website www.trusthomeopathy.org).

*General Osteopathic Council:* 176 Tower Bridge Road, London, SE1 3LU, UK (tel 020-7357 6655; Website www.osteopathy.org.uk).

*Institute of Biomedical Science:* 12 Coldbath Square, London EC1R 5HL, UK (tel 020-7713 0214; fax 020-7436 4946; e-mail mail@ibms.org Website www.ibms.org).

*Pharmaceutical Society of Northern Ireland:* 73 University Street, Belfast BT7 1HL, UK.

*Royal College of Anaesthetists:* 48-49 Russell Square, London WC1B 4JY, UK.

*Royal College of Midwives:* 15 Mansfield Street, London W1M 0BE, UK (tel 020-7312 3535; fax 020-7312 3536).

*Royal College of Nursing:* 20 Cavendish Square, London W1M 0AB, UK (tel 020-7409 3333; fax 020-7355 1379; Website www.rcn.org).

*Royal College of Obstetricians and Gynaecologists:* 27 Sussex Place, Regents Park, London NW1 4RG, UK (tel 020-7772 6263; fax 020-7772 6359; Website www.rcog.org.uk).

*Royal College of Ophthalmologists:* 17 Cornwall Terrace, Regents Park, London NW1 4QW, UK (tel 020-7935 0702; fax 020-7935 9838).

*Royal College of Pathologists:* 2 Carlton House Terrace, London SW1Y 5AF, UK (tel 020-7930 5863; fax 020-7321 0523).

*Royal College of Psychiatrists:* 17 Belgrave Square, London SW1X 8PG, UK (tel 020-7235 2351; fax 020-7245 1231; Website www.rcpsych.ac.uk).

*Royal College of Radiologists:* 38 Portland Place, London W1N 4JQ, UK (tel 020-7636 4432; fax 020-7323 3100; e-mail enquiries@rcr.ac.uk Website www.rcrad.org.uk).

*Royal College of Speech and Language Therapists:* 2/3 White Hart Yard, London SE1 1NX, UK (tel 020-7378 1200; fax 020-7403 7254; e-mail postmaster@rcslt.org Website www.rcslt.org).

*Royal Pharmaceutical Society of Great Britain:* 1 Lambeth High Street, London SE1 7JN, UK (tel 020-7735 9141; fax 020-7735 7629; e-mail enquiries@rpsgb.org.uk).

*Society of Chiropodists and Podiatrists:* 53 Welbeck Street, London W1M, UK 7HE (tel 020-7486 3381; fax 020-7935 6359; e-mail eng@scpod.org Website www.feetforlife.org).

*Society of Homeopaths:* 4a Artizan Road, Northampton, NN1 4HU, UK (tel 01604-621400; fax 01604-622622; Website www.homeopathy.org.uk). Non-medically qualified homeopaths.

*Society of Radiographers:* 2 Carriage Row, 183 Eversholt Street, London, NW1 1BU, UK (tel 020-7391 4500; fax 020-7391 4504; Website www.sor.org).

## USEFUL ADDRESSES

*British Acupuncture Council:* 63 Jeddo Road, London W12 9HQ, UK (tel 020-8735 0400; fax 020-8735 0404; e-mail info@acupuncture.org.uk Website www.acupuncture.org.uk).

*The British Council:* Information Centre, 10 Spring Gardens, London SW1A 2BN, UK (tel 020-7389 4383; Website www.britishcouncil.org).

*Council for Complementary and Alternative Medicine:* 179 Gloucester Place, London NW1 6DX (tel 020-7724 9103).

*Council for Professions Supplementary to Medicine:* Park House, 184 Kennington Park Road, London SE11 4BU, UK (tel 020-7582 0866; fax 020-7820 9684).

*Dental Technicians Education and Training Advisory Board:* 5 Oxford Court, St James' Road, Brackley, NN13 7XY, UK (tel 01280-702600).

*Department of Trade and Industry (European Community and Trade Relations Division 1B):* Room 212, Kingsgate House, Victoria Street, London SW1E

6SW, UK (tel 020-7215 4405; fax 020-7215 4489).

*English National Board for Nursing, Midwifery and Health Visiting (Careers Service):* Victory House, 170 Tottenham Court Road, London W1P 0HA, UK (tel 020-7388 3131; fax 020-7383 4031; Website www.enb.org.uk ).

*General Dental Council:* 37 Wimpole Street, London W1M 8DQ, UK (tel 020-7887 3800; fax 020-7224 3294).

*General Medical Council:* 44 Hallam Street, London W1N 6AE, UK.

*Home Office, Immigration and Nationality Directorate:* Lunar House, Wellesley Road, Croydon, Surrey CR9 2BY, UK (tel 020-8686 0688).

*Homoeopathy:* British Homoeopathic Association Journal, 27A Devonshire Street, London W1N 1RJ, UK.

*Institute for Complementary Medicine:* PO Box 194, London SE16 1QZ (tel 020-7237 5165).

*Local Government Management Board:* Layden House, 76-86 Turnmill Street, London EC1M 5QU, UK (tel 020-7296 6585; fax 020-7296 6666).

*National Advice Centre for Postgraduate Medical Information (NACPME):* Medical Information Assistant, British Council, Bridgewater House, 58 Whitworth Street, Manchester, M1 6BB, UK (tel 0161-957 7214/8; fax 0161-957 7029; Website www.britishcouncil.org/health/nacpme).

*National Board for Nursing, Midwifery and Health Visiting for Northern Ireland:* Centre House, 79 Chichester Street, Belfast BT1 4JE, UK (tel 01232-238152; e-mail enquiries@nbni.n-i.nhs.uk Website www.n-i.nhs.uk/NBNI/index.htm).

*National Board for Nursing, Midwifery and Health Visiting for Scotland (Careers Information Team):* 22 Queen Street, Edinburgh EH2 1NT, UK (tel 0131-225 2096; fax 0131-226 2492; Website www.nbs.org.uk).

*United Kingdom Central Council for Nursing, Midwifery and Health Visiting:* 23 Portland Place, London, W1N 3JT, UK (tel 020-7333 9333; fax 020-7636 6935; Website www.ukcc.org.uk in English, French, German and Spanish).

*United Kingdom Homecare Association Ltd:* 42b Banstead Road, Carshalton Beeches, Surrey SM5 3NW, UK (tel 020-8288 1551; fax 020-8288 1550; Website www.ukhca.co.uk).

*Welsh National Board for Nursing, Midwifery and Health Visiting:* 2nd Floor, Golate House, 101 St Mary Street, Cardiff CF1 1DX, UK (tel 02920-261400; fax 02920-261499; e-mail info@wnb.org.uk Website www.wnb.org.uk in English and Welsh).

## OTHER AGENCIES

The organisations listed below are involved in various aspects of health recruitment in the UK, and may be able to help you in your job search. Professional Connections have offices in several countries to place nursing staff in the UK.

*Grafton Recruitment:* 35-37 Queen's Square, Belfast, Northern Ireland, BT1 3FG (tel 028-9024 2824; fax 028-9024 2897; Website www.grafton group.com).

*O'Grady-Peyton International* 332 Congress Street, Boston, Massachusetts 02210, USA, (tel +1-617-422 0300; fax 617-422 0399; Website www.opginc.com).

*Professional Connections IRL Oy:* Aleksanterinkatu 48A, 3 krs, FIN-0100 Helsinki, Finland (tel +358-9-4155 6611; fax 9-4155 6612; e-mail ProfessionalConnections@profco.com).

*Professional Connections Ltd:* 5 City Gate, Bridge Street Lower, Dublin 8, Ireland (tel +353-1-679 2277; fax 1-679 2396; e-mail profconn@iol.ie).

*Professional Connections AB:* Radmansgatan 48 bv, S-113 57 Stockholm, Sweden (tel +46-8-673 1490; fax 8-673 1491).

*Professional Connections (UK) Ltd:* 10 Stratton Street, London, W1X 5FD, UK (tel 020-7544 6848; 020-7544 6849; e-mail profcoldn@aol.com Website www.profco.com).

*Universal Care:* Chester House, 9 Windsor End, Beaconsfield, Bucks HP9 2JJ, UK (tel 01494-678811; fax 01494-671259; e-mail universal.care@olcs.net website www.olcs.net/universal.care).

# Other Western European Countries

Some useful addresses are included here for several countries where opportunities are likely to be rare.

## ICELAND

*Icelandic Embassy:* Suite 1200, 1156 15th Street, NW, Washington, DC 20005-1704, USA (tel 202-265-6653; fax 202-265-6656; e-mail icemb.wash@utn.stjr.is Website www.iceland.org).

*Icelandic Embassy:* 1 Eaton Terrace, London SW1W 8EY, UK (tel 020-7730 5131/2; fax 020-7730 1683).

*Icelandic Consulate-General:* Suite 300, 246 Queen Street, Ottawa, Ontario K1P 5E4, Canada (tel 613-238-7412; fax 613-238-1799).

*International Telephone Code:* +354

### Visas and Work Permits

Citizens of the EU/EEA, Nordic nations, the USA, Australia and New Zealand do not need visas for stays of up to three months. Longer stays require visas and residence permits, with the exception of citizens of Nordic nations. As is the case in many countries the employer applies for the work permit from the Ministry of Social Affairs. EU/EEA nationals do not require work permits. Further information and confirmation of your immigration status can be obtained from the Immigration Service, Audbrekka 6, IS-200 kopavogur, Iceland (tel +354-554 4400; fax 562 3375).

### Professional Organisations and Useful Addresses

*Directorate of Health:* Laugavegur 116, IS-150 Reykjavik, Iceland (tel 562 7555; fax 562 3716).

Felag Islenskra Sjukrapjalfara: (physiotherapists) Box 5023, IS-125 Reykjavik, Iceland (tel 568 7661; fax 588 9239; e-mail physio@simnet.is Website www.physio.is).

*Icelandic Dental Association:* Tanaeknafélag Islands, PO Box 8596, IS-128 Reykjavik, Iceland.

*Icelandic Dietetic Association:* c/o Mrs AE Asgeirdottir, St Josejsspitali Landaroti, IS-101 Reykjavik, Iceland.

*Icelandic Medical Association:* Hlioasmara 8, 200 Kópavogur, Iceland (tel 164 4100; fax 164 4106).

*Icelandic Nurses' Association:* Sudurlandsbraut 22, IS-108 Reykjavik, Iceland (tel 568 7575; fax 568 0727).

*Icelandic Nurses' Association of Radiological Nurses:* Heidarlundur 6, IS-10 Gardabaer, Iceland.

*Icelandic Occupational Therapy Association:* Postholf 8845, IS-128 Reykjavik, Iceland.

*Ministry of Education* (for recognition of professional qualifications) Sölvhólsgata

4, IS-150 Reykjavik, Iceland (tel 560 9500; fax 562 3068; e-mail postur@mrn.stjr.is Website www.mrm.stjr.is).
*Ministry of Health and Social Security:* Laugavegur 116, IS-150 Reykjavik, Iceland (tel 560 9700; fax 551 9165).
*University of Iceland, Faculty of Medicine:* Laeknagarthur, Vatnsmyrarvegur 16, IS-101 Reykjavik, Iceland.

## LIECHTENSTEIN

*Liechtensteinischer Ärzteverein* (Liechtenstein Medical Association) Zwischenbäch 12, 9496 Balzers, Liechtenstein (tel 384 15 16).
*Physioterapeuten-Verband Furstentum Liechtenstein* (physiotherapists) Postfach FL 603, Schaan, Liechtenstein (tel +423-371 1140; fax 371 1141; e-mail yvonne@odoni.loli.li)

## MALTA

At the present time the only foreign doctors working in Malta are specialists employed in government hospitals; there are no foreign doctors or dental surgeons working in private practice. The situation may alter if Malta is admitted to the European Union. There are two private hospitals in Malta, which started operating only recently; it is not yet possible to say whether they will be permitted to employ foreign doctors or under what conditions.

*Embassy of the Republic of Malta:* 2017 Connecticut Avenue, NW, Washington, DC 20008, USA (tel 202-462-3611/2; fax 202-387-5470).
*High Commission for the Republic of Malta:* Malta House, 36-38 Piccadilly, London W1V 0PP, UK (tel 020-7292 4800; fax 020-7734 1832).
*Consulate-General of the Republic of Malta:* 3461 North Cliffe, Montréal, Québec H4A 3K8, Canada (tel 514-284-3627; fax 514-284-1860).
*International Telephone Code:* +356

### Professional Organisations

*Association of Occupational Therapists:* c/o Occupational Therapy Department, St Luke's Hospital, G'Mangia MSD 07, Malta (tel 241251; fax 240176).
*Dental Association of Malta:* Federation of Professional Bodies, Medisle Village, St Andrews STJ 07, Malta.
*Malta Association of Physiotherapists:* Marwin, Carob Street, Msida MSD 03, Malta (tel 312367; e-mail jxdc@orbit.net.mt).
*Malta Nurses' Association:* PO Box 63, Hamrun, Malta.
*Medical Association of Malta:* Medisle Village, St Andrews STJ 14, Malta (tel 338851; fax 235638).
*Medical Council:* Castellania Palace, 15 Merchants Street, Valletta, Malta (tel 224071/7).

# Switzerland

*Swiss Embassy:* 2900 Cathedral Avenue, NW, Washington, DC 20008, USA (tel 202-745-7900; fax 202-387-2564).
*Swiss Embassy:* 16-18 Montagu Place, London W1H 2BQ (tel 020-7723 0701; fax

020-7724 7001).
*Swiss Embassy:* 5 Marlborough Avenue, Ottawa, Ontario K1N 8E6, Canada (tel 613-235-1837; fax 613-563-1394).
*Currency:* 1 Swiss Franc (SFr) = 100 Rappen.
*Exchange rate:* £1 = SFr2.5; $1 = SFr1.89.
*Capital:* Berne (Bern).
*International Telephone Code:* +41
*Population:* 6,908,000.
*Area:* 41,300 sq. km.
*Languages:* German, French, Italian, Rhaeto-Romanic

Famous for mountains, skiing secretive bankers and watchmaking, Switzerland is at the the heart of Europe geographically, but steadfastly remains outside the EU/EEA. Historically Switzerland has remained firmly independent, and it is now well established as a centre for numerous international organisations, including the International Red Cross and various departments of the United Nations.

Switzerland is a federal state consisting of 26 canton; these regions have considerable autonomy and have their own constitutions, parliaments, governments and courts. The cantons are further subdivided into a total of approximately 3000 communes.

## HEALTH SERVICES

The health system is decentralised in Switzerland, and although there is a Federal Office of Public Health (*Bundesamt für Gesundheitswesen*) it is essentially the cantons that determine how their public health systems are run. The construction and management of hospitals and clinics are the responsibility of the cantons and communes, and with the exception of one military hospital there are no health care facilities run by the Federal Government. There is therefore no single body in Switzerland responsible for health service provision and planning.

The private sector plays a very significant role in the organisation of the health care system, although that is not to say that the system is run solely according to market forces. The involvement of the public and private sectors in funding health care varies according to the type of service. The public authorities, for example, heavily subsidise hospitals and medical home care services, whereas there is essentially no contribution from the public authorities for visits to surgeries, the costs involved being covered by social and health insurance and by the patients themselves. Dental care is almost entirely paid for by the patients.

Switzerland has a high density of doctors and hospital beds, and the country's small size and efficient transport network mean that the population can easily reach the excellent health care facilities and services that are available.

The Swiss health system employs over 300,000 people – about 9% of the working population of the country. This figure includes doctors, nursing and paramedical staff, as well as the staff of various institutions and administrative and support services.

Out-patient health care services form the backbone of the Swiss health system – each inhabitant consults a doctor on average 11 times each year as an out-patient. On the in-patient side there are over 300 hospitals – the majority of which receive substantial public subsidies – alongside 100 psychiatric and geriatric clinics; together these employ about 106,000 people. There are also 100 private clinics receiving no or very little public money.

'Non-hospital' health care establishments include homes for the elderly and various institutions and treatment centres.

# SKILLS AND QUALIFICATIONS

As noted, the responsibility for health care in Switzerland rests mainly with the cantons, and because of this the Federal Office of Public Health is not involved in assessing the validity of foreign medical degrees and other qualifications. Such assessment is carried out by the individual cantonal health authorities, and so those wanting to work in a particular canton will need to contact the relevant health authority directly.

Doctors must have passed the Swiss state examination before they are allowed to practise independently; in principle, only Swiss citizens are admitted to this examination.

# VISAS AND WORK PERMITS

Switzerland is not a member of the European Union, and so the free movement of labour and individuals does not apply as it does in the EU countries.

Switzerland does not issue 'work permits' in the usual sense; the Swiss equivalent is the Residence Permit, a combination of both a residence and a work permit entitling the holder to live in a particular canton and work for a specified employer.

The Swiss Government's restrictive immigration policy means that it is very difficult to obtain a Residence Permit with a view to taking up employment. Generally only those who have been offered jobs that can not be done by Swiss nationals have a chance of obtaining Residence Permits; as a result the jobs that are available are usually in an occupation of a highly specialised nature. The standard one-year or 'B' permit is issued for a specific job and is valid for a limited period, usually 1 year, and renewable.

Residence Permits are actually issued after arrival in Switzerland, but only to those holding a passport and an 'Assurance of a Residence Permit' (*Zusicherung der Aufenthaltsbewilligung*). These are obtained by the prospective employer applying to the cantonal authorities on the would-be employee's behalf; if a Residence Permit is granted, then the 'Assurance' is sent to the employee's address outside Switzerland. Alternatively, for those who require a visa to work in Switzerland (most non-Europeans come into this category) a 'visa for the purpose of employment' is needed in addition to a passport; in this case the prospective employee applies for a work visa at the same time as the employer applies for a permit in Switzerland; once the latter has been granted, an authorisation to issue a work visa is sent to the appropriate Swiss Embassy or Consulate.

All those arriving in Switzerland to work are required to undergo a medical examination.

# JOB OPPORTUNITIES

Switzerland is unique in being the only country in western Europe that is neither a member of the European Union nor the European Economic Area, they have however joined the European Free Trade Area. This means that EU/EEA nationals have no advantages when looking for work over professionals from non-european nations.

Normally only Swiss citizens are allowed to practise as doctors, dentists and pharmacists, but where there is a shortage of qualified staff exceptions are possible. If a particular hospital or surgery wants to employ a doctor with foreign medical qualifications they have to apply for a work permit from the cantonal authorities. However the already high density of doctors in Switzerland means that it may prove difficult for a foreign doctor to find work.

The most effective means of finding out about the current employment situation is likely to be contacting directly the cantonal authorities in which you are interested in working; the central office for the authorities (address below) should be able to provide you with addresses. Alternatively you can contact the hospitals themselves; the Association of Swiss Hospitals and the Swiss Association of Private Clinics will be able to provide you with lists. The weekly *Schweizerische ärztezeitung (Swiss Medical Journal*; address below) includes details of all the hospital and surgery vacancies.

The Swiss Embassy is unable to assist in finding work in Switzerland, and does not have lists of potential employers, agencies and organisations available.

## PROFESSIONAL ORGANISATIONS

*Association Suisse des Infirmières et Infirmiers* (Swiss Nurses' Association) Secrétariat Central, Case Postale, CH-3001 Bern (tel 031-388 3636; fax 031-388 3635).

*ErgotherapeutInnen Verband Schweiz/Association Suisse des Ergotherapeutes* (occupational therapists) Stauffacherstrasse 96, Postfach, CH-8026 Zurich, Switzerland (tel 01-242 5464; fax 01-291 5440).

*Federation Suisse des Physiotherapeutes* (physiotherapists) Oberstadt 8, CH-6204 Sempach-Stadt, Switzerland (tel 041-462 7060; fax 041-462 7061; e-mail info@physioswiss.ch Website www.physioswiss.ch).

*Schweizerischer Fachverband der diplomierten medizinischen Laborantinnen und Laboranten* (medical laboratory technologists) c/o V Weber, Waisenhausstrasse 14, CH-9000 St Gallen, Switzerland.

*Schweizerischer Verband diplomierter ErnahrungsbeaterInnen* (dietitians) Oberstadt 11, CH-6204 Sempach-Stadt, Switzerland (tel 041-99 33 84).

*Société Suisse d'Odonto-Stomatologie* (dentists) Münzgraben 2, CH-3000 Bern 7, Switzerland.

*SVMTRA* (radiographers/radiological technologists) AWM Grabenstrasse 6, CH-3600 Thun, Switzerland

## USEFUL ADDRESSES

*International Committee of the Red Cross:* 19 Avenue de la Paix, CH-1202 Geneva, Switzerland (tel 22-734 6001; fax 22-733 2057; e-mail dc_com_cip.gva@icrc.org Website www.icrc.org (English) www.cicr.org (French/Italian)).

*Schweizerische Ärztezeitung:* Hans Huber Verlag, Länggassstrasse 76, CH-3000 Bern 9, Switzerland (tel 031-300 4500; fax 031-300 4591).

*Schweizerische Sanitätsdirektoren-Konferenz:* Terrassenweg 18, CH-3012 Bern, Switzerland (tel 031-301 2152). This is the central office for the cantonal health authorities; contact it for details of the authorities themselves.

*Schweizerische Vereinigung der Privatkliniken* (Swiss Association of Private Clinics) Postfach 29, Moosstrasse 2, CH-3073 Gümligen-Bern, Switzerland (tel 031-952 6133; fax 031-952 7683).

*Vereinigung Schweizerischer Krankenhäuser (VESKA)* (Association of Swiss Hospitals) Rain 32, CH-5001 Aarau, Switzerland (tel 062-824 1222; fax 062-822 3335).

# EASTERN EUROPE

## Czech Republic

*Embassy of the Czech Republic:* 3900 Spring of Freedom Street, NW, Washington DC 2008, USA (tel 202-274 9100; fax 202-966 8540; e-mail washington@embassy.mzv.cz Website www.czech.cz/washington).
*Embassy of the Czech Republic:* 26-30 Kensington Palace Gardens, London, W8 4QY, UK (tel 020-7243 1115; fax 020-7727 9654).
*Embassy of the Czech Republic:* 541 Sussex Drive, Ottawa, Ontario, K1N 6Z6, Canada (tel 613-562 3875; fax 613-562 3878; e-mail ottawa@embassy.mzv.cz).
*Currency:* 1 Crown/Koruna (CSK) = 100 Haléru.
*Exchange rate:* £1 = 58.75; $1 = 35.50.
*Capital:* Prague (Praha).
*International Telephone Code:* +420
*Population:* 10,500,000.
*Area:* 78,864 sq. km.
*Languages:* Czech, Slovak and German.

The Czech Republic came into being in 1993, with the peaceful seperation of Czechoslavakia's Czech and Slovak ethnic entities into two nation states. Once part of the Austro-Hungarian Empire Czechoslavakia gained brief independence in the 1920s and 30s before being absorbed first by Germany and then Russia. However, in 1989 the 'Velvet Revolution' saw communist authority collapse and the country swiftly embraced western market economics, before dividing. Although the economy has faced several problems since then the Czech Republic is currently on the verge of joining the European Union as it expands, having joined NATO in March 1999.

### HEALTH SERVICES

Public healthcare is universally available to citizens of the Czech Republic. As in many european nations the system is funded by a public insurance scheme, although there are options for private treatment and care, as not all types of treatment are provided by the public system. At present the system is undergoing changes, health establishments are obliged to have a contract with the insurance scheme, but individual professions are often not included in legislation so their position is ambiguous, physiotherapy is a case in point.

### SKILLS AND QUALIFICATIONS

At the time of writing the only specific information on working in the Czech Republic was supplied by the physiotherapists' association UNIFY. However, as the country is soon to join the EU it is probable that regulations applicable in those countries will soon apply to health professionals wishing to work in the Czech health system. It is therefore advisable to contact local professional organisatiosn and the Ministry of Health for clarification on the acceptance of non-Czech qualifications.

## Physiotherapy

Non-Czech physiotherapists can obtain work in the republic if their training course is similar to that of the Czech Republic's and lasted for at least three years. They should then obtain an 'acknowledgment of validity', to get one of these notarised copies, translated into Czech, of certificates and training curiculae should be presented to either the Ministry of Education (for degree courses) or the District Education Office, nearest the intended place of work (for non-degree courses).

Although there are no recognition agreements at the moment with foreign national organisations, a twinning project is under development between *Unie Fyzioterapeutu Ceske Republiky* (UNIFY) and the British Chartered Society of Physiotherapy. Currently the average salary for Czech physiotherapists is KCs 6,000-7,000 per month.

## VISAS AND WORK PERMITS

British and US passport holders do not require a visa to enter the Czech Republic and may remain for up to 30 days before they need to apply for a residence permit. Work permits are arranged by the employer at local Employment Offices, and a photocopy of your passport and qualifications / diplomas are required. Residence permits should be applied for prior to departure from a Czech Embassy abroad and the applicant should hold a valid work permit. Those working in the Czech Republic must register within three days at the local police station, where they may obtain an Identity Card for Foreigners.

Voluntary workers need a certificate from the relevant organisation, but do not have their visa stamped 'work permit'; these visas for voluntary workers are issued free of charge.

## JOB OPPORTUNITIES

At present the unemployment rate is 7% which some EU states would envy, and as a potential new entry to the EU there is obvious hope for expansion in the job market which would also be of interest to health professionals. There are two American medical centres in Prague, a Canadian medical centre and a Polyclinic for Foreigners, so there is scope for anglophone staff to be employed.

It should be taken as common sense that some fluency in Czech will be required.

## PROFESSIONAL ORGANISATIONS

*Ceska Stomatologická Spolecnost* (dentists) Karlovo nam 32, 121 11 Prague 2, Czech Republic.

*Czech Medical Association J.E. Purkyne:* PO Box 88, Sokolská 31, 120 26 Prague 2, Czech Republic (tel 2-24 91 51 95; fax 2-24 21 68 36; e-mail czma@cls.cz Website www.cls.cz/eCLS8.htm).

*Czech National Association of Nurses:* I. interní Klinika, U nemocnice 2, 12808 Prague, Czech Republic (tel 2-29 00 65; fax 2-29 79 32).

*Society for Radiological Technicians:* Sekce Radiologikych Laborantu, CS Lekarske Spolennosti J.E. Purkyne, Prague, Czech Republic.

*Unie Fyzioterapeutu Ceske Republiky (UNIFY):* (physiotherapists) Antala Staska

1670/80, CZ-140 46 Prague 4, Czech Republic (tel 2-6100 6441; fax 2-6100 6446; e-mail unify@oku-kl.cz Website www.oku-kl.cz/unify.htm).

## USEFUL ADDRESSES

*Grafton Recruitment:* Karlovo Nam 17, 120 00 Prague, Czech Republic (tel 22198 6450; fax 22198 6460; e-mail grafton@mbox.vo.cz Website www.graftongroup.com).

*Ministry of Education, Youth and Sports:* Karmelitská 5, CZ-110 00 Prague 1, Czech Republic.

*Ministry of Health:* Palackého nám., CZ-120 00 Prague 2, Czech Republic.

*The Prague Post:* (English language newspaper) Nai Porici 12, CZ-115 30 Prague 1, Czech Republic (tel 2-2487 5000; fax 2-2487 5050; e-mail news@praguepost.cz website www.praguepost.cz).

# Other East European Countries

## VOLUNTARY ORGANISATIONS

A large number of voluntary and aid organisations are involved in providing health services in eastern Europe; such as *CARE International* and *VSO. MERLIN* and *Médecins Sans Frontières* are involved in providing relief in regions affected by war, famine or natural disaster, such as Chechnya and the former Yugoslavia. *International Health Exchange* helps provide health workers for programmes in eastern Europe.

A programme of special interest to those looking to put their skills to use in eastern Europe is the VSO initiative East European Partnership, which places volunteers in a range of positions in several eastern European countries.

For all of these agencies, further information, addresses and telephone numbers are included in the directory starting on page 48.

## PROFESSIONAL ORGANISATIONS

The agencies mentioned above provide the most convenient way of finding out about what opportunities exist, but if you have a particular interest in a certain country (or countries) the addresses below will be useful for obtaining more information.

### Baltic Republics

*Association of Estonian Laboratory Technologists:* Söle 16, 0006 Tallinn, Estonia.

*Estonina Kinesitherapy Association:* Puusepa 1A, EE-2400 Tartu, Estonia (tel +372-27-449168; fax 27-428528; e-mail margusmu@cut.ee).

*Estonian Nurses' Association:* Paldiski mnt. 68, 0006 Tallinn (tel 2-471 856; fax 2-476 156).

*Latvian Association of Nurses:* 3 J Asara Street, Riga 226009 (tel/fax 2-273 340).

*Latvian Dental Association:* 20 Dzirciema Street, 1007 Riga, Latvia.

*Latvian Physicians Association:* Skolas Street 3, 1050 Riga, Latvia (tel 2-22 06 61/22 06 57; fax 2-22 06 57).

*Lithuanian Medical Association:* PO Box 1011, 3007 Kaunas, Lithuania (tel/fax 7-733 607).

*Lithuanian Nurses' Association:* PO Box 2450, 2051 Vilnius, Lithuania (tel 2-636 230; fax 2-263 640)

## Bulgaria

*Association Médicale Scientifique Républicaine de Stomatologie* (dentists) G Sofiisky, Sofia 1, Bulgaria.

*Bulgarian Association of Kinesitherapists and Rehabilitators* (physiotherapists) 1 Gurgulyat Street, Dept of Kinesitherapy NSA, 1000 Sofia, Bulgaria (tel +359-2-981 5228; fax 2-88 30 64).

*Bulgarian Medical Association:* 15 D Nestorov Street, 1431 Sofia, Bulgaria (tel 2-59 30 96; fax 2-59 91 26)

## Slovak Republic

*Slovak Chamber of Dentists:* PO Box 1, 917 01 Trnava, Slovakia

## Hungary

*Association of Hungarian Physiotherapists:* Frankel Leo u. 62, 1023 Budapest, Hungary (tel +36-1-386 2055; e-mail physioth@c3.hu Website www.c3.hu/~pysioth).

*Egeszegugyi Dolgozok Szakszervete* (radiographers/radiological technologists) Munnich Ferenc u. 32, 1363 Budapest, Hungary.

*Federation of Hungarian Medical Societies (MOTESZ):* Nádor u. 36 – POB 145, 1443 Budapest, Hungary (tel 1-112 3807; fax 1-111 6687).

*Hungarian Dental Association:* Mikszath K ter 5, 1088 Budapest, Hungary.

*Hungarian Nursing Association:* Karolina 19/21 IIe, 26 Budapest, H-1518, POB 200 (tel/fax 1-371 0401)

## Poland

*Polish Medical Association:* Al Ujazdowskie 24, 00-478 Warsaw, Poland (tel 22-288 699; fax 22-50 40).

*Polish Nurses' Association:* ul Koszykowa 8, 00-564 Warsaw, Poland (tel/fax 22-621 5066).

*Polish Society of Physiotherapy:* Zarzad Glowny, AWF – Katedra Rehabilitacji, ul Mikolowska 72, 40-065 Katowice, Poland (tel +48-32-2-510225; fax 32-2-511097; Website www.awfkatowire.edu.pl).

*Polish Stomatological Association* (dentists) Maxillofacial Surgery II Clinic, Lindle'a Street 4, 02-005 Warsaw, Poland

## Romania

*Romanian Association of Private Practising Medical Stomatologists:* Str Presei 6, Sector 1, Bucharest, Romania.

*Romanian Medical Association:* Str Progre Sului 10, Sector 1, Bucharest COD 70754, Romania (tel 1-3141071/3141062/3141817; fax 1-3121357)

## Former Yugoslavia

*Croatian Dental Society:* University of Zagreb, Gunduliceva 5, 4100 Zagreb, Croatia.

*Croatian Medical Association:* Subiceva Ulica 9, 41000 Zagreb, Croatia (tel/fax 41-416 820).

*Croatian Nurses' Association:* Kispaticeva 12, Zagreb, Croatia (tel 41-233 233; fax 41-212 247).

*Macedonian Medical Association:* Dame Gruev Br 3, PO Box 174, 91000 Skopje, Macedonia (tel 91-232577; fax 91-232577/111828).

*Nurses Association of Slovenia:* Vidovdanska 9, 61000 Ljubljana, Slovenia (tel/fax 61-316 055).

*Society of Radiologic Technologists of Slovenia:* Klinicni Centre-Institut za radiologijo, Zaloska 7, 61000 Ljubljana, Slovenia.

*Slovenian Association of Physiotherapists:* Institute for Rehabilitation, Linhartova 51, 61000 Ljubljana, Slovenia (tel 61-1375 188; fax 61-1372 070).

*Slovenian Medical Society:* Komenskega 4, 61001 Ljubljana, Slovenia (tel 61-323 469; fax 61-301 955).

*Slovenian Stomatologic Association:* Komenskega 4, 61001 Ljubljana, Slovenia

# AUSTRALIA & NEW ZEALAND

## Australia

*Embassy of the Commonwealth of Australia:* 1601 Massachusetts Avenue, NW, Washington, DC 20036, USA (tel 202-797-3000; fax 202-797-3168).
*High Commission of the Commonwealth of Australia:* Australia House, The Strand, London WC2B 4LA, UK (tel 020-7379 4334; fax 020-7240 5333).
*Australian High Commission:* Suite 710, 50 O'Connor Street, Ottawa, Ontario K1P 6L2, Canada (tel 613-236-0841; fax 613-236-4376).
*Currency:* Australian Dollar (A$).
*Exchange rate:* £1 = A$2.5; $1 = A$1.57.
*Capital:* Canberra.
*International Telephone Code:* +61
*Population:* 17,292,000.
*Area:* 7,682,000 sq. km.
*Language:* English

Australia is a modern, developed country, and the only country in the world to occupy an entire continent. Much of Australia is uninhabited, with the majority of the population concentrated along the eastern coast and the south-eastern corner of the continent. This uneven distribution brings with it extreme contrasts in lifestyle, and also presents problems in transportation and the provision of essential services – including health care – to all of the country's population.

Australia has a federal system of government and is divided into six independently governed states – New South Wales, Queensland, South Australia, Tasmania, Victoria and Western Australia – and two territories – the Northern Territory and the Australian Capital Territory (ACT). Together these states and territories form the Commonwealth of Australia. The states have significant autonomy, and there are significant differences in the laws and regulations that apply in the different states and territories.

There is a considerable strength of feeling in Australia that the country should become a republic, independent of its historical link with Britain. At present the Head of State is Queen Elizabeth II, and a recent referendum to determine public feeling towards an independent Australian Republic with an Australian Head of State resulted in a slim victory for the status quo, mostly due to public dissatisfaction with the methods offered by the government for presidential selection.

# HEALTH SERVICES

The Australian health care system consists of a mixture of public and private sector involvement: private medical practitioners provide primary and specialist care, and both public and private hospitals provide comprehensive services (of the 1100 hospitals throughout the country, 65% are public). The programme of community health services is presently being expanded. Responsibility for providing public health services lies with state and local governments, although the Commonwealth government has become increasingly involved in recent years – for example, in developing and coordinating national policies, and in a wide range of specific health issues. Health services were traditionally administered centrally in each state, but there has been a growing tendency towards regionalising these services, thereby devolving decision-making to a level closer to the communities concerned.

All towns and cities of a certain size have public hospitals, nursing homes and community health services. There are also special services for rural and remote areas, such as the well known Royal Flying Doctor Service.

The national health funding system in Australia is called Medicare, and it aims to provide all Australian residents with access to affordable health care; it is funded by the Commonwealth and state governments through taxation. It does not cover certain specific health areas, including physiotherapy, and chiropractic and most dental treatment.

## Where Health Professionals Work

There are about 42,000 doctors in active practice: 50% work as general practitioners (primary care), 30% as specialists and 20% in salaried employment. About 190,000 registered nurses work in public and private hospitals, nursing homes, home-nursing agencies, occupational health nursing services, school health services and community health activities. Nurses may also work in uniquely Australian situations – for example, in isolated health centres in the Northern Territory where the nurse may be the most senior practitioner, with a doctor visiting once a week. There are over 7000 dentists in Australia, most of whom work in private practice. Others work in the public sector for government, school dental services, universities and dental and general hospitals.

Occupational therapists in Australia practise in various settings, including hospitals, nursing homes, community centres and corrective institutions. Private practice opportunities are increasing rapidly, and there is now a greater demand for therapists to work in positions outside of government. Physiotherapists work with patients who are in hospital or who attend as out-patients. They may practise in a general or specialised hospital, or in a specialised unit – for example, intensive care, paediatrics, geriatrics or obstetrics. They may also practise in special schools, community health centres, health clinics, nursing homes, psychiatric clinics, government agencies, industry, sports clinics or they may establish a private practice. Some patients are treated at home, or, in some states, through domiciliary nursing care centres. Most podiatrists in Australia work in private practice; others work in hospitals, local government clinics, community health centres and nursing homes.

Most pharmacists in Australia practise in the community – i.e. retail businesses – or in hospitals. A small number work in the pharmaceutical industry, academic and government institutions, the public sector or the armed services. Most of those engaged in medical laboratory science are employed in public hospitals, while some work in private laboratories. The majority of dietitians in Australia are employed in public and private hospitals and community health centres. Some are also employed in industry – for example, in product development or in occupational health and safety.

## SKILLS AND QUALIFICATIONS

The majority of health professionals must be registered in order to be able to practise in Australia. Such registration comes under the purview of national boards, professional organisations, state health boards or the National Office of Overseas Skills Recognition (NOOSR). Generally a national body oversees registration or accreditation of qualifications, which are then presented to the health board in the state where you wish to practise and be registered. It is possible to move later on as many state boards operate 'mutual recognition' of qualifications, although there are sometimes minor differences regarding accreditation of qualifications or training requirements.

NOOSR produces a series of booklets covering the various professions, and these provide essential information on registration requirements, examination procedures, the nature of the professions, and which institutions around the world award qualifications that are acceptable in Australia. Contact NOOSR to obtain a copy of the booklet for your profession.

A comprehensive knowledge of English is essential to work in most of the professions described below in Australia, and if English is not your first language you will need to pass the Occupational English Test (OET) administered by the Language Australia, further details can be obtained from them (see *Useful Addresses*).

### Dentistry

To practise dentistry in Australia you must be registered with the local State or Territory Dental Board. Registration requirements vary from state to state, but generally you can only apply if you hold a Bachelor of Dental Surgery from an Australian, New Zealand, or UK university. Those whose qualifications are not immediately acceptable can take the written and clinical examinations conducted by the Australian Dental Council (ADC) to obtain registration under the auspices of the National Office of Overseas Skills Recognition (NOOSR). The procedure consists of the OET (see above), the Preliminary Examination, and the Final Examination, which is held over 3 to 5 days and can only be taken in Australia. The ADC certificate entitles you to apply for registration with any of the Dental Boards.

The 'Trans-Tasman' mutual recognition agreement allows dentists from New Zealand to work in Australia, with the requirements that they register with the dental council of the state they wish to live and work in.

### Dietetics

In Australia dietitians are nutritionists who are also qualified to provide counselling and clinical care of people with food and nutritional problems.

Most Australian dietitians work in public or private hospitals and community health centres. Although there are no legal requirements for registration, if you want to work in the public sector then you will be expected to have qualifications which meet the eligibilty requirements of the Dietitians Association of Australia and accreditation as an Accredited Practising Dietitan. The DAA's accreditation programme is a means of professional self-regulation to help maintain high professional standards. To obtain accreditation qualifications gained overseas are assessed by the DAA and then a professional examination is set, including the OET (see above). Full details can be obtained from the DAA and their website.

### Medical Laboratory Science

There are two levels of practice in medical laboratory science: medical scientists (or medical laboratory scientists), and medical laboratory technical officers (or medical technical officers), who work under the direction of the former. In Australia medical laboratory science comprises eight distinct professional disciplines: blood transfusion, clinical biochemistry, cytology, haematology, histopathology, immunology, microbiology and virology.

In Australia, a directed medical laboratory science degree from an Australian university or other qualification according to the guidelines approved by the Australian Institute of Medical Scientist (AIMS) is equired for employment as a medical scientist.

Registration is not a prerequisite for recognition or practice in Australia although membership of AIMS may enhance employment prospects. The AIMS is also the body that assesses overseas qualifications in this field. Further information about assessment can be obtained from the Institute.

## Medical Radiation Science

This broad term covers several distinct professional areas: diagnostic radiography, medical imaging, radiation therapy and sonography. With the exception of qualifications gained in New Zealand, the United Kingdom or from Hong Kong polytechnic anyone who wishes to work in these areas must have their qualifications assessed by the Australian Institute of Radiography (AIR). Anyone who wishes to work in medical radiation science must be able to provide accreditation from either the AIR or the Australia and New Zealand Society of Nuclear Medicine Technologists (ANZSMT).

In Australia the position of medical imaging technologist is broadly equivalent to that of diagnostic radiographer in the UK (other closely related job titles include medical radiation technologist, medical radiographer, medical imaging practitioner and sonographer); similarly the position of radiation therapist is broadly equivalent to that of therapeutic radiographer (other similar titles include radiotherapy technologist, radiation oncology technologist and therapy radiographer). According to AIR a newly qualified medical radiation scientist will earn between A\$26,000-A\$28,000 per year (allowing for variations from state to state) rising to A\$36,000-A\$40,000 after 6 years. The institute also provides medical indemnity insurance for all members paying residential membership subscriptions.

## Medicine

Medical registration in Australia is the responsibility of the Australian Medical Council and the State and Territory Medical Boards. Before medical practitioners can practise, they must be registered in the state or territory in which they intend to live and work.

All overseas trained doctors who wish to practise medicine in Australia, must be approved for immigration or hold permanent residence status and pass the Australian Medical Council (AMC) examination. The AMC examination consists of theoretical and clinical examinations (for which candidates must travel to Australia), and an OET (see above) for those of a non-English-speaking background. Because of Australia'a 'mutual recognition' scheme, a doctor with registration in one state or territory is able to gain automatic registration in another, however, this does not confer an automatic right to practise and the individual state medical boards should be contacted for clarification.

At present some rural areas of Australia have been designated as 'areas of need' where there is a shortfall in the number of medical practitioners. To relieve this some medical boards may register doctors with formal qualifications in general practice, after assessment of the qualification and register them without their having taken the AMC exam. These doctors will be registered for general practice only and will be required to work in the area for a minimum of five years.

A recent oversupply of doctors in Australia has resulted in the federal government restricting the number of overseas trained doctors permitted to practise. One important measure of the government's policy was to impose a point penalty on overseas-trained doctors seeking to migrate permanently to Australia under the immigration points test, meaning that a greatly reduced number of doctors can meet the pass mark. Full details on the points test and migration are available from your nearest Australian Embassy, High Commission or the Department of Immigration and Multicultural Affairs.

Registration with conditions may be available in one of several categories – for example, for overseas doctors who wish to undergo postgraduate training in Australia, or if they are specialists in the country in order to train others in their particular techniques. Specialists may also be able to obtain conditional registration in order to practise, following assessment by the relevant specialist college.

## Practical Information
### Provider Numbers
Assuming that you successfully register, those working in private practice will need to apply for a 'Provider Number' from the Health Insurance Commission (HIC), more commonly referred to as Medicare. The Commission is the source of payment to practitioners for persons entitled to free or subsidised medical treatment. On completion of the requisite form 'Application for Provider Number for a Medical Practitioner' your application should take about one week to be processed. The HIC also require you to attend an orientation session, these are usually held on Tuesday afternoons, but in order to attend you should already have your provider number. Those doctors working in the public sector do not require provider numbers.

### Doctor's Bags
The Australian Government provides a quantity of emergency drugs on a monthly basis for doctors. These can be obtained by completing and returning a 'Doctor Bag Order Form' which will be issued to you at HIC orientation, although you will need to provide your own bag.

## Nursing/Midwifery
There are two levels of nurse in Australia: the registered nurse and the enrolled nurse. Registered nurses are required to hold a Bachelor of Applied Science (Nursing) degree or its equivalent. They are licensed to practise their profession in the field(s) in which they are registered without supervision. Enrolled nurses are increasingly educated through advanced certificate or associate diploma level courses. They are 'second level' nurses and work under the supervision of registered nurses. Within Australia the Australian Nursing Federation negotiates on pay and conditions at a national level for all types of nurse.

Nurses are legally required to be registered or enrolled with the regulatory authority in the state or territory in which they intend to practise. A nurse can be registered as a midwife after appropriate education but must first be a registered nurse, in most states and territories. As midwifery courses are at postgraduate level in Australia, people holding only midwifery qualifications need to undertake a nursing course before they can be eligible for registration as a midwife in most states.

The Australian Nursing Council Inc (ANCI) sets national standards of nursing competency and assesses the qualifications of nurses resident overseas for migration purposes. However if the ANCI determines that you are eligible for registration, this does not ensure that every nurses' registration board will accept you for registration without requiring you to undergo a further period of supervised practice or a bridging programme, as the regulations specified by the boards vary. An example being New South Wales where nurses qualifying in Canada, Hong Kong, Ireland, Singapore, South Africa, the United Kingdom, the USA and Zimbabwe can have their qualifications assessed by post from outside Australia. Although 'mutual recognition' applies to certain categories of staff across state boundaries and for nursing staff from New Zealand.

Overseas-qualified nurses may apply for an assessment of their qualifications provided they have completed a pre-registration/pre-enrolment course of training overseas; have been registered or enrolled as a nurse in the country where they were trained; have a current registration, practising certificate or licence in the country where they are practising; and have practised in the branch of nursing for which they are seeking registration within the previous 5 years. If English is not their first language they must also have passed the nursing version of the OET (see above), or the International English Language Testing System (IELTS) Academic Test with an overall score of 7 and not less than 6.5 on any section.

Nurses living overseas should contact their nearest Australian Embassy, High Commission or Consulate in the first instance, for information on applying to the ANCI. You may also want to contact the ANCI to obtain a copy of their booklet *Nursing in Australia*, which provides information relevant to overseas nurses. The ANCI strongly recommends that nurses coming to Australia on working holiday visas get their qualifications assessed before leaving their home country, as this helps to avoid inconvenient delays in obtaining registration once in Australia.

Generally nurses from the UK who have undertaken at least three years training and have been registered with the UKCC are eligible for registration in Australia. The Working Holiday scheme also allows nurses to bypass ANCI assessment, although they should apply directly to the state they plan to work in, prior to depature for Australia.

## Occupational Therapy

At present occupational therapists must be registered to practise in Queensland, South Australia, Western Australia and the Northern Territory. Registration is through the local registration boards. Therapists with overseas qualifications first need to pass the NOOSR occupational therapy examination before they can register.

Registration is not required in Tasmania, New South Wales, Victoria or the ACT. However, if you want to work in a government-funded agency such as a public hospital or a community health centre you will need qualifications acceptable to the Australian Association of Occupational Therapists (AAOT) – again, this means that you will need to pass the NOOSR examination.

It is only possible to take this examination if you are a permanent resident of Australia, have been given permission to work in Australia, or have applied to migrate to Australia; are recognised as an occupational therapist in the country where you trained or practised; and have completed a degree or diploma in occupational therapy that NOOSR considers appropriate.

The examination procedure includes the OET (see above) and the occupational therapy examination itself, both of which can be taken at any Australian Embassy, High Commission or Consulate. Once you have received a NOOSR certificate you will be entitled to apply for membership of the AAOT and registration where required.

## Pharmacy

To practise pharmacy in Australia you must be registered with the local state or territory pharmacy registration authority. Pharmacists licenced to practise in the

UK, Ireland and New Zealand are accepted for registration by all such authorities, although a short period of supervised practical experience in Australia may be necessary first. Those whose qualifications are not immediately acceptable can undertake the examination procedure conducted by the Australian Pharmacy Examining Council (APEC). This procedure includes the OET (see above), two stages of examinations, an interview and counselling, and a period of supervised practice in an Australian pharmacy (usually 1 year). Pharmacists wanting to migrate to Australia on the basis of their pharmacy skills should note that the necessity of the supervised period excludes anyone from the examination procedure whose right of entry to Australia has not already been granted. Furthermore the interview and the Stage II examination can take place only in Australia. Once you have obtained an APEC Certificate, you can apply for registration with any of the pharmacy registering authorities.

## Physiotherapy

To practise physiotherapy in Australia you must be registered with the local State or Territory Physiotherapists' Board. Some overseas qualifications are acceptable for immediate registration; these include courses validated by the Chartered Society of Physiotherapy in the UK, and some qualifications gained in Hong Kong. For those with qualifications that are not immediately acceptable, assuming that certain eligibility criteria are met it is possible to go through an examination procedure conducted by the Australian Examining Council for Overseas Physiotherapists (AECOP); for qualifications from most physiotherapy schools in Canada, Ireland, New Zealand and South Africa, this means sitting a screening examination (which can be taken at an Australian Embassy, High Commission or Consulate abroad). If you complete the procedure you will receive an AECOP Final Certificate, which entitles you to apply for registration.

Further information on eligibility criteria and registration is included in the NOOSR booklet *Recognition of Physiotherapy Qualifications in Australia*.

## Podiatry (Chiropody)

The NOOSR booklet *Recognition of Podiatry Qualifications in Australia* provides a summary of the knowledge and competencies expected of a podiatrist. In Australia podiatry is regarded as a 'primary contact' profession, and it shares with medicine and dentistry the legal rights and responsibilities of diagnosis.

Overseas podiatry qualifications are not automatically recognised in Australia, and all overseas-trained podiatrists must undertake at least the Stage II (clinical) and perhaps also the Stage I (theoretical) examination of the Australian Podiatry Council.

Registration with a state podiatry board is a prerequisite for practising as a podiatrist in all Australian states and territories. Enquiries about the procedure involved should be made to the Australian High Commission, NOOSR, or the Executive Officer at the Australian Podiatry Council; the latter can also provide a list of state and territory registration boards and podiatry schools.

# VISAS AND WORK PERMITS

The procedure for entering Australia to take up employment can be complicated and very involved. It is important that you contact the nearest Australian Embassy or High Commission or the Department of Immigration and Multicultural Affairs for the latest details relevant to your own situation.

If you want to work in Australia for a short period you will need a temporary residence visa. These are issued to people who intend to enter Australia to engage in short-term employment (or one of several other activities). The categories of most interest to health professionals looking for work are *Specialist (category 414)*, which allows employers to recruit skilled workers from overseas on a short-term basis, when they can not recruit suitable people in Australia for the position; *Working Holiday Maker (category 417)*, which allows people up to 30 years old from selected countries (Canada, Ireland, Japan, Korea, Malta, the Netherlands and the United Kingdom) to combine a travelling holiday with work; *Educational (418)*, which allows qualified staff to work in Australian educational and research institutions; and *Medical Practitioner (422)*, which allows medical practitioners to enter the country, when the relevant State or Territory Medical Board recognises the applicant's medical qualifications as suitable to practise in that State or Territory, and there is a demonstrable need to employ a non-australian.

There is also a variety of categories for application for permanent residence. The *Skill Migration* category is likely to be the most appropriate for health professionals and there is a series of subdivisions including *Independent*. A points system operates for immigration; this means that an applicant is awarded a certain number of points according to their qualifications, age, skills, number of relatives resident in Australia, and so on. Points for skill are based on the applicant's usual occupation and the qualifications required to work in that occupation in Australia.

## JOB OPPORTUNITIES

Many professional organisations (listed below) produce journals and magazines that include details of vacancies. In many cases writing directly to hospitals in the state or territory where you want to work could be worthwhile. A list of public hospitals, divided by regions, can be obtained from Australia House in London, or from your nearest Embassy, High Commission or Consulate.

**N.B.** For agencies mentioned under the following headings, further information, addresses and telephone numbers are included in the directory on page 48. Agencies not in the directory are included at the end of this chapter.

### Medicine

There are areas of special need throughout the country and a range of short-term opportunities, although in general it is very difficult for overseas-trained doctors to obtain employment in Australia. Some state branches of the Australian Medical Association (AMA) run locum services, or are able to direct interested doctors to the appropriate locum agencies. Overseas doctors are often recruited to fill specific vacancies in designated 'areas of need' identified by the state health authorities. *AMAQ Services* provides such a service for locum GP positions in Queensland.

Not all agencies operate with a regional focus; *Morgan & Banks* recruits overseas medical staff for positions throughout Australia, especially GP trainees, training registrars, and consultants to work in 'areas of need'. In addition the *Auckland Medical Bureau* occasionally has information on locum positions for doctors in general practice and hospitals in Australia. *The Anaesthetists Agency* is a British one-specialty medical agency that occasionally places locum anaesthetists in posts in Australia.

Note that there are differences in nomenclature between levels of medical officer appointments in Australian hospitals and the British and Irish systems, and you should confirm with the hospital or your agency that you know which level in your home country the position in Australia corresponds to.

### Nursing

Nursing positions are widely advertised in Australian newspapers. Information concerning employment can be obtained from state and territory health departments. *Worldwide Healthcare Exchange (WHE)* is a network of healthcare recruitment companies that specialises in placing English-speaking nurses in posts in Australia. *Jenrick Medical* has information on vacancies for nurses in Australia. *STA Health Services* of Perth recruit general and specialist nurses for Western Australia, while *Code Blue Specialist Nurses Agency* recruits through interviews in major cities in the UK

## Other Professions

The universities in Australia that offer physiotherapy degree courses generally produce enough graduates each year to meet the country's demand for physiotherapists. However, some states such as New South Wales alllow physiotherapists to register and work under the working holiday scheme.

Australia currently has an oversupply of dentists in all states and territories; opportunities for overseas dentists are therefore rare.

## PROFESSIONAL ORGANISATIONS

The organisations listed below will be able to provide the addresses of the state and territory registration boards for their professions, where appropriate; alternatively this information is also available from NOOSR. Many of these organisations also publish journals that include information on employment opportunities in their profession.

*Australian Association of Occupational Therapists (AAOT):* 6 Spring Street, Fitzroy VIC 3065, Australia (tel 03-9416 1021; fax 03-9416 1421; e-mail otausnat@ozemail.com.au).

*Australian College of Rural and Remote Medicine:* Level 1, 467 Enoggera Road, Alderley QLD 4051, Australia (tel 07-3352 8600; fax 07-3356 2167; e-mail acrrm@acrrm.org.au Website www.acrrm.org.au).

*Australian Dental Association:* PO Box 520, St Leonards, NSW 1590, (75 Lithgow Street, St Leonards NSW 2065), Australia (tel 02-9906 4412; fax 02-9906 4917; e-mail adainc@ada.org.au Website www.ada.org.au).

*Australian Institute of Medical Scientists:* PO Box 1911, Milton Qld 4064, Australia (tel 07-3876 2988; fax 07-3876 2999; e-mail aimsnat@medserv.com.au Website wwwaims.org.au).

*Australian Institute of Radiography (AIR):* PO Box 1169 (1st Floor, 32 Bedford Street) Collingwood VIC 3066, Australia (tel 03-9419 3336; fax 03-9416 0783).

*Australian Medical Association:* PO Box E115, Queen Victoria Terrace, Parkes ACT 2600, Australia (tel 06-270 5400; fax 06-270 5499; Website www.ama.com.au).

*Australian and New Zealand Society of Nuclear Medicine (ANZSNM):* PO Box 27, Parkville VIC 3052, Australia (tel 03-9347 9633; fax 03-9347 4547; Website www.anzsnm.org.au).

*Australian and New Zealand College of Anaesthetists:* Ulimaroa, 630 St Kilda Road, Melbourne VIC 3004, Australia (tel 03-9510 6299; fax 03-9510 6786).

*Australian Nursing Federation:* Level 2, 21 Victoria Street, Melbourne VIC 3000, Australia (tel 03-9639 5211; fax 03-9652 0567; Website http://avoca.vicnet.au/anfed/).

*Australian Osteopathic Association:* PO Box 242, Thornleigh NSW 2130, Australia (tel 02-9980 8511; fax 02-9980 8466; e-mail aoa@tpgi.com.au Website www.osteopathic.com.au).

*Australian Physiotherapy Association:* PO Box 6465, Melbourne, VIC 3004, Australia (tel 03-9534 9400; fax 03-9534 9199).

*Australian Acupuncture and Traditional Chinese Medicine Association Ltd:* PO Box 5142, West End, QLD 4101, Australia.

*Australian Psychological Society:* 1 Grattan Street, Carlton South, VIC 3053, Australia (tel 03-9663 6166; fax 03-9663 6177; e-mail natloff@psychsociety.com.au Website www.aps.psychsociety.com.au).

*Australasian College for Emergency Medicine:* 17 Grattan Street, Carlton VIC 3053, Australia (tel 03-9663 3800; fax 03-9663 8013).

Australasian College of Dermatologists: PO Box 1065, Boronia Park NSW 2111, Australia (tel 02-9879 6177; fax 02-9816 1174; e-mail austcollderm@bigpond.com).

*Chiropractors Association of Australia:* PO Box 241, Springwood, NSW 2777, or PO Box 6248, South Penrith DC, NSW 2750, Australia (tel 02-4751 5644; fax 02-4751 5856; e-mail caa—nat@pnc.com.au Website caa.com.au).

*Dietitians' Association of Australia:* 1/8 Phipps Close, Deakin ACT 2600, Australia (tel 02-6282 9555; fax 02-6282 9888; e-mail daacanb@ncn.net.au Website www.daa.com.au).

*Orthoptists Association of Australia Inc:* 140 Hobury Road, Greenbank, QLD 4124, Australia (tel 3-9521 9844; fx 3-9597 0990).

*Optometrists Association Australia:* PO Box 185, Carlton South VIC 3053, Australia (tel 03-9663 6833; fax 03-9663 7478; e-mail ausoptom@ozemail.com.au).

*Pharmaceutical Society of Australia:* Pharmacy House, 44 Thesiger Court, Deakin ACT 2600, Australia (tel 02-6283 4777; fax 02-6285 2869; e-mail psa.nat@psa.org.au).

*Royal Australasian College of Physicians:* (Australian HQ) 145 MacQuarie Street, Sydney NSW 2000, Australia (tel 02-9256 5444; fax 02-9252 3310; e-mail racp@racp.edu.au Website www.racp.edu.au/).

*Royal Australasian College of Surgeons:* Surgeons Gardens, Spring Street, Melbourne VIC 3000, Australia (tel 03-9249 1200; fax 03-9249 1219; Website www.racs.edu.au).

*Royal Australian and New Zealand College of Pyschiatrists:* 309 La Trobe Street, Melbourne VIC 3000, Australia (tel 03-9640 0646; fax 03-9642 5652).

*Royal Australian and New Zealand College of Radiologists:* Level 9, 51 Druitt Street, Sydney NSW 2000, Australia (tel 02-9264 3555; fax 02-9264 7799).

*Royal Australian College of General Practitioners:* 1 Palmerston Crescent, South Melbourne VIC 3205, Australia (tel 03-9214 1414; fax 03-9214 1400; e-mail racgp@racgp.org.au Website www.racgp.org.au).

*Royal Australian College of Physicians:* 145 Macquarie Street, Sydney NSW 2000, Australia (tel 02-9256 5444; fax 02-9252 3310).

*Royal College of Nursing, Australia:* 1 Napier Close, Deakin ACT 2600, Australia (tel 02-6282 5633; fax 02-6282 3565; Website www.rcna.org.au).

*Speech Pathology Association of Australia:* 2nd Floor, 11-19 Bank Place, Melbourne VIC 3000, Australia (tel 03-9642 4899; fax 03-9642 4922; e-mail sppathau@vicnet.au Website http://home.vicnet.au/~sppathau/).

## USEFUL ADDRESSES

*Australian Acupuncture Ethics and Standards Organisation:* PO Box 84, Merrylands NSW 2160, Australia.

*Australian Dental Council:* Suite 1, Level 2, 112 Wellington Parade, East Melbourne, VIC 3002, Australia (tel 3-9415 1638; fax 3-9415 1669).

*Australian Federation of Homeopaths:* PO Box 806, Spit Junction NSW 2088, Australia.

*Australian Hospital Association:* 42 Thesiger Court, Deakin ACT 2600, Australia.

*Australian Medical Council:* PO Box 4810, Kingston ACT 2604, Australia (tel 02-6270 9777; fax 02-6270 9799; e-mail ama@amc.org.au Website www.amc.org.au).

*Australian Nursing Council Inc:* 1st Floor, 20 Challis Street, Dickson ACT 2602, Australia (tel 02-6257 7960; fax 02-6257 7955; e-mail anci@anci.org.au Website www.anci.org.au).

*Australian Pharmacy Examining Council (APEC):* c/- NOOSR (see address below; tel 06-240 7614; fax 06-240 7636).

*Australian Podiatry Council:* 41 Derby Street, Collingwood VIC 3066, Australia (tel 03-9416 3111; fax 03-9416 3188).

*Australian Red Cross:* PO Box 196, Carlton South, (155 Pelham Street, Carlton) VIC 3053, Australia (tel 03-9345 1800; fax 03-9348 2513; e-mail redcross@nat.redcross.org.au Website www.redcross.org.au).

*Department of Employment, Education and Training (DEET):* Derwent House, University Avenue, Canberra ACT 2601, Australia.

*Department of Immigration and Multicultural Affairs:* Central Office, Benjamin Offices, Chan Street, Belconnen ACT 2617, Australia (tel 02-6264 1111; 02-6264 1021).

*IELTS Australia:* GPO Box 2006, Canberra ACT 2601, Australia (tel 02-6285 8222; fax 02-6285 3233; e-mail ielts@idp.edu.au Website www.ielts.org/).

*Language Australia:* Level 2, 255 William Street, Melbourne VIC 3000, Australia (tel 03-9926 4779; fax 03-9926 4780; e-mail annl@la.ames.vic.edu.au Website www.sunsite.anu.edu.au/language-australia).

*National Office of Overseas Skills Recognition (NOOSR):* GPO Box 1407, Canberra ACT 2601, Australia (tel 06-240 8111; fax 06-240 7636; e-mail noosr@deetya.gov.au; Website www.deetya.gov.au/noosr).

*New South Wales Health Professionals Registration Board:* 28-36 Foveaux Street, Surry Hills NSW 2000, Australia (tel 02-281 0939; fax 02-281 2030).

*The Optometry Council:* PO Box 185, Carlton South VIC 3053, Australia (tel 03-9663 2733; fax 03-9663 7478; e-mail ocanz@ozemail.com.au). Optometry registration for Australia and New Zealand.

## AUSTRALIAN MEDICAL ASSOCIATION STATE BRANCHES

*AMA Australian Capital Territory Branch:* PO Box 560, Curtin ACT 2605, Australia (tel 02-6281 2144; fax 02-6285 2050; e-mail ama.act@dynamite.com.au).

*AMA New South Wales Branch:* PO Box 121, St Leonards NSW 2065, Australia (tel 02-9439 8822; fax 02-9438 3760; e-mail enquiries@nswama.com.au Website www.nswama.com.au).

*AMA Northern Territory Branch:* PO Box 4106, Casuarina NT 0811, Australia (tel 08-8927 7004; fax 08-8927 7475; e-mail amant@octa4.com.au).

*AMA Queensland Branch:* PO Box 123, Red Hill QLD 4059, Australia (tel 07-3872 2222; fax 07-3856 4727; e-mail amaq@amaq.com.au Website www.amaq.com.au).

*AMA South Australian Branch:* PO Box 134, North Adelaide SA 5006, Australia (tel 08-8267 4355; fax 08-8267 5349; e-mail admin@amasa.org.au Website ww.amasa.org.au).

*AMA Tasmanian Branch:* 2 Gore Street, South Hobart TAS 7004, Australia (tel 03-6223 2047; fax 03-6223 6469; e-mail admin@amatas.com.au).

*AMA Victorian Branch:* PO Box 21, Parkville VIC 3052, Australia (tel 03-9280 8722; fax 03-9280 8786; e-mail donnar@amavic.com.au Website www.amavic.com.au ).

*AMA Western Australian Branch:* PO Box 133, Nedlands WA 6909, Australia (tel 08-9273 3000; fax 08-9273 3073; e-mail mail@wa.ama.com.au Website www.wa.ama.com.au/).

## STATE & TERRITORY HEALTH DEPARTMENTS

*Australian Capital Territory, Department of Health and Community Care:* GPO Box 825 Canberra City ACT 2601, Australia (tel 02-6205 5111; fax 02-6205 0830; Website www.act.gov.au).

*New South Wales Health Department:* NSW Health Dept., Locked Mail Bag 961, North Sydney NSW 2059, Australia (tel 02-9391 9000; fax 02-9391 9101; Website www.health.nsw.gov.au).

*Northern Territory Health Services:* GPO Box 40596, Casuarina NT 0811, Australia (tel 08-8999 2400; fax 08-8922 8233).

*Queensland Health:* GPO Box 48, Brisbane QLD 4001, Australia (tel 07-3234 0111; fax 07-3234 0062; Website www.health.qld.gov.au).

*South Australia, Department of Human Services:* PO Box 39, Rundle Mall SA 5000, Australia (tel 08-8226 7000; fax 08-8226 6649).

*Tasmanian Department of Community and Health Services:* GPO Box 125B, Hobart TAS 7001, Australia (tel 03-6233 8011; fax 03-6233 6392; Website www.dchs.tas.gov.au).

*Department of Human Services:* GPO Box 4057, Melbourne VIC 3001, Australia (tel 03-9616 7777; fax 03-9616 7350; Website www.dhs.vic.gov.au).

*Western Australia Health:* PO Box 8172, Stirling Street, Perth WA 6849, Australia (tel 08-9222 4222; fax 08-9222 4009).

## MEDICAL BOARDS

*Medical Board of the Australian Capital Territory:* PO Box 1309, Tuggeranong ACT 2901, Australia (tel 02-6205 1599; fax 02-6205 1602).

*New South Wales Medical Board:* PO Box 104, Gladesville NSW 2111, Australia (tel 02-9879 6799; fax 02-9816 5307).

*Northern Territory Medical Board:* GPO Box 4221, Darwin NT 0801, Australia (tel 08-89469542; fax 08-8946 9550).

*Medical Board of Queensland:* GPO Box 2438, Brisbane QLD 4001, Australia (tel 07-3227 7111; 07-3225 2527).

*Medical Board of South Australia:* PO Box 359, Stepney SA 5069, Australia (tel 08-8362 7811; fax 08-8362 7906).

*Medical Council of Tasmania:* 2 Gore Street, South Hobart TAS 7000, Australia (tel 03-6223 8466).

*Medical Board of Victoria:* GPO Box 821, Melbourne VIC 3205, Australia (tel 03-9695 9500; fax 03-9614 0382).

*Medical Board of Western Australia:* PO Box 788, West Perth WA 66872, Australia (tel 08-9481 1011; fax 08-9321 1744).

## NURSING BOARDS

*Nurses Board of the ACT:* Ground Floor, Centrepoint Building, Anketell Street, Tuggeranong ACT 2900, Australia (tel 02-6205 1599; fax 02-6205 1602).

*New South Wales Nurses Registration Board:* Level 2, 28-36 Foveaux Street, Surry Hills NSW 2010, Australia (tel 02-9281 4300; fax 02-9281 2030; e-mail nursesreg@doh.health.nsw.gov.au).

*Nurses Board of the Northern Territory:* PO Box 4221, Darwin NT 0801, Australia (tel 08-8946 9545; fax08-8946 9550; e-mail nurses.board@nt.gov.au).

*Nurses Registration Board of Queensland:* GPO Box 2928, Brisbane QLD 4001, Australia (tel 07-3223 5160; fax 07-3223 5115)..

*Nurses Board of South Australia:* 200 East Terrace, Adelaide SA 5000, Australia (tel 08-8223 9700; fax 08-8223 9717; e-mail registrations@ nursesboard.sa.gov.au).

*Nursing Board of Tasmania:* 15 Princes Street, Sandy Bay, TAS 7005, Australia (tel 03-6224 3991; fax 03-6224 3995).

*Nurses Board of Victoria:* GPO Box 4932, Melbourne VIC 3001, Australia (tel 03-9613 0333; fax 03-9629 2409).

*Nurses Board of Western Australia:* 165 Adelaide Terrace, East Perth WA 6892, Australia (tel 08-9421 1100; fax 08-9421 1022).

## Other Agencies

*Code Blue Specialist Nurses Agency:* tel 03-9792 9611/9866; Website www.codeblue.com.

*NT Medic Pty Ltd:* GPO Box 2893, Darwin NT 0801, Australia (tel 08-8941 1819; fax 08-8941 0712).

*STA Health Services:* Perth, Australia (tel 08-9389 7774; fax 08-9386 8535; e-mail sta@q-net.au).

---

# New Zealand

---

*New Zealand Embassy:* 37 Observatory Circle, NW, Washington, DC 20008, USA (tel 202-328-4800; fax 202-667-5227).

*New Zealand High Commission:* New Zealand House, 80 Haymarket, London SW1Y 4TQ, UK (tel 020-7930 8422; fax 020-7839 4580).

*New Zealand High Commission:* Suite 727, Metropolitan House, 99 Bank Street, Ottawa, Ontario K1P 5G4, Canada (tel 613-238-5991; fax 613-238-5707).

*Currency:* New Zealand Dollar (NZ$).
*Exchange rate:* £1 = NZ$3.25; $1 = NZ$2.2.
*Capital:* Wellington.
*International Telephone Code:* +64
*Population:* 3,454,000.
*Area:* 271,000 sq. km.
*Language:* English

New Zealand 'the land of the long white cloud' is a modern country with some amazing and unspoiled countryside. Although New Zealand and the UK are of comparable size, New Zealand has only one-twentieth the population. The two islands that make up New Zealand are a popular destination for international travellers and for those looking to work in an English-speaking country with an inviting climate. The population is made up of the native Maori and european and asian immigrants. In many respects New Zealand will feel familiar to european expatriates, but it has a style and way of life entirely its own.

# HEALTH SERVICES

Health care standards in New Zealand are generally high, although some poverty related diseases are on the rise again due to the social stresses of economic restructuring. Life expectancy is the same as in the UK but there are significant differences between ethnic groups.

The provision of health care has been a major political issue over the last decade; apart from payment for doctor's fees and some prescription charges, for many years the health service was provided free of charge. However, the increasing cost of specialist health services coupled with the reduction in the number of tax paying workers has brought about a partial user-pays service. The criteria for public health funding is being constantly debated by politicians and senior health care workers. Health spending follows social welfare as a major item of government expenditure, with 75% of the money spent on health services coming from the government, and this expenditure accounting for 16% of government spending. In April 1998 $6.2 billion was allocated for health care (7.8% of GDP).

The public health system in New Zealand is organised such that primary health care (GPs, prescriptions, out-patients visits to hospitals) is funded by a mix of public subsidy and private fees while secondary health care is provided free. About 60% of New Zealanders have supplementary private medical insurance, to cover the additional costs of using the public system and to cover the costs of private hospital care. The costs of health care not covered by the state are between $30-$40 for a visit to a doctor, prescription charges at $15 per item maximum, optometrists (opticians) and dentists charges at around $80 per visit. People on low incomes can get a Community Services Card which entitles them to cheaper primary care, but not dental care. As in Britain, the GPs provide most basic health care. It is not necessary to register with just one doctor, although for obvious reasons people tend to stay with the same doctor.

Hospital funding and management is currently in a state of upheaval due to the introduction of an internal market system similar to the NHS internal market. Hospitals were renamed Crown Health Enterprises for some years but in 1998 it was announced that the 23 CHEs are now to be called 'hospitals' again. These hospitals compete for the available funds on a regional basis. The Government has yet to define what services it expects hospitals to provide free of charge, but at least the ambition of turning hospitals into profit making ventures, has been abandoned. The quality of care in the public hospital sector does not seem to have declined from its previous high standards but more services are being provided on 'user-charge' basis, public hospitals still provide free operations but the waiting lists are growing. Recently a points based system has been introduced so that people of high priority are dealt with first. As a result, a great number of people have taken out medical insurance and elect to go to a private hospital; unlike in the UK there are no private beds in public hospitals.

Private hospitals exist but cater mainly for elective surgery and for those who prefer a private room and more choice of when they have their operation. Waiting lists for standard surgical routines in public hospitals are shorter than in the UK.

Dental care for adults is only subsidised by the government in a special low income adult programme which some practitioners have joined, but is provided free for all primary school children through the school dental system.

# SKILLS AND QUALIFICATIONS

## Acupuncture

At the time of writing anyone could set up as an acupuncturist in New Zealand, however those who wished to join the New Zealand Register of Acupuncturists (NZRA) would have to meet its training requirements. There are currently 70 different colleges from Australia, Canada, China, Hong Kong, Japan, Korea, the UK and the USA who's training is recognised as suitable by the NZRA. Membership of the register allows the practitioner to provide acupuncture services under the Accident Insurance Act 1998 (a government insurance scheme that covers all New Zealanders) with the benefits of indemnity and malpractice insurance. The NZRA has a recognition agreement with the Australian Acupuncture and Traditional Chinese Medicine Association and can arrange locum work for registered acupuncturists for up to 12 weeks.

## Chiropody/Podiatry
Training approved for State Registration in the UK by the British Society of Chiropodists and Podiatrists is generally acceptable in New Zealand, but it is still a question of applying for individual registration to the Podiatrists Board, and a pre-entry examination must be completed.

## Dentistry
Holders of degrees in dentistry from British and Australian universities are eligible to apply for registration to practise as a dentist on arrival in New Zealand. Applicants will need to produce evidence that a position as a registered dental practitioner is available to them in the country. All other overseas dentists must apply to sit the overseas registration examination. Full details of the registration procedure and the fees involved are available from the Dental Council of New Zealand. If you wish to be recognised as a specialist you must first register as a dentist and then apply for specialist registration.

Overseas-trained dental technicians need to pass an entry examination in order to register. Technicians need to have completed at least 3 years' training and to hold overseas registration. Further information is available from the Dental Technicians Board.

Overseas dental therapists' qualifications are currently not recognised in New Zealand, and to practise in this area you must have attended an approved training course in the country. In New Zealand dental therapists are school dental nurses working in school dental clinics.

Dentists employ auxiliaries to work as dental hygienists – there is no such designation in New Zealand. Registration is not required for these positions and the dentist assumes responsibility for their work. Dental surgery assistants do not require qualifications, and have no registration procedure.

## Dietetics
Only registered dietitians can practise dietetics in New Zealand. To obtain registration you must sit the Overseas Candidates Registration Examination (OCRE). Applicants are required to have completed a tertiary level programme of dietetic training of at least 3 years' duration, including a practical component, leading to a degree, diploma or other qualification approved by the Dietitians Board. Applicants must be registered, licensed or otherwise officially recognised as dietitians in the country in which they trained. They must also present with their applications details and evidence of training undertaken and examinations passed; details of work experience; a certificate of good character; and evidence of English proficiency.

## Homeopathy
At present anyone who has a work permit may set up as a homeopath in New Zealand, however, this may change soon. The New Zealand Council of

homoeopaths currently acts as a register of medical doctors trained in homeopathy and can give information on current trends and requirements.

## Medical Laboratory Technology

To work as a medical laboratory technologist in New Zealand you must be registered with the Medical Laboratory Technologists Board. Certain qualifications from Australia, Canada and the UK are accepted for registration, though you will also need medical laboratory training and experience. If you have other qualifications you will need to have them assessed by the New Zealand Qualifications Authority (the Board can forward your application for assessment).

You may work as a laboratory assistant, under the supervision of a registered health professional, without being registered with the Board.

## Medical Radiation Technology

This is a broad term that covers diagnostic radiography, therapeutic radiography, radionuclide imaging (nuclear medicine) ultrasound imaging and magnetic resonance imaging. To work as a medical radiation technologist (equivalent to radiographer in the UK) you must be registered with the Medical Radiation Technologists Board. Some British qualifications are recognised for registration purposes by the Board; in other cases qualifications need to be assessed by the appropriate New Zealand authority. Contact the Board for further information.

## Medicine

The Medical Council of New Zealand authorises the registration of medical practitioners under the regulations of the Medical Practitioners Act of 1995. Under this act no one may practise medicine using the term 'medical practitioner' unless they are registered, or hold temporary registration and have a valid annual practising certificate. Graduates of medical schools in Australia are entitled to apply for probationary or general registration in New Zealand without examination. Doctors who have graduated from medical schools in the UK, Ireland, Canada and South Africa are no longer automatically eligible for probationary or general registration unless they meet specific examination requirements. Graduates from medical schools in other countries will need to apply for probationary registration, and either pass the New Zealand Registration Examination (NZREX) or be assessed as eligible for admission to the vocational register.

The supervised probationary period, prior to admission to general registration, is normally 12 months.

Temporary registration without examination will continue to be available for a maximum of 3 years to doctors visiting New Zealand for particular reasons, if they graduated from medical schools listed in the *World Directory of Medical Schools* published by WHO. These reasons are: to give postgraduate instruction; to obtain postgraduate training and experience as sponsored trainees; and to serve in shortage specialties, for a limited period, on the understanding that they will leave New Zealand when the training or experience is concluded.

Further details about the NZREX can be obtained from the Medical Council in Wellington which will also answer queries on eligibility for registration and from the NZ Health On-line website www.nzhealth.co.nz/jobs/register.

## Nursing/Midwifery

All nurses and midwives seeking employment must be registered by the Nursing Council of New Zealand. The Council will require evidence of your qualifications – you must have undertaken a nursing or midwifery programme similar in content and length to the equivalent programme in New Zealand – and these must show an ability to meet the competency requirements of the registers for nurses and midwives. The Nursing Council has an overseas registration procedure and details of this are on their website (www.nursingcouncil.org.nz/reg). Nurses must also be fluent in English and the Council may require applicants to sit an English examination. Once registration/enrolment is approved you may then apply for a practising certificate.

There are no regulatory bodies or national standards of practice for nurse aides and carers. Employers assess these staff according to their skills and experience, and recognise any certificates and other qualifications that they have.

## Pharmacy

The Pharmaceutical Society of New Zealand is the statutory body for the registration of pharmacists. A reciprocal arrangement exists between the Society and its corresponding organisations in the UK, Ireland and Australia; this means that a pharmacist registered in these countries can become registered in New Zealand on application to the Society. You will need to produce evidence of good standing from the Pharmaceutical Society that you are registered with and to work in a supervised environment for 4 weeks. After this period you will be interviewed to ensure that you have adapted to the New Zealand pharmacy environment.

Pharmacists who gained their qualifications in other countries must go through an assessment process before they are admitted to the New Zealand register. They will need to provide proof that they are registered in the country in which they gained their pharmacy qualification; a statement from their registration authority confirming that they are in good standing with that authority; evidence of eligibiity for permanent residence in New Zealand; and evidence of English proficiency. Applicants must submit details of their degree/diploma curriculum including all marks gained, hours studied etc, this documentation must be supplied by the awarding establishment. They must also submit a full curriculum vitae with accompanying evidence of all post-graduate qualifications and work experience. This documentation will then be considered by a board of assessors to confirm if the applicant's knowledge is equivalent to that of a New Zealand pharmacy graduate. If so then the applicant must then successfully complete 26 weeks of full-time training in an approved community or hospital pharmacy. Applicants must also pass an examination in pharmacy law, those who's training is not deemed equivalent to that of a New Zealander will need to undertake further study prior to reassessment.

## Psychology

It is not compulsory to be registered in New Zealand, but registration will enhance your employment options. Only registered psychologists can be employed in the state sector, and working for other employers often requires registration. In order to practise psychologists also need to have obtained an Annual Practising Certificate from the Psychologists Board.

Overseas psychologists can register, but will need to satisfy the New Zealand Psychologists Board that their qualifications are equivalent to those required of New Zealand psychologists. For this reason they may be examined by the Board in the theory and practice of psychology. Overseas applicants may also need to provide evidence of competence in the English language, and to undergo a supervised period of practice.

Further advice on registering with overseas qualifications is available from the Secretary of the Board.

## Occupational Therapy

To work as an occupational therapist in New Zealand you must first obtain registration with the Occupational Therapy Board, which can be quite a time-consuming process. For graduates of colleges in the UK, Australia and Canada, registration should not be difficult to obtain.

## Physiotherapy

Registration is a legal requirement for practising physiotherapy in New Zealand, and all physiotherapists intending to work in the country must register with the Physiotherapy Board. The Board grants either full or temporary registration: full registration entitles a physiotherapist to practise anywhere in New Zealand, subject to the holding of an annual practising certificate; temporary registration may be available to those not eligible for full registration who wish to work or undertake postgraduate physiotherapy studies, but restricts practice to a specified place for a specified period of time. An applicant must have a definite offer of employment (or study) before applying for temporary registration.

To be eligible for registration, overseas physiotherapists need to meet various criteria, including suitability of qualifications, proficiency in English and sufficient clinical experience. Full details of the procedure are included in the Physiotherapy Board's booklet *Registration Procedures for Overseas Physiotherapists*.

Special legislation governs the use of ultrasonic therapy apparatus in New Zealand and every physiotherapist using such equipment must hold an ultrasonic licence. As the use of ultrasonic therapy is likely in any position held in New Zealand, overseas-qualified physiotherapists should apply for the licence at the same time as they apply for registration.

## Speech & Language Therapy

Most employers require speech therapists to have their qualification assessed by the New Zealand Speech Language Therapy Association, to confirm that it meets the Association's criteria for membership.

# VISAS AND WORK PERMITS

Many countries now have visa exempt status for their citizens to enter New Zealand, although you should obtain a visitor's permit on arrival (these generally last three months initially but can be extended) and be able to show that you will have sufficient funds to support yourself during your stay. Sufficient funds being deemed to be NZ$1000 per month.

If you find or wish to take up employment in New Zealand you will need to obtain a work visa (Australian citizens are exempt from this requirement) which can be applied for from outside New Zealand or within the country should you arrive with the intention of looking for work. When you apply for it, your employer will need to provide details of your job title, responsibilitites, pay and conditions, duration of employment and proof that the vacancy could not be filled by a New Zealand resident. The period of time you are allowed to stay in the country varies according to where the visa was applied for; from outside New Zealand the visa will be valid for up to 3 years, but only 9 months if applied for from inside the country.

If you are planning to move permanently to New Zealand or work there for longer than the 3 years allowable with the temporary work permit, you will need a residence visa. Health professionals may be eligible for this visa under the General Skills category, which operates on a points system. The qualities of potential immigrants are assessed according to factors such as English language ability, qualifications, work experience, possession of a job offer, age, 'settlement factors' and family sponsorship. If registration in your profession is required by law, then you must be registered before you can claim points for your professional qualification.

There is also the *Working Holiday Visa* which allows people up to 30 years old from selected countries (Canada, Ireland, Japan and the United Kingdom) to combine a travelling holiday with work. Details of this scheme and visa and work permit regulations can be obtained from the New Zealand Immigration Service, or the nearest embassy or High Commison.

## JOB OPPORTUNITIES

In addition to the agencies listed below and in Part II, those seeking employment in New Zealand can often arrange a position directly with the hospitals or health services. There are also several internet sites listing vacancies in New Zealand, some operated by the regional health services. One such http://www.hospitals.co.nz/jobs/job.html provides employment and immigration information. The weekly journal *Health Employment Gazette* is a source of employment and vacancy information and the most recent two issues are available on their website.

### Dentistry

Most work opportunities for dentists in New Zealand are through private practice, either as assistants or locums, or by actually purchasing a practice. There are some appointments in hospitals, some in the armed services and very few in administration. There is just one school of dentistry, located in Dunedin, which occasionally has appointments available.

Overall the number of vacancies for overseas dentists is not great. In a country with approximately 1450 dentists and 900 private practices, about 14 hospitals that employ dentists, and one dental school, there are very limited work opportunities outside private practice. There are limited general practice positions as locums and assistants, but these are less available now than in the past, due to an increasing number of New Zealand dentists choosing to remain in their own country, and more overseas dentists qualifying to practise. There are very few positions available in hospital and state-funded dentistry, as there is now a very limited service and apart from senior hospital dental appointments, any work tends to go to first and second-year graduates. There is currently no significant unemployment of dentists, except for those who have a special area that they wish to practise in.

There are no locum agencies for dentists in New Zealand, due to the size of the country. The New Zealand Dental Association keeps a card file for dentists seeking work, and also carries advertisements in its two main publications, *The Dental Journal* and the *NZDA News*, which between them are published nine times a year. It may also be worth contacting Craig Alexander at NZ Dental Insurance (155 Remuera Road, Auckland 5, New Zealand; tel 09-523 3349; fax 09-523 3609), who may have details of some vacancies.

### Medical Laboratory Technology

Overseas-trained technologists could write to individual medical laboratories for information on any vacancies that are available. A list of hospital and private laboratories is produced by the New Zealand Institute of Medical Laboratory Science, and should also be available from the Medical Laboratory Technologists Board.

## Medical Radiation Technology

All overseas qualified MRTs must register with the Medical Radiation Technology Board in order to be employed in New Zealand. MRTs are usually in short supply from April onwards as new graduates enter the workforce in December, and many seek work experience outside New Zealand. Sonographers are very sought after at the moment and there are often locum places open for all specialisations. Salaries for MRTs are between NZ$30,000-NZ$47,000, while sonographers can earn NZ$40,000-NZ$49,000.

## Medicine

The number of foreign doctors registering with the Medical Council has increased in recent years and there are fears that this may result in an oversupply of medical personnel. This situation seems to be mainly the result of an increase in numbers of skilled immigrants, particularly from South Africa. The situation in New Zealand has traditionally been the reverse of this, with qualified New Zealanders going abroad, and leaving opportunities for professional migrants in their wake. The New Zealand Medical Association may be able to provide an up-to-date assessment of employment opportunities.

Doctors considering a period of employment in New Zealand may want to contact the Association of Salaried Medical Specialists for information on pay and employment benefits.

### Agencies

Several agencies are involved in the recruitment of medical staff *Jenrick* sometimes has vacancies for doctors in New Zealand. The *Auckland Medical Bureau* places doctors in locum and permanent positions in general practice and hospitals throughout the country.

Some hospitals are involved in recruiting staff directly: *Coast Health Care* recruits overseas staff in a range of medical specialisations, for example, and *Northern Clinical Training Network* recruits medical staff at most levels for hospital and health services in the Auckland area. Positions are also advertise in the *BMJ*, *Australian Medical Journal*, online at www.nzjobs.co.nz and in local papers.

## Nursing/Midwifery

Recently the employment situation has not been particularly good for general nurses, although there have been more opportunities for experienced nurses and midwives with specialist skills. Nursing positions are advertised in the daily newspapers, and also in *Kai Tiaki: Nursing New Zealand* (the monthly magazine of the New Zealand Nurses Organisation) and on the Internet (as mentioned above). Direct application to hospitals may also be worthwhile, at present *Health Waikato* is trying to recruit registered nurses for ten departments. You may also wish to contact the Hospital Association and Residential Care NZ Inc for advice on positions in the private sector.

The New Zealand Nurses Organisation represents nurses, midwives, care givers and support staff in New Zealand, and can provide professional advice to its members, though it does not act as an employment agency.

Independently practising nurses are not yet very common in New Zealand; there are a few nursing practices that offer a range of services. Many midwives are employed by public hospitals, and qualified midwives may also practise independently and many have formed into midwifery provider groups. The New Zealand Nurses Organisation may be able to provide you with further information on work in these areas.

## Agencies

Several agencies are involved in placing nursing and care staff in placements in New Zealand, but you should get in touch with them before you arrive in New Zealand so that you can get the process of obtaining registration underway. *Coast Health Care* recruits overseas theatre nurses, and *Jenrick* normally has some vacancies for nurses in New Zealand. *Worldwide Healthcare Exchange (WHE)* is a network of healthcare recruitment companies that specialises in placing English-speaking nurses in posts in New Zealand. *Panacea Healthcare* places nurses, hospital aides and carers in both clinical and community settings in the Auckland and Hamilton regions.

## Pharmacy

Positions are normally advertised in trade journals and magazines; the two main trade journals in New Zealand are *Pharmacy Today* and *NZ Pharmacy* (addresses below). Overseas pharmacists looking for work can advertise their availability before they arrive in the country. Also *Jenrick Medical* may have vacancies for pharmacists in New Zealand.

## Therapy

The NZ Health website has banner displaysindicating that of all the categories of therapist – occupational therapists, physiotherapists and speech & language therapists – are in the most demand, particularly as a result of recruitment agencies enticing these professionals overseas with higher salaries and other incentives such as free travel.

# PROFESSIONAL ORGANISATIONS

*Australian and New Zealand College of Anaesthetists:* Ulimaroa, 630 St Kilda Road, Melbounre VIC 3004, Australia (tel 03-9510 6299; fax 03-9510 6786).

*Homeopathic Society Inc:* PO Box 67-095, Mt Eden, Auckland, New Zealand.

*New Zealand Association of Occupational Therapists:* PO Box 12-506 (Royal Society of New Zealand Offices, 4 Halswell Street, Thorndon), Wellington 6001, New Zealand (tel 04-473 6510; fax 04-473 1841).

*New Zealand Association of Optometrists Inc:* PO Box 30-545, Lower Hutt, New Zealand.

*New Zealand Association of Psychotherapists:* 50 Connaught Terrace, Wellington 2, New Zealand.

*New Zealand Audiological Society Inc:* PO Box 33465 Takapuna, New Zealand.

*New Zealand Chiropractors Association Inc:* PO Box 7144, Wellesly Street, Auckland, New Zealand.

*New Zealand College of Midwives:* PO Box 21 106, Edgeware, Christchurch, New Zealand (tel 03-37 2732; fax 03-377 5662; e-mail nzcom@clear.net.nz Website http://webnz.com/midwives/).

*New Zealand Council of Homeopaths:* PO Box 51-195, Tawa, Wellington, New Zealand.

*New Zealand Dental Association:* PO Box 28 084, Auckland 5, New Zealand (tel 09-524 2778; fax 09-520 5256; e-mail nzda@nzda.org.nz).

*New Zealand Dental Therapists Association:* 9 Miriam Corban Heights, Henderson, Auckland, New Zealand.

*New Zealand Dietetic Association Inc:* PO Box 5065, Wellington, New Zealand.

*New Zealand General Practitioners' Association:* PO Box 10 789, 28 The Terrace, Wellington, New Zealand (tel 04-472 8992; fax 04-499 3607).

*New Zealand Institute of Dental Technologists:* 543 Main Highway, Hatfields Beach, Orewa, New Zealand.

*New Zealand Institute of Medical Laboratory Science:* PO Box 3270, Christchurch, New Zealand (tel 03-313 4761; fax 03-313 20989; e-mail nzimls@ exevents.co.nz Website www.nzimls.org.nz).

*New Zealand Institute of Medical Radiation Technology:* PO Box 25 668, St Heliers, Auckland, New Zealand (tel 09-528 1087).

*New Zealand Medical Association:* PO Box 156, Wellington, New Zealand (tel 04-472 4741; fax 04-471 0838; Website www.nzma.org.nz).

*New Zealand Nurses Organisation:* PO Box 2128, Wellington, New Zealand (tel 04-385 0847; fax 04-382 9993; e-mail nurses.org.nz).

*New Zealand Private Physiotherapists' Association:* PO Box 26 454, Epsom, Auckland 1003, New Zealand (tel 09-630 5943; fax 09-630 5933; e-mail nzppaadmin@clear.net.nz).

*New Zealand Psychological Society Inc:* PO Box 4092, Wellington, New Zealand (tel 04-801 5414; fax 04-801 5366; e-mail office@psychology.org.nz Website www.psychology.org.nz).

*New Zealand Register of Acupuncturists:* PO Box 9950, Wellington 6001, New Zealand (tel 04-476 4866: e-mail nzra@acupuncture.org.nz Website www.acupuncture.org.nz).

*New Zealand Society of Naturopaths:* PO Box 90 170, Auckland, New Zealand (tel 09-360 2772; Website www.naturopath.org.nz).

*New Zealand Society of Physiotherapists Inc:* PO Box 27 386 (Level 3, Wang House, 195-201 Willis Street), Wellington (tel 04-801 6500; fax 04-801 5571; e-mail nzsp@mail.netlink.co.nz).

*New Zealand Society of Podiatrists Inc:* PO Box 14 697, Wellington, New Zealand (Website www.podiatry.org.nz).

*New Zealand Speech-Language Therapists Association:* Suite 369, 63 Remuera Road, Newmarket, Auckland (tel 03-235 8257; fax 03-235 8850 Website www.nzsta-speech.org.nz).

*Nurses Association Inc:* PO Box 2128, Wellington, New Zealand.

*Pharmacy Guild of New Zealand Inc:* (PO Box 127 139)Pharmacy House, 124 Dixon Street, Wellington, New Zealand (tel 04-802 8200; fax 04-384 8055; e-mail p.guild@pharmacy-house.org.nz Website www.pgnz.org.nz).

*Pharmaceutical Society of New Zealand:* PO Box 11-640, Wellington, New Zealand (tel +64-4-802 0030; fax 04-382 9297; Website www. psnz.org.nz).

*Royal Australasian College of Physicians:* (New Zealand HQ) 5th Floor, St John House, 99 The Terrace, Wellington, New Zealand (tel 04-472 6713; fax 04-472 6718; e-mail jo.jones@racp.org.nz Website www.racp.edu.au/).

*Royal Australasian College of Radiologists (New Zealand Branch):* Dept of Radiology, Christchurch Hospital, Private Bag, Christchurch, New Zealand

*Royal New Zealand College of General Practitioners:* PO Box 10 440, Wellington, New Zealand (tel 04-496 5999; fax 04-496 5997; e-mail rnzcgp@rnzcgp.org.nz Website www.rnzcgp.org.nz).

## USEFUL ADDRESSES

*Association of Salaried Medical Specialists:* PO Box 10763, Wellington, New Zealand (tel 04-499 1271; fax 04-499 4500; Website www.asms.org.nz).

*Chiropractic Board:* PO Box 10-140, Wellington, New Zealand (tel 05-499 7979; fax 04-472 2350).

*Dental Council of New Zealand:* Level 8, 108 The Terrace, PO Box 10-448, Wellington, New Zealand (tel 04-499 4820; fax 04-499 1668).

*Dental Technicians Board:* PO Box 11-053, Ellerslie, Auckland, New Zealand (tel 09-579 7096; fax 09-525 1169).

*Dietitians Board:* PO Box 10-140, Wellington, New Zealand (tel 04-499 7979; fax 04-472 2350).

*Dispensing Opticians Board:* PO Box 10-140, Wellington, New Zealand (tel 04-499 7979; fax 04-472 2350).

*Health Employment Gazette:* Snedden & Cervin Publishing Ltd, 1st Floor, 38 East Street, Newton, Auckland, New Zealand (tel 09-358 2255; fax 09-358 2393; e-mail health@scpublishing.co.nz Website www.scpublishing.co.nz).

*Hospital Association:* PO Box 74 059, Market Road, Auckland, New Zealand (tel 09-524 2611).

*Medical Council of New Zealand:* PO Box 11-649, Wellington, New Zealand (tel 04-384 7635; fax 04-385 8902).

*Medical Laboratory Technologists Board:* PO Box 10-140, Wellington, New Zealand (tel 04-499 7979; fax 04-472 2350).

*Medical Radiation Technologists Board:* PO Box 10-140, Wellington, New Zealand (tel 04-499 7979; fax 04-472 2350).

*Ministry of Health:* PO Box 5013 (133 Molesworth Street), Wellington, New Zealand (tel 04-496 2000; fax 04-496 2340).

*Natural Health Professions Accreditation Board:* PO Box 38-678, Howick 1705, Auckland, New Zealand (tel 09-537 6602).

*New Zealand Charter of Health Practitioners Inc:* (natural health practitioners) PO Box 36-588, Northcote, Auckland, New Zealand (tel 09-443 6255; fax 09-443 2336; e-mail email@healthcharter.org.nz Website www. healthcharter.org.nz).

*New Zealand Council of Homoeopaths:* PO Box 51, 195 Tawa, Wellington, New Zealand.

*New Zealand Health Employment Gazette:* Snedden & Cervin Publishing Ltd, 1st Floor, 38 East Street, PO Box 68-450, Newton, Auckland, New Zealand (tel 09-358 2255; fax 09-358 2393).

*New Zealand Psychologists Board:* PO Box 10 140, Wellington, New Zealand (tel 04-499 7979; fax 04-472 2350).

*New Zealand Qualifications Agency:* 79 Tarnaki Street, PO Box 160, Wellington, New Zealand (tel 04-802 3000; fax 04-802 3112; Website www.nzqa.gvt.nz).

*New Zealand Red Cross:* Red Cross House, 14 Hill Street, Wellington 1, PO Box 12-140, New Zealand (tel 04-472 3750; fax 04-473 0315).

*Northern Clinical Training Network:* Private Bag 92024, Auckland 1, New Zealand (tel 09-366 1623; fax 09-366 1635; e-mail crew@nctn.co.nz).

*Nursing Council of New Zealand:* PO Box 9644, Wellington, New Zealand (tel 04-385 9589; fax 04-801 8502; e-mail oseas@nursingcouncil.org.nz Website www.nursingcouncil.nz).

*NZ Pharmacy* (journal) PO Box 105483, Auckland, New Zealand.

*Occupational Therapy Board:* PO Box 10-140, Wellington, New Zealand (tel 04-499 7979; fax 04-472 2350).

Optometrists Board: PO Box 10-140, Wellington, New Zealand (tel 04-499 7979; fax 04-472 2350).

*The Optometry Council:* PO Box 185, Carlton South VIC 3053, Australia (tel 03-9663 2733; fax 03-9663 7478; e-mail ocanz@ozemail.com.au). Optometry registration for Australia and New Zealand.

*Pharmacy Today* (journal) PO Box 6599, Auckland, New Zealand.

*Physiotherapy Board:* PO Box 10-140, Wellington, New Zealand (tel 04-499 7979; fax 04-472 2350).

*Podiatrists Board:* PO Box 10-140, Wellington, New Zealand (tel 04-499 7979; fax 04-472 2350).

*Psychologists Board:* PO Box 10-140, Wellington, New Zealand (tel 04-499 7979; fax 04-472 2350).

*Residential Care NZ Inc:* PO Box 560, Wellington, New Zealand (tel 04-499 4156).

## HOSPITAL AND HEALTH SERVICES

*Auckland Healthcare:* PO Box 92 024, Auckland, New Zealand (tel 09-379 7440; fax 09-631 0743).

*Canterbury Health:* Private Bag 4710, Christchurch, New Zealand (tel 03-364 0137; 03-364 0438).

*Capital Coast Health:* PO Box 7902, Wellington South, New Zealand (tel 04-385 5900; fax 04-472 5869; e-mail info@wnhealth.co.nz Website www. wnhealth.co.nz).

*Coast Health Care:* PO Box 387, Greymouth, New Zealand (tel 03-768 2801; fax 03-768 2791).

*Eastbay Health:* Whakatane Hospital, PO Box 241, Whakatane, New Zealand (tel 07-307 8840; fax 07-307 0451).

*Good Health Wanganui:* Wanganui Hospital, Private Bag, Wanganui, New Zealand (tel 06-345 3909; fax 06-345 1759).

*Hawke's Bay Health:* Private Bag, Napier, New Zealand (tel 06-835 9241; fax 06-835 0666).

*Health South Canterbury Services:* Private Bag 911, Timaru, New Zealand (tel 03-688 1079; fax 03-688 0238).

*Health Waikato:* Private Bag 3200 or PO Box 934, Hamilton, New Zealand (tel 07-839 8667; fax 07-834 3613).

*Healthcare Otago:* Private Bag 1921, Dunedin, New Zealand (tel 03-474 0999; fax 03-474 7623).

*Healthlink South:* 3rd Floor, 10 Oxford Terrace, Christchurch, New Zealand (tel 03-364 0150; fax 03-364 0318).

*Hutt Valley Health:* Hutt Hospital, Pilmuir House, Pilmuir Street, Lower Hutt, New Zealand (tel 04-566 6999; fax 04-566 9083).

*Lakeland Health:* Rotorua Hospital, Private Bag 3023, Rotorua, New Zealand (tel 07-348 1199; fax 07-349 1309).

*MidCentral Health:* PO Box 2056, Palmerston North, New Zealand (tel 06-350 8913; fax 06-355 0616).

*Nelson/Marlborough Health:* PO Box 132, Nelson, New Zealand (tel 03-546 1723; fax 03-546 9326).

*Northland Health:* PO Box 742, Whangarei, New Zealand (tel 09-430 4101; fax 09-430 8010).

*Pacific Health:* Private Bag 12024, Tauranga, New Zealand (tel 07-577 8000; fax 07-577 8487; Website www.wbhealth.co.nz).

*South Auckland Health:* Private Bag 93311, Otahuhu, Auckland, New Zealand (tel 09-276 0000; fax 09-276 0023).

*Southern Health:* PO Box 828, Invercargill, New Zealand (tel 03-214 4009; fax 03-214 2496).

*Tairawhiti Health Ltd:* Private Bag 7001, Gisborne, New Zealand (tel 06-868 0001;

fax 06-867 8527).

*Taranaki Healthcare:* PO Box 2016, New Plymouth 4620, New Zealand (tel 06-753 6139; fax 06-753 7770; Website www.thcl.co.nz).

*Wairarapa Health:* Masterton Hospital, PO Box 96, Masterton, New Zealand (tel 06-378 2099; fax 06-378 2110).

*Waitemata Health:* PO Box 93503, Takapuna, Auckland, New Zealand (tel 09-486 1491; fax 09-486 8908).

# NORTH AMERICA

## Canada

*Canadian Embassy:* 501 Pennsylvania Avenue, NW, Washington, DC 20001, USA
(tel 202-682-1740; fax 202-682-7726).
*Canadian High Commission:* Macdonald House, 1 Grosvenor Square, London
W1X 0AA, UK (tel 020-7258 6600; fax 020-7258 6333).
*Currency:* Canadian Dollar (Can$; Can$1 = 100 cents).
*Exchange rate:* £1 = Can$2.38; $1 = Can$1.48.
*Capital:* Ottawa.
*International Telephone Code:* +1
*Population:* 27,409,000.
*Area:* 9,971,000 sq. km.
*Languages:* English, French

Canada is a huge country, second in size only to Russia. It consists of a
confederation of ten provinces and three territories. The country has a very uneven
population distribution; the territories which account for one third of Canada's land
area are home to a mere 1% of the population, three-quarters of Canadians live
within 150 km of Canada's border with the USA, and 77% live in urban areas,
particularly the major cities of Toronto, Montréal, Vancouver, Ottawa and
Edmonton.

Canada remains strongly influenced by its historical links with Britain and
France, the secession movement in the French-speaking province of Québec is a
powerful political force. Canada has been a popular migration destination
throughout its history, and a recent United Nations report concluded that it is the
best place to live, based on forty factors including life expectancy and education.

### HEALTH SERVICES

Canada has excellent health care facilities, similar to those available in the USA.
Health care is the responsibility of the provincial governments, although the federal
government contributes funds and the way the system works is similar to the
National Health Service in the UK. A publicly funded system of hospital and
medical care has been in place since 1968.

Health responsibilities of the provincial and territorial governments include the
administration of hospital and medical insurance plans and the provision of other
general health services. Public insurance plans cover standard hospital care,
physician's services, and other costs. Health care is guaranteed to all, and is
cheaper and more equitable than in the USA. Increased attention is being placed in
Canada on preventive services. The use of hospital and long-term care facilities is
greater in Canada than in most other Western countries.

Private extended medical and dental insurance is popular for treatments and services not covered under provincial insurance plans.

The health system is widely regarded as operating under considerable strain at the moment. Some of the changes currently taking place in the system involve restraints in the government funding of hospitals and reduced employment opportunities in some areas.

## SKILLS AND QUALIFICATIONS

The provinces have their own authorities in charge of regulating the various health professions, and so it is important to find out how the system works in the particular regions of the country in which you are interested.

One very useful website for professionals wishing to find work in Canada is that of the Canadian Information Centre for International Credentials (www.cicic.ca), which has details of almost all professions and the regulatory and training requirements for their practice in Canada. Each section also has the addresses of regional boards and associations, thus allowing you to contact them directly for information on regional variations in registration. The centre also produces fact sheets on working in Canada as well as having links to immigration and employment websites.

Although Canada is a bilingual country, English and French are not equally useful in all places. You must have a knowledge of French to work professionally in Québec. New Brunswick and Ontario are the two provinces where English and French come closest to being equally acceptable. In the other provinces and territories English dominates. Wherever you are in the country, however, proficiency in both languages is undoubtedly an asset.

### Dentistry

Licensure is mandatory in order to practise dentistry in Canada, and is administered at the provincial level, with each province having its own licensing body. Each licensing body is able to grant permission to practise only within its own province. However, certification by the National Dental Examining Board of Canada (NDEBC) is a prerequisite for licensure in all but one province. In order to become certified you will need to sit the NDEBC's examination, and detailed information on the procedure is available directly from the NDEBC. The one exception to the NDEBC licence requirement is Quebec where for a review of your qualifications you should contact the L'Ordre des dentistes du Québec. Prior to sitting the certification exam the applicants qualifications will be reviewed by either board, this review is to ascertain eligibility to sit the exam and does not guarantee recognition of credentials.

The Royal College of Dentists of Canada (RCDC) offers examinations in all the recognised dental specialties in Canada. Once again, the granting of permission to practise in your specialty by a provincial licensing body is valid only in that province. Contact the RCDC for information on their examinations.

### Dental Hygiene

In order to practise as a dental hygienist you must have registered with the provincial regulatory authority, certification by the National Dental Hygiene Certification Board (NDHCB) is a prerequisite for registration in most provinces. To obtain certfication the applicant must have graduated from an accredited training programme or have successfully taken the NDHCB exam. Details of accredited courses and the examination are available from the NDHCB. Canadian Dental Hygiene courses last 2-3 years at college or universities, with hygienists going on to work in public hospitals, health schemes or private practices.

## Dietitians

Nutritionists and dietitians are also regulated professions and provisional authorities set standards and issue licences to practice. Foreign trained dietitians should contact the Dietitians of Canada for assessment of their qualifications prior to arrival in Canada. This assessment requires the submission of academic transcripts, in either English or French, certification of completed practical training and any degrees awarded outside of Canada must be assessed for equivalency. This is done by forwarding a copy to Comparative Education Services at the University of Toronto. The association can provide more details on regulatory requirements and provide addresses of regional bodies.

## Medical Radiation Technology

To work in Canada MRTs will have to pass the Canadian Association of Medical Radiation Technologists national certification examination in their discipline (nuclear medicine, magnetic resonance, radiation therapy and radiological technology). This exam costs Can$375 plus an off-shore handling fee of Can$250, the results of this exam are accepted nationally and are valid for five years. Passing of this exam allows the applicant to register with the provincial association of the province that they wish to work in.

## Medicine

In Canada each of the provinces and territories has its own regulatory framework for licensing physicians, coordinated by provincial medical councils or Colleges of Physicians and Surgeons. Addresses of these licensing authorities are available from the Medical Council of Canada, and you will need to contact the appropriate authority for the province or territory in which you would like to practise in order to find out their licensing requirements. The examination requirements for medicine, however, are national and are specified by the Medical Council.

The Licentiate of the Medical Council of Canada (LMCC) is granted to graduate physicians who have passed an Evaluating Examination and the Qualifying Examination Parts I and II, and then successfully completed 1 year of postgraduate medical training. The LMCC is one of the requirements for licensure to practise medicine with all licensing authorities in Canada (except Québec) and thus all foreign doctors will have to take postgraduate training in Canada in order to gain the licence and practise there. Postgraduate training places can be arranged through the Canadian Resident Matching Service, however, at present there are few training places available. Doctors who have graduated from accredited medical schools in the USA are exempt from the Evaluating Examination.

Further information on all stages of the examination procedure is available from the Council. Health Canada has prepared a publication entitled *Medical Licensure in Canada – Information for Graduates of Foreign Medical Schools*, which is available on-line through a link from the Canadian Information Centre for International Credentials or from the Health Canada website (www.hc-sc.gc.ca/) as well as by post. This is a valuable source of information for all doctors considering working in Canada.

## Nursing

In order to practise nursing in Canada you must be licensed or registered in the province or territory in which you want to work. Whether nurses are licensed or registered depends on the legislation in their particular province or territory. The terms licensure and registration have slightly different meanings relating to the titles used by nurses. A list of registering and licensing authorities is available from the Canadian Nurses Association.

All Canadian provinces and territories require that you sit the Canadian Nurses Association Registration/Licensure Examination as part of the registration/licensure process. At present this examination can only be taken in Canada on the recommendation of a provincial or territorial nurses association.

## Occupational Therapy

Regulation of occupational therapy is administered at the provincial level. The addresses of the regulatory organisations of the provinces and territories are available from the Canadian Association of Occupational Therapists (CAOT).

Generally international qualifications are recognised in Canada. The Association advises that therapists looking to live and work in Canada for an open period and who wish to have the freedom to move around the country should apply for 'landed immigrant' status; occupational therapists are in demand and these visas may be granted without evidence of an offer of employment. Nevertheless a job offer will assist your application. Alternatively occupational therapists can first find employment and then obtain an entry permit – this will commit the therapist to working for one employer for the life of the permit, usually 1 year. Both procedures involve applying for membership of the CAOT in order to obtain the Statement of Candidacy to sit the CAOT Certification Examination.

## Physiotherapy

The Canadian Alliance of Physiotherapy Regulators has established a foreign credential assessment process to determine the eligibility of applicants to sit the Physiotherapy National Exam, successful passing of which is required prior to licensing by provincial authorities. Details of the exam can be found in the alliance's annual *Candidate's Handbook*.

## Psychology

A psychologist must be licensed in each province or territory where they provide services or perform activities that fall within the 'scope or practice' of the pyschology licensure or practice act of that region. Differences in legislation and the interpretation of that statement can make life hard for the psychologist seeking work. The Association of State and Provincial Psychology Boards (ASPPB) has two programmes to facilitate professional mobility, the Certificate of Professional Qualification in Pyschology and the ASPPB Agreement of Reciprocity.

The ASPPB is an alliance of territorial, provincial and state agencies responsible for the licensure and certification of psychologists throughout Canada and the USA. The board encourages mutual recognition of qualification and advises member boards on education, the verification of credentials, professional and legislative issues. Details of their programmes and local pyschology boards can be obtained from them on their website.

# VISAS AND WORK PERMITS

For information regarding immigration or visas you should contact your nearest Canadian Embassy or High Commission. It is very likely that you will be required to have an offer of employment.

In general overseas workers who intend to work temporarily in Canada require 'employment authorisations' – these are issued abroad at a visa office (for example, the Canadian High Commission in London or the Canadian Embassy in Washington, DC), once it has been established that qualified Canadians or residents would not be adversely affected by the employment of a foreign worker (a process called 'job validation').

If you have been offered a temporary job in Canada your prospective employer must first contact his nearest Canada Employment Centre to seek approval ('validation') of the job offered. If approval is given, the Canada Employment Centre will contact the Canadian Embassy/High Commission through which you are applying, and they will forward your application forms.

Employment authorisations are not issued for the purpose of seeking a job in Canada.

## JOB OPPORTUNITIES

Because health is a provincial responsibility, the health care system is not centralised and there is no one place where health professionals can apply for work. Therefore they need to apply directly to individual employers. At present though Canada is raising its immigration limits to an annual level of 300,000, this can only mean that entering Canada will become somewhat easier for professional staff.

The Canadian Hospital Association publishes a large directory that lists and gives addresses for hospitals, health centres, nursing homes, health associations and health education programmes; the directory may be available through public libraries or your nearest Canadian Embassy or High Commission. However, Canadian diplomatic missions are not able to help people find employment in Canada, and do not keep information about employment opportunities. Staff at Canada Employment and Immigration Centres are unable to help non-residents of Canada find a job. Information on jobs in Canada can be obtained by reviewing Canadian newspapers or professional journals.

### Dentistry

The national professional association for dentists in Canada is the Canadian Dental Association (CDA), and it may be able to provide information on the current employment situation. There are also provincial dental associations for information on a more local level; the CDA can supply addresses.

### Medicine

The Medical Council of Canada advises that there are currently almost no opportunities in Canada for overseas medical graduates to pursue the postgraduate medical training necessary to obtain medical licensure. There are also sufficient doctors in most areas to meet the needs of the population. Nevertheless there is an under-supply of physicians in the less populated regions of Canada. One approach to targeting those vacancies that are available is through services such as Health Match BC (see below).

The Canadian Medical Association (CMA) publishes the *Canadian Medical Association Journal*, *Canadian Journal of Surgery*, *Canadian Association of Radiologists Journal* and *Canadian Journal of Respiratory Therapy*, each of which has a jobs section. The CMA also produces a free leaflet called *Medical Practice in Canada*, which provides information on registration and appointments, and also lists the addresses of provincial medical associations and their various requirements.

### Health Match BC

Health Match BC is recognised as the primary recruitment service for health professionals in the Province of British Columbia. It operates under the auspices of the non-profit Health Employers Association of British Columbia (HEABC) and is funded by the British Columbia Ministry of Health. It provides a unique, no-fee service in all aspects of recruitment to both the communities of British Columbia (BC) and healthcare professionals. Specifically, the purpose of this service is two-fold: to work with communities in remote or rural areas that have difficulty filling vacancies; and to provide assistance to physicians and other health professionals in finding employment outside the major metropolitan areas. General practice, specialist, locum and nursing positions are available. Practitioners within Canada and from abroad can find placements using this service

Foreign-trained physicians are eligible for temporary licensure as set out in the regulations of the BC College of Physicians and Surgeons. Physician incomes may be 'fee-for-service' or salaried. Nurses must be approved by the Registered Nurses Association of British Columbia (RNABC) before they can be placed in a community. Nursing salaries are arranged by negotiation with nursing unions. The process for obtaining a temporary licence is somewhat complex and differs according to a number of factors. Health Match BC can provide answers to questions about licencing, billing and immigration procedures (full details are available on their website www.healthmatchbc.org). They also advertise in the *British Medical Journal*, the *South African Medical Journal* and in similar publications in Australia and New Zealand.

## Nursing

The majority of nurses in Canada work within the publicly funded health sector, a minority work in the private sector and a small number of nurses are self-employed.

Nurses with skills and experience in speciality areas – for example, psychiatry and intensive care units – and those willing to work in smaller or more isolated communities will have a better chance of obtaining a position. It may be worthwhile contacting the registration/licensing authorities for information on employment opportunities – they may have a referral service or be able to direct you to the appropriate journals to find advertised positions or employer contacts and some have links from their websites which may turn up vacancy information.

## Other Professions

For information on the current employment situation in other health professions, contact the appropriate professional organisations. Although they are unlikely to have information on specific employment opportunities, they may be able to provide useful guidance.

## PROFESSIONAL ORGANISATIONS

*Acupuncture Foundation of Canada Institute:* Suite 204, 2131 Lawrence Avenue East, Scarborough, Ontario M1R 5G4, Canada (tel 416-752 3988; fax 416-752 4398; e-mail info@afcinstitute.com Website www.afcinstitute.com).

*Association des chirugiens généreaux du Quebec (Quebec Associationof General Surgeons):* 2 Complex Desjardins, Porte 3000, CP 216 Succursale Desjardins, Montréal, Quebec H5B 1G8, Canada (tel 514-350 5107; fax 514-350 5157; e-mail chirugie@acgq.qc.ca Website www.acgq.qc.ca).

*Association des médecins spécialistes en médecins nucléaire du Quebec:* 2 Complex Desjardins, CP 216 Succrsale Desjardins, Montréal, Quebec H5B 1G8, Canada (tel 514-350 5133; fax 514-350 5151).

*Canadian Association of Medical Radiation Technologists:* Suite 1510, 130 Albert Street, Ottawa, Ontario K1P 5G4, Canada (tel 613-234 0012; fax 613-234

1097; Website www.camrt.ca).

*Canadian Association of Nuclear Medicine:* 774 Echo Drive, Ottawa, Ontario K1S 5N8, Canada (tel 613-730 6254; fax 613-730 1116; e-mail canm@rcpsc.edu).

*Canadian Association of Occupational Therapists:* Carleton Technology & Training Centre, Suite 3400, 1125 Colonel By Drive, Ottawa, Ontario K1S 5R1, Canada (tel 613-523 2268; fax 613-523 2552; Website www.caot.ca/).

*Canadian Association of Speech-Language Pathologists and Audiologists:* 2006-130 Albert Street, Ottawa, Ontario K1P 5G4, Canada (tel 613-567 9968; fax 613-567 2859; e-mail caslpa@caslpa.ca Website www.caslpa.ca).

*Canadian Chiropractic Association:*1396 Eglinton Avenue West, Toronto, Ontario M6C 2E4, Canada (tel 416-781 5656; fax 416-781 7344; e-mail ccachiro@ccachiro.org Website www.ccachiro.org).

*Canadian College of Osteopathy:* 39 Alvin Avenue, Toronto, Ontario, Canada (e-mail ceo@ceo.edu Website www.ceo.edu/index).

*Canadian Dental Assistants' Association:* 1785 Alta Vista Drive, Suite 105, Ottawa, Ontario K1G 3Y6, Canada (tel 613-521 5495; fax 613-521 5572; e-mail cdaa@cyberus.ca Website www.cdaa.ca).

*Canadian Dental Association:* 1815 Alta Vista Drive, Ottawa, Ontario K1G 3Y6, Canada (tel 613-523 1770; fax 613-523 7736; e-mail reception@cda-adc.ca Website www.cda-adc.ca).

*Canadian Dental Hygienists' Association:* 96 Centrepointe Drive, Nepean, Ontario K2G 6B1, Canada (tel 613-224 5515; fax 613-224 7283; e-mail info@cdha.ca Website www.cdha.ca).

*Canadian Dental Therapists Association:* PO Box 2275, Fort Macleod, ALberta T0L 0Z0, Canada.

*Canadian Medical Association:* Box 8650, Ottawa, Ontario K1G 0G8, Canada (tel 613-731 9331; fax 613-731 9013).

*Canadian Nurses' Association:* 50 The Driveway, Ottawa, Ontario K2P 1E2, Canada (tel 613-237 2133; fax 613-237 3520; e-mail prr@cna-nurses.ca Website www.cna-nurses.ca).

*Canadian Pharmacists Association:*1785 Alta Vista Drive, Ottawa, Ontario K1G 3Y6, Canada (tel 613-523 7877; fax 613-523 0445; Website www.cdnpharm.ca).

*Canadian Physiotherapy Association:* 2345 Yonge Street, Suite 410, Toronto, Ontario M4P 2E5, Canada (tel 416-932 1888; fax 416-932 9708; e-mail information@physiotherapy.ca Website www.physiotherapy.ca).

*Canadian Podiatric Medical Association:* 900-45 Sheppard Avenue E., Toronto, Ontario M2N 5W9, Canada (tel 416-927 9111; fax 416-733 2491; e-mail info@podiatrycanada.org Website www.podiatrycanada.org).

*Canadian Psychological Association/Societe Canadienne de Pyschologie:* 151 Slater Street, Suite 205, Ottawa, Ontario K1P 5H3, Canada (tel 613-237 2144; fax 613-237 1674; e-mail cpamemb@cpa.ca Website www.cpa.ca).

*Canadian Society for Medical Laboratory Science:* PO Box 2830, LCD1 Hamilton, Ontario L8N 3N8, Canada (tel 905-528 8642; fax 905-528 4968; Website www.csmls.org).

*Canadian Society of Hospital Pharmacists:* 1145 Hunt Club Road, Suite 350, Ottawa, Ontario K1V 0Y3, Canada (tel 613-736 9733; fax 613-736 5660; Website www.cshp.ca).

*Canadian Society of Nuclear Medicine:* 774 Promenade Echo Drive, Ottawa, Ontarion K1S 5N8, Canada (tel 613-730 6278; fax 613-730 1116; e-mail csnm@rcpsc.edu Website http://csnm.medical.org).

*Collége des Médecins du Québec:* 2170 boul, René-Lévesque Ouest, Montréal, Québec H3H 2T8, Canada (Website www.cmq.org).

*College of Family Physicians of Canada:* 2630 Skymark Avenue, Mississauga, Ontario L4W 5A4, Canada (Website www.cfpc.ca/).

*Dietitians of Canada:* 480 University Avenue, Suite 604, Toronto, Ontario M5G 1V2, Canada (tel 416-596 0857; fax 416-596 0603; Website www.dietitians.ca).

*Federation of Medical Women of Canada:* 225-267 O'Connor Street, Ottawa, Ontario K2P 1V3, Canada (tel 613-569 5881; fax 613-569 4432; e-mail secal60@ibm.net Website www.cyberus.ca/fmwc/).

*L'Ordre des dentistes du Québec:* 625 boul. René-Lévesque Ouest, 15e étage, Montrél, Québec H3B 1R2, Canada (tel 514-875 8511; fax 514-393 9248; Website www.odq.qc.ca).

*Royal College of Dentists of Canada:* 365 Bloor Street East, Suite 1706, Toronto, Ontario, Canada (tel 416-929 2722; fax 416-929 5924; e-mail office@rcdc.ca Website www.rcdc.ca).

*Royal College of Physicians and Surgeons of Canada:* 774 promenade Echo Drive, Ottawa, Ontario K1S 5N8, Canada (tel 613-730 8177; fax 613-730 8830; Website www.rcpsc.medical.org).

*Society of Rural Physicians:* PO Box 893 Shawville, Quebec J0X 2Y0, Canada (tel 613-647 3971; Website www.srpc.ca).

## USEFUL ADDRESSES

*Association of State and Provincial Psychology Boards:* PO Box 4389, Montgomery, AL 36103, USA (tel 334-832 4580; e-mail asppb@asppb.org Website www.asppb.org).

*Canadian Alliance of Physiotherapy Regulators:* 230 Richmond Street West, 10th Floor, Toronto, Ontario M5V 1V6, Canada (tel 416-591 1784; fax 416-591 1759; e-mail email@alliancept.org Website www.physiotherapy.ca/cpacoll.htm).

*Canadian Information Centre for International Credentials:* 252 Bloor Street West, Suite 5-200, Toronto, Ontario M5S 1V5 (tel 416-964 1777; fax 416-64 2296; e-mail info@cicic.ca Website www.cicic.ca).

*Canadian Healthcare Association:* 17 York, Ottawa, Ontario K1N 9J6, Canada (tel 613-241 8005; fax 613-241 5055).

*Canadian Hospital Association:* 17 York Street, Suite 100, Ottawa, Ontario K1N 9J6, Canada.

*Canadian Resident Matching Service:* 151 Slater Street, Suite 802, Ottawa, Ontario K1P 5H3, Canada (tel 613-237 0075; e-mail carmsmail@carms.ca Website www.carms.ca/).

*Commission on Dental Accreditation of Canada:* 1815 Alta Vista Drive, Ottawa, Ontario K1G 3Y6, Canada (tel 613-523 1770; fax 613-523 7489).

*Comparative Education Services:* University of Toronto, 315 Bloor Street West, Toronto, Ontari M5S 1A3, Canada (tel 416-978 2185; fax 416-978 7022).

*Federation of Medical Licensing Associations of Canada:* PO Box 8234, Ottawa, Ontario K1G 3H7, Canada (tel 613-738 0372; fax 613-738 8977; e-mail fmlac@aol.com).

*Health Employers Association of British Columbia:* #200, 1333 West Broadway, Vancouver, BC V6H 4C6, Canada (tel 604-736 5909; fax 604-736 2715).

*Health Canada:* A.L. 0913A, Ottawa, Ontario K1A 0K9, Canada (fax 613-941 5366; website www.hc-sc.gc.ca).

*Health Match BC:* 200-1333 West Broadway, Vancouver, British Columbia V6H 4C6, Canada (tel 604-736 5920; fax 604-736 5963; e-mail recruit@healthmatchbc.org Website www.healthmatchbc.org).

*Medical Council of Canada:* PO Box 8234, Station 'T', Ottawa, Ontario K1G 3H7,

Canada (tel 613-521 6012; fax 613-521 9417; Website www.mcc.ca/).
*National Dental Examining Board:* 100 Bronson Avenue, Suite 203, Ottawa,
Ontario K1R 6G8, Canada (tel 613-236 5912; fax 613-236 8386).
*National Dental Hygiene Certification Board:* PO Box 58006, Orleans, Ontario
K1C 7H4, Canada (tel 613-837 2727; fax 613-837 6971; e-mail
exam@ndhcb.ca Website www.ndhcb.ca).
*Ordre des pharmaciens du Québec:* 266 Notre Dame ouest, Bureau 301, Montréal,
Québec H2Y 1T6 (tel 514-284 9588; fax 514-284 3420).
*Pharmacy Examining Board of Canada:* Suite 603, 123 Edward Street, Toronto,
Ontario M5G 1E2 (tel 416-979 2431; fax 416-599 9244).
*Royal College of Dentists of Canada:* 365 Bloor Street E, Ste 1706, Toronto,
Ontario M4W 3L4, Canada (tel 416-929 2722; fax 416-929 5924)

## VOLUNTARY ORGANISATIONS

The Mennonite Central Committee places nurses in public health programmes and
inner-city hospitals in North America, in addition to its overseas work; see page 89
for further information. The Canadian Red Cross (1800 Alta Vista Drive, Ottawa,
Ontario K1G 4J5, Canada; tel 613-739-3000; fax 613-731-1411) is involved in a
range of voluntary programmes.

## OTHER AGENCIES

The following organisations are involved in various aspects of the health care
employment market in Canada, and may be able to help you in your job search:.

*Helen Ziegler & Associates Inc:* 2403-180 Dundas Street West, Toronto, Ontario
M5G 1Z8, Canada (tel 416-977 6941; fax 416-977 6128; e-mail
hza@hziegler.com).
*The Lennox Partnership:* #2001, 500-4 Avenue South West, Calgary, Alberta T2P
2V6, Canada (fax 403-264 8523; e-mail lennox@cybersurf.net).
*MDS Metro Laboratory Services:* Human Resources, 3680 Gilmore Way, Burnaby,
British Columbia V5G 4V8, Canada (tel 604-412 4448).

---

# USA

---

*United States Embassy:* 24-31 Grosvenor Square, London W1A 1AE, UK (tel 020-
7499 9000; visa information 020-7499 6846).
*United States Embassy:* PO Box 866, 100 Wellington Street, Station B, Ottawa,
Ontario K1P 5T1, Canada (tel 613-238-5335; fax 613-238-8750).
*Currency:* US Dollar ($; $1 = 100 cents).
*Exchange rate:* £1 = $1.60.
*Capital:* Washington, DC.
*International Telephone Code:* +1
*Population:* 255,082,000.
*Area:* 9,373,000 sq. km.
*Language:* English

The last global superpower, the United States of America will always be high on
the list of places to go for people from practically every other country on the

planet. This is perhaps partially why America has such tough rules on immigration, with severe penalties for those 'tourists' who take up work while visiting. Stretching from the cold North Atlantic to the sunshine of the Caribbean and across a continent to the Pacific the United States is as physically varied a country as it is possible to be. Americans generally enjoy a high standard of living, especially amongst the professional classes. America's dominance in the mindset of most people comes from the vast number of films and television programmes produced there. Some of these programmes are exported around the world such as *Friends*, *The X-Files*, *Buffy the Vampire Slayer* and of course *ER*; although you don't have to be George Clooney to get a medical licence.

The USA is made up of states and jurisdictions, each of which is an autonomous entity operating within a federal framework. Those looking to find work need to bear this in mind; a license to practise obtained in one state will not necessarily be recognised in another. Levels of taxation can also fluctuate dramatically between states, which may influence where overseas professionals consider looking for work.

## HEALTH SERVICES

Government supported universal health insurance is not provided in the US. For the most part, the costs of health care are met by insurance schemes paid for by employers or payroll deductions. Medical care for the elderly is provided through a government health insurance programe called 'Medicare', and medical care for the unemployed is provided by the combination federal and state programme 'Medicaid'. Although in 1994 the Clinton administration failed to push reforms through to make public healthcare more widespread it appears that the issue may be central to the Presidential election of 2000. Certainly all the candidates have talked about reforms of one form or another.

Around 15% of american citizens do not have health insurance and are dependent on Medicare/Medicaid and other charitable schemes. While many Americans do have private insurances to cover all aspects of care, much emergency care is provided free by city and county hospitals supported by municipal authorities. The provision of healthcare to those on low incomes is a matter of concern for the medical community and the government.

More and more frequently health care is being provided by 'health management organisations' which enter into arrangements with patients to provide all of their care for a set fee rather than by the system whereby several individual physicians would provide medical services for fees related to the care provided.

Hospitals in the USA are supported by public or private funding and many were initially established by religous organisations. Most hopsitals at present supply healthcare supported by payments from health insurance companies, government grants, charitable contributions and private payments from patients.

Health workers are well paid in the USA, although the income levels for physicians have declined slightly in recent years. Health care accounts for 14% of the USA's GDPand the ratio of physicians to population is around 2.6 per 1,000. Currently there are about 650,000 physicians in the USA with almost a quarter of them having graduated from foreign medical schools.

## SKILLS AND QUALIFICATIONS

The individual states have their own authorities in charge of regulating the various health professions, and so it is important to find out how the system works in the region in which you are interested. At present the licence gained in one state does not permit you to practice outside that state. Infomation on state licensing boards can be obtained from professional associations.

## Dentistry

State licensure is required to practise in the USA. However a license obtained in one state does not allow a dentist to practise in another. Furthermore, the requirements for licensure vary from one state to the next, and so it is essential to obtain the latest information directly from the appropriate state board. The American Dental Association produces *Dentistry in the United States:* an excellent booklet for overseas dentists considering dentistry in the USA; it is available free from the address below. The three main requirements for licensure are that the applicant meets educational requirements and can pass a written and a clinical exam. The educational requirement is that the candidate holds a degree from an accredited dental school, accreditation for dental schools is the responsibility of the Commission on Dental Accreditation. Only dental schools in the USA are evaluated for accreditation, schools in Canada are approved indirectly through a reciprocal agreement. Dental schools outside the USA and Canada are considered non accredited, although this does not mean that the entire dental course has to be repeated in the USA. Graduates from outside the USA and Canada can have their dental training verified by Educational Credential Evaluators Inc (PO Box 514070, Milwaukee, Wisconsin 532-3470, USA).

The most standardised part of the licensing process is the written exam, all US licensing bodies require the candidate to have passed the National Dental Board Examination (NDBE), administered by the Joint Commission on National Dental Examinations. Some states augment this exam with one of their own; these can include local laws, oral diagnosis and treatment planning. NDBEs are only carried out in the USA or Canada, sample examinations can be purchased from the American Student Dental Association.

The final part of the educational requirement is the clinical exam, non-US graduates may also have to take a pre-clinical 'bench-test'. The clincal exams are sometimes administered by regional boards acting for several licensing bodies. However, any enquiries about the requirements of the clinical exam should always be directed to the individual state board.

## Medicine

Graduates of medical schools in other countries, except in the rarest of cases, can only gain licenses to practice in the USA after completing a period of graduate medical training. In order to obtain a residency training place foreign medical graduates must be certified by the Educational Commission for Foreign Medical Graduates (ECFMG) as ready to take up the postgraduate training. This involves passing steps I and II of the US Medical Licencing Exam (USMLE), an English language test and an assessment of clinical skills. The last part can only be tested in Philadelphia while the first two exams are now computer based and can be examined in Sylvan Technology Centres around the world. For information about the computer based exams it is worth looking at the ECFMG website which has a list of frequently asked questions and a link to Sylvan Technology where you can find details of the nearest exam site (www.sylvanprometric.com).

Candidates for an ECFMG certificate are eligible for appointment to residency training and should apply directly to a residency programme, these are listed in the *Graduate Medical Education Directory*, which is available in medical libraries and US Consulates General. The programmes are also listed on the American Medical Association website under the heading 'FRIEDA' (www.ama-assn-org/frieda). Applicants should also apply to take part in the National Resident Matching

Programme which assists graduates in finding training places.

A few licensing jurisdictions will allow graduates of foreign medical schools to take the USMLE step III exam without residency training, one such is the New York State Board for Medicine.

The period of graduate training required varies from state to state, in most cases it is three years for a licence and hospital appointment. Some states will licence physicians 'of international reputation', while others will grant licences limited to practice in a specific institution. As these are obviously limited it is easier to go through the rigmarole of obtaining full licensure.

If entering on a J-1 Educational Exchange visa you should bear in mind that usually you must return to your home country for at least two years before you can apply for an immigration visa. However, exchange visitors who entered the USA for medical training are currently exempt from this, although you should obtain confirmation from the nearest US Embassy or consulate, or the Immigration and Naturalization Service.

## Specialists

Specialists may be eligible for partial exemption from a Residency Program, or in the case of experienced consultants perhaps even immediate licensure. To assess your situation first write to the appropriate specialist college in the USA to find out how they view your specialist qualifications; the address of the college will be available from the corresponding college in your own country, or from the American Medical Association. Then contact the relevant licensing authority for the state(s) in which you are interested.

## Nursing

To practise as a nurse in the USA you must first pass a state licensing examination. The Commission on Graduates of Foreign Nursing Schools (CGFNS) sets an examination that it is necessary to pass in order to sit for the National Council of State Boards of Nursing Licensure Examinations (NCLEX). Passing the CGFNS is a requirement of the H1-A (Registered Nurses) visa, and you must have an offer of full-time work from a US employer.

## Nurse-Midwifery

Midwifery is known as 'nurse-midwifery' in the USA. Overseas midwives will need to complete a pre-certification programme in order to be able to practise. Details of programmes and certification requirements are available from the American College of Nurse-Midwives.

## Occupational Therapy

In order to practice as an occupational therapist in the USA, you must meet the requirements of the state board where you wish to work. Some states do not regulate therapists, others require you to register and obtain a licence, but all states require that you have completed all the requirements for Occupational Therapist certification. The National Board for Certification in Occupational Therapy (NBCOT) is the national certifying agency which determines the academic, field and examination requirements which US and foreign trained occupational therapists must meet if they wish to become certified as an Occupational Therapist Registered (OTR). The NBCOT can provide full details of the certifcation process including verifying your training, the English test for non-native speakers and the addresses of state boards and the currnt requirements for practice in each state.

To obtain a license you must first submit evidence of successful completion of the (NBCOT) certification examination for Occupational Therapist Registered, in order to receive approval to sit the licensing examination. Once you have this approval you can apply to the state in which you want to work for a license to practise. Some states will issue a temporary license that will enable you to start working before you sit the licensing examination, which you must pass in order to get a full license.

Recently the NBCOT has been empowered to act as a visa credential verification authority, thus the board can certify that individuals have sufficient skills and knowledge of English to enter on a permanent basis in order to ease shortages in occupational therapy.

## Physiotherapy
You will need a license to practise as a physiotherapist in the USA. Each of the states has its own licensing requirements, and almost all expect you to have the equivalent of a US degree in physiotherapy. You must also be fluent in English.

The Federation of State Boards of Physical Therapy, acts to promote public safety and uniformity within physical therapy practice. To this end they reccomend best practices, the equivalency of foreign qualifications and administer the National Physical Therapy Examination for state boards. Details of the examination requirements, the status of your training and the addresses of state boards can be obtained from the federation. In addition to its educational work the federation acts as a clearing house for information on physical therapy practice.

## Podiatry (Chiropody)
To practise as a podiatrist in the USA it is necessary to have a license. Licensure is administered at state level. All 50 states and the District of Columbia require graduation from a US college of podiatric medicine, plus successful completion of a qualification examination. In addition all states require passing state licensure examinations. Thirty-five states also require 1 year of postgraduate training from an approved programmefor eligibility. To find out about the specific licensing requirements for a particular state, contact the licensing authority in that state; the address will be available from the American Podiatric Medical Association or the Federation of Podiatric Medical Boards.

Overseas-trained podiatrists may be able to find work as unlicensed podiatric medical assistants; they may not practise independently.

## Psychology
A psychologist must be licensed in each state where they provide services or perform activities that fall within the 'scope or practice' of the pyschology licensure or practice act of that state. Differences in legislation and the interpretation of that statement can make life hard for the psychologist seeking work. The Association of State and Provincial Psychology Boards (ASPPB) has two programmesto facilitate professional mobility, the Certificate of Professional Qualification in Pyschology and the ASPPB Agreement of Reciprocity.

The ASPPB is an alliance of state, territorial and provincial agencies responsible for the licensure and certification of psychologists throughout the USA and Canada. The board encourages mutual recognition of qualification and advises member boards on education, the verification of credentials, professional and legislative issues. Details of their programmes and local pyschology boards can be obtained from them by post or on their website.

## Radiologic Technology
35 US states require the technologist to be licensed in order to practise, generally involving registration with the American Registry of Radiologic Technologists

(ARRT) or the passing of an examination. Whether you are considering practising in a licensing state or not ARRT registration will improve the number of employment opportunities available.

The ARRT provides certification in three disciplines of radiologic technology – radiography, nuclear medicine technology and radiation therapy. All candidates for certification must be graduates of an educational programme accredited by a body recognised by the ARRT. This can mean the Joint Review Committee on Education in Radiologic Technology (JRCERT) or a regional agency. Foreign trained staff who do not meet this requirement should seek advanced placement and graduation from an accredited programme.

## VISAS AND WORK PERMITS

The USA recently initiated a Visa Waiver Programme, whereby almost any nationality can enter the USA for a holiday or on business for 90 days. There are certain restrictions on this programme so check with your nearest consulate or embassy in advance of any travel.

Anyone going to the USA with the intention of working there for whatever length of time must obtain a non-immigrant visa unless they plan to settle permanently in which case they should apply for an immigrant visa, although these are obviously rather harder to obtain.

Non-immigrant visas are for specific positions with employment prearranged with a US employer. There are two categories of non-immigrant work visa 'H & L', the ones used by professional staff are the *H-Temporary Work Visas*, these are required by a foreigner who is to perform a prearranged professional or highly skilled job for a temporary period, or to fill a temporary position for which there is a shortage of US workers. The employment must be approved in advance by an office of the Immigration and Naturalization Service in the USA on the basis of an application filed by the prospective employer. The limit on H1-B visas has been raised from 65,000 to 115,000 with another possible rise in Congress, these rises are capped though and the number of H1-B visas will drop back to 65,000 in 2003.

Students can obtain *Academic Student* (F-1) or *Exchange Visitor* (J-1) visas. These are usually limited to taking up a prearranged appointment under an officially approved programme sponsored by an educational or other non-profit institution. The programme sponsor provides the applicant with a *Certificate of Eligibility for Exchange Visitor Status*, which is required for the visa application. Holders of these visas are not permitted to take on any paying work so they are of limited value.

An immigrant visa is required by those who want to work and/or reside in the USA permanently. Categories under which foreigners may qualify for immigration include 'immediate relatives of US citizens', 'family-sponsored immigrants', and 'employment-based immigrants'; the latter category includes:.

*Priority Workers:* including 'persons of extraordinary ability in the sciences, education and business; and outstanding professors and researchers';

*Members of the Professions:* including 'professionals holding advanced degrees and persons of exceptional ability in the sciences and business';

*Professionals, Skilled and Unskilled Workers:* 'professionals holding baccalaureate degrees, skilled workers with at least 2 years' experience, and other workers whose skills are in short supply in the USA';

*Special Immigrants:* including 'certain international organisation employees and their immediate family members, and specially qualified and recommended current and former employees of the US government'.

For further information on these categories, contact the Visa Branch of your nearest US Embassy with full details of the job being taken, including the name of the employer, the length of the appointment and the type of work to be performed. A stamped, self-addressed envelope must accompany your request.

## JOB OPPORTUNITIES

To find out about vacancies in your profession you will find that most associations have jobs listings on their websites, and that vacancies are advertised in professional journals, as well as the national and local press. Address details for the latter can be found in books such as Vacation Work's *Live & Work in the USA and Canada*, (see page 256) while information on US specialist journals for the various professions is included in *Benn's International Media Directory*, which you should be able to obtain through your local library.

In 1999 the Immigration and Naturalisation Service brought in interim immigration rules which make it easier for nurses, occupational therapists and physiotherapists to enter the USA to work. There are certain limits; the applicant must be applying through either the Commission on Graduates of Foreign Nursing Schools, the National Board for Certification in Occupational Therapy or the Foreign Credentialing Commission on Physical Therapy and they must have been exempted from or have passed an English Language test.

**N.B.** For agencies mentioned under the following headings, further information, addresses and telephone numbers are included in the directory on page 48.

### Dentistry

The American Dental Association notes that overseas dental graduates often seek employment as 'allied dental personnel' – i.e. dental hygienists, dental assistants (equivalent to dental surgery assistants in the UK) and dental laboratory technicians – until they succeed in attaining dental licensure. Overseas dentists who are interested in working as a dental hygienist in the USA first need to contact the state board of dentistry in the state(s) in which they are interested, in order to find out if the state's licensure requirements make provision for overseas dentists in this way. The American Dental Association's free booklet *Dentistry in the United States* contains the addresses of the appropriate boards.

### Medicine

The excellent facilities and high salaries mean that working in medicine in the USA is a prospect that most overseas doctors continue to find very attractive. The north-east, where many overseas doctors would probably like to work, has the highest doctor-to-patient ratio, while medical practitioners are in shorter supply in the southern states.

The salary for the first and second years of a Residency Programme (see above) is about $30,000. Once you have reached the last few years of your programme your salary is likely to be in the region of $52,000. Consultants earn considerably more, depending on the amount of private work they do and their speciality; a first-year consultant with little private practice will earn around $100,000.

There are also opportunities for doctors on the non-clinical side – for example, in researching and testing drugs in the pharmaceutical industry.

### Nursing

There is a shortage of nurses in the USA, and it is currently a favoured destination for overseas nurses and midwives. At the time of writing *Western Arizona Regional*

*Medical Centre* had taken to advertising in the UK press and in July 1999 a bill was ready for approval which would allow 500 more nurses into the USA per year on new H1-C visas. This approval would be lmited to hospitals in 'health professional shortage areas' and foreign nurses can only make up one third of the total nursing staff, however the H1-C visa would be valid for three years and nurses will be paid the same as local staff.

*Nursing Management Services* and *Stateside Nursing* are agencies specialising in placing nurses in the USA, in facilities ranging from small community hospitals to county-operated facilities. Stateside Nursing can also provide information aand help with registering as a nurse in the USA. The National League for Nursing has a countrywide vacancy list on its website (www.nln.org).

## Radiologic Technology

The job market for radiographers in the USA is strong, particularly in the areas of diagnostic medical sonography, radiation therapy and nuclear medicine. Many areas of the USA began to experience shortages of sonographers and radiation therapists in late 1998, and the shortages are expected to continue for the next several years.

Demand for radiographers varies by geographic region, but the US Department of Labour predicts steady growth in the field through 2005.

The American Society for Radiologic Technologists (ASRT) is the national professional organisation representing radiographers, radiation therapists, nuclear medicine technologists and sonographers in the USA. It offers an internet-based employment service (www.asrt.org).

Entry level salaries in radiologic professions vary according to region, size of hospital and other factors, below are income figures based on a 1998 survey of annual salary ranges:

| | |
|---|---|
| Diagnostic medical sonographer | $20,000–$36,857 |
| Mammographer | $18,000–$24,757 |
| Nuclear medicine technologist | $28,000–$35,300 |
| Radiographer | $19,200–$27,871 |
| Radiation therapist | $29,000–$36,122 |

*DSI Staff RX* (see page 54) is a temporary staffing agency that specialises in the fields of diagnostic imaging and radiation therapy. It places staff throughout the USA, and can find positions in a wide range of speciality areas.

## Therapy

The American Occupational Therapy Association (AOTA) and the American Physical Therapy Association (APTA) can provide information on employment opportunities; in particular the AOTA produces *OT Week*, a weekly job information publication, there is also a seperate weekly journal *Advance for Occupational Therapists* which carries vacancy listings.

A recent shortage in physiotherapists now appears to have eased and some budgetary changes are forcing some physiotherapists to take reductions in pay, so it may not be easy for a foreign trained physiotherapist to find a place.

# PROFESSIONAL ORGANISATIONS

*American Academy of Family Physicians:* 11400 Tomahawk Creek Parkway, Leawood, KS 66211-2672, USA (tel 913-906 6000; e-mail fp@aafp.org Website www.aafp.org).

*American Academy of Opthamology:* PO Box 7424, San Francisco, CA 94120-7424, USA (Tel 415-561 8500; Website www.eyenet.org).

*American Association of Medical Dosimetrists:* PO Box 1498, Galesburg, Illinois 61401, USA.

*American Association of Pharmaceutical Sciences:* 1650 King Street, Suite 200, Alexandria, Virginia 22314-2747, USA (tel 703-548 3000; fax 703-684 7349; e-mail aaps@aaps.org Website aaps.org).

*American Association of Physicists in Medicine:* One Physics Ellipse, College Park, MD 20740, USA (tel 301-209 3350; fax 301-209 0862; e-mail aapm@aapm.org Website www.aapm.org).

*American Chiropractic Association:* 1701 Clarendon Boulevard, Arlington, VA 22209, USA (fax 703-243 2593; Website www.amerchiro.org).

*American College of Nurse-Midwives:* 818 Connecticut Avenue, NW, Suite 900, Washington, DC 20006, USA (tel 202-728 9860; fax 202-728 9897).

*American College of Radiology:* 1891 Preston White Drive, Reston, Virginia 22091, USA (tel 703-648 8900; e-mail info@acr.org Website www.acr.org).

*American College of Surgeons:* 633 North Saint Clair Street, Chicago, IL 60611-3211, USA (tel 312-202 5000; fax 312-202 5001; e-mail Postmaster@facs.org Website www.facs.org).

*American Dental Association:* 211 East Chicago Avenue, Chicago IL 60611, USA (tel 312-440 2500; fax 312-440 2800; Website www.ada.org).

*American Dietetic Association:* 216 West Jackson Boulevard, Chicago, Illinois 60606-6995, USA (tel 312-899 0040; e-mail cdr@eatright.org Website www.eatright.org).

*American Medical Association:* 515 North State Street, Chicago, Illinois 60610, USA (tel 312-464 4677; fax 312-464 4567; Website www.ama-assn-org).

*American Medical Women's Association:* 801 N. Fairfax Street, Suite 400, Alexandria, VA 22314, USA (tel 703-838 0500; fax 703-549 3864; e-mail info@amwa-doc.org Website www.amwa-doc.org).

*American Nurses Association Inc:* 600 Maryland Avenue, SW, Suite 100 West, Washington DC 20024 (tel 202-651 7134; fax 202-651 7001; Website www.ana.org).

*American Occupational Therapy Association Inc:* 4720 Montgomery Lane, PO Box 31220, Bethesda, Maryland 20824-1220, USA (tel 301-652 2682; fax 301-652 7711; e-mail accred@aota.org Website www.aota.org).

*American Osteopathic Association:* 142 East Ontario Street, Chicago, Illinois 60611, USA (tel 312-202 8000; Website www.aoa-net.org).

*American Pharmaceutical Association:* 2215 Constitution Avenue, NW, Washington, DC 20037, USA (tel 202-628 4410; fax 202-783 2351; e-mail membership@mail.aphanet.org Website www.aphanet.org).

*American Physical Therapy Association:* 1111 North Fairfax Street, Alexandria, Virginia 22314, USA (tel 703-684 2782; fax 703-684 7343; Website www.apta.org).

*American Podiatric Medical Association:* 9312 Old Georgetown Road, Bethesda, Maryland 20814-1698, USA (tel 301-571 9200; e-mail askapma@apma.org Website www.apma.org).

*American Psychological Association:* 750 First Street, NE, Washington DC 20002-4242, USA (tel 202-336 5500; e-mail education@apa.org Website www.apa.org).

*American Society for Clinical Laboratory Science:* 7910 Woodmont Avenue, Suite 530, Bethesda, Maryland 20814, USA (tel 301-657-2768; fax 301-657-2909; Website www.ascls.org).

*American Society of Radiologic Technologists:* 15000 Central Avenue SE,

Albuquerque, New Mexico 87123-3917, USA (tel 505-298 4500; fax 505-298 5063; Website www.asrt.org).

*American Speech-Language Hearing Association:* 10801 Rockville Pike, Rockville, Maryland 20852, USA (tel 888-321 ASHA; Website www.asha.org).

*American Student Dental Association:* Suite 1160, 211 East Chicago Avenue, Chicago IL 60611, USA (tel 312-440 2795).

*National Acupuncture and Oriental Medicine Alliance:* 14637 Starr Road SE, Olalla, Washington 98359, USA (tel 253-851 6896; fax 253-851 6883; Website www.AcuAll.org).

*National Association of Emergency Medical Technicians:* 408 Monroe Street, Clinton, MS 39056-4210, USA (tel 800 34 NAEMT; Website www.naemt.org).

*National Association of Womens Health Professionals:* 175 W. Jackson Boulevard, Chicago, IL 60604-0260, USA (tel 312-786 1468).

*National Center for Homeopathy:* 801 North Fairfax Street, Suite 306, Alexandria, Virginia 22314-1757, USA (tel 703-548 7790; Website www.homeopathic.org).

*National League for Nursing:* 61 Broadway, New York, NY 10006, USA (tel 212-363 5555; fax 212-812 0393; e-mail nlnweb@nln.org Website www.nln.org).

*National Paramedic Society:* 408 Monroe Street, Clinton, MS 39056-4210, USA (e-mail nps@naemt.org; Website www.naemt.org).

*San Francisco Paramedic Association:* 657 Mission Street, Suite 302, San Francisco CA 94105, USA (tel 415-543 1161; fax 415-543 0415; e-mail sfpa@slip.net Website www.sfparamedics.org).

*Society of Nuclear Medicine:* 1850 Samuel Morse Drive, Reston, Virginia 22090-5316, USA.

*Southern Medical Association:* 35 Lakeshore Drive, Birmingham, AL 35209, USA (tel 205-945 1840; Website www.sma.org).

## USEFUL ADDRESSES

*Accreditation Commission for Acupuncture and Oriental Medicine:* 1010 Wayne Avenue, Suite 1270, Silver Spring, MD 20910, USA (tel 301-608 9680; fax 301-608 9576).

*Advance for Occupational Therapists:* Merion Publications Inc, 650 Park Avenue, Box 61556, King of Prussia, PA 19406-0956, USA (tel toll-free 800-355 1088; Website www.advanceweb.com)

*American Academy of Osteopathy:* 3500 DePauw Boulevard, Suite 1080, Indianapolis, Indiana 46268-139, USA (tel 317-879 1881).

*American Council of Graduate Medical Education:* 515 North State Street, Chicago, Illinois 60610, USA.

*American Association of Colleges of Nursing:* One Dupont Circle, NW, Suite 530, Washington DC20036, USA (tel 202-463 6930; fax 202-785 8320; Website www.aacn.nche.edu).

*American Healthcare Radiology Administrators:* PO Box 334, Sudbury, Massachusetts 01776, USA.

*American Hospital Association:* One North Franklin, Chicago, Illinois 60606, USA (tel 312-422 3000).

*American Registry of Radiologic Technologists:* 1255 Northland Drive, St Paul, Minnesota 55120-1155, USA (tel 651-687 0048; Website www.arrt.org).

*Association of State and Provincial Psychology Boards:* PO Box 4389, Montgomery, AL 36103, USA (tel 334-832 4580; e-mail asppb@asppb.org Website www.asppb.org).

*Commission on Graduates of Foreign Nursing Schools (CGFNS):* 3600 Market Street, Suite 400, Philadelphia, Pennsylvania 19104-2651, USA (tel 215-349

8767; fax 215-222 8454; e-mail info@cgfns.org Website www.cgfns.org).

*Council of Medical Specialty Societies:* PO Box 70, Lake Forest, Illinois 60045, USA.

*Educational Commission for Foreign Medical Graduates (ECFMG):* 3624 Market Street, Philadelphia, Pennsylvania 19104-2685, USA (tel 215-386 5900; fax 215-387 9963; Website www.ecfmg.org).

*Federation of Podiatric Medical Boards:* PO Box 33285, Washington, DC 20033, USA (tel 202-659 3112).

*Federation of State Medical Boards:* Federation Place, 400 Fuller Wiser Road, Suite 300, Euless, TX 76039-3855, USA (tel 817-868 4000; fax 817-868 4098; Website www.fsmb.org).

*Federation of State Boards of Physical Therapy:* 509 Wythe Street, Alexandria, VA 22314, USA, (tel 703-299 3100; fax 703-299 3110; Website www.fsbpt.org/).

*Joint Commission on National Dental Examinations:* American dental Association, Suite 846, 211 East Chicago Avenue, Chicago, Illinois 60611, USA (tel 312-440 2500).

*National Board for Certification in Occupational Therapy Inc:* 800 S Frederick Avenue, Suite 200, Gaithersburg, Maryland 20877-4150, USA (tel 301-990 7979; fax 301-869 8492; Website nbcot.org).

*National Certification Agency for Medical Laboratory Personnel:* 8310 Nieman Road, Lenexa, Kansas 66214, USA.

*National Council of State Boards of Nursing:* 676 N St Clair Street, Suite 550, Chicago, Illinois 60611-2921, USA (tel 312-787 6555; e-mail info@ncsbn.org Website ncsbn.org); the Council can provide addresses for the State Boards of Nursing.

*National Resident Matching Program:* 2501 M Street, NW, Suite 1, Washington DC 20037-1307, USA (tel 202-828 0566; Website http://nrmp.aamc.org/nrmp).

*New York State Board for Medicine:* Empire State Plaza, Albany, NY 12230, USA (e-mail medbd@mail.nysed.gov Website www.nysed.gov).

*US Department of Justice, Immigration and Naturalization Service:* 25 E Street, NW, Washington DC 20538, USA (tel 202-663 1225).

*OT Week:* c/o AOTA, 4720 Montgomery Lane, PO Box 31220, Bethesda, MD 20824-1220, USA (tel 301-652 2682; fax 301-652 7711; Website www.otweek.org).

## VOLUNTARY ORGANISATIONS

In addition to its overseas work, the Mennonite Central Committee places health workers in programmes in North America; see page 89 for further information. The American Red Cross Society is at 17th and D Streets, NW, Washington, DC 20006, USA (tel 202-728 6600; fax 202-775 0733).

## OTHER AGENCIES

The following organisations are involved in various aspects of the health care employment market in the USA, and may be able to help you in your job search:.

*Ac'cent Group Ltd:* 20 Henderson Drive, Avon, Connecticut 06127-0280, USA (tel 860-677 1288).

*Dunhill of Tampa:* 4350 W Cypress Street 814, Tampa, Florida 33607-0416, USA (tel 813-872 8118).

*Ethan Allen Personnel:* 50 Academy Street, Poughkeepsie, New York 12601-0411, USA (tel 914-471 9700).

*Executive Search of New England:* 131 Ocean Street, South Portland, Maine 04106, USA (tel 207-741 4110).

*Health Examinetics;* 10920 Via Frontera, San Diego, California 92127-0170, USA (tel 858-485 0933).

*Medical Professionals for Home Healthcare:* 7928 S. King Drive, Chicago, IL60619-0370, USA (tel 773-487 2400).

*Med Search Physician Service:* 300 2nd Avenue, Long Branch, NJ 07740-0630, USA (tel 732-870 5500).

*O'Grady-Peyton International:* 332 Congress Street, Boston, Massachusetts 02210, USA, (tel 617-422 0300; fax 617-422 0399; Website www.opginc.com).

*O'Grady-Peyton International:* 349 Mall Bvld, Savannah, Georgia 31406-0474, USA (tel 912-353 9366).

*Professional Medical:* 4350 Georgetown Square, Atlanta, GA 30338-0620, USA (tel 770-458 1648).

*Professional Medical Agency:* 2210 Wynnton Road, Columbus, GA 31906-0580, USA (tel 706-320 0307); Home Health Agencies & Service Nurses.

*RT Temps Inc:* PO Box 104, Devon, Pennsylvania 19333, USA (tel 1-800-67STAFF, in the USA only).

*RTT Temps:* 750 Downtowner Loop W, Mobile, Alabama 36609, USA.

*Sierra Recruitment Services Inc:* PO Box 6103, Hollywood, Florida 33081, USA (tel 954-680-2660; fax 954-680-0995); occupational therapists.

*Supplemental Health Care:* 2829 Sheridan Drive, Buffalo, New York 14150, USA.

*Tech Group Inc:* Spokane, Washington 99206, USA (tel 1-800-523-3968, in the USA only).

*Trillium Human Resources Inc:* RR #3, Ayr, Ontario N0B 1E0, Canada (fax 519-632-8364)

*Western Arizona Regional Medical Centre:* Human Resources, 2000 West Bethany Home Road, Phoenix, AZ 85015, USA (fax 602-246 5769).

# CENTRAL & SOUTH AMERICA

## INTRODUCTION

The main opportunities for health professionals in Central and South America are likely to be through international voluntary organisations. Opportunities in the state and private health sectors are rare and in many countries financial instability means that while there is a demand for the skills of overseas health professionals, there is no budget for the tools and equipment which they are used to. Nonetheless there is nothing to stop you enquiring of voluntary agencies and appropriate professional organisations in any countries in which you have an interest.

## VOLUNTARY ORGANISATIONS

Numerous agencies are involved with aid and development work throughout Latin America; these include: *VSO*; *Care International*; *Health Unlimited* which sends medical teams to Guatemala, El Salvador, Nicaragua, Brazil and Bolivia; the *Institute for International Cooperation and Development:* which sends volunteers to work on health programmes in the region (for example, in Nicaragua); the *International Federation of Red Cross and Red Crescent Societies*, which undertakes long-term community health projects; *International Cooperation for Development*; *CUSO*, which sends Canadian volunteers to work on health projects; *Save the Children Fund*; and *United Nations Volunteers*. *International Health Exchange* is an excellent source of information for health professionals wanting to work in Latin America.

The *International Committee of the Red Cross* and *Médecins sans Frontières* are both involved in health programmes in countries affected by war, famine and natural disaster.

## DENOMINATIONAL ORGANISATIONS

Several missionary and other religious agencies combine health care with their evangelical activities in Latin America. The *Baptist Missionary Society, Catholic Medical Mission Board, Latin Link* and the *Mennonite Central Committee* are involved with health initiatives throughout central and Latin America. *HCJB World Radio* has health professionals working just in Ecuador. *Christoffel Blindenmission* recruits eye care and other health specialists for various projects in Latin America.

## THE CARIBBEAN

Voluntary organisations such as *Concern Worldwide, CUSO* and *International Cooperation for Development*, are involved in health projects in the Caribbean. Of the denominational organisations, the *Catholic Medical Mission Board* is active in the region. **N.B.** For all of the voluntary and denominational agencies mentioned above, further information, addresses and telephone numbers are included in the directories in Part II of this book.

# PROFESSIONAL ORGANISATIONS

## Argentina

*Asociacion Argentina de Pedicuros del Litoral*, Pte Roca 1028, 2000 Rosario, Sante-Fe, Argentina.

*Argentine Medical Association:* Sante Fe 1171-1059 Buenos Aires, Argentina (tel +54-11 4811 1633; fax 11-4814 0634).

*Asociación Odontológica Argentina*: Junin 959, 1113 Buenos Aires, Argentina (tel +54-11-4961 6141; fax 11-4961 1110; e-mail aoa@aoa.org.ar Website www.aoa.org,ar).

*Federación Argentina de Enfermeria* (nurses' association) Av Rivadavia 3518, Casilla de Correo 59 – Sucursal 53, CP 1204 Buenos Aires, Argentina (tel/fax 1-865 1512)

## Brazil

*Associaçao Brasileira de Enfermagem* (nurses' association) SGAN, Av L2 Norte, Quadra 603 Módulo B, CEP 70830-30 Brasilia DF, Brazil (tel 61-226 0653; fax 61-225 4473).

*Associaçao Brasileira de Odontologia* (dental association) Rua Alvaro Alvim 33/37, Salas 514-517, 20031 Rio de Janeiro, Brazil.

*Associaçao Brasileira de óptica e Optometria:* Venâncio II bloc H n°26 sala 504, CEP 70393900 Brasíla, Brazil (tel +61-323 9200; e-mail saveiga@ nutecnet.com.br Website www.brnet.com.br/pages/saveiga/abpoo)

*Associação Médica Brasileira* (medical association) Rua São Carlos do Pinhal 324, Bela Vista-São Paulo, SP 01333-903, Brazil (e-mail administracao@amb.org.ar Website amb.org.ar).

## Chile

*Colegio de Dentistas de Chile* (dental association) Avenida Santa Maria 1990, Casilla 252 V, Santiago, Chile.

*Colegio de Enfermeras de Chile* (nurses' association) Miraflores 563, Casilla No 9752–Correo Plaza de Armas, Santiago, Chile (tel/fax 2-639 8556).

*Colegio Médico de Chile* (medical association) Esmeralda 678 – Casilla 639, Santiago, Chile (tel 2-633 0505/0884; fax 2-633 0940/6732).

## Colombia

*Asociación Nacional de Enfermeras de Colombia* (nurses' association) Carrera 27 – No 46 21, Apartado Aéreo No 059871, Bogotá DE, Colombia (tel 1-268 3535/244 3991; fax 1-269 2095).

*Federación Médica Colombiana* (medical association) Calle 72 – No 6-44, Piso 11, Bogotá DE, Colombia (tel 1-211 0208/212 6082).

*Federación Odontológica Colombiana* (dental association) Calle 71 No 11-10 Of 1101, Apartado Aéreo 52925, Bogotá DE, Colombia

## Costa Rica

*Colegio de Cirujanos Dentistas de Costa Rica:* Apartado Postal 698/1000, San José, Costa Rica.

*Colegio de Enfermeras de Costa Rica* (nurses' association) Avenida 10 Calles 14 y 16, contiguo a la Cruz Roja – Costarricense, San José, Costa Rica (tel 257 9541; fax 257 9854).

*Unión Médica Nacional* (medical association) Apartado 5920-1000, San José, Costa Rica (tel 232 6230/3433; fax 231 7373)

## Mexico

*Asociación Dental Mexicana AC:* Ezequiel Montes No 92, Col Revolucion, Delegacion Cuahtemoc, 06030 México DF.

*Asociación Nacional de Colegios* (medical association) Médicos Estatales (Mexico) Rosalio Bustamante No 224, Col. Esfuerzo Nacional, CD, Madero, Tams, CP 89470, Mexico (tel 12-17 03 88/17 09 18/17 08 58; fax 12-13 19 69).

*Colegio Nacional de Enfermeras AC* (nurses' association) Czda Obrero Mundial 229, Cal del Valle, Apartado Postal 12-986, 03100 México DF (tel 5-543 6637; fax 5-669 4031)

## Panama

*Asociación Odontológica Panamena* (dental association) Apartado 6777, Panamá 5, Panama.

*Asociación Médica Nacional de la República de Panamá* (medical association) Apartado Postal 2020, Panamá 1, Panama (tel 637622; fax 231462).

*Asociación Nacional de Enfermeras de Panamá* (nurses' association) Apartado 5272, Panamá 5, Panama (tel 225 4717/8120; fax 227 5320)

## Peru

*Colegio Médico del Perú* (medical association) Malecón Armendariz No 791, Miraflores, Lima, Peru (tel 14-463690; fax 14-474930).

*Colegio Odontológica del Perú* (dental association) Los Próceres 261, Santa Constanza-Monterrico, Zona 33, Casilla 4027, Lima, Peru.

*Federación de Enfermeros del Peru* (nurses' association) Jirón Washington No 1651 – Oficina No 201, Lima, Peru (tel 14-330418; fax 14-300602/300614)

## Uruguay

*Asociación Odontológica Uruguaya* (dental association) Durazno 937, Montevideo CP 11100, Uruguay.

*Colegio de Enfermeras del Uruguay* (nurses' association) Colonia 1854, Piso 6, Escritorio 607, CP 11200 Montevideo, Uruguay (tel/fax 2-49 09 00).

*Sindicato Médico del Uruguay* (medical association) Bulevar Artigas 1515, CP 11200 Montevideo, Uruguay (tel 2-41 47 01; fax 2-49 16 03).

*Union Uruguaya de Pedicuros y Podologos:* Sede Social Propia, Florida 1276-Piso 50-ESC 611, Montevideo, Uruguay

## Venezuela

*Colegio de Odontólogos de Venezuela* (dental association) Apartado de Correos 1341, Caracas, Venezuela.

*Federación de Colegios de Enfermeras de Venezuela* (nurses' association) Av Luís Roche, entre 8va y 9na Transversal, Qta Acuarela Altamira, Caracas 1062, Venezuela (tel 2-261 3444/3794; fax 2-576 5256).

*Federación Médica Venezolana* (medical association) Avenida Orinoco con Perijé, Las Mercedes – Caracas, Venezuela (tel 2-993 0073/5227; fax 2-993 2890/9027)

## The Caribbean

*Antigua & Barbuda Medical Association:* Deanery Lane, PO Box 1374, St Johns, Antigua (tel +1-268-462 3710).

*Bahamas Dental Association:* PO Box N1617, 4 Collins Avenue, Nassau, Bahamas (tel +1-809-322 3375; fax 809-326 1534).

*Jamaican Dental Association:* 7 Upper Musgrave Avenue, Kingston 6, Jamaica (tel +876-960 5070; fax 968-4742; Website www.infochan.com/JDA/).

*Medical Association of the Bahamas:* PO Box N4463, 315 Terrace East, Nassau, Bahamas (tel +1-809-356 3536).

*Medical Association of Jamaica:* 3a Paisley Avenue, Kingston 5, Jamaica (tel +876-929 9227; fax 929-5829; e-mail info@maj.org.jm Website www.maj.org.jm).

# MIDDLE EAST

## Jordan

*Embassy of the Hashemite Kingdom of Jordan:* 3504 International Drive, NW, Washington, DC 20008, USA (tel 202-966-2664; fax 202-966-3110).
*Embassy of the Hashemite Kingdom of Jordan:* 6 Upper Phillimore Gardens, London W8 7HB, UK (tel 020-7937 3685; fax 020-7937 8795).
*Embassy of the Hashemite Kingdom of Jordan:* Suite 701, 100 Bronson Avenue, Ottawa, Ontario K1R 6G8, Canada (tel 613-238-8090; fax 613-232-3341).
*Currency:* Jordanian Dinar (JD) (1 JD = 1000 fils).
*Exchange rate:* £1 = JD1.13; $1 = JD0.71.
*Capital:* Amman.
*International Telephone Code:* +962
*Population:* 4,145,000.
*Area:* 98,000 sq. km.
*Language:* Arabic; some English spoken

The majority of the Jordanian population are of Palestinian origin. Christians (including both Roman Catholics and Protestants) make up about 5%. Amman is by far the biggest city, containing almost half of the population.

Jordan is a constitutional monarchy and the King has extensive powers: he appoints the Prime Minister, is Commander-in-Chief of the armed forces and approves laws. The Jordanian press is relatively free, although those foreign newspapers that are available in Amman are subject to government censorship.

The Jordanian economy benefited in the 1970s from the oil boom and the civil war in Lebanon. More recently Jordan has suffered as a result of the Gulf War and falling oil prices, but it achieved strong economic growth in the early 1990s and its prospects seem good. The standard of health care in Jordan is generally high and there are a large number of hospitals and specialists in Amman.

### VISAS AND WORK PERMITS

Visas are required by all foreign nationals, except nationals of most Middle Eastern countries. Nationals of EU countries, the USA, Canada, Australia, New Zealand and Japan can obtain visas on arrival. Work permits will normally be arranged through the agency arranging your placement; for details on requirements contact your nearest Jordanian Embassy.

### PROFESSIONAL ORGANISATIONS

*Jordan Association of Occupational Therapy:* Farah Royal Jordan Rehabilitation Centre, King Hussain Medical City, Amman, Jordan.

*Jordan Dental Association:* PO Box 1326, Amman, Jordan.
*Jordan Nurses and Midwives Council:* PO Box 10076, Amman, Jordan (tel 6-689468).
*Jordanian Physiotherapy Society:* PO Box 510489, Amman 11151, Jordan (tel 6-840840; fax 6-682299).

# Saudi Arabia

*Royal Embassy of Saudi Arabia:* 601 New Hampshire Avenue, NW, Washington, DC 20037, USA (tel 202-342-3800).
*Royal Embassy of Saudi Arabia:* 30 Charles Street, London W1X 7PM, UK (tel 020-7917 3000; fax 020-7917 3330).
*Royal Embassy of Saudi Arabia:* Suite 901, 99 Bank Street, Ottawa, Ontario K1P 6B9, Canada (tel 613-237-4100-3; fax 613-237-0567).
*Currency:* Riyal (SRl; SRl1 = 100 halalahs).
*Exchange rate:* £1 = SRls6; $1 = SRls3.75.
*Capital:* Riyadh.
*International Telephone Code:* +966
*Population:* 14,870,000.
*Area:* 2,240,000 sq. km.
*Language:* Arabic

Saudi Arabia is well known as a destination for health professionals looking for overseas work. The abundance of modern and very well equipped health care facilities actively looking for qualified Western staff, together with the availability of comprehensive packages for those interested in working in Saudi Arabia, make it an attractive prospect for many. There are, however, sharp cultural differences between the country (and indeed the Middle East in general) and the West, which Westerners should consider before committing themselves to a position; these are described below.

The religion of Saudi Arabia is Islam. Islam, however, is not only a religion but also the basis for the country's legal system and a national way of life, laying down rules for behaviour in private, social and business activities. The country has no formal constitution; government structure and actions are based on Islamic law and royal decrees.

The Saudi government operates according to the Hegira calendar, the ninth month of which is known as Ramadan. This is a period of day-time fasting, and it can significantly disrupt the normal pattern of working, something Westerners should be aware of. There are other important festivals, including the Haj (the pilgrimage to Mecca), which occurs during the first 10 days of the twelfth Hegira month (Dhu al-Hijjah).

## Saudi Arabian Law
There are a number of laws in force in Saudi Arabia that to a Westerner may seem either unusual or severe. Several of these derive from Islam, others from the country's desire to protect its national security. Professionals contemplating working in Saudi Arabia should be aware of the following laws in particular:

- women are not allowed to drive;
- aerial photography and photography of government buildings, defence establishments and royal residences are forbidden;
- the drinking of alcohol is forbidden;
- no drugs or barbiturates can be brought into the country without a letter of authorisation;
- the possession of weapons is forbidden;
- no mixed bathing is allowed in public places;
- no pork products may be consumed in or brought into the country;
- pornography is forbidden;
- non-Muslims may not enter the Holy Cities of Mecca and Medina;
- unions and strikes are illegal.

In addition a dress code applies for foreigners, published by the Society for the Encouragement of Virtue and the Elimination of Vice, an institution whose laws and regulations are enforced by the *Mutaww'in* (the 'Religious Police'). The code is directed principally at women, and would-be foreign residents should consult their nearest Saudi Arabian consulate or the agency through which they are arranging employment for information on what is regarded as 'proper' attire.

## HEALTH SERVICES

The health care industry in Saudi Arabia is very modern and involves a range of health care providers. There are many hospitals that attain Western standards. The Ministry of Health provides 63% of hospital beds, followed by the private sector with 13%, the Ministry of Defence and Aviation with 8%, the Ministry of Higher Education with 7%, the National Guard with 3%, and the General Organisation for Social Insurance, the Royal Commission and the Ministry of the Interior with 2% each. The government is the major provider of financial support to health services at all levels.

The Ministry of Health is concerned with providing primary health care by means of hospitals and clinics throughout the country; hospitals are located in the main population centres, and are supplemented by smaller clinics in towns and villages. There are also mobile clinics serving rural areas.

Some Saudi hospitals are internationally famous, such as the King Khaled Eye Specialist Hospital and the King Faisal Specialist Hospital and Research Centre. These two hospitals employ approximately 40% and 50% Western staff, respectively, and many other hospitals – such as those of the National Guard and the Ministry of the Interior – employ similar proportions of health professionals from Western countries.

## SKILLS AND QUALIFICATIONS

Western staff recruited to work in hospitals with a high proportion of fellow Western professionals will generally have qualifications at the same level as required to practise their profession in their own country. However the countries whose qualifications are acceptable and the amount of experience required can vary between posts with different hospitals or organised through different hospital management organisations, and any queries should be addressed to the agency (or agencies) through which you are trying to find work.

## VISAS AND WORK PERMITS

Employment in Saudi Arabia is contingent upon the Saudi Arabian consulate issuing the prospective employee with an entry visa. The visa will be for work in Saudi Arabia under the sponsorship of a specific employer. Health professionals finding employment in Saudi Arabia through a recruitment agency will normally have a visa obtained on their behalf.

## JOB OPPORTUNITIES

As mentioned above, large numbers of Western-trained health professionals are employed in Saudi Arabian hospitals. These hospitals are often managed by hospital management organisations, which may also have been responsible for establishing them in the first place. Recruitment to these positions generally takes place through agencies specially set up for the purpose, which advertise and actively recruit in selected Western countries for high-calibre health professionals. These hospitals generally provide English-speaking working environments, particularly so with the high numbers of Western professionals they employ.

### Saudisation

The Saudisation programme is intended to train Saudi nationals to be able to take over from the numerous foreign workers in the country. Therefore if the designation of a particular post changes from 'Westerner' to 'Saudi' during the course of an overseas health professional's placement, they will not be able to renew their contract. However the programme has proved to be more difficult to implement than was originally envisaged, and so it seems that foreign workers will be required for the forseeable future.

## AGENCIES

The following agencies have fuller listings and contact details in the directory section of *Part II*.

*BML Recruitment* have ten years experience of placing staff in the Middle East. *HCA International* recruits specifically for the King Faisal Specialist Hospital and Research Centre in Riyadh. *United Medical Enterprises Ltd* recruits medical staff, GPs, dentists, nurses and paramedical staff for a hospital management organisation. *Arabian Careers Ltd* places doctors, dentists, nurses, laboratory technicians, radiographers, physiotherapists, dieticians and other health professionals in hospitals across the country. *Network Overseas* and *Choice Personnel* recruit staff at all levels up to chiefs of medical staff for countries throughout the region, on a variety of contracts.

### Other Agencies

The following organisations are involved in various aspects of health recruitment in Saudi Arabia, and may be able to help you in your job search. *Professional Connections* with offices in four countries recruit medical staff at various levels in all specialities and nursing staff for permanent and contract positions at five hospitals in Saudi Arabia.

*Athena Saudi Arabia:* PO Box 61587, Riyadh 11575, Saudi Arabia (tel 01-464 8245; fax 01-461 5012).
*Network Overseas:* 34 Mortimer Street, London W1N 8JR, UK (tel +44-20-7580 5151; fax 020-7580 6242; e-mail medical@networkoverseas.cc website networkoverseas.cc).
*O'Grady-Peyton International:* 332 Congress Street, Boston, Massachusetts 02210, USA, (tel +1-617-422 0300; fax 617-422 0399; Website www.opginc.com).
*Grafton Recruitment Ltd:* 35-37 Queens Square, Belfast BT1 3FG, UK (tel 028-9024

2824; fax 028-9024 2897); recruits qualified and experienced medical personnel at all levels.

*Gulf Link:* PO Box 15331, Manama, Bahrain (tel 240090; fax 240040); recruits a wide variety of management, technical and medical staff for hospitals in Saudi Arabia and Bahrain.

*Professional Connections IRL Oy:* Aleksanterinkatu 48A, 3 krs, FIN-0100 Helsinki, Finland (tel +358-9-4155 6611; fax 9-4155 6612; e-mail ProfessionalConnections@profco.com).

*Professional Connections Ltd:* 5 City Gate, Bridge Street Lower, Dublin 8, Ireland (tel +353-1-679 2277; fax 1-679 2396; e-mail profconn@iol.ie).

*Professional Connections AB:* Radmansgatan 48 bv, S-113 57 Stockholm, Sweden (tel +46-8-673 1490; fax 8-673 1491).

*Professional Connections (UK) Ltd:* 10 Stratton Street, London, W1X 5FD, UK (tel +44-020-7544 6848; 020-7544 6849; e-mail profcoldn@aol.com Website www.profco.com).

*Witikar Saudi Arabia Ltd:* 2009 Massachusetts Avenue, NW, Washington, DC 20036, USA (tel 1-800-999-9725, in the USA only; 202-877-3046).

# United Arab Emirates

*Embassy of the United Arab Emirates:* Suite 600, 3000 K Street, NW, Washington, DC 20007, USA (tel 202-338-6500; fax 202-337-7029).

*Embassy of the United Arab Emirates:* 30 Prince's Gate, London SW7 1PT, UK (tel 020-7581 1281; fax 020-7581 9616).

*Currency:* UAE Dirham (UAE Dh1 = 100 fils).

*Exchange rate:* £1 = UAE Dh5.8; $1 = UAE Dh3.67.

*Capital:* Abu Dhabi.

*International Telephone Code:* +971

*Population:* 2,083,000.

*Area:* 78,000 sq. km.

*Language:* Arabic

The country of the United Arab Emirates (UAE) – formerly known as the Trucial States – was formed in 1971, and consists of seven Emirates (former sheikhdoms). The Emirates initially came under British influence in the 1820s, when Britain sought control of the Gulf to protect India. Britain withdrew from the Gulf in 1971, and in the years since independence the UAE have undergone dramatic economic development, particularly as a consequence of the discovery of oil.

Abu Dhabi is the largest and richest of the Emirates and is the largest oil producer. Along with Dubai and Sharjah, Abu Dhabi provides aid to the remaining Emirates and exerts considerable influence within the UAE.

Islam is the official religion of the country and it has a major influence on the country's life. Westerners should note that a dress code applies (directed particularly at women).

## HEALTH SERVICES

As part of the country's overall economic development in recent years, health care has advanced markedly and all members of the population now have access to high quality medical care often staffed by western professionals, but with a growing body of highly trained native staff. Facilities are of a high standard but are very expensive, so health insurance is essential. The UAE Ministry of Health has plans to double the bed capacity of the nation's hospitals over the next ten years, a programme which would take current capacity to 6,000 beds by next year. 17 new hospitals are to be created in the northern emirates alone.

## VISAS AND WORK PERMITS

You should contact your nearest UAE embassy for information on visa requirements. Work permits will normally be arranged through the agency arranging your employment.

## JOB OPPORTUNITIES

Given the expansion of health provision in the Emirates health employment in the UAE would seem to be a booming industry.

### Agencies

Several of the recruitment agencies involved in the Middle East place staff in the UAE. *United Medical Enterprises Ltd* recruits senior hospital medical staff, GPs, dentists, RGNs and paramedical staff for hospitals in Abu Dhabi and Dubai. *Professional Connections* with offices in four countries (see p.228) recruits medical staff at various levels in all specialities and nursing staff for permanent and contract positions at the Tawam and three other hospitals in the Emirates.

### Tawam Hospital

PO Box 15258, Al Ain, Abu Dhabi, UAE (tel 3-677410; fax 3-671228).
This Ministry of Health hospital is a 277-bed referral/acute care general hospital serving the national population. It is the referral centre for oncology, neurosurgery and paediatric surgery within the UAE.

The hospital actively recruits overseas staff, and a package including airfares, medical and emergency dental care, and an end-of-service award is available. The hospital has a multinational staff, but English is the official language. All candidates must pass a full medical examination on site, and a residency visa (valid for 5 years) is arranged following successful completion of this. Single females must live on the hospital compound.

### Useful Addresses

*American Hospital Dubai:* Human Resources, PO E, Dubai, UAE (fax 014-336 0068; e-mail hr@dubai.com Website www.abudhabi.com/site/employment).
*Dubai London Clinic:* PO Box 12119, Dubai, UAE (tel 04-446663; 04-446191).
*El Maghraby Eye & Ear Centre:* PO Box 655, Abu Dhabi, UAE (tel 02-345000; fax 02-343940; Website www.elmaghraby.com).
*The Gulf Diagnostic Centre:* PO Box 30702, Abu Dhabi, UAE (tel 02-658090; fax 02-658084; e-mail gdcmktg@emirates.net.ae).
*New Medical Centre Hospital Abu Dhabi:* PO Box 6222, Abu Dhabi, UAE (tel 02-323296; fax 02-320878; e-mail nmc@emirates.net.ae).
*New Medical Centre Hospital Dubai:* PO Box 7832, Dubai, UAE (tel 04-683131; fax 04-682353).
*New Medical Centre Hospital Sharjah:* PO Box 25262, Sharjah, UAE (tel 06-536936; fax 06-536378).

*UAE University:* Faculty of Medicine: PO Box 17666, Al Ain, UAE (fax 03-672 001; Website www.uaeu.ac.ae).

# Other Middle Eastern Countries

## INTRODUCTION

In addition to the countries described above, there are some employment opportunities in other parts of the Middle East. Once again, these positions are largely available through agencies specialising in the region, including some of those already mentioned above. *BML Recruitment International* finds work in the Middle East. Many of the agencies listed on page 228 that operate in Saudi Arabia are also able to place staff in other countries throughout the Middle East.

In the Gaza trip area of Israel the *Ahli Arab Hospital* often requires volunteer nursing staff. Details can be obtained from The Director, Ahli Arab Hospital, PO Box 72, Palestine Square, Gaza, Israel.

In the Sultanate of Oman the 500-bed Sultan Qaboos University Hospital has a continuing need for highly experienced doctors, nurses, physiotherapists and laboratory technicians. Further information is available from the Director of Administration & Finance, Sultan Qaboos University Hospital, PO Box 38, Al-Khod 123, Sultanate of Oman (tel 513355; fax 513009).

## VOLUNTARY ORGANISATIONS

Many international relief agencies are involved in providing medical and health care assistance in the most unsettled parts of the Middle East. These include the *International Committee of the Red Cross*, which provides health care in areas of armed conflict; *Médecins sans Frontières*; and *MERLIN*, which provides emergency medical care in Yemen. Many more are involved in longer-term projects, including the *International Federation of Red Cross and Red Crescent Societies, International Cooperation for Development; International Service Medical Aid for Palestinians*, which works in the West Bank, the Gaza Strip and Lebanon; *United Nations Volunteers*; and *VSO*.

**N.B.** For all of the agencies mentioned above, further information, addresses and telephone numbers are included in the directories in Part II of this book.

# AFRICA

## South Africa

*South African Embassy:* 3051 Massachusetts Avenue, NW, Washington, DC 20008,
 USA (tel 202-232-4400; fax 202-265-1607/232-3402).
*South African High Commission:* Trafalgar Square, London WC2N 5DP, UK (tel
 020-7930 4488; fax 020-7451 7284).
*South African High Commission:* 15 Sussex Drive, Ottawa, Ontario K1M 1M8,
 Canada (tel 613-744-0330; fax 613-741-1639).
*Currency:* Rand (R; R1 = 100 cents).
*Exchange rate:* £1 = R9.8; $1 = R6.13.
*Capitals:* Pretoria (administrative); Cape Town (legislative).
*International Telephone Code:* +27
*Population:* 40,436,000.
*Area:* 1,221,000.
*Languages:* Afrikaans, English; there are also nine main African languages

The newly democratised South Africa has inherited enormous problems, however,
and faces economic uncertainty and continuing social conflict. The recent
retirement of Nelson Mandela, has added to the uncertainty, but the Rainbow
Nation is looking to the future. The problems off the past still haunt the nation as
many white professionals emigrate to New Zealand, and high unemployment has
lead to high crime figures.

## HEALTH SERVICES

South Africa's health services have until now been fragmented and to a large extent
ineffective with a very poor distribution of resources. The years of apartheid
produced huge inequalities in the provision of health care to the white and black
sections of the population. Black townships were often lacking even basic health
facilities, while internationally renowned hospital capable of carrying out heart
transplants were open only to whites. Although admission into properly equipped
hospitals on the basis of skin colour is a thing of the past, the inherited problems
can obviously not be changed overnight and conditions are still very poor in many
rural hospitals, with insufficient staff and basic drugs and equipment lacking. A
recent government audit revealed that R8 billion is required to bring hospitals up to
scratch. Staffing levels remain a major problem in the provision of adequate health
care; the Barragwanath hospital, for example, which serves the township of
Soweto, is desperately short of doctors, and in Benoni hospital east of
Johannesburg 45 doctors serve 2 million people.
    One of the priorities established by the national Reconstruction and
Development Programme (RDP) was that all the different health care services and

operators should be drawn together into a co-ordinated national health system including both the public and private sectors. This will involve a fundamental restructuring of the health care system. Ultimately health authorities at the national, provincial and district levels are envisaged, with the district health authorities responsible for all primary health care services, including GP's and community hospitals. Retraining and 'reorienting' of all existing health workers is planned, corresponding to a shift in budget allocation from curative hospital services to primary health care. Ambitious immunisation programmes and schemes to improve the nutrition of the population are also planned for the years ahead.

Free medical treatment became available to certain categories of patient in 1994, including pregnant women, new mothers and young children. There is, however, no national medical insurance programme as such, and there are 172 private medical schemes.

At present the provincial health administrations provide and manage hospitals, clinics and community health centres. The local authorities are also responsible for providing primary health care. There are also over 200 private hospitals, many of which are owned by consortiums of private physicians or large businesses. The mining industry also contributes to the number of private hospitals. In 1999 there were 26,452 medical practitioners registered with the Health Professions Council of South Africa (HPCSA), of whom 7167 had specialist qualifications. Many of these doctors were working in private practice. There were 4029 dentists, 331 dental and oral specialists, 787 oral hygienists, 180 dental therapists and 1151 dental technicians. All dental workers provide services in the private as well as public sector. There were 9622 pharmacists registered with South African Pharmacy Council, about 1174 of whom were employed in provincial and state hospitals. There were 158,538 registered and enrolled nurses and nursing auxiliaries. There were also 377 qualified chiropractors and homeopaths registered with the Chiropractors, Homeopaths and Allied Health Service Profession Council.

## SKILLS AND QUALIFICATIONS

The Health Professions Council of South Africa is directly concerned with medical practitioners, dentists and psychologists – registration with the Council is a prerequisite for practising in any of these professions. In addition there are a number of 'supplementary health service professions' that register with the Council, although almost all of these have their own regulatory bodies.

The Council advises that the question of registration is relatively complex, and health professionals considering working in South Africa should contact the Council directly for a discussion of their situation on an individual basis. However some general details on particular professions are included below.

### Medicine

At present original qualifications are accepted from UK, Ireland and Belgium. For the past three years the South African Medical Association has been anticipating a new registration system which will no longer automatically accept these degrees. Foreign qualified doctors will then have to sit a form of registration exam which would (as present for other countries) make them eligible for work in the public service. Specialist qualifications would again only be accepted after review, and for public service.

If a doctor aims to go into private practice in South Africa country he/she will need to take the equivalent of the South African 6th year exam, possibly repeat an internship period and complete a period of community service.

## Nursing

The South African Nursing Council controls the practice of nursing in South Africa. It sets the minimum requirements for the training of nurses and midwives, and registers those nurses who have acquired one or more of the basic or post-basic qualifications. You should contact the Council to see if your qualifications can be recognised for practice in South Africa. The Council advises that nurses from the UK rarely have problems in having their training and experience recognised, but this is not the case for all European countries. Nowadays in South Africa nurses play an enormous role in health promotion and the prevention of illness at a community level.

## Occupational Therapy

Every foreign therapist coming to South Africa has to register with the Health Professions Council of South Africa (HPCSA) via the Professional Board for Occupational Therapy and Medical Orthotics/Prosthetics. To become an occupational therapist in South Africa involves full time study for four years to obtain a Bachelor's degree, either a BScOccTher or a BOccTher. This is offered at eight universities and includes extensive clinical practice under supervision. Entry requirements into these university courses are relatively stringent, often including high school subjects like maths, science and biology. In the past, foreign applicants simply had to submit their qualifications, academic transcripts and course outlines to the Board for review. Currently, however, a registration examination is being introduced. Further information can be obtained from the HPCSA.

In general, therapists trained in World Federation for Occupational Therapy member countries will have been trained to the same sort of minimum standards. This means that it would usually be easier for foreign-trained OTs from WFOT countries to obtain registration in South Africa than for those from non-WFOT countries – however, no assumptions can be made and each would-be registrant is treated on her/his merits.

The rates of pay are quite widely variable, depending on where the occupational therapist is employed. Starting salaries in the public sector are between R40,000 and R50,000 p.a., while private sector work may start higher than this. At senior levels, salaries will usually reach or exceed R100,000 p.a. and may be substantially above this.

The Occupational Therapy Association of South Africa (OTASA) is the officially recognised professional association for OT staff (OTs, OT Assistants and OT Technicians) in South Africa, it represents around 1300, out of a total of about 2300 registered occupational therapy staff countrywide. Services to members include professional indemnity insurance, an information service and resources such as position papers on a variety of topics. Their refereed journal (the *South African Journal of Occupational Therapy*) is published twice annually.

## Pharmacy

To be able to practise as a pharmacist in South Africa, you will first need to obtain registration with the Pharmacy Council. To do this you will need: evidence of registration as a pharmacist in your country of origin; a letter of good standing from your registering authority; evaluation of your pharmacy degree by the Human Sciences Research Council; and evidence of having completed at least 12 months' practical training. Applicants should be living in South Africa in order to be registered.

## Physiotherapy

Physiotherapy in South Africa is currently a 4-year University degree. Master &

PhD programme is available. The South African Society of Physiotherapy is the only body representing physiotherapists in South Africa. It ensures ethical and clinical standards, maintains and promotes the profession.

All practising physiotherapists in South Africa are required by law to register with the Health Profession Council of South Africa, the registering body of physiotherapists being the Professional Board of Physiotherapy. An examination process has been instituted. This will be taken in South Africa prior to acceptance on the register. Further details are available from the Health Professions Council of South Africa.

Pay in the public sector is from R40, 000.00 – R80, 000.00 per annum. Private employment is more uncreative 80% work in the private sector but only 20% of the public have access to this.

## VISAS AND WORK PERMITS

All overseas health professionals intending to work in South Africa must apply for a visa/work permit, which must be obtained before entry into the country, as they are not issued to visitors after arrival. An application for a temporary work permit can be made once you are in possession of an official letter of employment from a South African employer, stating your position, salary and so on. Note that the authorities' overriding consideration in dealing with applications for temporary work permits is whether the vacancy can be filled by a person already in South Africa.

Professionals wishing to enter South Africa in order to secure employment may apply to their nearest diplomatic mission for a work seeker's permit. Once approval for the permit has been granted, the job-seeker can enter the country and, should he or she be successful in obtaining employment, apply to the Department of Home Affairs to change their status accordingly.

Applicants in countries where South Africa is not represented may send their applications for visas/work permits to the Director-General for Home Affairs (address below).

### Health Requirements

Yellow fever immunisation is a requirement if your journey to South Africa starts or entails passing through the yellow fever belt of Africa or South America by any means other than by a scheduled air service. Malaria is endemic in certain areas of the Northern Province, Eastern Lowveld and Northern Natal.

## JOB OPPORTUNITIES

Useful publications include the *South African Medical Journal*, which is published fortnightly and is available from the Medical Association of South Africa. The *South African Journal of Surgery* is quarterly and available from the same address. Both of these journals include current vacancies. Nurses will find the South African Nursing Association's monthly magazine *Nursing News* a useful source of job advertisements.

Newspapers are also a source of information on vacancies in the health field; try the classified advertisements in the Johannesburg *Sunday Times*. Your nearest South African Embassy or High Commission will probably have a selection of newspapers available for consultation.

### Medicine

There is currently a moratorium on registration of foreign qualified physicians. Recent developments indicate that the Department of Health (DoHA) will start to issue new limited period contracts (1 year at first, renewable 1, 3 or 5 years). Although application for work permits will be annual, the Department of Home Affairs has indicated that they will issue work permits at regional level for the period of the contracts. The DoHA will ask for proof that the foreign trained physician either has special skills, and/or that they are not taking a job from a South African. Doctors wanting to do post-graduate studies will probably be required to work in super-numerary posts (unpaid) and return to their country of origin. Their qualifications may not necessarily be recognised for practice in South Africa, depending on the level of first qualification. The Rural Doctors Association may be willing to assist doctors looking for one or two year contracts.

The following are approximate annual basic rates for 40 hour week (excluding rural allowance R20 000 for select hospitals):

| | |
|---|---|
| Interns | R59 000 |
| Medical Officer | R90 000 |
| Senior Medical Officer | R111 700 |
| Principal Medical Officer | R130 000 |
| Chief Medical Officer | R157 000 |
| Principal Specialist | R178 300 |
| Chief Specialist | R205 400 |

One agency dealing with opportunities for medical staff is *Foreign Placements*; write to the following address for further details: PO Box 912, Somerset West 7129, South Africa (tel 04457-7677; fax 04455-32680).

## Occupational Therapy

There are some foreign occupational therapists working voluntarily in South Africa, mainly in rural hospitals through the VSO.

## Supplementary Health Professions

There is an extreme shortage of health professionals working in these areas, including physiotherapy, dietetics and radiography. The appropriate professional organisation in each case (see list below) will be able to provide more detailed information on where the employment opportunities are. The South African Society of Physiotherapy can supply a list of institutes and centres throughout the country that physiotherapists can contact to find out about current opportunities – these include provincial hospitals, mine hospitals, rehabilitation centres, industrial clinics and schools for handicapped children.

The number of job opportunities for radiographers at any one time is hard to determine, but for information on vacant posts in the public service you can contact the Directorate for Radiation Control, and information about vacancies in the private sector may be obtained by writing to the President of the Radiological Society of South Africa.

# PROFESSIONAL ORGANISATIONS

*Association for Dietetics in South Africa:* PO Box 4309, Randburg 2125, South Africa (tel 011-886 8130).

*Chiropractic Association of South Africa:* 929 Pretorius Street, Arcadia, Gauteng, South Africa (tel +27-12-434832).

*Colleges of Medicine of South Africa:* 17 Milner Road, Rondebosch 7700, South Africa (tel 21-689 3161; fax 21-685 3766; e-mail csma-adm@iafrica.com Website www.collegemedsa.ac.za).

*Democratic Nursing Organisation of South Africa (DENOSA):* PO Box 1280, Pretoria 0001, South Africa (tel 012-343 2315/6/7; fax 012-344 0750; e-mail denosahq@cis.co.za).

*Dental Association of South Africa:* Private Bag 1, Houghton 2041, South Africa (tel 011-484 5288, fax 011-642 5718 e-mail dasa@jhb.lia.net Website www.dasa.co.za).

*Homeopathy Association of West Cape:* PO Box 426, Rondebosch, West Cape, South Africa (tel +27-21-689 5061).

*Medical Association of South Africa:* PO Box 20272, Alkantrant 0005 (428 King's Highway, Lynnwood, Pretoria), South Africa (tel 012-476101; fax 012-471815).

*National Society for Community Nurses of South Africa:* Department of Nursing, University of the Free State, PO Box 339, Bloemfontein 9300, South Africa.

*Occupational Therapy Association of South Africa (OTASA):* (tel/fax 11-885 2031; e-mail piplee@global.co.za Website www.linx.co.za/occther).

*Radiological Society of South Africa:* PO Box 3475, Cresta 2118, South Africa (tel 011-888 5982; fax 011-888 1065; e-mail radsoc@aztec.co.za; web page http://www.imed.co.za/rssa).

*Society of Medical Laboratory Technologists of South Africa:* PO Box 6014, Roggebaai 8012, South Africa (tel 021-419 4857).

*Society of Midwives in Southern Africa:* PO Box 704, Florida Hills 1716, South Africa (tel 011-489 2795; fax 011-489 2411).

*Society of Radiographers of South Africa:* PO Box 6014, Roggebaai 8012, South Africa (tel/fax 011-463 3159).

*South African Association of Occupational Therapists:* 946 Shoeman Street, Arcadia 0083, South Africa.

*South African Dental Laboratory Association:* PO Box 95340, 0145 Waterkloof, South Africa.

*South African Medical Association:* PO Box 74789, Lynwood Ridge, Pretoria 0040, South Africa (tel 012-481 2000; fax 012-481 2100).

*South African Nursing Association:* PO Box 1280, Pretoria 0001, South Africa (tel 012-343 2315; fax 012-344 0750).

*South African Society of Anaesthetists:* 101 Cargo Corner, Rosebank 2196, South Africa (tel 011-880 8418).

*South African Society of Physiotherapy:* PO Box 92125, Norwood 2117, South Africa (tel 011-485 1467; fax 011-485 1613; e-mail secretary@saphysio.co.za).

## USEFUL ADDRESSES

*Chiropractic, Homeopathic and Allied Health Services Professional Council:* PO Box 17005, Groenkloof 0027, South Africa.

*Department of Health:* Private Bag X828, Pretoria 0001, South Africa (fax 012-325 5706).

*Department of Home Affairs:* Private Bag X114, Pretoria 0001, South Africa (tel 012-314 8911; fax 012-326 4571).

*Directorate: Radiation Control:* Private Bag X62, Belville 7535, South Africa (fax 021-946 1589).

*Health Professions Council of South Africa:* PO Box 205, Pretoria 0001, South Africa (tel 12-328 6680).

*Hospital Personnel Association:* PO Box 3284, Pretoria 0001, South Africa (tel 012-322 2739).

*Human Sciences Research Council:* Private Bag X41, Pretoria 0001, South Africa (tel 012-202 9111).

*Professional Board for Physiotherapy:* c/o South African Medical and Dental Council.

*South African Medical and Dental Council:* PO Box 205, Pretoria 0001, South Africa (tel 012-328 6680; fax 012-328 5120; e-mail samdc2@cis.co.za).

*South African Nursing Council:* PO Box 1123, Pretoria 0001, South Africa (tel 012-343 0121; fax 012-343 5400).

*South African Pharmacy Council:* PO Box 40040, Arcadia 0007, South Africa (tel 012-21 1477; fax 012-21 1492)

## VOLUNTARY ORGANISATIONS

A large number of voluntary organisations provide vital health services in South Africa. The South African Red Cross, for example, provides a wide range of emergency, health and community services. A comprehensive list of South African voluntary organisations operating in the health field is included in the *Hospital and Nursing Year Book of Southern Africa:* which may be available through libraries or for consultation at your nearest South African Embassy. In addition, several of the agencies operating in some of the less developed African countries are also involved in health projects in South Africa – see page 239.

*South African Red Cross Society:* 21 Broad Road, Wynberg 7800, South Africa (tel 021-797 8620; fax 021-797 9147; e-mail Redxnatgadija@cybertrade.co.za).

*Flight for Life:* Air Ambulance Service, c/o Johannesburg Hospital, Private Bag X39, Johannesburg 2000, South Africa (tel 011-488 4162).

*Hospital Christian Fellowship:* PO Box 353, Kempton Park 1620, South Africa (tel 011-972 2934).

*Medic Alert Foundation:* PO Box 4841, Cape Town 8000, South Africa (tel 021-461 7328; fax 021-461 6654).

*Medical Rescue International:* Heerengracht, De Korte St, Johannesburg 2001, South Africa (tel 011-403 7080; fax 011-339 6897).

## OTHER AGENCIES

*Charisma Verpleegagentskap:* PO Box 3281, Kempton Park 1620, South Africa (tel 011-394 4155).

*Dynamic Nurses:* PO Box 7776, Pretoria 0001, South Africa (tel 012-807 3013).

*East Rand Nursing Agency:* PO Box 14866, Farrarmere 1518, South Africa (tel 011-425 2509).

*Grafton Recruitment:* 3rd Floor, NW Tower, The Piazza, cnr Republic & Jan Smuts Avenue, Randburg, Craighall 2024, South Africa (tel 011-789 9591; fax 011-789 9502; e-mail grafton1@iafrica.com Website www.grafton group.com).

*Home Nursing Care:* 10 St John Street, George 6530, South Africa.

*Lauderdale Nursing Services:* PO Box 53220, Kenilworth 7745, South Africa (tel 021-683 4113).

*Lowveld Nursing Services:* PO Box 2833, Nelspruit 1200, South Africa (tel 013-782 5869)

*Maylen Nursing Services:* PO Box 28040, Sunnyside 0132, South Africa (tel 012-46 8992).

*Nightingale Nursing Services:* PO Box 8230, Johannesburg 2000, South Africa (tel 011-682 2948).

*Nursing Emergencies:* PO Box 5891, Johannesburg 2000, South Africa (tel 011-725 0396).

*Promed Services:* PO Box 70445, Die Wilgers, Pretoria 0041 (tel 012-807 1697).

*Quality Nursing Services:* PO Box 23010, Joubertpark 2044, South Africa (tel 011-482 8755).

*Robert Coleman Associates:* 2 London Wall Buildings, London Wall, London EC2M 5UU, UK (tel 020-7628 5001; fax 020-7628 5002; e-mail info@robertcoleman.com).

---

# Other African Countries

---

## INTRODUCTION

A huge number of overseas organisations are involved in the provision of health care in Africa, both in the governmental and non-governmental/voluntary sectors.

There is a welcome trend towards promoting long-term sustainability in health projects, rather than increasing the dependence of African countries on overseas aid. This shift is apparent both on the part of African governments and international organisations; the Tanzanian government, for example, is not keen on there being more expatriates than necessary working within its borders, as there are qualified local health staff who need employment; similarly many British charities or voluntary groups are keen to involve local people and promote self-sufficiency in health projects wherever possible.

One local organisation which recruits the occasional expatriate professional is the St Giles Medical Rehabilitation Centre ( PO Box A224, Avondale, Harare, Zimbabwe; tel +263-4-704691), which had vacancies for Speech Language Therapists in 1999.

**N.B.** For the agencies mentioned below, further information, addresses and telephone numbers are included in the directories in Part II of this book.

## VOLUNTARY ORGANISATIONS

Many voluntary organisations are involved in emergency relief in various parts of Africa – the current violent rest in the central African republics is just one region requiring urgent aid. Organisations geared up to responding to crises in areas affected by war, political upheaval, natural disaster and famine include the *International Committee of the Red Cross*; *Médecins sans Frontières*; and *MERLIN*, which have recently been involved in providing emergency medical care in Ethipoia, Sierra Leone and Rwanda.

In addition there are several agencies involved in longer-term projects – some in countries throughout the continent, others in particular regions. In the former category are *Care International,* which is involved in relief and development work; the *International Federation of Red Cross and Red Crescent Societies,* which is involved in long-term community health projects in developing countries; *International Cooperation for Development; Save the Children Fund; VSO*; and *WaterAid. CUSO* places Canadian volunteers on health projects in Africa.

A wide range of health professionals work for *Action Health* in Tanzania and Uganda; and for *Concern Worldwide* in Angola, Democratic Republic of Congo Ethiopia, Mozambique, Rwanda, SIerra Leone, Somalia, Tanzania and Uganda. *Health Projects Abroad* has community health workers active in Tanzania and Cameroon; *Health Unlimited* has medical teams working in twelve african nations; the *Institute for International Cooperation and Development* places volunteers on health programmes in countries such as Zimbabwe and Zambia; and *International*

*Service* places volunteers on projects in western Africa. *Skillshare Africa* runs health projects in Botswana, Lesotho and Mozambique. Bear in mind that the work of these agencies is subject to changes in the situation on the ground; it may be necessary, for example, to divert resources to regions where they are more urgently needed, or a particular project may come to an end, with responsibility for the work passing to members of the local community. It is therefore important to contact the agencies directly to find out about their current activities and personnel requirements in the health field.

## DENOMINATIONAL ORGANISATIONS

There is an astonishing number of religious groups working in Africa, coupling the provision of much-needed health care with 'spreading the word' of their particular faith. These include *Action Partners Ministries*, which takes on health workers to work in Cameroon, Chad, Egypt, Kenya, Ghana, Nigeria, Sudan and Zaire; *CORD*, which has health staff in Mozambique, Rwanda and Tanzania; the *Mid-Africa Ministry*, which places health professionals and volunteer workers in Rwanda, Burundi, Uganda and the Democratic Republic of Congo; the *Volunteer Missionary Movement*, which places health professionals in Central Africa; and *WEC International*, which carries out medical work in Gambia, Guinea Bissau, Ghana, Chad and Congo.

The *Catholic Medical Mission Board*, *Christians Abroad*, the *Mennonite Central Committee* and *Tear Fund* all need health professionals to fill positions in various parts of Africa.

Organisations with more specialised requirements include *Christoffel Blindenmission*, which takes on eye care and other health specialists to work in Africa, and *The Leprosy Mission*, which needs health professionals to work with leprosy patients.

# ASIA

## Hong Kong

With the return of Hong Kong to Chinese rule, all entry, visa and work permit enquiries are dealt with by the Chinese embassies.

*Embassy of The People's Republic of China:* 2201 Wisconsin Avenue, NW, Washington, DC 20007, USA; tel 202-338 6688; fax 202-588 9760.

*Embassy of The People's Republic of China:* 49-51 Portland Place, London, W1N 3AH; tel 020-7262 0253.

*Embassy of The People's Republic of China:* 515 St. Patrick Street, Ottawa, Ontario, K1N 5H3, Canada; tel 613-789 3434; fax 613-789 1911.

*Currency:* Hong Kong Dollar (HK$).

*Exchange rate:* £1 = HK$12.48; $1 = HK$7.77.

*International Telephone Code:* +852

*Population:* 6,500,000.

*Area:* 1091 sq. km.

*Language:* Cantonese; English widely spoken

Hong Kong was a British colony leased from China until July 1997 when it returned to Chinese rule. Under British rule Hong Kong had developed into the main financial services area for Asia and its stock exchange was one of the world's most important. The government of the People's Republic of China, concluded a treaty with Britain which will preserve Hong Kong's current economic system for fifty years and so Hong Kong has become a special administrative region, and continues to trade and act as a market economy. In effect nothing has changed except the uniforms of the policemen on the street. Hong Kong itself is a sprawling, crowded city on several islands around a large natural harbour. Its streets, hawkers and restaurants all attract tourists, while its businesses have continued to thrive even through the recent slump.

## HEALTH SERVICES

Hong Kong is well provided with 31,000 beds in 40 hospitals and health care facilities that match the best Western standards, and a comprehensive range of public and private medical services is available. This adds up to a bed-population ratio of 4.7 beds per 1,000 inhabitants. Despite the British connection there is no direct equivalent to the UK's National Health Service, and medical advice and treatment have to be paid for, although government medical services are available to all at a nominal charge. An interesting aspect of health care in Hong Kong is that although China has a centuries old tradition of herbal medicine and practices which are viewed as 'alternative' or 'complimentary' therapies by the western health system, Western medicine is entirely acceptable to the Chinese population.

The government/public sector consists of hospitals and clinics located throughout the territory. Private practitioners and hospitals, for which patients have to pay all costs, provide a complementary service, and the private sector co-operates with the government to provide the School Medical Service and clinics in public housing estates. Other preventive programmes implemented by the government include Family Health Services, the Port Health Service, the School Dental Service and many other community health services. All of these have contributed to the high standard of health, and have kept Hong Kong free from epidemics of the major communicable diseases, despite its being one of the world's most densely populated cities.

Private GPs, specialists and traditional Chinese medical practitioners account for about 85% of all out-patient consultations. Public clinics (run by the Department of Health) account for the remaining 15%. About 93% of in-patient admissions take place in public hospitals operated by the Hospital Authority, and 7% in private profit-making and non-profit-making hospitals run by a number of religious and commercial organisations. Public health care services are heavily subsidised from general revenue. About 15% of the population is covered by medical insurance, mainly provided by employers as a fringe benefit. Currently there are 9,289 doctors registered in Hong Kong, thus the ratio of doctors to every 1000 people is 1.4.

A detailed review of the health care system in Hong Kong is published in the annual Hong Kong yearbook, available in libraries.

## SKILLS AND QUALIFICATIONS

Members of the following healthcare professions are legally required to register with the appropriate board or council before they can work in Hong Kong: Dentists, Medical Practitioners, Medical Laboratory Technologists, Midwives, Nurses, Occupational Therapists, Optometrists, Pharmacists, Physiotherapists and Radiographers. The various registration requirements can be obtained from the different boards at the Department of Health. Those mentioned above which do not have a board or council of their own are regulated by a specialist section of the Supplementary Medical Professions Council.

## VISAS AND WORK PERMITS

As mentioned above visas and work permits for the Hong Kong Special Administrative Region (HKSAR) are handled by the diplomatic missions of the People's Republic of China. Those nationalities which did not need a visa to visit Hong Kong before July 1997 (ie Britons, citizens of most European and Commonwealth countries and the USA), are still able to do so, unless they intend to live, work or study there, in which case a visa is required. Visas would also be required for anyone travelling into China from Hong Kong.

## JOB OPPORTUNITIES

Hong Kong's advanced economy requires people of most professions and skills, but the high standards of qualifications and experience possessed by the local population mean that competition is keen. The job market for expatriates is largely confined to the professions or specialist posts.

Positions with the Hospital Authority may also be advertised in professional journals and newspapers in overseas countries. Normally overseas nationals will work with the Authority on contracts lasting 1-3 years, at a salary level comparable to that of local recruits. The Department of Health has a small number of permanent foreign staff – overseas medical personnel holding recognised qualifications and registered with the Medical Council of Hong Kong can apply for vacancies when they arise. For current information on recruitment in the Hospital Authority and the Department of Health you should contact these organisations directly.

Jobs in the private sector are normally found by replying to advertisements in the local press or by making direct approaches to potential employers, i.e. the private hospitals and clinics themselves.

In Hong Kong the *South China Morning Post* is the major source of classified job advertisements; the Saturday edition comes with several supplements full of vacancies, one of which includes 'recruitment features' on health care and social welfare – full-page advertisements for positions with the Hospital Authority, for example, appear here. The other English-language newspaper that you might wish to consult is the *Hong Kong Standard* (address below).

## PROFESSIONAL ORGANISATIONS

*BMA Hong Kong Branch:* c/o Federation of Medical Societies of Hong Kong, 4/F Duke of Windsor Social Services Building, 15 Hennesy Road, Wanchai, Hong Kong (tel 2527 8858; fax 2865 0345).

*College of Nursing:* 221 Gloucester Road, 12th Floor, Hyde Centre, Wanchai, Hong Kong (tel 2572 9255; fax 2838 6280).

*Hong Kong Association of Occupational Therapists:* PO Box 98241, Tsim Sha Tsui Post Office, Kowloon, Hong Kong.

*Hong Kong Dental Association:* Duke of Windsor Building, 8th Floor, 15 Hennessy Road, Wanchai, Hong Kong (tel 2528 5327; fax 2529 0755; e-mail hkda@hkda.org Website www,hkda.org).

*Hong Kong Medical Association:* Duke of Windsor Building, 5th Floor, 15 Hennessy Road, Wanchai, Hong Kong (tel 2527 8452; fax 2865 0943; e-mail hkma@hkma.com.hk Website www.hkma.com.hk).

*Hong Kong Medical Technicians and Technologists Association:* 7/F Sai Ying Pun Jockey Club Polyclinics, 134 Queens Road west, Sai Ying Pun , Hong Kong (tel 2857 4079; fax 2858 2684).

*Hong Kong Occupational Therapy Association:* Box 98241, Tsim Sha Tsui Post Office, Hong Kong (Website http://hkpu15.polyu.edu.hk/~hkota/).

*Hong Kong Physiotherapy Association:* PO Box 10139, Hong Kong (tel 2336 0172; fax 2338 0252).

*Hong Kong Radiological Technologists' Association:* PO Box 73549, Kowloon Central Post Office, Hong Kong (tel 2358 6535; fax 2335 0074)

*Pharmeceutical Society of Hong Kong:* 4/F Duke of Windsor Social Services Building, 15 Hennesy Road, Wanchai, Hong Kong (fax 2808 0162; e-mail pharmacisthk@hotmail.com).

## USEFUL ADDRESSES

*Government of Hong Kong, Special Administrative Region, Department of Health:* Wu Chung House, 17th & 21st Floors, 213 Queen's Road East, Wan Chai, Hong Kong (tel 2961-8894; fax 2836-0071; Website www.info.gov.hk/dh/).

*Government Publications Office:* Ground Floor, Low Block, Queensway Government Offices, 66 Queensway, Hong Kong.

*Hong Kong Academy of Medicine:* Jockey Club Building, 99 Wong Chuk Hang Road, Aberdeen, Hong Kong.

*Hong Kong Medical Journal:* Pearson Professional (Hong Kong) Ltd, suite 1808, Asian House, 1 Hennessy Road, Wan Chai, Hong Kong (tel 2863-2655; fax 2520-6954; Website www.hkmj.org.hk).

*Hong Kong Standard:* Sing Tao Building, 4th Floor, 1 Wang Kwong Road,

Kowloon Bay, Hong Kong (tel 2798-2859; fax 2750-5584; Website www.hkstandard.com).
*Hospital Authority:* Hospital Authority Building, 147B Argyle Street, Kowloon, Hong Kong.
*Immigration Department:* Immigration Tower, 7 Gloucester Road, Wan Chai, Hong Kong (tel 2824 6111; fax 2877 7711).
*Secretary for Health and Welfare:* 19th Floor, Murray Building, Garden Road, Central, Hong Kong.
*Social Welfare Department:* Wu Chung House, 8th Floor, 213 Queen's Road East, Wan Chai, Hong Kong (tel 2892 5323; fax 2838 0114; e-mail swdenq@swd.gcn.gov.hk Website www.info.gov.hk/swd).
*South China Morning Post:* Morning Post Building, Tong Chong Street, Hong Kong.

## PROFESSIONAL BOARDS/COUNCILS

*Dental Council:* 17/F Wu Chung House, 213 Queen's Road East, Wanchai, Hong Kong (tel 2961 8648; Website www.dchk.org.hk).
*Medical Council of Hong Kong:* (Registration Office) 1/F Wu Chung House, 213 Queen's Road East, Wanchai, Hong Kong (tel2961 8648; fax 2891 7946; Website www.mchk.org.hk).
*Midwives Council:* 17/F Wu Chung House, 213 Queen's Road East, Wanchai, Hong Kong (tel 2527 8351; fax 2527 2272; Website www.mwchk.org.hk).
*Nursing Council:* 1/F Shun Feng International Centre, 182 Queen's Road East, Wanchai, Hong Kong (tel 2527 8325; fax 2527 2277; Website www.nchk.org.hk).
*Pharmacy and Poisons Board:* Department of Health, 17/F Wu Chung House, 213 Queen's Road East, Wanchai, Hong Kong (tel 2961 8648).
*Supplementary Medical Professions Council:* Department of Health, 17/F Wu Chung House, 213 Queen's Road East, Wanchai, Hong Kong (tel 2961 8647; fax 2961 8652).

# Japan

*Embassy of Japan:* 2520 Massachusetts Avenue, NW, Washington, DC 20008, USA (tel 202-939-6700; fax 202-328-2187).
*Embassy of Japan:* 101-104 Piccadilly, London W1V 9FN, UK (tel 020-7465 6500; fax 020-7491 9348).
*Embassy of Japan:* 255 Sussex Drive, Ottawa, Ontario K1N 9E6, Canada (tel 613-241-8541; fax 613-241-2232).
*Currency:* Yen (Y).
*Exchange rate:* £1 = Y166; $1 = Y104.
*Capital:* Tokyo.
*International Telephone Code:* +81
*Population:* 123,587,000.
*Area:* 378,000 sq. km.
*Language:* Japanese

Made up of four major islands, Japan is a country synonymous with modern technology and innovation. Although its manufacturers have yet to gain the cachet of having a product universally named after them (as with *Hoover* and vacuum cleaners) there are very few electrical goods shops or car showrooms that do not have a Japanese product on sale in Europe or the Americas. Since the Second World War Japan has been the economic and manufacturing powerhouse of the Pacific nations, and many Japanese companies play an important role in western business. Apart from televisions, videos and microwave ovens, Japan is famous for geisha girls, samurai, karate, animé and sumo wrestling. Although it has recently experienced an economic recession, it remains a major industrial force, and continues to attract many Westerners keen to work in the country and explore its fascinating culture.

## HEALTH SERVICES

Health care in Japan is the responsibility of three different ministries: the Ministry of Health and Welfare is in charge of most health care services; the Ministry of Education, Science and Culture has authority over health care for school children; and the Ministry of Labour is in charge of health care for workers.

Health care services are provided in a variety of hospitals, medical clinics and community health centres. Japan has over 9000 general hospitals, over 1000 psychiatric hospitals and over 1100 geriatric hospitals. The total number of hospital beds is over 1.5 million.

In Japan a medical clinic is a medical facility with 19 or fewer beds. There are at present around 24,000 such clinics. These clinics are mainly concerned with patients with minor illnesses or disabilities, and care is provided principally through consultation with a doctor. Patients with more serious problems are referred to large hospitals or are visited at home.

Community health centres are involved in improving and promoting public health. Each centre serves a population of about 100,000. There are over 850 throughout Japan; about half are in urban areas, but many are in villages or serve thinly populated areas. The public health nurses employed by health centres provide the main part of the centres' individualised health care, and coordinate the work of the community health team. Their work includes home visits, group health screening and health counselling.

As a result of advances in medical treatment and shorter hospital stays, a growing number of patients with serious illnesses now receive treatment at home rather than in hospital. The health care system is also faced with increasing numbers of people living longer.

Japan has a system of health insurance to cover the expense of medical examinations and the treatment of illness and injury. Since 1961 all Japanese have been covered by some type(s) of health insurance scheme. This insurance is guaranteed with public money, when payments can not be made due to illness or unemployment.

## SKILLS AND QUALIFICATIONS

For a health professional to practise in Japan it will normally be necessary to pass a licensure examination. The professional organisations listed at the end of this section will be able to provide details of what is involved.

### Nursing

In order to practise in Japan, overseas nurses are required to take and pass the national board licensure examination. Applicants must take this examination in Japanese, although there is no specific language test as part of the procedure. The examination is offered twice annually. However, according to the Japanes Nursing Association it is very difficult for a foreign nurse to even arrange to take the exam.

In order to apply for recognition of existing qualifications, an overseas nurse must appear in person and submit the necessary documents (with Japanese translations) to the Medical Affairs Division of the Ministry of Health and Welfare, together with an application for confirmation of their examination qualification; these documents include the nurse's CV/résumé, their license to practise in their own country, confirmation of their nursing examination result, a copy of their nursing diploma or other certificate (with curriculum details and grades), a certificate of good health, and their certificate of alien registration. These documents are then verified by the Ministry (a procedure that will normally take between 6 months and a year); if all is in order, the Ministry will award the applicant the national examination qualification.

## VISAS AND WORK PERMITS

Europeans, Americans, Canadians and citizens of most Commonwealth nations do not require visas for visitor entry to Japan, although the length of stay permitted varies according to which country you are from. Australians, on the other hand do require visas even as tourists. Canadian citizens may also take advantage of a working holiday scheme, for those under 30, agreed between the two countries; visas issued under this scheme are valid for twelve months. Other nationalities will need to obtain a Working Visa, these vary according to your profession or intended area of work. Visitor visas can not be changed to working visas within Japan, and any application for a working visa must be supported by an employer who will sponsor you and arrange for your certificate of eligibility.

## JOB OPPORTUNITIES

If you are interested in working in Japan, your main source of information will be the Japanese equivalent of your own professional organisation; addresses for these are included below. They will be able to provide information on how easy it is for overseas professionals to have their qualifications recognised and practise, and what kind of opportunities are available.

## PROFESSIONAL ORGANISATIONS

*Japan Association of Radiologic Technologists:* 3-3-2 Minato, Chuo-ku, Tokyo 104, Japan.

*Japan Dental Association:* 4-1-20 Kudan-kita, Chiyoda-ku, Tokyo 102-0073, Japan (tel 03-3262 9213; fax 03-3262 9885; e-mail jdent@jda.org.jp Website www.jda.org.jp/).

*Japan Medical Association:* 2-28-16 Honkomagome, Bunkyo-ku, Tokyo 113, Japan (tel 03-3946 2121/3942 6489; fax 03-3946 6295).

*Japanese Association of Medical Technologists:* c/o Ichigaya Hoso Building 1-5, 4-Chome, Kudan-kita, Chiyoda-ku, Tokyo 102, Japan.

*Japanese Association of Occupational Therapists:* 2-2-8 Nishi-Waseda, Shinjuku-ku, Tokyo 162, Japan (tel 03-3203 1286).

*Japanese Dietetic Association:* 1-39 Kanda-Jinbocho, Chiyoda-ku, Tokyo 101, Japan (tel 03-3295 5151).

*Japanese Midwives' Association:* 1-8-21 Fujimi, Chiyoda-ku, Tokyo 102, Japan (tel 03-3262 9953).

*Japanese Nursing Association:* 8-2, 5 Chome, Jingumae, Shibuya-ku, Tokyo 150-0001, Japan (tel 03-400 8331; fax 03-400 8336; Website www.nurse.or.jp).

*Japanese Physical Therapy Association:* Health Department, School of Medicine, Hiroshima University, 1-1-89 Higashisenda, Naka-ku, Hiroshima, Japan (tel 082-241 1221; fax 082-241 0508; e-mail mfujimu@ue.ipc.hiroshima-u.ac.jp); 2-5-18-602 Toyo, Koto-ku, Tokyo 135, Japan (tel 03-3699 1242).

*Japan Psychiatric Nursing Association:* 3-54-15 Momijigaoka, Fuchu-shi, Tokyo 183, Japan (tel 0423-63 6663)

## USEFUL ADDRESSES

*International Nursing Foundation of Japan:* 3-2-4 Kudan-kita, Chiyoda-ku, Tokyo 102, Japan (tel 03-3264 6667).

*Japan Association for Working Holiday Makers:* P-Face 3F, 1-3-20 Arato, Chuoku Fukoka-shi, Fukoka 810, Japan (tel 092-713 0854; fax 092-752 2415).

*Japan Hospital Association:* 2-14 Kojimachi, Chiyoda-ku, Tokyo 102, Japan (tel 03-3265 0077).

*Japanese National Council of Social Welfare:* 3-3-2 Kasumigaseki, Chiyoda-ku, Tokyo 100, Japan (tel 03-3581 7851).

*JNA News:* (nursing journal) 8-2, 5 Chome, Jingumae, Shibuya-ku, Tokyo 150-0001, Japan (tel 03-400 8331; fax 03-400 8336).

*Kimi Information Centre:* Oscar Building, 8F 2-42-3, Toshima-ku, Tokyo 171-0014, Japan, (tel 03-3986 1604; fax 03-3986 3037). Information centre for accommodation and jobs.

*Ministry of Education, Culture and Science:* 3-2-2 Kasumigaseki, Chiyoda-ku, Tokyo 100, Japan (tel 03-3581 4211).

*Ministry of Health and Welfare, Health Policy Bureau, Department of Nursing:* 1-2-2 Kasumigaseki, Chiyoda-ku, Tokyo 100-0013, Japan (tel 03-3503 1711).

*Ministry of Labour:* 1-2-2 Kasumigaseki, Chiyoda-ku, Tokyo 100, Japan (tel 03-3593 1211)

## EMPLOYMENT AGENCIES

*Borgnan Human Development Institute:* Daisan Taihei Building, 1-25-3 Higashi-Ikebukuro, Toshima-ku, Tokyo 170, Japan (tel 03-3989 8151; fax 03-3983 4897).

*Cambridge Corporation:* 1-11-45 Akasaka, Minato-ku, Tokyo 107, Japan (tel 03-3582 8931).

*OA Consultants:* 1405-2-1, Udagawa-cho, Shibuya, Tokyo 150, Japan (tel 03-3496 9443).

*Selnate Co:* Fujibo Building, 2nd Floor, 22-10-28 Fujimi, Chiyoda-ku, Tokyo 102, Japan (tel 03-3234 5071).

---

# Singapore

---

*Embassy of the Republic of Singapore:* 3501 International Place, NW, Washington, DC 20008, USA (tel 202-537-3100; fax 202-537-0876).

*High Commission for the Republic of Singapore:* 9 Wilton Crescent, London SW1X 8SA (tel 020-7235 8315/235 5441 (visa section); fax 020-7245 6583).

*Consulate of the Republic of Singapore:* Suite 1305, 999 West Hastings Street, Vancouver, British Columbia V6C 2W2, Canada (tel 604-669-5115; fax 604-669-5153).

*Currency:* Singapore Dollar (S$).

*Exchange rate:* £1 = S$2.69; $1 = S$1.68.

*International Telephone Code:* +65

*Population:* 2,818,000.

*Area:* 641.4 sq. km.

*Languages:* Malay, Chinese (Mandarin), Tamil, English; Malay is the national language, English is the language of administration

Singapore is a small island republic situated less than a mile from the Malayan Peninsula, its history dates as far back as the 7th century, but modern Singapore was founded by Sir Stamford Raffles in 1819. The British turned Singapore into a thriving free port, attracting many immigrant settlers from the Malay Peninsula, the Indonesian islands, China and India. Singapore has operated as an independent state since 1965. Currently Singapore is famous for the penalties meted out to drug traffickers and the high rise blocks which dominate its business district. It is now a prosperous city-state with a parliamentary system of government. Living conditions in Singapore are among the best in Asia and Singaporeans enjoy a high standard of living.

As Singapore is a multi-racial society, it is useful for newcomers to be aware of the festivals, celebrations and customs of the Chinese, Malay and Indian communities.

## HEALTH SERVICES

Health standards in Singapore are high, due to a decline in the incidence of communicable diseases, high living standards, easy access to health services and stringent health control measures. Both the government and the private sector provide comprehensive health care services. Government health services are heavily subsidised to ensure that health care is available to everyone, but medical insurance is nonetheless popular. There are 10 public and 12 private hospitals in Singapore. Of the public hospitals 8 are 'restructured'; which means that they are owned by the government and provide subsidised services but operate as autonomous entities.

Government polyclinics provide 'one-stop' health services and are found in all the major Housing and Development Board (HDB) town centres and estates. Services include out-patient medical care for acute and chronic diseases, maternal and child health care, immunisation, family planning, screening for commonly occurring and communicable diseases, medical attention for the elderly, psychiatric services, laboratory, X-ray and pharmacy services, dental treatment and health education.

The hospitals provide specialist out-patient services. Most HDB estates have several private clinics to serve the needs of their residents.

## SKILLS AND QUALIFICATIONS

Admission to four health professions in Singapore – dentistry, medicine, nursing and pharmacy – is controlled by statutory regulatory authorities. Regulation is strict – particularly in medicine, as in recent years there has been an over-supply of doctors. The Ministry of Health produces a comprehensive booklet *The Handbook on the Accreditation of Medical Specialists* which gives details of the training requirements for 35 medical specialisations, and where this training can be acquired.

### Dentistry

Overseas dentists who graduated from one of 36 approved dental schools can apply for registration – the Singapore Dental Board will review applications from graduates of other schools only in special cases. The approved schools are in Australia, Canada, Hong Kong, Ireland, New Zealand, the UK and the USA. It is necessary to obtain an offer of employment before applying for registration. There is generally no requirement for further training or examinations, although the

Board may set an examination in certain cases.

## Medicine

Overseas doctors who obtained their basic medical degrees from one of 20 recognised universities will be considered for registation; these universities are in Australia, Canada, the UK and the USA. The Singapore Medical Council is the body responsible for the registration of doctors. Registration does not involve examinations or periods of supervised training, but an official offer of employment must be attached to the application.

The Council has the discretion to review special applications for registration in certain circumstances. However this is rare, and only takes place when the doctor has carried out internationally renowned research or has sought-after clinical skills that are not available in Singapore.

## Nursing

There is no list of recognised overseas nursing schools – the Singapore Nursing Board reviews each application on its own merits. However nursing qualifications from countries such as the UK, the USA, Australia and New Zealand (and European countries where English is widely spoken) are normally acceptable for registration. Assistant nurses and more junior positions do not need to be registered.

## Pharmacy

Overseas pharmacists who wish to work in Singapore have to be registered with the Singapore Pharmacy Board and must obtain work permits from the Ministry of Manpower. Pharmacy qualifications from overseas will be considered by the Singapore Pharmacy Board on a case by case basis. At the time of writing the board had registered pharmacy graduates from those universities in UK, Australia, New Zealand, USA and Canada, where the pharmacy training was consider equivalent to the Singapore Pharmacy Degree.

The Department of Pharmacy at the National University of Singapore (NUS) offers a four-year degree course in Pharmacy, awarding the Bachelor of Science (Pharmacy). Upon graduation, pharmacy graduates are required to undergo a 12-month pre-registration training in an approved training centre. Upon successful completion of the pre-registration, graduates are eligible to be registered to practice pharmacy in Singapore. The Department of Pharmacy, also offers post graduate programmes towards Master Degree or Phd.

The Singapore Pharmacy Board will consider the application for registration only after the pharmacist has received a job offer from one of the approved institutions for pre-registration training. Applications for registration should include the following documents: proof of identity, CV (giving details of basic education, pharmacy training including post graduate training and work experience), details of academic results and course content or syllabus, certificate of registration/licence to practice pharmacy from the Pharmacy Board/Licensing Authority in the last country of practice, documentary proof of pre-registration training, a letter of Good Standing from the Pharmacy Board, references and a confirmation of their appointment from the prospective employer in Singapore.

New pharmacy graduates with no post-registration experience can expect to be paid between $2,200 to $2,500 per month.

## VISAS AND WORK PERMITS

Visas to enter Singapore are not required of EU/EEA, American or Commonwealth citizens in possession of a valid passport, a Social Visit pass will be stamped by the immigration official at the port of entry; these are valid for two weeks to three months. Work permits can be applied for within Singapore but you will probably have to leave the state while it is being processed. However, only your employer can apply for a permit on your behalf and they will need to show that no-one in Singapore could do the job. Work permits can be applied for through employers from your homeland but until you recieve notification from the immigration service you will not be able to obtain entry or employment in Singapore.

## JOB OPPORTUNITIES

You can visit Singapore for the purposes of finding a job, and will not need a visa if you are a national of a country in western Europe or North America, Australia, New Zealand, Japan, Hong Kong or an ASEAN country.

The classified job advertisements in the *Straits Times:* an English-language daily published in Singapore, as well as other local papers, are a good source of information on current vacancies.

Consulting the Singapore Economic Development Board (EDB) may also be useful to you during your job search. The EDB helps employers in Singapore to recruit skilled people from overseas. If you are a professional, a manager or a researcher, or are technically qualified, or are a graduate or postgraduate, and are interested in a career in Singapore, you can contact the EDB's Manpower and Capability Development Division. The Division maintains a database of employers and individuals, and also provides literature on recent developments in Singapore, advises on immigration requirements and helps successful candidates to enter and work in Singapore.

### Dentistry

As with medical positions, the best way to find out about employment opportunities in dentistry is to contact the hospitals and clinics where dentistry is practised. Hospital addresses are included at the end of this section; addresses for dental clinics should be available from the Dental Board.

### Medicine

Recruitment for the polyclinics and public hospitals remains under the control of the Ministry of Health – for information on employment opportunities, you should contact the recruitment officer in the personnel department of the hospital(s) in which you are interested (see addresses below). The 'restructured' hospitals are independent of the Ministry in employment matters, and again you should write to those hospitals in which you are interested directly.

### Nursing

Singapore is presently keen to recruit nurses from overseas, and interested nurses should write directly to the hospitals for information on employment opportunities.

As mentioned above, assistant nurses and more junior positions do not need to be registered; they can apply to hospitals/clinics directly, and if they are successful in finding work they can apply for a work permit.

## PROFESSIONAL ORGANISATIONS

*Singapore Association of Occupational Therapists:* Orchard, PO Box 0475, Singapore 9123, Republic of Singapore.

*Singapore Dental Association:* 2 College Road, Singapore 169850, Republic of Singapore (tel 220 2588).

*Singapore Dietetic Association:* Tanglin, PO Box 180, Singapore 9124, Singapore.

*Singapore Medical Association:* Level 2, Alumni Medical Centre, 2 College Road, Singapore 169850, Republic of Singapore (tel 223 1264; fax 224 7827; e-mail sma@sma.org.sg).

*Singapore Nurses' Association:* 77 Maude Road, Singapore 208353 (tel 392 0770; fax 392 7877; e-mail sna@pacific.net.sg; Website www.sna.org.sg).

*Singapore Physiotherapy Association:* Tanglin, PO Box 442, Singapore 9124, Republic of Singapore (tel 329 0331; fax 227 3738).

*Singapore Society of Radiographers:* c/o Dept of Diagnostic Imaging, National University Hospital, 5 Lower Kent Ridge Road, Singapore 0511, Singapore.

## USEFUL ADDRESSES

*Academy of Medicine:* College of Medicine Building, 16 College Road #01-01, Singapore 169854, Republic of Singapore (tel 223 8968; fax 225 5155).

*British Council:* 30 Napier Road, Singapore 258509, Republic of Singapore (tel 473-1111; fax 472-1010).

*Dental Board:* (see Medical Council address).

*Economic Development Board (Manpower and Capability Development Division):* 250 North Bridge Road #24-00, Raffles City Tower, Singapore 179101, Republic of Singapore (tel 330 6836; fax 337 8552).

*National University of Singapore, Lower Kent Ridge Road, Singapore 119074 (tel 874 3300; fax 773 1462).*

*Ministry of Community Development:* MCD Building, 512 Thomson Road, Singapore 298136, Republic of Singapore.

*Ministry of Health:* College of Medicine Building, 16 College Road, Singapore 169854, Republic of Singapore (tel 325 9220; fax 224 1677; e-mail mohinfo@moh.gov.sg; Website www.moh.gov.sg)).

*Ministry of Manpower, Employment Pass Dept.:* 10 Kallang Road, Singapore 208718 (tel 297 5443; fax 293 2138).

*Pharmacy Board:* c/o Ministry of Health.

*Singapore Immigration and Registration:* SIR Building, 10 Kallang Road #08-00, Singapore 208718, Republic of Singapore (tel 391 6100; fax 298 0843; Website www.str.gov.sg).

*Singapore Medical Council:* College of Medicine Building, 16 College Road, Singapore 169854, Republic of Singapore (tel 223 7777; fax 224 1677; e-mail moh_smc@moh.gov.sg).

*Singapore Nursing Board:* (see Medical Council address)

*Straits Times:* Singapore Press Holdings, Times House, 390 Kim Seng Road, Singapore 0923, Republic of Singapore (tel 737 0011; fax 732 0131; e-mail straits@cyberway.com.sg Website http://straitstimes.asia1.com.sg/).

## HOSPITAL ADDRESSES

### Government Hospitals

*Alexandra Hospital:* Alexandra Road, Singapore 159964 (tel 473-5222; fax 479-3183). 400 beds

*Ang Mo Kio Community Hospital:* 17 Ang Mo Kio Avenue 9, Singapore 569766 (tel 453-8033; fax 454-1729). 180 beds

*Changi General Hospital:* 2 Simei Street 3, Singapore 529889 (tel 788 8833; fax 788 0933; Website www.cgh.com.sg/). 801 beds

*KK Women's & Children's Hospital:* 100 Bukit Timah Road, Singapore 229899 (tel 293 4044; fax 293 7933; Website www.kkh.com.sg/). 898 beds

*National University Hospital:* 5 Lower Kent Ridge Road, Singapore 119074 (tel 1-

800-772 5555; fax 779 5678; Website www.nuh.com.sg/). 957 beds
*Singapore General Hospital:* Outram road, Singapore 169608 (tel 222 3322; fax 222 1720; Website www.sgh.gov.sg). 1708 beds
*Tan Tock Seng Hospital:* 11 Jalan Tan Tock Seng, Singapore 308433 (tel 256-6011; fax 252-7282; Website www.ttsh.gov.sg/). 1068 beds
*Woodbridge Hospital:* 10 Buangkok Green, Singapore 539747 (tel 385 0411; fax 385-1050). 3114 beds.

## Speciality Centres

*National Cancer Centre:* 11 Hospital Drive, Singapore 169610 (tel 436 8000 (professional enquiries tel 436 8388); fax 225 6283; e-mail corporate@nccscomsg Website www.nccs.com.sg).
*National Heart Centre:* Mistri Wing, 17 Third Hospital Avenue, Singapore 168752 (tel 4367800; fax 2210944; e-mail nhc@nhc.com.sg Website www.nhc.com.sg/).
*National Neuroscience Institute:* 11 Jalan Tan Tock Seng Singapore 308433 (tel 357 7153; fax 256 4755; Website www.nni.com.sg/).

## Private Hospitals

*Adam Road Hospital:* 19 Adam Road, Singapore 289891 (tel 466 7777; fax 467 0254; e-mail arh@arhcomsg Website http://home2.pacific.net.sg/~arh/). 56 beds.
*East Shore Hospital:* 321 Joo Chiat Place, Singapore 427 990 (tel 344 7588; Website www.esh.parkway.com.sg). 157 beds.
*Gleneagles Hospital:* 6A Napier Road, Singapore 258 500 (tel 473 7222). 328 beds.
*HMI Balestier Hospital:* 363 Balestier Road, Singapore 329784 (tel 253 3818; fax 251-0530). 62 beds.
*Kwong Wai Shiu Hospital:* Serangoon Road, Singapore. 30 beds.
*Mount Alvernia Hospital:* 820 Thomson Road, Singapore 574623 (tel 253 4818; fax 255-6303; Website www.mtalvernia-hospital.org). 300 beds.
*Mount Elizabeth Hospital:* Singapore (tel 737 2666). 505 beds.
*Ren Ci Hospital:* 10 Buangkok Green, Singapore 539747 (tel 385 0288; fax 385 0388). 174 beds.
*Thomson Medical Centre:* 339 Thomson Road, Singapore 307677 (tel 256 9494; fax No 253-4468). 191 beds.

# Other Asian Countries

## VOLUNTARY ORGANISATIONS

A large number of organisations are involved in development and aid work in many of the less-developed Asian countries, much of which is concerned with improving health. These agencies include the *International Federation of Red Cross and Red Crescent Societies:* which is involved in long-term community health projects; *Care International*; *Save the Children Fund*; *United Nations Volunteers*; *VSO*; and *WaterAid*. *CUSO* sends Canadian volunteers to work on health projects in various parts of Asia. Many agencies operate in specific regions:

*Action Health* has a wide range of health professionals working in India; *Concern Worldwide* has health workers in Bangladesh, Cambodia and Laos; and *Health Unlimited* sends medical teams to Burma, Laos, Cambodia and China.

*International Health Exchange* is an excellent source of information on opportunities in health care in countries throughout Asia.

Organisations especially concerned with providing medical aid in areas affected by war, famine and other disaster situations include the *International Committee of the Red Cross*; *MERLIN* which provides emergency medical care in Siberia, Sri Lanka and Afghanistan; and *Médecins sans Frontières*.

## DENOMINATIONAL ORGANISATIONS

In addition to the voluntary organisations mentioned above, many religious missions in Asia combine the provision of health care with converting the masses to their particular faith. Several of these operate in Nepal; the *International Nepal Fellowship* has various health professionals working on a range of initiatives, including leprosy and TB control programmes; and the *Nepal Leprosy Trust* also has health workers in the country. *The Leprosy Mission* has health professionals working with leprosy patients throughout southern and south-east Asia.

Eye care is another specialist area in which several agencies operate; *Christoffel Blindenmission* recruits eye care and other health specialists; and *SAO Cambodia* has health workers involved in eye-care projects in Cambodia.

Other denominational organisations working in Asia include the *Catholic Medical Mission Board*, which has doctors and nurses in India and Papua New Guinea; *CORD*, which has health staff in Cambodia; the *Mennonite Central Committee*; *Tearfund*; and *WEC International*.

**N.B.** For all of the voluntary and denominational agencies mentioned above, further information, addresses and telephone numbers are included in the directories in Part II of this book.

## PROFESSIONAL ORGANISATIONS

### India
*Indian Dental Association:* 20A Dewan Bahadur Road, RS Puram, Coimbatore 641-002, Tamilnadu, India.
*Indian Medical Association:* Indraprastha Marg, New Delhi 110 002, India (tel 11-331 8819/331 9009; fax 11-331 6270)

### Indonesia
*Indonesian Dental Association:* PO Box 4541, Jakarta Pusat 10000, Indonesia.
*Indonesian Medical Association:* Jalan Dr Sam Ratulangie No 29, Jakarta 10350, Indonesia (tel 21-315 0679; fax 21-390 0473)

### Malaysia
*Malaysian Dental Association:* 69-2 Medan Setia 1, Plaza Damansara, Kuala Lumpur 50490, Malaysia (tel +60-3-255 1532; fax 3-254 4670; e-mail mda@po.jaring.my Website www.mda.org.my/).
*Malaysian Medical Association:* 4th Floor, MMA House, 124 Jalan Pahang, 53000 Kuala Lumpur, Malaysia (tel +60-3-442 0617; fax 3-441 8187; e-mail mma@tm.net.my Website www.mma.org.my).
*Malaysian Medical Council:* Ministry of Health, Kuala Lumpur, Malaysia.
*Malaysian Nurses Association:* PO Box 11737, General Post Office, 50756 Kuala

Lumpur, Malaysia (tel 3-25 43 84 6).
*Malaysian Society of Radiographers:* Dept of Diagnostic Imaging, Jalan Pahang, 50586 Kuala Lumpur, Malaysia.
*Ministry of Health:* Jalan Cenderasari, 50590 Kuala Lumpur, Malaysia

## Philippines
*Philippine Dental Association:* Ayala Avenue, Cor Komagong St, Makati, Metro Manila 1200, Philippines.
*Philippine Medical Association:* PO Box 4039, Manila, Philippines (tel 2-97 35 14; fax 2-97 49 74).
*Philippine Nurses Association:* 1663 FT Benitez Street, Malate, Manila 1004, Philippines (tel 2-58 30 92/50 15 45; fax 2-58 30 92)

## South Korea
*Korean Dental Association:* 81-7 Songjung-dong, Songdong-ku, Seoul 133-160, South Korea (tel +82-2-498 6320; fax 02-468 4655; e-mail kda001@chollian.net Website http://kda.infostar.co.kr).
*Korean Medical Association:* Central PO Box 2062, Seoul, South Korea (tel 2-794 2476/7; fax 2-792 1296/793 8702).
*Korean Nurses Association:* 88-7 Sang Lim Dong, Choong Ku, Seoul, South Korea (tel 2-279 36 18/19; fax 2-278 37 63).
*Korean Radiological Technologist Association:* 250 Yang jae-dong, Seocho-ku, Seoul, South Korea

## Taiwan
To work as a nurse in Taiwan the applicant would have to sit the national professional qualifying exam (in Chinese). Prior to this they should also have submitted copies of their certificates and licences from their homeland to the Ministry of Education.
*Association of Radiologic Technologists of the Republic of China:* 280 Section 4, Jen-ai Road, Taipei, Taiwan.
*Chinese Taipei Association for Dental Sciences:* 4F No 52, Hsing Sheng South Road, Section 3, Taipei 106, Taiwan.
*Chinese Taipei Medical Association:* 201 Shih-pai Rd, Section 2, PO Box 3043, Taipei 11217, Taiwan (tel 2-875 7358; fax 2-874 1097).
*Taiwan Nurses Association:* 4F, 281 Section 4 Hsin-Yi Road, Taipei 106, Taiwan (tel +886-2-2755 2291; fax 2-2701 9817; e-mail twnna@ms38.hinet.net)

## Thailand
*Dental Association of Thailand:* PO Box 355, Samsennai Post Office, Bangkok 10400, Thailand.
*Medical Association of Thailand:* 2 Soi Soonvichai, New Petchburi Road, Bangkok 10310, Thailand (tel 2-314 4333/314 6305/6; fax 2-314 4333).
*Nurses Association of Thailand:* 12/21 Rang Nam Road, Bangkok 10400 (tel 2-247 4463/4464; fax 2-247 4470)

# Appendix 1 – Useful Publications

*Allied Health Education Directory* (1996). A general guide to the various health professions in the USA, including brief descriptions of each occupation. It also includes lists of schools offering programmes for each career area. Published by the American Medical Association (515 North State Street, Chicago, Illinois 60610, USA).

*International Handbook of Medical Education* (1994) Eds. Sajid, McGuire, Veach, Aziz, Gunzburger; Greenwood Press ISBN 0313 284237; £93.50. Although this weighty study is beyond many pockets it provdes a useful reference for those professionals looking for work elsewhere. Intended as a reference work for the provision of health services in developing countries, the text covers 28 countries. Given its scope this can probably be found in medical or reference libraries.

*Live & Work in ....* A series of guides to living and working abroad, including detailed information on visas, employment regulations and looking for a job. Titles published so far are: *Australia & New Zealand; Belgium, The Netherlands & Luxembourg; France; Germany; Italy; Japan; Russia & Eastern Europe; Scandinavia; Spain & Portugal,* and *The USA & Canada.* Published by Vacation Work.

*Medical Careers – A General Guide* (1998, 4th edition). A highly useful guide designed to help medical students and newly qualified doctors in the UK make their career choices. It describes the postgraduate training pathways of the main branches of medicine, career choices and prospects, and includes detailed information on the immigration rules for overseas doctors. It is available for £10 (including postage) from the BMJ Bookshop, 1 Burton Street, London WC1H 9JR (tel 020-7383 6244/6638).

*Medical Information on the Internet* (2nd ed) R. Kiley; Churchill Livingstone ISBN 0443061947; £18.95. This guide to the internet and how it can be of use to medical professionals comes with a free CD-rom, which gives access to the pages discussed in addition to its role as a learning tool.

*Nursing in Europe* (1997) J. Salvage & S. Heijwen; WHO Regional Publications No. 74 ISBN 9289013389; £74. A comprehensive overview of nursing throughout Europe, full of information on nursing, professional bodies, and the health ministries amd health services of the different nations. Its size and cost mean that this is another one to look up rather than buy.

*Overseas Clinical Elective* (1997) R. Adomat; Blackwell Science UK ISBN 0632041021; £12.99. A guide to the potential for overseas work during training for medical students, which is becoming more common amongst nursing students.

*The Essential Medical Secretary* (1998) S.J. Green; Baillière Tindall ISBN 0702021032; £15.95. Approved by AMSPAR (see page 15) this book is designed to support the diploma in medical secretarial studies. Apart from its usefulness as a textbook, it provides an up-to-date guide to working practices within medical administration.

*UCAS Handbook*. Annually updated directory of undergraduate degree, HND and DipHE courses in the UK. Published by the Universities and Colleges Admissions Service, and available free from schools and colleges. Essential reading for anyone considering undertaking a first degree.

# Appendix 2 – Abbreviations

| | |
|---|---|
| ECFMG | Educational Commission for Foreign Medical Graduates (USA). |
| EEA | European Economic Area. |
| EU | European Union. |
| GP | General Practitioner. |
| NGO | Non-Governmental Organisation. |
| NHS | National Health Service (UK). |
| NRMP | National Resident Matching Programme(USA). |
| PLAB | Professional and Linguistic Assessments Board (UK). |
| RN | Registered Nurse. |
| RGN | Registered General Nurse. |
| RMHN | Registered Mental Handicapped Nurse. |
| RPN | Registered Psychiatric Nurse. |
| RSCN | Registered Sick Children's Nurse. |
| USMLE | United States Medical Licensing Examination. |
| WHO | World Health Organisation. |

# Vacation Work publish:

| | Paperback | Hardback |
|---|---|---|
| The Directory of Summer Jobs Abroad | £9.99 | £14.95 |
| The Directory of Summer Jobs in Britain | £9.99 | £14.95 |
| Supplement to Summer Jobs in Britain and Abroad *published in May* | £6.00 | – |
| Work Your Way Around the World | £12.95 | – |
| The Good Cook's Guide to Working Worldwide | £11.95 | – |
| Taking a Gap Year | £11.95 | – |
| Working in Tourism – The UK, Europe & Beyond | £11.95 | – |
| Kibbutz Volunteer | £10.99 | – |
| Working on Cruise Ships | £9.99 | – |
| Teaching English Abroad | £11.95 | – |
| The Au Pair & Nanny's Guide to Working Abroad | £10.99 | – |
| Working in Ski Resorts – Europe & North America | £10.99 | – |
| Working with Animals – The UK, Europe & Worldwide | £11.95 | – |
| Accounting Jobs Worldwide | £11.95 | – |
| Working with the Environment | £11.95 | – |
| Health Professionals Abroad | £11.95 | – |
| The Directory of Jobs & Careers Abroad | £11.95 | £16.95 |
| The International Directory of Voluntary Work | £10.99 | £15.95 |
| The Directory of Work & Study in Developing Countries | £9.99 | £14.99 |
| Live & Work in Saudi & the Gulf | £10.99 | – |
| Live & Work in Japan | £10.99 | – |
| Live & Work in Russia & Eastern Europe | £10.99 | – |
| Live & Work in France | £10.99 | – |
| Live & Work in Australia & New Zealand | £10.99 | – |
| Live & Work in the USA & Canada | £10.99 | – |
| Live & Work in Germany | £10.99 | – |
| Live & Work in Belgium, The Netherlands & Luxembourg | £10.99 | – |
| Live & Work in Spain & Portugal | £10.99 | – |
| Live & Work in Italy | £10.99 | – |
| Live & Work in Scandinavia | £10.99 | – |
| Panamericana: On the Road through Mexico and Central America | £12.95 | – |
| Travellers Survival Kit: Mauritius, Seychelles & Réunion | £10.99 | – |
| Travellers Survival Kit: Madagascar, Mayotte & Comoros | £10.99 | – |
| Travellers Survival Kit: Sri Lanka | £10.99 | – |
| Travellers Survival Kit: Mozambique | £10.99 | – |
| Travellers Survival Kit: Cuba | £10.99 | – |
| Travellers Survival Kit: Lebanon | £10.99 | – |
| Travellers Survival Kit: South Africa | £10.99 | – |
| Travellers Survival Kit: India | £10.99 | – |
| Travellers Survival Kit: Russia & the Republics | £9.95 | – |
| Travellers Survival Kit: Western Europe | £8.95 | – |
| Travellers Survival Kit: Eastern Europe | £9.95 | – |
| Travellers Survival Kit: South America | £15.95 | – |
| Travellers Survival Kit: USA & Canada | £10.99 | – |
| Travellers Survival Kit: Australia & New Zealand | £11.95 | – |

## Distributors of:

| | | |
|---|---|---|
| Summer Jobs USA | £12.95 | – |
| Internships (On-the-Job Training Opportunities in the USA) | £16.95 | – |
| Sports Scholarships in the USA | £16.95 | – |
| Scholarships for Study in the USA & Canada | £14.95 | – |
| Colleges & Universities in the USA | £15.95 | – |
| Green Volunteers | £10.99 | – |

**Vacation Work Publications, 9 Park End Street, Oxford OX1 1HJ**
**Tel 01865–241978    Fax 01865–790885**

**Visit us online for more information on our unrivalled range of titles for work,**
**travel and adventure, readers' feedback and regular updates:**
**Web site http://www.vacationwork.co.uk**